Lecture Notes in Computer Science

T0238406

Commenced Publication in 1973
Founding and Former Series Editors:
Gerhard Goos, Juris Hartmanis, and Jan van Leeuwen

Editorial Board

David Hutchison
Lancaster University, UK
Takeo Kanade
Carnegie Mellon University, Pittsburgh, PA, USA
Josef Kittler
University of Surrey, Guildford, UK
Jon M. Kleinberg
Cornell University, Ithaca, NY, USA
Friedemann Mattern
ETH Zurich, Switzerland
John C. Mitchell
Stanford University, CA, USA
Moni Naor
Weizmann Institute of Science, Rehovot, Israel
Oscar Nierstrasz
University of Bern, Switzerland
C. Pandu Rangan
Indian Institute of Technology, Madras, India
Bernhard Steffen
University of Dortmund, Germany
Madhu Sudan
Massachusetts Institute of Technology, MA, USA
Demetri Terzopoulos
University of California, Los Angeles, CA, USA
Doug Tygar
University of California, Berkeley, CA, USA
Moshe Y. Vardi
Rice University, Houston, TX, USA
Gerhard Weikum
Max-Planck Institute of Computer Science, Saarbruecken, Germany

Markus Lumpe   Wim Vanderperren (Eds.)

Software Composition

6th International Symposium, SC 2007
Braga, Portugal, March 24-25, 2007
Revised Selected Papers

 Springer

Volume Editors

Markus Lumpe
Swinburne University of Technology
Faculty of Information and Communication Technologies
Hawthorn, VIC 3122, Australia
E-mail: mlumpe@ict.swin.edu.au

Wim Vanderperren
Vrije Universiteit Brussel
System and Software Engineering Lab - ETRO
Pleinlaan 2, 1050 Brussel, Belgium
E-mail: wvderre@vub.ac.be

Library of Congress Control Number: 2007941317

CR Subject Classification (1998): D.2, D.1.5, D.3, F.3

LNCS Sublibrary: SL 2 – Programming and Software Engineering

ISSN   0302-9743
ISBN-10   3-540-77350-9 Springer Berlin Heidelberg New York
ISBN-13   978-3-540-77350-4 Springer Berlin Heidelberg New York

This work is subject to copyright. All rights are reserved, whether the whole or part of the material is concerned, specifically the rights of translation, reprinting, re-use of illustrations, recitation, broadcasting, reproduction on microfilms or in any other way, and storage in data banks. Duplication of this publication or parts thereof is permitted only under the provisions of the German Copyright Law of September 9, 1965, in its current version, and permission for use must always be obtained from Springer. Violations are liable to prosecution under the German Copyright Law.

Springer is a part of Springer Science+Business Media

springer.com

© Springer-Verlag Berlin Heidelberg 2007
Printed in Germany

Typesetting: Camera-ready by author, data conversion by Scientific Publishing Services, Chennai, India
Printed on acid-free paper   SPIN: 12206353   06/3180   5 4 3 2 1 0

Preface

On behalf of the Organizing Committee we are pleased to present the proceedings of the 2007 Symposium on Software Composition (SC 2007). The goal of SC 2007 was to bring together the research and industrial communities in order to address the challenges of the component-based software development approach. SC 2007 was the sixth symposium on software composition in the SC series that seeks to develop a better understanding of how software components may be used to build and maintain large software systems.

This LNCS volume contains the revised versions of the papers presented at SC 2007, which was held as a satellite event of the European Joint Conferences on Theory and Practice of Software (ETAPS) in Braga, Portugal, March 24–25, 2007. The symposium began with a keynote on "Composition by Anonymous Parties" by Farhad Arbab (CWI and Leiden University). The main program consisted of six technical sessions related to specific aspects of component-based software development.

In response to the call for papers, we received 59 submissions from over 20 countries and 6 continents. Each paper was reviewed by at least three Program Committee members. The entire reviewing process was supported by Microsoft's Conference Management Toolkit. In total, 15 submissions were accepted as full papers and 5 submissions were accepted as short papers.

We would like to express our gratitude to the General Chair, Judith Bishop, for her invaluable support and guidance that made the symposium in Braga possible. We would like to thank the European Network of Excellence on Aspect-Oriented Software Development (AOSD-Europe), the International Federation for Information Processing, Technical Committee on Software: Theory and Practice (IFIP, TC 2), and IBM Zurich for sponsoring this event. We are also thankful to the System and Software Engineering Lab at the Vrije Universiteit Brussel for the administrative support in hosting the symposium's Web page. Last but not least, we would like to thank the organizers of ETAPS 2007 for hosting and providing an organizational framework for SC 2007.

September 2007
Markus Lumpe
Wim Vanderperren

Organization

General Chair

Judith Bishop   University of Pretoria, South Africa

General Co-chairs

Markus Lumpe   Iowa State University, USA
Wim Vanderperren   Vrije Universiteit Brussel, Belgium

Program Committee

Uwe Aßmann   Dresden University of Technology, Germany
Brian Barry   Bedarra Research Labs, Canada
Alexandre Bergel   Trinity College, Dublin, Ireland
Vittorio Cortellessa   University of L'Aquila, Italy
Thierry Coupaye   France Telecom, France
Birgit Demuth   Dresden University of Technology, Germany
Maja DHondt   CWI, The Netherlands
Flavio De Paoli   University of Milan, Italy
Dieter Fensel   DERI Galway/Innsbruck, Ireland/Austria
Dimitra Giannakopoulou   RIACS/NASA Ames Research Center, USA
Volker Gruhn   University of Leipzig, Germany
Thomas Gschwind   IBM Research, Switzerland
Arno Jacobsen   University of Toronto, Canada
Mehdi Jazayeri   Vienna University of Technology, Austria
Wouter Joosen   Katholieke Universiteit Leuven, Belgium
Joe Kiniry   University College Dublin. Ireland
Kung-Kiu Lau   The University of Manchester, UK
Welf Löwe   University of Växjö, Sweden
Karl Lieberherr   Northeastern University, USA
Jeff Magee   Imperial College, London, UK
Klaus Ostermann   Technical University of Darmstadt, Germany
Claus Pahl   Dublin City University, Ireland
Arnd Poetzsch-Heffter   Kaiserslautern University of Technology, Germany
Elke Pulvermüller   University of Luxembourg, Luxembourg
Ralf Reussner   University of Oldenburg, Germany
Lionel Seinturier   University of Lille, France
Jean-Guy Schneider   Swinburne University of Technology, Australia
Mario Südholt   École des Mines de Nantes, France
Ragnhild Van Der Straeten   University of Brussels, Belgium
Éric Tanter   University of Chile, Chile

External Referees

Adina Sirbu
Adrian Mocan
Andrea Maurino
Andrew McVeigh
Charles Zhang
Christoph Bockisch
Cuong Tran
Daniel Sykes
Ellen Van Paesschen
Emilia Cimpian
Faris M. Taweel
Fintan Fairmichael
Florian Heidenreich
Frank-Ulrich Kumichel
Guillaume Pothier

Ilie Savga
Ioannis Ntalamagkas
James Scicluna
Jan Schafer
Jean-Marie Gaillourdet
Karl Klose
Kathrin Geilmann
Katja Lehmann
Ling Ling
Maarten Bynens
Marco Comerio
Mick Kerrigan
Mikolas Janota
Mirko Seifert
Nicole Rauch

Pasqualina Potena
Patrick Michel
Perla Velasco
Radu Grigore
Robin Green
Rodolfo Toledo
Shane Brennan
Simone Roettger
Sören Blom
Steffen Zschaler
Stijn Mostinckx
Vinod Muthusamy
Vladyslav Ukis
Wouter Horre
Zhengdao Xu

Sponsoring Institutions

IFIP, Laxenburg, Austria
IBM Zurich, Switzerland
AOSD-Europe, European Network of Excellence in AOSD, Lancaster, UK
Vrije Universiteit Brussel, Belgium
Microsoft Research, Redmond, WA

Table of Contents

Composition by Anonymous Third Parties

Farhad Arbab

Center for Mathematics and Computer Science (CWI), Amsterdam and
Leiden Institute for Advanced Computer Science, Leiden University
The Netherlands

Composition of algorithms has dominated software composition since the inception of programming. The ubiquitous subroutine call acts as the primary composition operator in virtually all programming models and paradigms, appearing in various guises such as function call, method invocation, remote procedure call, etc. The inadequacies of the tight coupling imposed by such composition mechanisms and the need for more flexible alternatives have become clearer along the evolution through object-oriented to component-based, and now, service oriented computing.

Interaction arises out of how a composition allows the active entities in a composed system to play against one another. Communication primitives used in classical models of concurrency to allow interaction among processes in a composed system share the targeted message passing nature of function calls: in order to interact, they generally require a process to directly address foreign entities, such as other processes or channels, that belong to the environment of the process. Interaction constitutes the most interesting and the most difficult aspect of concurrent systems. We have studied protocols for, and various aspects of, interaction in concurrency theory. Curiously, however, no model of concurrency has hitherto considered interaction as a first-class concept! This makes dealing with interaction protocols more difficult than necessary, by erecting a level of indirection that acts as an obstacle between the concrete structures constructed and manipulated in a model, on the one hand, and interaction as the subject of discourse, on the other.

Recognizing the need to go beyond the success of available tools sometimes seems more difficult than accepting to abandon what does not work. Our concurrency and software composition models have served us well-enough to bring us up to a new plateau of software complexity and composition requirements beyond their own effectiveness. In this sense, they have become the victims of their own success. Dynamic composition of behavior by orchestrating the interactions among independent distributed components or services has recently gained prominence. We now need new models for software composition to tackle this requirement.

In this presentation, I describe our on-going work on a compositional model for construction of complex concurrent systems out of simpler parts, using interaction as the only first-class concept. This leads to a simple, yet surprisingly expressive, connector language, together with effective models and tools for composition of complex systems of distributed components and services.

M. Lumpe and W. Vanderperren (Eds.): SC 2007, LNCS 4829, p. 1, 2007.
© Springer-Verlag Berlin Heidelberg 2007

Defining Component Protocols with Service Composition: Illustration with the **Kmelia** Model

Pascal André, Gilles Ardourel, and Christian Attiogbé

LINA CNRS FRE 2729 - University of Nantes
F-44322 Nantes Cedex, France
(Pascal.Andre,Gilles.Ardourel,Christian.Attiogbe)@univ-nantes.fr

Abstract. We address in this article the description and usage of component protocols viewed as specific services. In addition to inter-component service composition, our Kmelia component model supports vertical structuring mechanisms that allow service composition inside a component. The structuring mechanisms (namely state annotation and transition annotation) are then used to describe protocols which are considered here as component usage guides. These structuring mechanisms are integrated in the support language of our component model and are implemented in our COSTO toolbox. We show how protocol analysis is performed in order to detect some inconsistencies that may be introduced by the component designers.

Keywords: Component, Service, Composition, Protocols, Property Analysis.

1 Introduction

In this work we address the description and usage of component protocols viewed as specific services and described as such. In [9] Meyer suggests a property classification for a Component Quality Model that may lead to trusted components. We consider the *assertions* and *usage documentation* properties which range in the *Behaviour* category from the classification. The first property requires formal descriptions which are helpful to ensure the correctness of the components and their assemblies. The *usage documentation* property requires specific abstraction means in order to help the component-based system developer to build correct assemblies. Clearly, this component documentation property participates in the development of trusted components: this motivates our work. In this context, component documentation should therefore be more than a list of available services (like IDL descriptions); it should overview the component behaviour and constraints, provide some guidelines to use services, describe precisely the usage conditions of services and the interaction conditions. These requirements are fulfilled by the present work which builds on the Kmelia component model [4] which is an abstract component model based on services. Kmelia services are more than simple operations: they enable complex interactions and are the key

M. Lumpe and W. Vanderperren (Eds.): SC 2007, LNCS 4829, pp. 2–17, 2007.
© Springer-Verlag Berlin Heidelberg 2007

element to model components and to connect them to make assemblies. The use of service is central to the verification of compatibility when assembling components according to four compatibility layers: signature, structure, contracts and behaviours layers. In a previous article [4] we presented the Kmelia model and we studied the definition and the verification of component assemblies which are based on a *horizontal service composition*. In the present article we extend the service composition.

In the horizontal composition, services of the same level in various components are composed, with respect to the four compatibility levels, to define new services.

To enforce the idea of component documentation, we consider a methodological layer between services and components. This layer deals with the good usage of the components: which services can be used to fulfil a given need and in what order these services should be called. This layer corresponds to the concept of *component protocol* already used in various component models. Compared with related approaches (see Section 4) which are provider-oriented protocols, our proposal suggests user-oriented protocols. This means that the Kmelia component protocols are not a component life-cycle or a component constraint but merely *macro-services* which play an important role in component composition. To support protocols in Kmelia we now introduce a *vertical service composition*, based on hierarchical structuring operators, to build new provided services from existing ones. Building protocols with service composition is beneficial because: the component model stays simple; protocols can be combined and can play a central role in component composition and last, the verification support of service composition may be reused.

The contribution of this article is twofold: new vertical service composition operators are introduced with their formal descriptions; the definition of powerful component protocols, using service composition, to structure the component interface. From the verification point of view we reuse the existing techniques developed for the service level and we adapt them to the protocol level.

The article is structured as follows. Section 2 is a brief overview of the Kmelia formal component model. In Section 3 we define the vertical service composition. Component protocols are developed in Section 4; first we discuss the concept and compare it with related approaches; then we define protocols in Kmelia and illustrate with an example of a bank Automatic Teller Machine system. The verification aspect is studied in Section 5. Last, we conclude in Section 6 and discuss some perspectives.

2   Overview of the **Kmelia** Component Model

Kmelia is a component model based on services [4]: an elementary Kmelia component encapsulates several services (Fig. 1). The service behaviours are captured with labelled transition systems. Kmelia makes it possible to specify abstract components, to compose them and to check various properties. A Kmelia abstract component is a mathematical model of an open multi-service system that supports synchronous communication with its environment. A component

```
Component C1                           Provided aService_1 ()
  Interface    <Interface descr>         Interface   <Interface descr>
  Types        <Type Defs>               Pre         <Predicate>
  Variables    <Var list>                Post        <Predicate>
  Invariant                              Behaviour
               <Predicate>               init        aStateI
  Initialisation                         final       aStateF
  ... // var. assignments                { state_i --label--> state_j
                                            ... }
  Services                             end
  ... // as described at side          Required aService_2 ()
end                                      ... //in the same way
```

Fig. 1. Overview of Kmelia syntax

specification language (also named Kmelia) and a prototype toolbox (COSTO) support the Kmelia model. The toolbox already permits formal analysis via Lotos/CADP[1] and Mec[2]. We recall (from [4]) in the following the main definitions and the related notations to facilitate the reading of the article.

Service Description. A *service* s of a component C is defined with an *interface* I_s and a (dynamic) *behaviour* $\mathcal{B}_s$: $\langle I_s, \mathcal{B}_s \rangle$. The interface I_s of a service s is defined by a 5-tuple $\langle \sigma, P, Q, V_s, S_s \rangle$ where σ is the service signature (name, arguments, result), P is a precondition, Q is a postcondition, V_s is a set of local declarations and the *service dependency* S_s is a 4-tuple $S_s = \langle sub_s, cal_s, req_s, int_s \rangle$ of disjoint sets where sub_s (resp. cal_s, req_s, int_s) contains the provided services names (resp. the services required from the caller, the services required from any component, the internal services) in the s scope.

The behaviour $\mathcal{B}_s$ of a service s is an *extended labelled transition system* (eLTS) defined by a 6-tuple $\langle S, L, \delta, S_0, S_F, \Phi \rangle$ with S the set of the states of s; L is the set of transition labels and δ is the transition relation ($\delta \in S \times L \to S$). S_0 is the initial state ($S_0 \in S$), S_F is the finite set of final states ($S_F \subseteq S$), Φ is a *state annotation* relation ($\Phi \in S \leftrightarrow sub_s$). The transitions in δ (with the$((ss, lbl), ts)$ abstract form) have the `ss--lbl-->ts` concrete form.

The transition labels are (possibly guarded) combinations of actions: `[guard] action*`. The actions may be either *elementary actions* or *communication actions*. An elementary action (an assignment for example) does not involve other services; it does not use a communication channel. A communication action is either a *service call/response* or a message *communication*.

Component Description. A component C is a 8-tuple $\langle \mathcal{W}, Init, \mathcal{A}, \mathcal{N}, I, \mathcal{D}_S, \nu, \mathcal{C}_S \rangle$ with:

---

[1] www.inrialpes.fr/vasy
[2] altarica.labri.fr

- $\mathcal{W} = \langle T, V, V_T, Inv \rangle$ the state space where T is a set of types, V a set of variables, $V_T \subseteq V \times T$ a set of typed variables, and Inv is the state invariant;
- $Init$ the initialisation of the V_T variables;
- $\mathcal{A}$ a finite set of elementary actions;
- $\mathcal{N}$ a finite set of service names;
- I the component interface which is the union of two disjoint finite sets: I_p the set of names of the provided services and I_r the names of required services.
- $\mathcal{D}_S$ is the set of service descriptions which is partitioned into the provided services $(\mathcal{D}_{S_p})$ and the required services $(\mathcal{D}_{S_r})$.
- $\nu : \mathcal{N} \to \mathcal{D}_S$ is the function that maps service names to service descriptions. Moreover there is a projection of the I partition on its image by ν: $n \in I_p \Rightarrow \nu(n) \in \mathcal{D}_{S_p} \wedge n \in I_r \Rightarrow \nu(n) \in \mathcal{D}_{S_r}$.
- $\mathcal{C}_S$ is a constraint related to the services of the interface of C in order to control the usage of the services.

The component behaviour relies on the behaviours of its services. The Kmelia components are composable via the interfaces of the involved services. Interface-compatible and behaviour-compatible services are composed at various levels to build *assemblies*. Assemblies and services can be encapsulated into a larger component called a *composition*.

3   Service Composition

In this section we consider two dimensions for service composition; each dimension is related to service behaviour (eLTS). The first dimension already presented in [4] deals with horizontal structuring mechanisms to compose services and components from existing ones on the basis of a client-supplier relation. The second dimension is introduced in this article; it deals with vertical structuring mechanisms for building new services.

3.1   Horizontal Structuring Mechanisms

Horizontal service composition is tightly coupled with component composition and hierarchical links between components. The horizontal structuring mechanisms are established by linking required services to services which are provided either internally or by the caller service or by a third component. These service calls are handled with communication mechanisms. The services are described in such a way that their interactions are made explicit via communication mechanisms. We use communication channels and the standard communication primitives ! and ?; they are complemented with ! ! and ?? to deal respectively with service call and service wait. Indeed as service interactions are not elementary, we distinguish their communication operators from the primitive ones.

The interacting services are viewed (from an observer) as one service. Inter-component interactions are based on service behaviour communications. The communications that support the interaction and hence the composition, are matching pairs: *send message(!)-receive message(?), call service(!!)-wait service start(??), emit service result(!!)-wait service result(??).*

Two services are composable if their signatures are matching (types), the assertions are consistent, the (hierarchical) service dependencies are not conflicting and their behaviours are compatible. When services are composed, they are linked via the information available in their interfaces. Provided services are linked to corresponding required services. In the same way, subservices are linked between the composed services. The transition labels of the service behaviours are used to perform the running of the resulting behaviour: either we have independent behaviours or a synchronising behaviour in the case of matching labels.

3.2   Vertical Structuring Mechanisms

In the following we consider and formalise two *vertical* structuring mechanisms that enable us to structure hierarchically the services: they are the *state annotation* mechanism and the *transition annotation* mechanism. Additionally to the flexibility of service description with *optional behaviours* (syntactically expressed as a state annotation) or *mandatory behaviours* (syntactically expressed as a transition annotation) the structuring mechanisms provide a means to reduce the LTS size, to share common services or subservices and to master the complexity of service specification, while preserving the pre/post condition contract at the begining/termination of services (both client and supplier constraints).

We maintain the principle that formally the unfolding of an eLTS should result in a LTS (in a recursive way). The unfolding of a service consists in the unfolding of all its annotated states (*state_unfold* in the sequel) and the unfolding of the annotated transitions (*transition_unfold* in the sequel). For the formalisation we use the (standard) operational semantics rules with premises and consequences separated by an horizontal line.

The << >> structuring operator. We use the << >> operator to denote an optional service call at any state of a service running. The principle is that the caller of a service s, of a component C, may call a service ss that belongs to the provided interface sub_s of s, when the running of s reaches a state e_i (of the LTS of s) annotated with ss.

This *optional* service call is syntactically noted with e_i <<ss>> in the eLTS of s. In [4] the state annotation mechanisms (called *branching states*) was informally introduced. According to the established link between a required and a provided service, there is a renaming which results in a uniform link name. Therefore, the service call is performed with _linkName!!serviceName(...) where _linkName (resp. serviceName) stands for the established link name (resp. the service name).

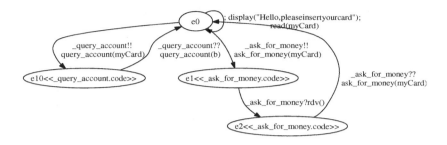

Fig. 2. An example of optional services in the USER_INTERFACE component

Let us illustrate with the example in the Figure 2[3]. It represents the main service of the user interface component of a bank ATM specification[4]. This service asks either for a withdrawal (`_ask_for_money!!ask_for_money`) or for a query account (`_query_account!!query_account`). The e1, e2 and e10 states are annotated with `<<code>>`; it means that the `code` service can be called from this state by the service which is interacting with the current one.

The relation $\Phi : S \leftrightarrow sub_s$ is used to manage the annotated states of a service specification (see Section 2). Now let formalise the structuring mechanisms introduced via state annotations. Let s be a service, e_j and e_i (annotated with ss) be two states of s. Let ss, a member of sub_s, be a service provided by (the interface of) s. The behaviour of a service ss is also an (extended) labelled transition system defined by a 6-tuple $\langle S_{ss}, L_{ss}, \delta_{ss}, \Phi_{ss}, S_{0_{ss}}, S_{F_{ss}} \rangle$.

The semantics of the unfolding of annotated states (in the domain of Φ) is as follows. We use the standard α-conversion to rename states and transitions to avoid name conflict. For this purpose, α_{state_s} denotes a renaming function that renames its parameters so as to avoid conflicts with the state names in s. The $\alpha_{transition_s}$ and α_{label_s} functions are used in the same way to denote transition and label renaming.

$$s \,\hat{=}\, \langle S_s, L_s, \delta_s, \Phi_s, S_{0_s}, S_{F_s} \rangle \ \ \wedge \ (e_i, ss) \in \Phi_s \ \ \wedge$$
$$ss \,\hat{=}\, \langle S_{ss}, L_{ss}, \delta_{ss}, \Phi_{ss}, S_{0_{ss}}, S_{F_{ss}} \rangle \ \ \wedge$$
$$S_{ss}^\alpha = \alpha_{state_s}(S_{ss}) \ \ \wedge \ L_{ss}^\alpha = \alpha_{label_s}(L_{ss}) \ \ \wedge \ \delta_{ss}^\alpha = \alpha_{transition_s}(\delta_{ss}) \ \ \wedge$$
$$ss_\alpha \,\hat{=}\, \langle S_{ss}^\alpha, L_{ss}^\alpha, \delta_{ss}^\alpha, \Phi_{ss}, S_{0_{ss}}^\alpha, S_{F_{ss}}^\alpha \rangle \ \ \wedge$$
$$S_s' = S_s \cup S_{ss}^\alpha \wedge L_s' = L_s \cup L_{ss}^\alpha \cup \{?? \ ss\} \ \ \wedge$$
$$\delta_s' = \delta_s \cup \delta_{ss}^\alpha \ \cup \ \{((e_i, ?? \ ss), S_{0_{ss}}^\alpha)\} \ \cup_{S_{f_{ss}} \in S_{F_{ss}}^\alpha} \{((S_{f_{ss}}, \epsilon), e_i)\} \ \ \wedge$$
$$\Phi_s' = \Phi_s - \{(e_i, ss)\} \ \ \wedge$$
$$S_{0_s}' = S_{0_s} \wedge S_{F_s}' = S_{F_s}$$

$$\overline{state\_unfold(s, ee) = \langle S_s', L_s', \delta_s', \Phi_s', S_{0_s}', S_{F_s}' \rangle}$$

---

[3] This picture is generated by the KmeliaToDot module of our COSTO toolbox.

[4] This ATM specification deals with the interaction between component services in order to enable some functionalities provided by the ATM: withdrawal, query account, etc. Some of these functionalities need the code or the amount from the user [4].

The rule expresses that after the unfolding of e_i, a transition labelled with ??ss goes from the annotated state to the initial state of the ss service; if there is a call to the service ss from the e_i state, provided that the precondition of ss is true, this transition (as the other matching action) will lead to the initial state of ss. To handle the end of the ss service, where the postcondition of ss is true, a transition labelled with ϵ relates the final states of ss and the annotated state; finally, all the transitions of ss are allowed in s provided that the control reaches ss (hence the inclusion of transition relations).

The [[ ]] structuring operator. The [[ ]] operator denotes *mandatory* service calls at any stage of a service running. To follow a transition annotated with [[ss]] the caller of a service s must call the service ss that belongs to the provided interface sub_s of s. Again pre/postcondition contract is preserved. Only one service name is allowed for this operator. In the same way as for state annotation, we extend the LTS of the service behaviour with a relation $\Psi : S \times S \leftrightarrow sub_s$ to capture the annotated transitions. Note that to preserve the service composition techniques and existing tools we do not modify the δ relation.

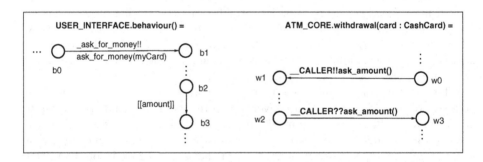

Fig. 3. An example of mandatory service in the USER_INTERFACE component

We use three components to describe the ATM example: the USER_INTERFACE component which provides the behaviour service and requires the amount service; the ATM_CORE component which provides the withdrawal service and requires the ask_amount service and the ATM_BASE component. The service withdrawal is linked with the ask_for_money one; the link name is _ask_for_money. In the same way the ask_amount service is linked with amount resulting in the ask_amount link. As depicted in the Figure 3, the amount service of the USER_INTERFACE must be called (here from the withdrawal service) after the b2 state.

In the same way as for the operator << >> we give the semantics of the [[ ]] operator. Consider a transition between e_i and e_j which is annotated with ss: we have $((e_i, e_j), ss)$ in Ψ. The semantics of the unfolding of the transition is as follows.

$$s \triangleq \langle S_s, L_s, \delta_s, \Phi_s, S_{0_s}, S_{F_s} \rangle \quad \wedge$$
$$((e_i, ss), e_j) \in \delta_s \quad \wedge (e_i, e_j) \in dom(\Psi) \quad \wedge \quad \Psi(e_i, e_j) = ss \wedge$$
$$ss \triangleq \langle S_{ss}, L_{ss}, \delta_{ss}, \Phi_{ss}, S_{0_{ss}}, S_{F_{ss}} \rangle \quad \wedge$$
$$S_{ss}^\alpha = \alpha_{state_s}(S_{ss}) \quad \wedge L_{ss}^\alpha = \alpha_{label_s}(S_{ss}) \quad \wedge \delta_{ss}^\alpha = \alpha_{transition_s}(\delta_{ss}) \quad \wedge$$
$$ss_\alpha \triangleq \langle S_{ss}^\alpha, L_{ss}^\alpha, \delta_{ss}^\alpha, \Phi_{ss}, S_{0_{ss}}^\alpha, S_{F_{ss}}^\alpha \rangle \quad \wedge$$
$$S'_s = S_s \cup S_{ss}^\alpha \wedge L'_s = L_s \cup L_{ss}^\alpha \cup \{?? \ ss\} \quad \wedge$$
$$\delta'_s = \delta_s \cup \delta_{ss}^\alpha - \{((e_i, ss), e_j)\}$$
$$\cup \{((e_i, ?? \ ss), S_{0_{ss}}^\alpha)\} \cup_{S_{f_{ss}} \in S_{F_{ss}}^\alpha} \{((S_{f_{ss}}, \epsilon), e_j)\} \quad \wedge$$
$$\Psi'_s = \Psi_s - \{((e_i, ss), e_j)\} \quad \wedge$$
$$S'_{0_s} = S_{0_s} \wedge S'_{F_s} = S_{F_s}$$

$$\overline{transition\_unfold(s, t_i) = \langle S'_s, L'_s, \delta'_s, \Phi'_s, S'_{0_s}, S'_{F_s} \rangle}$$

The semantic rule expresses that when a transition annotated with ss exists between the states e_i and e_j, then an expansion of the ss service is performed between e_i and e_j. The behaviour of ss is then reachable from the e_i state via a wait of a call (??ss) ensuring the precondition of ss; after the running of ss (one reaches a final state), the postcondition of ss is established and the execution proceeds from the e_j state due to the ϵ transition. A side effect is considered here; the Ψ relation that extends the service specification is also updated along the semantic rule. This rule is sufficient to deal with all annotation cases. The various cases of transition annotation are dealt with as follows:

– when an annotated transition is guarded $(((e_i, \mathtt{[g]} \ \mathtt{[[ss]]}), e_j) \in \delta)$, the firing of the transition depends on the value of the guard; in this case the semantics rule is slightly changed as follows;

$$s \triangleq \langle S_s, L_s, \delta_s, \Phi_s, S_{0_s}, S_{F_s} \rangle \quad \wedge$$
$$((e_i, \mathtt{[g]} \ ss), e_j) \in \delta_s \quad \wedge (e_i, e_j) \in dom(\Psi) \quad \wedge \quad \Psi(e_i, e_j) = ss \wedge$$
$$ss \triangleq \langle S_{ss}, L_{ss}, \delta_{ss}, \Phi_{ss}, S_{0_{ss}}, S_{F_{ss}} \rangle \quad \wedge$$
$$S_{ss}^\alpha = \alpha_{state_s}(S_{ss}) \quad \wedge L_{ss}^\alpha = \alpha_{label_s}(L_{ss}) \quad \wedge \delta_{ss}^\alpha = \alpha_{transition_s}(\delta_{ss}) \quad \wedge$$
$$ss_\alpha \triangleq \langle S_{ss}^\alpha, L_{ss}^\alpha, \delta_{ss}^\alpha, \Phi_{ss}, S_{0_{ss}}^\alpha, S_{F_{ss}}^\alpha \rangle \quad \wedge$$
$$S'_s = S_s \cup S_{ss}^\alpha \quad \wedge \quad L'_s = L_s \cup L_{ss}^\alpha \cup \{?? \ ss\} \quad \wedge$$
$$\delta'_s = \delta_s \cup \delta_{ss}^\alpha - \{((e_i, \mathtt{[g]} \ ss), e_j)\}$$
$$\cup \{((e_i, ?? \ ss), S_{0_{ss}}^\alpha)\} \cup_{S_{f_{ss}} \in S_{F_{ss}}^\alpha} \{((S_{f_{ss}}, \epsilon), e_j)\} \quad \wedge$$
$$\Psi'_s = \Psi_s - \{((e_i, ss), e_j)\} \quad \wedge$$
$$S'_{0_s} = S_{0_s} \wedge S'_{F_s} = S_{F_s}$$

$$\overline{unfold\_gtransition(s, t_i) = \langle S'_s, L'_s, \delta'_s, \Phi'_s, S'_{0_s}, S'_{F_s} \rangle}$$

– when an annotated transition is one of the output transition of a node (there is a choice of transitions), the used transition is the one which is involved in the current interaction with another service that call (or which is called by) the current one.

3.3 Component Maintenance and Consistency

Component maintenance. Decomposing a large behaviour into subservices is encouraged in Kmelia, but it bears consequences if the service was already used by other services. For instance, when the behaviour of an existing component service s is modified using the [[]] operator to exploit a part of it as a new service ss, the existing clients of s will cease to be compatible because they miss the (new) connection to ss. Indeed, the use of [[]] to modify s creates new transitions between s and ss: especially a call to ss which is of course not included in the previous client of s. This is what we called *interface granularity mismatch* in [2]: a client service considers that all the communications are made in the context of the unique old service while other newer clients use the new subservice ss. While being quite difficult to address in the general case, the granularity mismatch is easily avoided in the case of a maintenance or refactoring operation. For this reason we use a rather flexible operator noted [||] which expands in the same way as the (inflexible) [[]] operator but which adds new transitions that allow old clients to circumvent both the call to the subservice and the waiting for its termination. Likewise the flexible counterpart of (the inflexible) << >> is the <| |> operator.

Formally the flexible operators have rules very similar to their inflexible counterparts. We do not detail them here; the main point is that in the case of <| |> and [||] the final states of ss may not be reached, therefore an ϵ-transition relates each predecessor of these final states to e_j. Indeed the new clients call and wait for the termination, but the existing clients do not. In the case of this formalisation δ'_s is changed as follows:

$$\delta'_s = \delta_s \cup \delta^\alpha_{ss} \cup \{((e_i, \epsilon), S^\alpha_{0_{ss}})\} \cup_{e_p \in \{q_p | ((q_p, lx), s_{f_{ss}}) \in \delta_{ss}\}} \{((e_p, \epsilon), e_j)\}$$

Thanks to the flexible versions of the vertical structuring mechanisms, decomposing large services into subservices is expected to be a common refactoring. The systematic detection of occurrences where such refactorings are performed will be needed; but the adaptation of subservices that use parameters are out of the scope of this paper.

Impact of structuring on service consistency. The previous structuring mechanisms are independent of the service behaviour but they can impact on its consistency. The correct ordering of services may be checked using preconditions and postconditions. Therefore some control may already be performed at the provider side. We study these problems and provide some solutions in the following in the specific case of the component protocols.

Now we have a component model entirely equipped with service structuring mechanisms. The added vertical structuring mechanisms do not impact on composition since they are defined in terms of elementary LTS. However it is necessary to check for possible design errors. In the following section we reuse the service composition mechanisms to describe component protocols.

4   Component Protocols

Component behaviour protocols [14,12,8] have been introduced to extend static component interfaces to dynamic constraints such as valid sequences of message exchange, valid condition of service invocation, connection handling, etc.

4.1   The Component Protocol Concept

The concept of protocol already exists in several component or service models but its meaning varies from one model to another. In some approaches a protocol is a specific layer in a contractual vision including assertions [5,6,4,10] and non-functional constraints like the quality of service [5,6]. In other approaches [1,5,7,14] protocols are communication rules on connectors where adaptation is possible. Protocols can also be recursive [13,15] or subtyped [5,12,14].

In a short comparison[5], we use four criteria to compare the approaches: (1) contents of the protocols (service invocation, actions, message exchange, control structures...), (2) the attachment unit (component, interface, service, connector or architecture), (3) the formalism itself (finite state machine, statecharts, regular expressions, etc), (4) property specification and proof support techniques (temporal logic, markup language, algorithms, etc). We hereby classify these related approaches into three categories where the attachment unit is the main criteria:

1. The first category groups the approaches which define a protocol as a component *lifecycle* [5,8,11,13,15]. A single protocol is associated to the component (or with its single interface). The component is a process and the services are either atomic (messages) or defined by a specific behaviour [10].
2. In the second category a protocol defines a component view's lifecycle. In some of these approaches, a protocol is associated to an interface and several interfaces coexist in the component [3,6,12]. In other approaches [1,7,14] a protocol handles the communications on connection points (just like a usual communication protocol).
3. In the third category [4] a protocol describes a particular use of the component. Several protocols coexist within the component in one or several interfaces.

The above approaches are not different in terms of expression power but they are in terms of abstractions (concepts) from the component client point of view. For example, using a basic component model (single interface, single protocol), one can model every component system and in particular a system where connectors are considered as components and multiple interfaces as component compositions. In such a case the system architect should encapsulate the protocols in composite components and manage the interface consistency (close to the inheritance problems in Object-Oriented Design); this solution leads to heavy modelling. In other words, the approaches of category 1 and some of category 2 consider the protocol as a constraint rather than a guideline for the client. In Kmelia (third category) we rather emphasise the user point of view; this is more developed in the following section.

Protocols as Component Macro-services. When a component model does not have the protocol concept, any service of a component can be invoked at

---

[5] available at `lina.atlanstic.net/fr/equipes/team10/Kmelia/`

any time. This is acceptable for libraries of functions but not for components whose behaviour evolves with their service behaviours. Indeed the other solutions would be either to use non trivial preconditions for service specifications or to use comments to guide the users. We choose the use of protocol instead.

Component protocols enable the distinction between component state constraints (preconditions), sequencing constraints (ordering) and thereafter make easier the verification of each part. Protocols are both a constraint for the component supplier and a user guide for the component client (*e.g.* use case or scenario):

- A protocol defines the rules which are needed to preserve the component consistency.
- Protocols are helpful for the component system designer in describing guidelines: "which services one can use and in what order one can use them".
- Protocols are a coarse grain for component assemblies: instead of connecting each service, one can connect a pattern of services.

The protocols as considered above, are a means to model user sessions, processes, user classes or communication protocols.

4.2   Specification of Protocols in **Kmelia**

Within the Kmelia model a component protocol describes a *valid ordering* of service calls. Therefore we beneficially reuse vertical structuring mechanisms to describe protocols; for instance a sequence of mandatory service calls impose an ordering of the services. A protocol stands for a provided service that gives the access to other services of the same component. Thereby a protocol has a behaviour (eLTS). Among the provided services of a component, those used in a protocol description are called *controlled services*; those which are not used in the protocol descriptions are called *free services*. Thereby our model admits the existence of controlled services which are still offered (at any time) through the component interface.

A Kmelia component may provide one or several protocols. The provided protocols may be made *interruptible* by the component designer. The means to do that is the use of a property to qualify some services. Therefore the protocol interfaces have the following form:

```
provided protoName()
        Properties = {protocol, interruptible, ...}
```

A protocol which does not have the *interruptible* property is said *non-interruptible*; once it is started it cannot be interleaved with other runs.

Protocol Specification. A protocol p is a specific service; it needs an interface I_p and a behaviour description $\mathcal{B}_p$; therefore we use the same description as for a service: an eLTS. The behaviour of p is specified with $\langle S, L_P, \delta, \Phi, S_0, S_F \rangle$. But to deal with the protocol features, we need some restrictions on the labels of the transitions of protocols. The labels (L_P) are now either annotations (noted

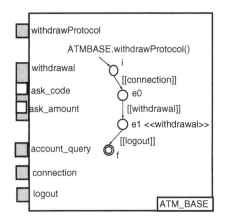

Fig. 4. A protocol of the ATM_BASE component

[[ss]] that corresponds to a service *ss* which should be called by the service that uses the protocol) or a local variable manipulation (that corresponds for example to a loop counting or a path predicate).

In the following we adopt the user's point of view, hence using *call to ss* to refer to the annotation of a state or a transition with a service *ss* using the vertical composition operators.

The Figure 4 stands for a component ATM_BASE that includes a protocol withdrawProtocol. The protocol gives the user guide of the services connection, withdrawal and logout. This protocol is rather simple, it does not include explicit loops, guards, basic actions on variables, etc. It appears in the component interface in the same way as the other provided services and can be called as such. The services that appear in the protocol (the controlled services) are called in the scope of the protocol in the same way as the subservices of a service are called. As far as the protocol withdrawProtocol is concerned, the services connection, withdrawal, logout are controlled but the service account_query is free.

5   Formal Analysis and Experimentations

We have undertaken the behavioural compatibility analysis of Kmelia component services [4]. The behaviours of linked services are checked for compatibility: the behavioural analysis is achieved by considering the simultaneous running of two (pairwise) services involved in a communication; the transitions are performed independently if they are labelled with elementary actions; the transitions labelled with communication actions should be matching pairs from both involved services. After the extension of service composition with the vertical structuring mechanisms, the behavioural compatibility analysis of services still works since the new mechanisms do not modify the behavioural structure of our services: we have the (unfolded) LTS of each service labelled with elementary actions or communication actions. Therefore component interaction *via* composition of services does not change. However, the behavioural compatibility should not hide the general compatibility rules which include assertion checking. The use of the vertical structuring mechanisms may lead to wrong orderings of services (if the user does not pay attention to pre/postconditions). For example, in order to perform *safely* a transition annotated with [[ss]] during the execution of a service *s*, the precondition of *ss* should be ensured. In the same way, the use of the structuring mechanisms to support protocol description requires a consistency analysis of the protocols. In the following section we investigate one kind of protocol analysis.

5.1   Analysis of Protocols: Inconsistency Checking

The absence of inconsistency within protocol descriptions is one of the criteria of a component correctness. For this reason, we need to detect inconsistency in protocols specified by component designers. A protocol of a component is *inconsistent* if one of its service sequences (from the protocol behaviour) is not feasible (*unfeasible sequences*). The following two cases of inconsistency may be detected:

- the existence of guarded sequences of service calls without other choice leading to a final state of the protocol;
- the existence in the protocol of a sequence of service calls $[s_i; s_{i+1}; \cdots ; s_j; s_k]$ such that the post-conditions of s_i to s_j imply the negation of the precondition of s_k; that means, some services called before s_k establish a context which is not altered by other services before the call of s_k and which is not consistent with s_k.

    For instance, if the service connection has *not connected* as precondition and *connected* as postcondition then the connection; connection sequence leads to an inconsistent protocol (in the same way as any protocol including this sequence).

To analyse and detect unfeasible sequences of service calls, we are experimenting the translation of our needs into properties that will be proved using existing theorem provers such as the Atelier B[6].

5.2   Analysis of Protocols: Inconsistency Detection

This section investigates the inconsistency cases of section 5.1. The goal is to help the component designer to write correct component equipped with protocols. Practically, the analysis of such components will output some warnings or errors showing the wrong parts of the component descriptions. Consider a protocol with its unfolded behaviour and the sub-chains of service calls going from the initial state to a final one (avoiding loops) of the protocol behaviour. For each chain we check for all its sub-chains $s_i; s_j$ (with $j = i + 1$) that

$$\boxed{\neg(post(s_i) \Rightarrow \neg pre(s_j))} \qquad (P1)$$

---

[6] www.atelierb.societe.com

This local property (where $pre(s)$ and $post(s)$ stand for the pre-condition and post-condition of s) should be extended to take into account the effect of a whole chain of calls that precedes a call to a service s_k.

Remind that the eLTS that specifies a protocol behaviour denotes a finite set of sequences which are made of the labels of the transitions. Therefore we have chains made of service calls and simple actions. Practically, a component protocol imposes an ordering of the component running, where each performed service has some effect on the component.

A service (say $s_i = \langle\langle\sigma, \ P_{s_i}, \ Q_{s_i}, \ V_{s_i}, S_{s_i}\rangle, \mathcal{B}_{s_i}\rangle$) is correctly performed if it starts with a state satisfying the required precondition P_{s_i}. $\mathcal{B}_{s_i}$ is the service behaviour; the effect of a service, via its $\mathcal{B}_{s_i}$ behaviour, is indicated by a post-condition Q_{s_i} together with a modification of the component state.

Consequently the initial $(P1)$ property is

$$\boxed{\neg(G_{s_i} \Rightarrow \neg P_{s_j})} \qquad (P2)$$

instead of $\neg(Q_{s_i} \Rightarrow \neg P_{s_j})$ for the chain $s_i; s_j$, where G_{s_i} is a global property. It expresses the cumulative effects of services $s_1..s_i$ on a component just before the call s_j that follows s_i in a chain of the given protocol.

This generalises the situation depicted as follows:

$$\underbrace{s_1}_{G_{s_1}} ; \ s_2; \ s_3; \ \cdots ; \ s_n$$

$$\underbrace{s_1 ; s_2}_{G_{s_2}}; \ s_3; \ \cdots ; \ s_n$$

$\cdots$

$$\underbrace{s_1; \ s_2; \ s_3; \ \cdots ; \ s_i; \ s_j; \ \cdots ; \ s_{n-1}}_{G_{s_{n-1}}}; \ s_n$$

The predicate P_{s_i} precondition of a service s_i is expressed with local variables (vl_i) that are the parameters of the service and with global variables (vg_k) of the component, together with typing information $(tl_i; tg_k)$ coming from the service and component interfaces:

$$vl_i : tl_i; \ vg_k : tg_k \ . \ P_{s_i}(vl_i, vg_k)$$

In the same way, the predicate P_{s_j} of a service s_j is expressed with local variables (vl_j) of the s_j service and with global variables (vg_k) of the component, together with typing information coming from the s_j service and from the component:

$$vl_j : tl_j; \ vg_k : tg_k \ . \ P_{s_j}(vl_j, vg_k)$$

As we are reasoning independently of the runtime context of the services, the values of local variables are not known (we assume in the best case that they have the right value for the truth of the predicates) when the service are called. The only working hypotheses are those on global variables; therefore we restrict $P_{s_i}(vl_i, vg_k)$ and $P_{s_j}(vl_j, vg_k)$ predicates to $P'_{s_i}(vg_k)$ and $P'_{s_j}(vg_k)$.

The previous property $(P1)$

$$\neg(vl_i : tl_i; vg_k : tg_k \ . \ Q_{s_i}(vl_i, vg_k) \Rightarrow \neg(vl_j : tl_j; vg_k : tg_k \ . \ P(vl_j, vg_k)))$$

is rewritten with

$$\neg(vg_k : tg_k \, . \, Q'_{s_i}(vg_k) \Rightarrow \neg(vg_k : tg_k \, . \, P'(vg_k)))$$

and is generalised with the following *proof obligation*:

$$\boxed{\neg(vg_k : tg_k \, . \, G'_{s_i}(vg_k) \Rightarrow \neg(vg_k : tg_k \, . \, P'(vg_k)))}$$

Finally, detecting inconsistencies results in the systematic checking of this proof obligation on components equipped with protocols. The obligation is yet restrictive (local variables are ignored) but it is possible to alleviate the imposed restrictions; however the obligation proofs will be very complex as we would have to explore some value constraints for local variables. The current compromise (i.e. considering only global variables) helps to detect some inconsistencies with proof obligations which are tractable. Therefore we should integrate, after preprocessing if needed to meet the input language of the prover, the G' and P' predicates with their contexts (types, variables) into the targeted prover. We are using the Atelier B prover as a support for our experimentations.

6   Conclusion and Perspectives

We have extended the horizontal structuring mechanisms of the Kmelia model with two vertical structuring mechanisms: state annotation to deal with optional service calls at some running stage and transition annotation to deal with mandatory service calls when they are needed by the component users. We have shown that these structuring mechanisms, first dedicated to service and component composition, are also appropriate for describing protocols. In this context component protocols are viewed as specific provided services. The behaviour of a protocol is described as a service using a LTS with restricted labels; for example they cannot include basic communication actions. The concept of protocol is added to the model without changing it. The inconsistency of service ordering may be detected through the protocols. Compared to the existing approaches, our abstract component model is easily extensible; it can be incrementally strengthened: in this case by defining the *protocol* property.

We studied protocol inconsistency detection using service pre/post conditions. That led to the generation of obligation proofs that can be managed using existing theorem provers. Robustness with respect to component maintenance was dealt with: when a service is restructured its clients are not broken. We have already implemented the structuring mechanisms within our COSTO toolbox that integrates: Kmelia specification parser, translators to LOTOS and MEC, static interoperability checkers, dynamic interoperability checkers, a translator of Kmelia services into dot (for the visualisation of service behaviours).

The challenge of building trusted components remains exciting. The Kmelia proposal does not yet overcome all aspects of this challenge; additionally to the improvement of the data and assertion part of the specification language, mechanised correctness analysis of services and components, equipped with protocols or not, are planned as short term research goals. We started some experiments with the Atelier B prover to deal with aspects reated to assertions and not covered by LOTOS or MEC. In this direction, further work is planned to mechanise the detection of inconsistency. The refinement of Kmelia model into executable framework such as Fractal and SOFA is also an exciting investigation area.

References

1. Allen, R., Garlan, D.: A Formal Basis for Architectural Connection. ACM Transactions on Software Engineering and Methodology 6(3), 213–249 (1997)
2. André, P., Ardourel, G., Attiogbé, C.: Coordination and Adaptation for Hierarchical Components and Services. In: WCAT 2006. Third International ECOOP Workshop on Coordination and Adaptation Techniques for Software Entities, pp. 15–23 (2006)
3. Attie, P.C., Lorenz, D.H.: Establishing Behavioral Compatibility of Software Components without State Explosion. Technical Report NU-CCIS-03-02, College of Computer and Information Science, Northeastern University (2003)
4. Attiogbé, C., André, P., Ardourel, G.: Checking Component Composability. In: Löwe, W., Südholt, M. (eds.) SC 2006. LNCS, vol. 4089, Springer, Heidelberg (2006)
5. Becker, S., Overhage, S., Reussner, R.: Classifying Software Component Interoperability Errors to Support Component Adaption. In: Crnković, I., Stafford, J.A., Schmidt, H.W., Wallnau, K. (eds.) CBSE 2004. LNCS, vol. 3054, pp. 68–83. Springer, Heidelberg (2004)
6. Beugnard, A., Jézéquel, J-M., Plouzeau, N., Watkins, D.: Making Components Contract Aware. Computer 32(7), 38–45 (1999)
7. Canal, C., Fuentes, L., Pimentel, E., Troya, J.M., Vallecillo, A.: Adding Roles to CORBA Objects. IEEE Trans. Softw. Eng. 29(3), 242–260 (2003)
8. Giannakopoulou, D., Kramer, J., Cheung, S-C.: Behaviour Analysis of Distributed Systems Using the Tracta Approach. ASE 6(1), 7–35 (1999)
9. Meyer, B.: The Grand Challenge of Trusted Components. In: Proceedings of 25th International Conference on Software Engineering, pp. 660–667. IEEE Computer Society, Los Alamitos (2003)
10. OMG. The OMG Unified Modeling Language Specification, V2.0 Rfp. Superstructure Specification Infrastructure Specification (2005), available at http://www.omg.org/docs/ptc/05-07-04.pdf, available at http://www.omg.org/docs/ptc/05-07-04.pdf
11. Pavel, S., Noye, J., Poizat, P., Royer, J-C.: Java Implementation of a Component Model with Explicit Symbolic Protocols. In: Gschwind, T., Aßmann, U., Nierstrasz, O. (eds.) SC 2005. LNCS, vol. 3628, Springer, Heidelberg (2005)
12. Plasil, F., Visnovsky, S.: Behavior protocols for software components, 2002. IEEE Transactions on SW Engineering 28(9) (2002)
13. Südholt, M.: A Model of Components with Non-regular Protocols. In: Gschwind, T., Aßmann, U., Nierstrasz, O. (eds.) SC 2005. LNCS, vol. 3628, pp. 99–113. Springer, Heidelberg (2005)
14. Yellin, D.M., Strom, R.E.: Protocol Specifications and Component Adaptors. ACM Transactions on Programming Languages and Systems 19(2), 292–333 (1997)
15. Zimmermann, W., Schaarschmidt, M.: Checking of Component Protocols in Component-Based Systems. In: Löwe, W., Südholt, M. (eds.) SC 2006. LNCS, vol. 4089, Springer, Heidelberg (2006)

Composite Contract Enforcement in Hierarchical Component Systems*

Philippe Collet[1], Jacques Malenfant[2], Alain Ozanne[1,2,3], and Nicolas Rivierre[3]

[1] University of Nice - Sophia Antipolis, I3S Laboratory, France
philippe.collet@unice.fr
[2] Laboratoire d'informatique de Paris 6, France
Jacques.Malenfant@lip6.fr
[3] France Telecom R&D, Issy les Moulineaux, France
{alain.ozanne,nicolas.rivierre}@orange-ftgroup.com

Abstract. Abadi and Lamport established a general theorem for composing specifications [1]. Based on an assume-guarantee principle, it enables one to prove the specification of a composite system from the ones of its components. But the general application of this theorem to software composition is not that straightforward because the resulting abstract specification of the composite depends upon the hidden guarantees of its subcomponents. In this paper, we investigate how this result can be exploited without blurring responsibilities between the different participants. Our contributions leverage an existing contracting framework for hierarchical software components [7], in which contracts are first-class objects during configuration and run times. This framework already associates specifications and responsibilities to software components, within the traditional *horizontal* form of composition. We show here how the *vertical* one can be made operational using the theorem as a sound formal basis. The resulting composite contracts make possible not only to detect violations, but also to determine and exploit precisely responsibilities upon them, related to both forms of composition.

1 Introduction

Reliably composing pieces of software crucially depends on how well these pieces observe constraints from each others. Beyond syntactic interfaces, which are taken into account by all component models, more semantic constraints are also tremendously important: behavior protocols, pre- and postconditions, and more and more QoS constraints are also deeply concerned [19]. Some of these constraints, expressed in specifications, can be proved at composition time. Others, because they are too hard to prove in the general case, or because they depend upon data known only at runtime (some QoS constraints, for example), can be checked at runtime, both to track down errors and to reason abductively about the component to blame when failures occur. The contract based approach has

* This work was partially supported by France Telecom under the collaboration contracts number 422721832-I3S and 46132097-I3S.

M. Lumpe and W. Vanderperren (Eds.): SC 2007, LNCS 4829, pp. 18–33, 2007.
© Springer-Verlag Berlin Heidelberg 2007

been used both to express and check, even at runtime, the assumptions and guarantees of components with regards to such constraints. Our ConFract platform [7,6] provides contracts as first-class objects, equipped with generic contract enforcement and blame-tracking mechanisms open to different kinds of contracts. However, as Goguen and Burstall [10] observed a quarter of century ago, composition is not only a matter of *horizontal* bindings between components but also the *vertical* nesting of subcomponents into more abstract composite ones. This vertical nesting entails obligations between the subcomponents and their outer composite, which need to be verified. Moreover, it has been argued that abstracting from the details of the inner obligations between composed components is essential to reason properly about horizontally composing at the composite level.

This paper therefore addresses the needs for abstract composite contracts working hand in hand with the nested composition of components to provide a well-founded tool to enforce obligations among composite components and between subcomponents and their outer composite. Among several different proposals to do so, we found our abstract composite contracts on the well-known Abadi's and Lamport's theorem [1]. This theorem makes explicit, under some assumptions and for some type of properties, the dependency between the specification of a component and the ones of its subcomponents.

One key observation in Abadi's and Lamport's theorem stems from the fact that when an abtract composite contract binding a composite A to its caller B fails, one cannot blame the horizontally composed B if any of the subcomponents fails to observe its own obligations towards A. Hence, to fruitfully apply the theorem, one needs to be able to monitor composite and hidden contracts and to correctly reason from effects to causes to blame the defective components either horizontally or vertically. It turns out that our ConFract model already associates specifications and some appropriate responsibilities to the corresponding software components, upon which it supports the *horizontal* form of composition. In this paper, we show how the *vertical* form can be made operational using the theorem as a sound formal basis. ConFract, extended with Abadi and Lamport based composite contracts, can guarantee that in all program runs, the specification of a component is well-founded on the base of its subcomponents, and that the vertical composition is sound against the contracted properties.

The rest of the paper is organized as follows. The next section briefly introduces the underpinnings of Abadi's and Lamport's theorem. In Section 3, a running example is described. Section 4 then presents our contract model and the case of composite contracts is studied in Section 5. Section 6 describes an application of our proposal with more complete specifications. Related works are discussed in Section 7 and Section 8 concludes this paper.

2   Foundation

An assume-guarantee specification of a system asserts that this system performs properly if its environment does [11,1]. It should not assert that its environment performs properly, as this would be unimplementable since the environment is not under the system control. This principle is adequate for rigourous composition of modular component specifications, and has lead to extensive research work since the 80s. We summarize here those aspects of the semantic model proposed by Abadi and Lamport [1], and adapted for the provision of end-to-end QoS guarantees in ODP systems [13]. This model is state-based and lies at the semantic level, i.e. does not depend upon a particular formalism.

Semantic Overview. A state describes observable parts of a relevant universe, i.e. the interfaces of all the agents (e.g. components) under consideration. The whole state is decomposed into the states attached to every component, where a component state may be accessed by other components only through explicit interactions. We assume, at this abstract level, that components interact by exchanging signals through their interfaces and that interactions are either controlled by a component or by its environment (one of those is responsible). Semantically, a state is an assignment of values to variables, a behavior is an infinite sequence of states and a transition of a behavior denotes an action in which an agent is responsible for changing the state. A property is true or false of a behavior[1] and is said a safety property if it is refutable in a finite time (e.g. the throughput cannot exceed a certain threshold) or a liveness property if it is never refutable in a finite time (e.g. an answer will eventually be delivered).

In the following, we assume that safety properties are sufficient in a first approach to deal with a large class of QoS or behavioral constraints (see [1] for the possible use of liveness properties). A safety property constrains a component if it can be violated only by this component, i.e. by a transition under its control, such as an internal action or an emitted signal, in which it is responsible for changing the state. An assume-guarantee specification attached to a component can be expressed in the form $E \dashrightarrow M$, where M is a safety property constraining this component, E is a safety property constraining its environment and $\dashrightarrow$ means that M must remain true as long as E does[2]. This temporal relation form is very useful for modular specifications of components, and for distinguishing responsibilities among components from the ones of its environment.

Composing specifications. It should be possible to prove the (QoS or behavioral) specification of a large system from the specifications of its components. The following result addresses this need and is basically the composition theorem established by Abadi and Lamport [1], in our component-oriented context considering only safety properties. It generalizes easily to n components.

Theorem 1. *Let C_1 and C_2 be two components with assume-guarantee specifications, respectively equal to $E_1 \dashrightarrow M_1$ and $E_2 \dashrightarrow M_2$, and E be a supplementary assumption on the environment of both components. Let us assume that M_1, M_2, E_1, E_2, E are safety properties such as:*

---

[1] Some notions (equivalent behaviors for stuttering, closure of a property...) are omitted here for the sake of brevity.

[2] A refinement of this temporal relation is discussed by Abadi and Lamport [2].

- M_1 and M_2 constrain respectively C_1 and C_2,
- E_1, E_2 and E constrain respectively $\neg\, C_1$, $\neg\, C_2$ and $\neg\,(C_1$ and $C_2)$.

Then the following inference rule is sound

$$\frac{E \cap M_1 \cap M_2 \subseteq E_1 \cap E_2}{(E_1 \dashrightarrow M_1) \cap (E_2 \dashrightarrow M_2) \subseteq (E \dashrightarrow M_1 \cap M_2)}. \tag{1}$$

This theorem provides an **agreement** criterion for the **composability** of C_1 and C_2 and a powerful technique to prove how the **resulting contract** can be guaranteed. More precisely, if the premise holds, one can obtain a contract specified as $(E \dashrightarrow M_1 \cap M_2)$, which is satisfied by the composition of C_1 and C_2. This contract **guarantees** that the safety properties M_1 and M_2 must remain true as long as E does. At runtime, any **violation** denotes an **observable** action (through some interface) in which either C_1, C_2 or their environment is **responsible** for changing the state. Furthermore, this contract is expressed as an assume-guarantee specification attached to a system composed of C_1 and C_2. The contract model proposed in this article, extended over this formal basis, provides an operational framework to enforce such compositional contracts. The resulting system is intended to be used during various phases (design, negotiation, etc.) of complex systems with QoS or behavioral constraints (see §6).

3   Running Example

Throughout this paper, we use a simplified cruise control system inspired from [14] as running example. This system is described using an usual component model, in which components are connected through their provided and required interfaces, and components may be composite. Currently, our work is validated on the *Fractal* component platform [4] that, among others, provides a Java implementation. In the sequel, references to types in the underlying programming language can be seen as Java interfaces.

The cruise control system is operated with three buttons: *resume, on* and *off*. When the car is running and *on* is pressed, the system records the current speed and maintains the car at this speed. When the accelerator, brake or *off* is pressed, the system disengages but retains the speed setting. If *resume* is pressed, the system accelerates or slows down the car back to the previously recorded speed (see Figure 1 for the architecture and the interfaces). From an

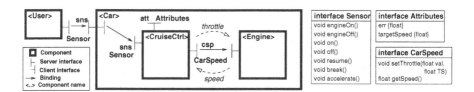

Fig. 1. The Cruise Control System

external point of view, the component <Car> provides the interface *sns*, of type *Sensor*, which methods permit to drive the car. Internally, the <Car> is made of two subcomponents. The component <CruiseCtrl> is the main control system, providing a *Sensor* interface and attributes representing its target speed and a possible error code. It also requires a *CarSpeed* interface in order to interact with the engine. The <Engine> provides an interface *csp*, of type *CarSpeed*, which methods permit to set the throttle and to get the current speed.

Composing specifications. Table 1 shows basic assume-guarantee specifications applying to the <CruiseCtrl> and <Engine> components (see Section 6 for a more complete illustration considering feedback control). We assume that the cruise is active, i.e. the button *on* or *resume* has been pressed, and that time intervals can be observed on the system execution.

The <CruiseCtrl> specification then guarantees that a *setThrottle* call is emitted periodically on its required interface *csp* (i.e. *periodic(csp.setThrottle)*). The <Engine> specification means: as long as it receives periodic *setThrottle* calls on its provided interface *csp* and the target speed (TS) is unchanged for r_{max} (i.e. $cst(TS, r_{max})$), it guarantees that the actual speed equals the target speed in less than r_{max} (i.e. $eq(speed, TS, r_{max})$).

Table 1. Specifications (the notation TS denotes $< CruiseCtrl > .att.targetSpeed$)

Participant	
<CruiseCtrl> offer	$TRUE \rightarrow periodic(csp.setThrottle)$
<Engine> offer	$periodic(csp.setThrottle) \wedge cst(TS, r_{max}) \rightarrow eq(speed, TS, r_{max})$
Environment E	$wait(D_1)$ // does nothing for the duration D_1
<User> requirement	$eq(speed, TS, D_2) \rightarrow TRUE$ // actual speed = target speed before D_2

The composition Theorem 1 can then be applied. To that end, it is easy to verify that the assume part of the specification of each component can be violated only by their respective environment, that the guarantee part can be violated only by itself and that all properties are safety properties. Thus, ignoring similar terms on both sides of the inclusion, the premise of Rule 1 can be written:

$$E \cap M_{<CruiseCtrl>} \cap M_{<Engine>} \subseteq E_{<CruiseCtrl>} \cap E_{<Engine>}, \qquad (2)$$
$$i.e. : \quad wait(D_1) \cap eq(speed, TS, r_{max}) \subseteq cst(TS, r_{max}). \qquad (3)$$

We note that $eq(speed, TS, r_{max})$ cannot be violated before $cst(TS, r_{max})$, unless the component <Engine> or <CruiseCtrl> violates its specification (cf. Table 1). Furthermore, since the environment of these two components is assumed to do nothing for the duration D_1 (denoted $wait(D_1)$ in Table 1), the target speed TS is unchanged for this period unless the environment violates its specification. A trivial condition for the premise to happen is then:

$$r_{max} < D_1.$$

If this agreement criterion is verified, the Theorem 1 proves that the conclusion of the inference rule is verified. Or in other terms that the composition of <CruiseCtrl> and <Engine> implements the following *contract* (in the sense of the theorem) $E \dashrightarrow M_{<CruiseCtrl>} \cap M_{<Car>}$, i.e.:

$$wait(D_1) \dashrightarrow periodic(csp.setThrottle) \cap eq(speed, TS, r_{max}), \qquad (4)$$

meaning that as long as the environment (the user) does nothing for D_1, the car system (composed of <CruiseCtrl> and <Engine>) guarantees that $setThrottle$ calls are emitted periodically and that the current speed equals the target speed in less than r_{max}.

In addition, we can consider that the user has the requirement shown in Table 1 (meaning that as long as the actual speed equals the target speed in less than D_2, he will be satisfied). We note that the form of this requirement is similar to the form of the offers of both components. Thus, it can be included in the composition. In that case, it is easy to verify that a trivial condition for the composition to be satisfactory for the user is $r_{max} < min(D_1, D_2)$.

4   Contract Model

The overall design of our contract model assumes that the collaboration between software entities (components, services, etc.) is driven by their architectural configuration. A complete and operational contract model is thus meant to verify properties of such configurations, and to determine the participating entities and their responsibilities. This implies that the used specifications should be explicit enough to allow a contracting system to determine the origin of a failure of a configuration. The model should also make it possible to express guarantees using various kinds of specification formalisms, provided that they can be interpreted in terms of contracts. Independently of the compositional relation that we focus on in this paper, we have previously stated the following properties as essential for a contract model [6]:

P1 - *Make explicit the conformance of individual components to their specifications.*

P2 - *Make explicit the compatibility of components specifications (between components of same level of composition, and between a composite and its subcomponents), on the base of their architectural configuration.*

P3 - *Make explicit the responsibilities of participating components against each specification they are involved in.*

P4 - *Support various specification formalisms and verification techniques (at configuration or run times).*

We develop a contracting system [7] that reifies different kinds of contracts. These contracts use executable assertions (P1), follow architectural configuration and reify responsibility (P3). We have shown [6] how this system is extended to explicit the conformance (P1), compatibility (P2) and responsibility (P3) properties, while providing an abstract model supporting P4.

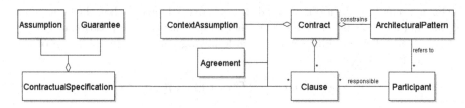

Fig. 2. Contracting framework

In order to make these properties hold, a contract in our model needs to be a first-class object, built from specifications at configuration time and that can check appropriate properties — and interpret violations — both at configuration and run times. The concepts that structure the contract are also partially inspired from real life contracts. A contract is thus a set of clauses constraining its participants, that are finally bound by an agreement.

Figure 2 shows a class diagram of the main reified concepts. Our contract model was originally meant to verify horizontal composition, but to deal with vertical one we will show next how the model meets the general assume-guarantee concepts used in the Abadi/Lamport theorem. A *Participant* is an object that refers to a compositional entity of the architecture, e.g. a service or a component. *Guarantee* and *Assumption* hold a predicate and the description of the observations on the system it constrains. For a given component, the guarantee constrains what it provides (its emitted messages..., as for the properties M_i in Theorem 1), the assumption constrains what it requires (its received messages, etc. as for the properties E_i in Theorem 1). According to the formalism used, their satisfaction can be evaluated at configuration or run times.

A *ContractualSpecification* is a predicate that binds together an assumption and a guarantee for a given component. It follows the assume-guarantee principle: as long as the assumption is true then the guarantee has to be also true (as for the temporal relation form $E \rightarrow M$). Consequently, our model applies to specification formalisms that are modular, i.e. a specification can be attached to a component, and that can also be interpreted in assume-guarantee terms, as shown in [6] (property **P4**).

A *Clause* is an object associating a contractual specification with a participant of the contract (property **P1**), which is then responsible for its guarantee (property **P3**). The model relies on architectural paths (APath, inspired from XPath) to navigate in the component structure. They allow a *Clause* to enforce its specification, by checking if its guarantee and assumption denote respectively observable actions under the control of the component it constrains (e.g. emitted calls) or of its environment (e.g. received calls). Moreover, strategy objects are associated to the evaluation of clauses, to detect if a guarantee is violated before its associated assumption.

An *Agreement* expresses the compatibility of the clauses (property **P2**) of the contract (as does the premise of the inference rule of Theorem 1). More precisely, it expresses that the assumptions of the collaborating parties are fulfilled by the their guarantees in a given environment. A *ContextAssumption* expresses a

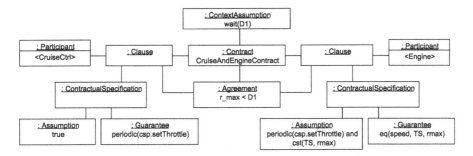

Fig. 3. Contract between <CruiseCtrl> and <Engine>

supplementary assumption on the environment of the components (as for the property E in Theorem 1), i.e. a predicate constraining the context in which they are composed.

Finally, an *ArchitecturalPattern* defines a configuration of relations between software entities. It is used to discern the entities to which the contract applies, and can be associated to a precise type of contract if needed. For instance, a very simple pattern is client-server, expressing that the contract participants are a client and a server bound by require/provide relationship in the architecture.

Figure 3 shows the object diagram of the contract constraining the <CruiseCtrl> and <Engine> components. This contract is related to the horizontal composition of the two components, following the specifications given in Section 3. For the sake of simplicity, the diagram the *ArchitecturalPattern* is not shown. The contract clauses are built from the specifications of the two participating components, as well as the assumption on their environment (cf. Table 1). In this case, the agreement expression is given by Formula 3 (the premise of the Rule 1), which is verified if $r_{max} < D_1$.

Responsibilities. Being able to determine the responsibility of a contract participant is the key in a contract model. In our model, a participating component in a clause can be either guarantor or beneficiary. As expected, the guarantor ensures the guarantee part of the component specification, whereas the beneficiary can rely on it as long as it does not violate the assume part. Responsibilities are automatically determined by the contracting system when contracts are built: for each clause, all participating components have their responsibilities set according to the type of contracts (client-server, composition, etc.) and their current configuration. More details on responsibilities and contract types are found in [7], and in the next section about vertical composition.

5 Composite Contract

Our current contract model supports and makes operational the horizontal composition of specifications, as long as they can be interpreted in assume-guarantee terms. We now describe our proposal to support the vertical composition of contracts relying on the Abadi/Lamport theorem presented in Section 2.

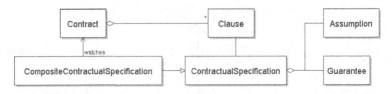

Fig. 4. Composite specification

Enforcing vertical composition consists in checking the compatibility between the specification of a composite and the composition of its subcomponents specifications. In order to support this, we extend our model with *CompositeContractualSpecification*, as shown in Figure 4 (the other concepts and their relations are described in Section 4). In this figure, the conclusion of the inference rule of Theorem 1 is linked to its premise. A *CompositeContractualSpecification* refers to a *Contract* between it subcomponents that reifies an agreement (the premise of the rule). It is itself an assume-guarantee *ContractualSpecification* obtained from the specifications of its subcomponents, and then stands for the conclusion of the rule. The application of this inference rule relies on several prerequisites, which are going to be either ensured by construction, or checked on the components by appropriate elements in the contract model:

- *A guarantee must constrain its guarantor, and its associated assumption must constrain the environment of the guarantor.* As stated in Section 4, the ConFract model enables *Clause* objects to check this prerequisite.
- *A guarantee must be true as long as its associated assumption is.* In ConFract, all clauses are evaluated following this rule (§4).
- *A composite specification must be implemented by a valid composition of components* (i.e. the premise of the inference rule holds). In our model, a *CompositeContractualSpecification* object watches (see Figure 4) the *Contract* between its subcomponents, to check if their *Agreement* (see Figure 3) is valid. It thus monitors the conditions of its own soundness.

Figure 5 shows a simplified object diagram of a composite specification, following the specifications given in Section 3. The *CompositeContractualSpecification* object is the composition of the <CruiseCtrl> and <Engine> components. The *Contract* (CruiseAndEngineContract) between these two components is detailed in Figure 3. The *Assumption* and *Guarantee* of the resulting composite specification are obtained from the Formula 4 on page 23 (the conclusion of the inference

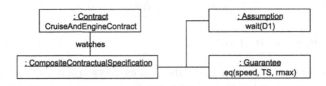

Fig. 5. Composite specification of the component <Car>

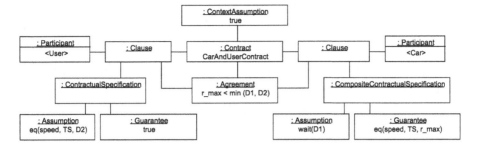

Fig. 6. Contract between <Car> and <User>

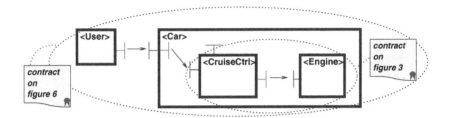

Fig. 7. Scope of the illustrated contracts

rule), by hiding the internal *setThrottle* events in order to attach them to the component <Car> (see Figure 1). As this component can itself be composed with the user, the contract between these two parties is shown in Figure 6. Applying again the inference rule, it is possible to infer a composite specification from this contract between the car and the user, etc... Figure 7 shows the scope of two of the contracts that are studied in the paper, with references to the respective figures.

Responsibilities. As a result, our framework makes possible to enforce responsibilities at several levels of abstraction. **Horizontally**, the framework handles clear responsibilities: a clause is violated only if its guarantee is violated before its assumption. The blame is on the component it constrains (the guarantor). When the assumption is violated first, the blame is on this component environment. If a contract is established, it is then possible to find a faulty participant, considering the architectural paths and the specification that cause the violation. For example, in Section 3, if the guarantee of the <Engine> component is violated first, this component is responsible. If its assumption is violated first, its environment is responsible. That is, the component <CruiseCtrl> considering the architectural paths and the specification. **Vertically**, at a composite level, when a clause of a contract is violated, the guarantor of this clause could be held responsible, following the rules described above. But considering the lower part of the inference rule of Theorem 1, we see that the conjunction of the subcomponent specifications implies what is represented as a *Composite-ContractualSpecification*. Consequently, if a *CompositeContractualSpecification* is not satisfied, we trivially deduce that a subcomponent specification is also not satisfied, as something false cannot be implied by something true. This reasoning is valid in our model since a *CompositeContractualSpecification* watches the contract between its subcomponents to ensure its own soundness (see Figure 4).

As the responsible components of the contract clauses are among the subcomponents, the mechanism for discovering responsibility can work at two levels of the component hierarchy: it can tell which component is to blame at a level of hierarchy, but also which part of this component did not behave properly in its content. For example, in Section 3, if we observe that the component <Car> violates its specification, we can relate this error to one of its subcomponents, that is the component <Engine>. In complex systems, this kind of reasoning (horizontal and vertical responsibilities) can help to analyse execution traces resulting from a property violation. It can be used automatically at runtime with appropriate monitoring mechanisms and/or at design time depending on the specification formalism used.

6   Application

We now consider a simplified feedback control for the speed at which the car is traveling when the cruise is active. The intent is to illustrate how classical results in linear control can be interpreted in contractual terms to constrain an architecture, rather than focusing on their mathematical treatments .

Transfer functions. As illustrated in Figure 1, the cruise controls the velocity of the car and forms a close-loop control system with the car engine. We use the following notations to represent the observable signals in the architecture:

- $y(t)$, the current velocity of the car. This signal is obtained by calling *getSpeed* on the provided interface *csp* of the component <Engine>. It is periodically observed by the component <CruiseCtrl> when the cruise is active.
- $r(t)$, the desired velocity of the car (reference input of the control loop). This signal changes when <CruiseCtrl> receives an *on* call on its provided interface *sns*. It then records the current value of $y(t)$ in its attribute *targetSpeed*.
- $e(t)$, the error represented here by $r(t) - y(t)$. This signal is recorded in the <CruiseCtrl> attribute *err* when the observed value of $r(t)$ or $y(t)$ changes.
- $u(t)$, the cruise controller output in reaction to $e(t)$. This signal is observed when the component <CruiseCtrl> emits *setThrottle* calls on its required interface *csp* to maintain the desired velocity of the car.

From classical results in linear control [8], we assume that the <CruiseCtrl> and <Engine> components (i.e. the controller and the system under control) are described by linear transfer functions $G_c(s)$ and $G_p(s)$. The <CruiseCtrl> and <Engine> output are then given by:

$$U(s) = G_c(s)E(s) = G_c(s)[R(s) - Y(s)] \quad and \quad Y(s) = G_p(s)U(s), \qquad (5)$$

where s is a frequency variable, and capital letters represent transforms in the frequency domain of the respective time functions $u(t)$, $e(t)$, $r(t)$ and $y(t)$.

Table 2. Specifications

Participant	
<CruiseCtrl> offer	$P_{E(s)} \rightarrow P_{U(s)}$ // guarantees a control output, assuming an error input
<Engine> offer	$P_{U(s)} \rightarrow P_{Y(s)}$ // guarantees a velocity output, assuming a control input
Environment E	$P_{R(s)}$ // the desired velocity, assumed from the two components environment
<User> requirement	$(\forall t > x : y(t) = r(t) \pm 5\%) \rightarrow TRUE$ // is satisfied, assuming a given precision

Composing specifications. Table 2 shows the individual assume-guarantee specifications applying to the <CruiseCtrl> and <Engine> components. For example, the reading of the <CruiseCtrl> specification means that[3]: as long as the input error signal $e(t)$ is described by $E(s)$ (assume part), the <CruiseCtrl> emits the control signal $u(t)$ described by $U(s)$ (guarantee part).

The composition Theorem 1 can be applied. To that end, it is easy to verify that the assume part of the specification of each component can be violated only by their respective environment, that the guarantee part can be violated only by itself and that all properties are safety properties (i.e. are refutable in a finite time). Thus, the premise of the inference Rule 1 can be written:

$$E \cap M_{<CruiseCtrl>} \cap M_{<Engine>} \subseteq E_{<CruiseCtrl>} \cap E_{<Engine>}, \tag{6}$$

$$i.e.: \quad P_{R(s)} \cap P_{U(s)} \cap P_{Y(s)} \subseteq P_{E(S)} \cap P_{U(s)}. \tag{7}$$

In this case, we observe that this is trivially verified by construction since $P_{U(s)}$ is similar on both sides of this inclusion and since the error $E(s) = R(s) - Y(s)$, i.e. $P_{E(s)}$ is verified by definition when $P_{R(s)}$ and $P_{Y(s)}$ are. Therefore, this agreement criterion proves that the composition of <CruiseCtrl> and <Engine> implements the following contract (cf. Theorem 1):

$$E \rightarrow M_{<CruiseCtrl>} \cap M_{<Engine>} \quad i.e. \quad P_{R(s)} \rightarrow P_{U(s)} \cap P_{Y(s)}, \tag{8}$$

meaning that as long as the reference input signal $r(t)$ for the desired velocity of the car is described by $R(s)$ (assume part), the closed-loop composed of <CruiseCtrl> and <Engine> emits the signals $u(t)$ and $y(t)$ described by $U(s)$ and $Y(s)$ (guarantee part). It turns out that $y(t)$, the actual velocity of the car, is the signal of interest for the user. By substituting $U(s)$ in $Y(s)$ in Formula 5, we know that the output signal $y(t)$ emitted by the closed-loop is described by:

$$Y(s) = [G_c(s)G_p(s)]/[1 + G_c(s)G_p(s)]R(s) = G(s)R(s), \tag{9}$$

and is guaranteed by Formula 8 as long as the desired velocity is described by $R(s)$. $G(s)$ represents the closed-loop transfer function relating the actual velocity to the desired velocity, a classical result in linear control systems.

Contract model. When the car system is undergoing test, the application of our contract model can be illustrated by the verification of the properties P1,

---

[3] The property P_X means that the signal x is described by the transfer function X.

P2 and P3 presented in Section 4. Using the ConFract system [7] extended to support the proposed model, contracts are built at configuration time on the whole architecture of the car system. Each component <CruiseCtrl>... is then monitored to check whether it respects its specification (P1). The responsible components (P3) can be precisely determined against a failure observed in P1. Moreover, as a result of the reification of the composite contract, and following the Abadi/Lamport theorem, the enforcement framework mechanisms discussed in Section 5 makes possible to deduce compositional responsibilities if the violated clause is the result of a vertical composition (P2).

For example, if the framework observes that the actual velocity (output signal) of the component <Car> is not described by $Y(s)$ (guarantee part), whereas the assumption on the desired velocity holds, then <Car> is responsible of the failure at the composite level. But the framework can deduce that a subcomponent is the actual responsible in the underlying composition: either <Engine> if its assumption holds, or <CruiseCtrl> if a propagation of failure has occured. The contract model makes operational this kind of reasoning. It can be exploited to propose versatile error handling mechanism, spanning from complete logs to precise identifications of the initial responsible component in a sequence of violations. This latter strategy is useful in complex hierarchical systems, where the same error can be observed at several level of nesting.

In practice, finally, control loops have well-known problems such as oscillations or physical systems that do not respond instantaneously. We briefly introduce how the contract model allows to support in uniform way **user requirements**. A user can be represented in the architecture by a component artifact (cf. Figure 1). As any other component, this artifact can handle individual specifications, participate in a composition to establish a contract, or be monitored to handle violations and responsibilities. Let us consider for illustration that the user (or designer) of the car system has the additional requirement specified in Table 2 (meaning that as long as the actual/desired velocity precision equals 5% after a delay x, he will be satisfied). We note that the form of this requirement is similar to the form of the offers of the other components. Thus, it can be included in the composition. In order to establish a contract with the car, whose contractual specification is given by Formula 8, the premise of the inference Rule 1 can be written:

$$P_{U(s)} \cap P_{Y(s)} \subseteq P_{R(s)} \cap (\forall t > x : e(t) = r(t) \pm 5\%). \tag{10}$$

Comparing to Formula 7, the verification of this new agreement criterion will require to know the transfer functions. Although such a mathematical treatment is out of the scope of this illustration, we note that user requirements for quality of service can be interpreted in contractual terms as for the other terms constraining the architecture. In particular, if the system analysis allows formula 10 to be verified, we can prove from Theorem 1 that the composition of <CruiseCtrl> and <Engine> satisfies the user requirement. We can then enforce that this composition is valid at configuration or runtime as long as the involved contracts are satisfied.

7   Related Work

Numerous works have provided rules for proving properties of systems by reasoning about the assume-guarantee specifications of their components. The first strong result, that could handle circularities for safety properties, is that of Misra [16] and was followed by extensive research works discussed by Abadi and Lamport [2]. This latter result supersedes the composition theorem 1 by providing rules for handling fairness properties, hiding and decomposition (wich eliminates the need to reason about the complete low-level system).

Besides, several works have proposed contract frameworks as a mean to apply formal results to concrete software systems. They all at least consider the conformance of components to their specifications (property P1 page 23). They handle quality of service [3,12] or behavioral [20] properties, but are then dedicated to one type of formalism (fail to meet P4). The compatibility of component specifications (P2) is generally considered, but often handled externally to the contract model with adequate solvers. For example, CQML [3] does not reify the compatibility but provides its expression considering the specifications of a component configuration taken as a whole, with no consideration for architecture. The architecture is taken into account in the contract model [20] but the compatibility is still not reified.

Some contract models are dedicated to specific concerns, such as correctness guarantees in the composition of web services [15]. Some others are implicit, e.g. the SOFA component model allows one to apply *implicit* behavior contracts in terms of both horizontal (client-service) and vertical (nesting) cooperation of components [17]. Leboucher and Najm [13] apply the Abadi's and Lamport's composition theorem to distributed systems. They propose it as a basis for an object oriented framework, with rigourous method for proving end-to-end QoS guarantees in ODP systems, but without a reified contract model.

In both the work of Reussner et al. [18] and the one of Jézéquel et al. [12], the contract model reifies the dependency between properties of provided and required services of a component. We also consider that this relationship is important and should be reified to study the component compatibility with its environment. We deal with this through a general assume-guarantee approach, and we also reify operationnally the global validity condition of an assembly of components for different formalisms. Moreover none of these consider the responsibilities of the contract participants.

Findler and Felleisen [9] show how the responsibility in behavioral subtyping of contracts expressed with assertions can be correctly assigned in object-oriented systems. They only determine the responsible part, but they can distinguish the client/provider relationship from the subtyping relationship between the authors of a class and its subclass. Our intentions are similar, but our model assigns fine-grained responsibilities to components, which makes possible to exploit them, for instance to renegotiate contracts in case of violation [5].

8   Conclusion

Reliably composing components is a long term but crucial goal. It intrinsically depends upon the capability to monitor the respective obligations both *horizontally*, between components, and *vertically*, from subcomponents to composite ones, in order to identify, trace back and blame the correct components when such obligations are broken and faults occur. Besides *horizontal* obligations of the traditional contract-based approach, in this paper we have proposed to extend this approach to address *vertical* composite contracts. Our new composite contract construct is formally founded in Abadi's and Lamport's theorem for composing specifications [1]. We are currently implementing this new form of contracts in our ConFract platform [7,6], which provides first-class contracts equipped with generic contract enforcement and blame-tracking mechanisms. The cruise control running example for composite contracts illustrates how the ConFract blame-tracking mechanism is able to exploit both *horizontal* and *vertical* compositions to find faulty components when obligations are no longer fulfilled.

ConFract is currently implemented over the Fractal hierarchical component model [4]. In this settings, the new composite contract works hand in hand with the hierarchical *vertical* composition to allow programmers to compose contracts as they compose components. However, the use of composite contracts is not limited to hierarchical component models. They can equally apply to the large class of models where the relationships between subcomponents and their composite remain implicit, such as non-hierarchical component models and Web services.

The current limitations of our composite contracts are linked to the need to reason about subcomponent specifications, following a bottom-up approach. In some circumstances, the formalism used will not allow to prove how a composite contract can be guaranteed, or it would be preferable to reason in a top-down approach, as proposed for behavior protocols [17]. Another valuable extension would be to compute the property of a component according to its context of reuse, as proposed for parametric contracts [18]. Further research is needed to overcome these limitations. However, the flexibility and the genericity of ConFract, as examplified in this paper, makes it an appropriate testbed and practical tool to this end.

References

1. Abadi, M., Lamport, L.: Composing specifications. ACM Trans. Program. Lang. Syst. 15(1), 73–132 (1993)
2. Abadi, M., Lamport, L.: Conjoining specifications. ACM Trans. Program. Lang. Syst. 17(3), 507–534 (1995)
3. Aegedal, J.O.: Quality of Service Support in Development of Distributed Systems. PhD thesis, University Of Oslo (2001)
4. Bruneton, E., Coupaye, T., Leclercq, M., Quéma, V., Stefani, J.-B.: An Open Component Model and Its Support in Java. In: Crnković, I., Stafford, J.A., Schmidt, H.W., Wallnau, K. (eds.) CBSE 2004. LNCS, vol. 3054, Springer, Heidelberg (2004)

5. Chang, H., Collet, P.: Fine-grained Contract Negotiation for Hierarchical Software Components. In: 31th EUROMICRO Conference 2005, Porto, Portugal, 30 August-3 September 2005, IEEE Computer Society Press, Los Alamitos (2005)
6. Collet, P., Ozanne, A., Rivierre, N.: Towards a versatile contract model to organize behavioral specifications. In: van Leeuwen, J., Italiano, G.F., van der Hoek, W., Meinel, C., Sack, H., Plášil, F. (eds.) SOFSEM 2007. LNCS, vol. 4362, Springer, Heidelberg (2007)
7. Collet, P., Rousseau, R., Coupaye, T., Rivierre, N.: A contracting system for hierarchical components. In: Heineman, G.T., Crnkovic, I., Schmidt, H.W., Stafford, J.A., Szyperski, C.A., Wallnau, K.C. (eds.) CBSE 2005. LNCS, vol. 3489, pp. 187–202. Springer, Heidelberg (2005)
8. D'azzo, J.J., Houpis, C.: Linear control system analysis and design: Conventional and modern. McGraw-Hill, New York (1995)
9. Findler, R.B., Felleisen, M.: Contract soundness for object-oriented languages. In: Proceedings of OOPSLA 2001 (2001)
10. Goguen, J.A., Burstall, R.M.: Cat, a system for the structured elaboration of correct programs from structured specifications. Technical Report CSL-118, SRI International, Computer Science Lab (1980)
11. Jones, C.B.: Specification and design of (parallel) programs. In: IFIP Congress, pp. 321–332 (1983)
12. Jézéquel, J.-M., Defour, O., Plouzeau, N.: An mda approach to tame component based software development. In: de Boer, F.S., Bonsangue, M.M., Graf, S., de Roever, W.-P. (eds.) FMCO 2003. LNCS, vol. 3188, pp. 260–275. Springer, Heidelberg (2004)
13. Leboucher, L., Najm, E.: A framework for real-time qos in distributed systems. In: IEEE Workshop on Middleware for Distributed Real-Time Systems and Service, San Francisco, California (1997)
14. Magee, J., Kramer, J.: Concurrency: state models & Java programs. John Wiley & Sons, Inc., Chichester (1999)
15. Milanovic, N.: Contract-based web service composition framework with correctness guarantees. In: Malek, M., Nett, E., Suri, N. (eds.) ISAS 2005. LNCS, vol. 3694, pp. 52–67. Springer, Heidelberg (2005)
16. Misra, J., Chandy, M.: Proofs of networks of processes. IEEE Transactions on Software Engineering 7(4), 417–426 (1981)
17. Plasil, F., Visnovsky, S.: Behavior protocols for software components. IEEE Transactions on Software Engineering 28(11) (November 2002)
18. Reussner, R., Poernomo, I., Schmidt, H.W.: Reasoning about software architectures with contractually specified components. In: Cechich, A., Piattini, M., Vallecillo, A. (eds.) Component-Based Software Quality. LNCS, vol. 2693, pp. 287–325. Springer, Heidelberg (2003)
19. Szyperski, C.: Component Software — Beyond Object-Oriented Programming. Addison-Wesley Publishing Co., Reading (1997)
20. Tran, H.-M., Bedu, P., Duchien, L., Nguyen, H.-Q., Perrin, J.: Toward structural and behavioral analysis for component models. In: SAVBCS 2004. 12th ACM SIGSOFT Symposium on the Foundation of Software Engineering, NewPort Beach, California, USA, ACM Press, New York (November 2004)

Towards a Unifying Theory for Choreography Conformance and Contract Compliance*

Mario Bravetti and Gianluigi Zavattaro

Department of Computer Science, University of Bologna, Italy

Abstract. In the context of Service Oriented Computing, contracts are descriptions of the externally observable behaviour of services. Given a group of collaborating services, their contracts can be used to verify whether their composition is sound, i.e., the services are compliant. In this paper, we relate the theory of contracts with the notion of choreography conformance, used to check whether an aggregation of services correctly behaves according to a high level specification of their possible conversations. The main result of this paper is the definition of an effective procedure that can be used to verify whether a service with a given contract can correctly play a specific role within a choreography. This procedure is achieved via composition of choreography projection and contract refinement.

1 Introduction

Service Oriented Computing (SOC) is a novel paradigm for distributed computing based on services intended as autonomous and heterogeneous components that can be published and discovered via standard interface languages and publish/discovery protocols. One of the peculiarities of Service Oriented Computing, distinguishing it from other distributed computing paradigms (such as component based software engineering), is that it is centered around the so-called *message oriented architecture*. This means that, given a set of collaborating services, the current state of their interaction is stored inside the exchanged messages and not only within the services. From a practical viewpoint, this means that it is necessary to include, in the exchanged messages, the so-called correlation information that permits to a service to associate a received message to the correct session of interaction (in fact, the same service could be contemporaneously involved in different sessions at the same time).

Web Services is the most prominent service oriented technology: Web Services publish their interface expressed in WSDL, they are discovered through the UDDI protocol, and they are invoked using SOAP.

Two main approaches for the composition of services are currently under investigation and development inside the SOC research community: service *orchestration* and service *choreography*. According to the first approach, the activities of the composed services are coordinated by a specific component, called the

---

* Research partially funded by EU Integrated Project Sensoria, contract n. 016004.

M. Lumpe and W. Vanderperren (Eds.): SC 2007, LNCS 4829, pp. 34–50, 2007.
© Springer-Verlag Berlin Heidelberg 2007

orchestrator, that is responsible for invoking the composed services and collect their responses. Several languages have been already proposed for programming orchestrators such as XLANG [Tha01], WSFL [Ley01] and WS-BPEL [OAS].

Choreography languages are attracting a lot of attention within W3C, where the most credited choreography language WS-CDL [W3C] is currently under development. Choreographies represent a "more democratic" alternative approach for service composition with respect to orchestrations. Indeed, orchestrations require the implementation of central points of coordination; on the contrary, choreography languages support a high level description of peer-to-peer interactions among services that directly communicate without the mediation of any orchestrator. Unfortunately, choreography languages are not yet popular due to the difficulties encountered while translating the high level description of the composed services into an actual system obtained as combination of autonomous, loosely coupled and heterogeneous components.

As an example of service composition, let us consider a travel agency service that can be invoked by a client in order to reserve both an airplane seat and a hotel room. In order to satisfy the client's request, the travel agency contacts two separate services, one for the airplane reservation and one for the hotel reservation. A choreographic specification of this service composition describes the possible flows of invocations exchanged among the four roles (the client, the travel agency, the airplane reservation service, and the hotel reservation service). A formal specification of a choreography of this kind can be found in the Example 1.

The problem that we consider in this paper can be summarized as follows: given a choreography, we want to define an automatic procedure that can be used to check whether a service correctly plays one of the roles described by the choreography. For instance, given a choreographic specification of the above travel agency example, and an actual travel agency service, we want to check whether the actual service behaves correctly according to the choreographic specification. The solution that we propose to this problem assumes that the services expose in their interface an abstract description of their behaviour. In the service oriented computing literature, this kind of information is referred to as the *service contract* [CL06]. More precisely, the service contract describes the sequence of input/output operations that the service intends to execute within a session of interaction with other services. In particular, we propose to combine choreography projection with service contract refinement. The former permits to extract the expected behaviour of one role and synthesize a corresponding service contract. The latter permits to characterize an entire class of contracts (that refine the contract obtained by projection), for which it is guaranteed that the corresponding services correctly play the considered role in the choreography.

An important property of our theory is that contract refinement is defined locally, i.e., given a correct implementation of a choreography based on the contracts $C_1, \cdots, C_n$, each contract C_i can be replaced by any refinement C_i', and the overall system obtained by composition of $C_1', \cdots, C_n'$ is still a correct implementation. This property permits to retrieve the actual services to be composed to implement the choreography independently one from the other (e.g. contemporaneously querying different service registries) collecting the services that either expose the contract obtained by projection, or one of its refined contracts.

The paper is structured as follows. In Section 2 we introduce our model for choreographies defined in terms of a process calculus. In Section 3 we report the theory of service contracts and refinement. This section is essentially an extension of our previous work [BZ06a]; the main novelty is that in the contract calculus we associate to contracts also an additional information indicating the location where the corresponding service is located. The presence of locations permits to prove new interesting results that did not hold in the theory reported in [BZ06a] (for this reason we need to completely revisit and extend the results already proved in [BZ06a]). Section 4 describes the exploitation of the theory of contract refinement in the context of choreography-based service composition. Finally, Section 5 reports some conclusive remarks and the comparison with the related literature. The proofs, not reported in the paper, can be found in [BZ06b].

2   The Choreography Calculus

Definition 1 (Choreographies). *Let* Operations, *ranged over by* $a, b, c, \cdots$ *and* Roles, *ranged over by* $r, s, t, \cdots$, *be two countable sets of operation and role names, respectively. The set of Choreographies, ranged over by* $H, L, \cdots$ *is defined by the following grammar:*

$$H \quad ::= \quad a_{r \to s} \quad | \quad H + H \quad | \quad H; H \quad | \quad H | H \quad | \quad H^*$$

The invocations $a_{r \to s}$ *means that role* r *invokes the operation* a *provided by the role* s. *The other operators are choice* $\_ + \_$, *sequential* $\_; \_$, *parallel* $\_|\_$, *and repetition* $\_^*$.

The operational semantics of choreographies considers two auxiliary terms **1** and **0**. They are used to model the completion of a choreography, which is relevant in the operational modeling of sequential composition. The formal definition is given in Table 1 where we take η to range over the set of labels $\{a_{r \to s} \mid a \in Operations, r, s \in Roles\} \cup \{\sqrt{}\}$ (the label $\sqrt{}$ denotes completion). The rules in Table 1 are rather standard for process calculi with sequential composition and without synchronization; in fact, parallel composition simply allows for the interleaving of the actions executed by the operands (apart from completion labels $\sqrt{}$ that are required to synchronize).

Choreographies are especially useful to describe the protocols of interactions within a group of collaborating services. To clarify this point, we present a simple example of a protocol described with our choreography calculus.

Example 1 **(Reservation via Travel Agency).** Let us consider the following choreography composed of four roles: *Client, TravelAgency, AirCompany* and

Table 1. Semantic rules for contracts (symmetric rules omitted)

$$a_{r \to s} \xrightarrow{a_{r \to s}} 1 \qquad\qquad 1 \xrightarrow{\sqrt{}} 0 \qquad\qquad H^* \xrightarrow{\sqrt{}} 0$$

$$\frac{H \xrightarrow{\eta} H'}{H+L \xrightarrow{\eta} H'} \qquad \frac{H \xrightarrow{\eta} H' \quad \eta \neq \sqrt{}}{H;L \xrightarrow{\eta} H';L} \qquad \frac{H \xrightarrow{\sqrt{}} H' \quad L \xrightarrow{\eta} L'}{H;L \xrightarrow{\eta} L'}$$

$$\frac{H \xrightarrow{\sqrt{}} H' \quad L \xrightarrow{\sqrt{}} L'}{H|L \xrightarrow{\sqrt{}} H'|L'} \qquad \frac{H \xrightarrow{\eta} H' \quad \eta \neq \sqrt{}}{H|L \xrightarrow{\eta} H'|L} \qquad \frac{H \xrightarrow{\eta} H' \quad \eta \neq \sqrt{}}{H^* \xrightarrow{\eta} H';H^*}$$

Hotel

$Reservation_{Client \to TravelAgency};$
$(\,(Reserve_{TravelAgency \to AirCompany}; ConfirmFlight_{AirCompany \to TravelAgency})\,|$
$(Reserve_{TravelAgency \to Hotel}; ConfirmRoom_{Hotel \to TravelAgency})\,);$
$Confirmation_{TravelAgency \to Client} + Cancellation_{TravelAgency \to Client}$

According to this choreography, the *Client* initially sends a reservation request to a travel agency, that subsequently contacts in parallel an airplane company *AirCompany* and a room reservation service *Hotel* in order to reserve both the travel and the staying of the client. Then, the travel agency either confirms or cancels the reservation request of the client.

Even if choreography languages represent a simple and intuitive approach for the description of the message exchange among services, they are not yet very popular in the context of service oriented computing. The main problem to their diffusion is that it is not trivial to relate the high level choreography description with the actual implementation of the specified system realised as composition of services that are usually loosely coupled, independently developed by different companies, and autonomous. More precisely, the difficult task is, given a choreography, to lookup available services that, once combined, are ensured to behave according to the given choreography.

In order to formally investigate this problem, we need also a calculus for the description of the behaviour of services. This calculus is reported in the next section; in Section 4 we will formalize a procedure to verify whether a given service can play a specific role within a given choreography.

3   The Theory of Contracts with Locations

We assume a denumerable set of action names $\mathcal{N}$, ranged over by $a, b, c, \ldots$. The set $\mathcal{N}_{con} = \{a_* \mid a \in \mathcal{N}\}$ is the set of contract action names. Moreover, we consider a denumerable set Loc of location names, ranged over by $l, l', l_1, \cdots$. The set $\mathcal{N}_{loc} = \{a_l \mid a \in \mathcal{N}, l \in Loc\}$ is the set of located action names. The set $\mathcal{A}_{con} = \mathcal{N}_{con} \cup \{\overline{a}_* \mid a_* \in \mathcal{N}_{con}\}$ is the set of input and output contract actions.

The set $\mathcal{A}_{loc} = \mathcal{N}_{loc} \cup \{\bar{a}_l \mid a_l \in \mathcal{N}_{loc}\}$ is the set of input and output located actions. We use $\tau \notin \mathcal{N}$ to denote an internal (unsynchronizable) computation. Given a set of located action names $I \subset \mathcal{N}_{loc}$, we denote: with $\bar{I} = \{\bar{a}_l \mid a_l \in I\}$ the set of output actions performable on those names and with $I_l = \{a \mid a_l \in I\}$ the set of action names with associated location l.

Definition 2 (Contracts and Systems). *The syntax of contracts is defined by the following grammar*

$$C ::= \mathbf{0} \mid \mathbf{1} \mid \tau \mid a_* \mid \tau;\bar{a}_* \mid a \mid \tau;\bar{a}_l \mid$$
$$C;C \mid C+C \mid C|C \mid C\backslash M \mid C^*$$

where $M \subseteq \mathcal{N}_{con}$. The set of all contracts C is denoted by $\mathcal{P}_{con}$. In the following we will omit trailing "$\mathbf{1}$" when writing contracts.
The syntax of systems (contract compositions) is defined by the following grammar

$$P ::= [C]_l \mid P\|P \mid P\backslash L$$

where $L \subseteq \mathcal{A}_{loc}$. A system P is well-formed if: (i) every contract subterm $[C]_l$ occurs in P at a different location l and (ii) no output action with destination l is syntactically included inside a contract subterm occurring in P at the same location l, i.e. actions $\bar{a}_l$ cannot occur inside a subterm $[C]_l$ of P. The set of all well-formed systems P is denoted by $\mathcal{P}$. In the following we will just consider well-formed systems and, for simplicity, we will call them just systems.

We take α to range over the set of syntactical actions $SAct = \mathcal{A}_{con} \cup \mathcal{N} \cup \{\bar{a}_l \mid a_l \in \mathcal{N}_{loc}\} \cup \{\tau\}$.

The operational semantics of contracts is defined by the rules in Table 2 (plus symmetric rules). The operational semantics of systems is defined by the rules in Table 3 plus symmetric rules. We take β to range over the set of actions executable by contracts and systems, $Act = \mathcal{A}_{con} \cup \mathcal{N} \cup \mathcal{A}_{loc} \cup \{\tau\}$. We take λ to range over the set of transition labels $\mathcal{L} = Act \cup \{\sqrt{}\}$, where $\sqrt{}$ denotes successful termination.

In the remainder of the paper we use the following notations: $P \xrightarrow{\lambda}$ to mean that there exists P' such that $P \xrightarrow{\lambda} P'$ and, given a sequence of labels $w = \lambda_1\lambda_2 \cdots \lambda_{n-1}\lambda_n$ (possibly empty, i.e., $w = \varepsilon$), we use $P \xrightarrow{w} P'$ to denote the sequence of transitions $P \xrightarrow{\lambda_1} P_1 \xrightarrow{\lambda_2} \cdots \xrightarrow{\lambda_{n-1}} P_{n-1} \xrightarrow{\lambda_n} P'$ (in case of $w = \varepsilon$ we have $P' = P$, i.e., $P \xrightarrow{\varepsilon} P$).

The main results reported in this paper are consequences of a property of systems that we call *output persistence*. This property states that once a system decides to execute an output whose location is not included in the system, its actual execution is mandatory in order to successfully complete the execution of the system. In order to formally prove this property we need to formalize two (easy to prove) preliminary lemmata. Given a system $P \in \mathcal{P}$, we use $loc(P)$ to denote the subset of Loc of the locations of contracts syntactically occurring inside P: e.g. $loc([C]_{l_1}\|[C']_{l_2}) = \{l_1, l_2\}$.

Table 2. Semantic rules for contracts (symmetric rules omitted)

$$1 \xrightarrow{\checkmark} 0 \qquad \alpha \xrightarrow{\alpha} 1$$

$$\frac{C \xrightarrow{\lambda} C'}{C+D \xrightarrow{\lambda} C'} \qquad \frac{C \xrightarrow{\lambda} C' \quad \lambda \neq \checkmark}{C;D \xrightarrow{\lambda} C';D} \qquad \frac{C \xrightarrow{\checkmark} C' \quad D \xrightarrow{\lambda} D'}{C;D \xrightarrow{\lambda} D'}$$

$$\frac{C \xrightarrow{a*} C' \quad D \xrightarrow{\overline{a}*} D'}{C|D \xrightarrow{\tau} C'|D'} \qquad \frac{C \xrightarrow{\checkmark} C' \quad D \xrightarrow{\checkmark} D'}{C|D \xrightarrow{\checkmark} C'|D'} \qquad \frac{C \xrightarrow{\lambda} C' \quad \lambda \neq \checkmark}{C|D \xrightarrow{\lambda} C'|D}$$

$$\frac{C \xrightarrow{\lambda} C' \quad \lambda \notin M \cup \overline{M}}{C\backslash M \xrightarrow{\lambda} C'\backslash M} \qquad C^* \xrightarrow{\checkmark} 0 \qquad \frac{C \xrightarrow{\lambda} C' \quad \lambda \neq \checkmark}{C^* \xrightarrow{\lambda} C';C^*}$$

Table 3. Semantic rules for contract compositions (symmetric rules omitted)

$$\frac{C \xrightarrow{a} C'}{[C]_l \xrightarrow{a_l} [C']_l} \qquad \frac{C \xrightarrow{\overline{a}_{l'}} C'}{[C]_l \xrightarrow{\overline{a}_{l'}} [C']_l} \qquad \frac{P \xrightarrow{\lambda} P' \quad \lambda \neq \checkmark}{P\|Q \xrightarrow{\lambda} P'\|Q}$$

$$\frac{P \xrightarrow{a_l} P' \quad Q \xrightarrow{\overline{a}_l} Q'}{P\|Q \xrightarrow{\tau} P'\|Q'} \qquad \frac{P \xrightarrow{\checkmark} P' \quad Q \xrightarrow{\checkmark} Q'}{P\|Q \xrightarrow{\checkmark} P'\|Q'} \qquad \frac{P \xrightarrow{\lambda} P' \quad \lambda \notin L}{P\backslash L \xrightarrow{\lambda} P'\backslash L}$$

Proposition 1 (Output persistence). *Let $P \in \mathcal{P}$ be a system such that $P \xrightarrow{w} P' \xrightarrow{\overline{a}_l}$, with $l \notin loc(P)$. We have that, for every P'' such that $P' \xrightarrow{w'} P''$ and $P'' \xrightarrow{\checkmark}$, the string w' must include $\overline{a}_l$.*

Note that, when we apply external restriction on outputs $\overline{a}_l$ to a system P such that $l \notin loc(P)$, i.e. we consider $P\backslash \overline{O}$, with $O \subset \mathcal{N}_{loc}$ such that $O_l = \emptyset$ for every $l \in loc(P)$, due to the absence of internal communication of actions of $\overline{O}$ inside the system, we obtain a transition system isomorphic to that of the system $P\{0/\alpha | \alpha \in \overline{O}\}$, i.e. the syntactical substitution of 0 for every syntactical occurrence of "α" such that $\alpha \in \overline{O}$. In the following we will use the abuse of notation "$C\backslash \overline{O}$" to stand for "$C\{0/\alpha | \alpha \in \overline{O}\}$": this allows us, e.g., to write a term $([C_1]_{l_1} \| [C_2]_{l_2})\backslash \overline{O}$ in the format considered above as $[C_1\backslash \overline{O}]_{l_1} \| [C_2\backslash \overline{O}]_{l_2}$. As far as inputs are concerned, we cannot perform a similar symmetric syntactic input action removal in the case of restriction on inputs $\overline{a}_l$ applied to a general system P such that $l \in loc(P)$. This because internal communication inside the system could make use of the inputs that we are considering for removal. However the property holds if we restrict to a system composed of a single contract. When we apply external restriction on input directly to a contract C, i.e. we consider $[C]_l\backslash I$, with $I = \{a_l \mid a \in M\}$ for some $M \subseteq \mathcal{N}$, we obtain a transition system isomorphic to that of $[C\{0/\alpha | \alpha \in M\}]_l$. In the following we will use the abuse of notation "$C \backslash M$" to stand for "$C\{\mathbf{0}/\alpha | \alpha \in M\}$": this allows us to write the term above simply as $[C \backslash M]_l$.

We now define the notion of correct composition of contracts. This notion is the same as in [BZ06a]. Intuitively, a system composed of contracts is correct if all possible computations may guarantee completion; this means that the system is both deadlock and livelock free (there could be an infinite computation, but given any possible prefix of this infinite computation, it can be extended to reach a successfully completed computation).

Definition 3 (Correct contract composition). *A system P is a correct contract composition, denoted $P \downarrow$, if for every P' such that $P \xrightarrow{\tau}^{*} P'$ there exists P'' such that $P' \xrightarrow{\tau}^{*} P'' \xrightarrow{\sqrt{}}$.*

3.1   Independent Subcontracts

We are now ready to define the notion of independent subcontract pre-order. Given a contract $C \in \mathcal{P}_{con}$, we use $oloc(C)$ to denote the subset of Loc of the locations of the destinations of all the output actions occurring inside C.

Definition 4 (Independent Subcontract pre-order). *A pre-order $\leq$ over $\mathcal{P}_{con}$ is an independent subcontract pre-order if, for any $n \geq 1$, contracts $C_1, \ldots, C_n \in \mathcal{P}_{con}$ and $C'_1, \ldots, C'_n \in \mathcal{P}_{con}$ such that $\forall i. C'_i \leq C_i$, and distinguished location names $l_1, \ldots, l_n \in Loc$ such that $\forall i. l_i \notin oloc(C_i) \cup oloc(C'_i)$, we have*

$$([C_1]_{l_1} \| \ldots \| [C_n]_{l_n}) \downarrow \quad \Rightarrow \quad ([C'_1]_{l_1} \| \ldots \| [C'_n]_{l_n}) \downarrow$$

We will prove that there exists a maximal independent subcontract pre-order; this is a direct consequence of the output persistence property. In fact, if we consider mixed choice it is easy to prove that there exists no maximal independent subcontract pre-order (see [BZ06a]).

We will show that the maximal independent subcontract pre-order can be achieved defining a more coarse form of refinement in which, given any system composed of a set of contracts, refinement is applied to one contract only (thus leaving the other unchanged). We call this form of refinement *singular subcontract pre-order.*

Intuitively a pre-order $\leq$ over $\mathcal{P}_{con}$ is a singular subcontract pre-order whenever the correctness of systems is preserved by refining just one of the contracts. More precisely, for any $n \geq 1$, contracts $C_1, \ldots, C_n \in \mathcal{P}_{con}$, $1 \leq i \leq n, C'_i \in \mathcal{P}_{con}$ such that $C'_i \leq C_i$, and distinguished location names $l_1, \ldots, l_n \in Loc$ such that $\forall k \neq i. l_k \notin oloc(C_k)$ and $l_i \notin oloc(C_i) \cup oloc(C'_i)$, we require

$$([C_1]_{l_1} \| \ldots \| [C_i]_{l_i} \| \ldots \| [C_n]_{l_n}) \downarrow \quad \Rightarrow \quad ([C_1]_{l_1} \| \ldots \| [C'_i]_{l_i} \| \ldots \| [C_n]_{l_n}) \downarrow$$

By exploiting commutativity and associativity of parallel composition we can group the contracts which are not being refined and get the following cleaner definition. We let $\mathcal{P}_{conpar}$ denote the set of systems of the form $[C_1]_{l_1} \| \ldots \| [C_n]_{l_n}$, with $C_i \in \mathcal{P}_{con}$, for all $i \in \{1, \ldots, n\}$.

Definition 5 (Singular subcontract pre-order). *A pre-order $\leq$ over $\mathcal{P}_{con}$ is a singular subcontract pre-order if, for any $C, C' \in \mathcal{P}_{con}$ such that $C' \leq C$, $l \in Loc$ such that $l \notin oloc(C_i) \cup oloc(C'_i)$, $P \in \mathcal{P}_{conpar}$ such that $l \notin loc(P)$ we have $([C]_l \| P){\downarrow}$ implies $([C']_l \| P){\downarrow}$.*

The following proposition, which shows that extending possible contexts with an external restriction does not change the notion of singular subcontract pre-order, will be used in the following Sect. 3.2. We let $\mathcal{P}_{conpres}$ denote the set of systems of the form $([C_1]_{l_1} \| \ldots \| [C_n]_{l_n}) \backslash L$, with $C_i \in \mathcal{P}_{con}$ for all $i \in \{1, \ldots, n\}$ and $L \subseteq \mathcal{A}_{loc}$.

Proposition 2. *Let $\leq$ be a singular subcontract pre-order. For any $C, C' \in \mathcal{P}_{con}$ such that $C' \leq C$, $l \in Loc$ such that $l \notin oloc(C_i) \cup oloc(C'_i)$, $P \in \mathcal{P}_{conpres}$ such that $l \notin loc(P)$ we have $([C]_l \| P){\downarrow}$ implies $([C']_l \| P){\downarrow}$.*

From the simple structure of their definition we can easily deduce that singular subcontract pre-order have maximum, i.e. there exists a singular subcontract pre-order includes all the other singular subcontract pre-orders.

Definition 6 (Subcontract relation). *A contract C' is a subcontract of a contract C denoted $C' \preceq C$, if and only if for all $l \in Loc$ such that $l \notin oloc(C_i) \cup oloc(C'_i)$ and $P \in \mathcal{P}_{conpar}$ such that $l \notin loc(P)$ we have $([C]_l \| P){\downarrow}$ implies $([C']_l \| P){\downarrow}$.*

It is trivial to verify that the pre-order $\preceq$ is a singular subcontract pre-order and is the maximum of all the singular subcontract pre-orders.

In order to prove the existence of the maximal independent subcontract pre-order, we will prove that every pre-order that is an independent subcontract is also a singular subcontract (Theorem 1), and vice-versa (Theorem 2).

Theorem 1. *If a pre-order $\leq$ is an independent subcontract pre-order then it is also a singular subcontract pre-order.*

Theorem 2. *If a pre-order $\leq$ is a singular subcontract pre-order then it is also an independent subcontract pre-order.*

We can, therefore, conclude that there exists a maximal independent subcontract pre-order and it corresponds to "$\preceq$".

3.2   Input-Output Subcontract Relation

We now define a notion of subcontract parameterized on the input and output alphabets of the contracts in the potential contexts. This will allow us to prove that, thanks to output persistency of contracts and the use of locations, we can characterize the subcontract relation "$\preceq$" in terms of a restricted set of contexts.

We first formally define the input and output alphabets of systems.

Definition 7 (Input and Output sets). *Given the contract* $C \in \mathcal{P}_{con}$, *we define* $I(C)$ *(resp.* $O(C)$*) as the subset of* $\mathcal{N}$ *(resp.* $\mathcal{N}_{loc}$*) of the potential input (resp. output) actions of* C. *Formally, we define* $I(C)$ *as follows (* $O(C)$ *is defined similarly):*

$$I(\mathbf{0}) = I(\mathbf{1}) = I(\tau) = I(a_*) = I(\tau; \overline{a}_*) = I(\tau; \overline{a}_{loc}) = \emptyset \quad I(a) = \{a\}$$
$$I(C;C') = I(C+C') = I(C|C') = I(C) \cup I(C') \qquad I(C \backslash M) = I(C^*) = I(C)$$

Note that the set M *in* $C \backslash M$ *does not influence* $I(C \backslash M)$ *because it contains only local names outside* $\mathcal{N}$. *Given the system* P, *we define* $I(P)$ *(resp.* $O(P)$*) as the subset of* $\mathcal{N}_{loc}$ *of the potential input (resp. output) actions of* P. *Formally, we define* $I(P)$ *as follows (* $O(P)$ *is defined similarly):*

$$I([C]_l) = \{a_l \mid a \in I(C)\} \qquad I(P \| P') = I(P) \cup I(P') \qquad I(P \backslash L) = I(P) - L$$

Note that, given $P = (C_1 \| \ldots \| C_n) \backslash I \cup \overline{O} \in \mathcal{P}_{conpres}$, *we have* $I(P) = (\bigcup_{1 \le i \le n} I([C_i]_{l_i})) - I$ *and* $O(P) = (\bigcup_{1 \le i \le n} O([C_i]_{l_i})) - O$. *In the following we let* $\mathcal{P}_{conpres,I,O}$, *with* $I, O \subseteq \mathcal{N}_{loc}$, *denote the subset of systems of* $\mathcal{P}_{conpres}$ *such that* $I(P) \subseteq I$ *and* $O(P) \subseteq O$.

Definition 8 (Input-Output Subcontract relation). *A contract* C' *is a subcontract of a contract* C *with respect to a set of input located names* $I \subseteq \mathcal{N}_{loc}$ *and output located names* $O \subseteq \mathcal{N}_{loc}$, *denoted* $C' \preceq_{I,O} C$, *if and only if for all* $l \in Loc$ *such that* $l \notin oloc(C_i) \cup oloc(C'_i)$ *and* $P \in \mathcal{P}_{conpres,I,O}$ *such that* $l \notin loc(P)$ *we have* $([C]_l \| P) \downarrow$ *implies* $([C']_l \| P) \downarrow$.

Due to Proposition 2, we have $\preceq = \preceq_{\mathcal{N}_{loc}, \mathcal{N}_{loc}}$. The following Proposition states an intuitive contravariant property: given $\preceq_{I',O'}$, and the greater sets I and O (i.e. $I' \subseteq I$ and $O' \subseteq O$) we obtain a smaller pre-order $\preceq_{I,O}$ (i.e. $\preceq_{I,O} \subseteq \preceq_{I',O'}$). This follows from the fact that extending the sets of input and output actions means considering a greater set of discriminating contexts.

Proposition 3. *Let* $C, C' \in \mathcal{P}_{con}$ *be two contracts,* $I, I' \subseteq \mathcal{N}_{loc}$ *be two sets of input channel names such that* $I' \subseteq I$ *and* $O, O' \subseteq \mathcal{N}_{loc}$ *be two sets of output channel names such that* $O' \subseteq O$. *We have:*

$$C' \preceq_{I,O} C \quad \Rightarrow \quad C' \preceq_{I',O'} C$$

The following Proposition states that a subcontract is still a subcontract even if we restrict its actions in order to consider only the inputs and outputs already available in the supercontract.

Proposition 4. *Let* $C, C' \in \mathcal{P}_{con}$ *be contracts and* $I, O \subseteq \mathcal{N}_{loc}$ *be sets of located names. We have*

$$C' \preceq_{I,O} C \quad \Rightarrow \quad C' \backslash (I(C') - I(C)) \preceq_{I,O} C$$
$$C' \preceq_{I,O} C \quad \Rightarrow \quad C' \backslash (O(C') - O(C)) \preceq_{I,O} C$$

All the results discussed so far do not depend on the output persistence property. The first relevant result depending on this peculiarity is reported in the following Proposition. It states that if we substitute a contract with one of its subcontract, the latter cannot activate outputs that were not included in the potential outputs of the supercontract.

Proposition 5. *Let $C, C' \in \mathcal{P}_{con}$ be contracts and $I, O \subseteq \mathcal{N}_{loc}$ be sets of located names and let $C' \preceq_{I,O} C$. For every $l \in Loc$, $l \notin oloc(C_i) \cup oloc(C_i')$, and $P \in \mathcal{P}_{conpres,I,O}$, $l \notin loc(P)$, such that $([C]_l \| P) \downarrow$,*

$$([C']_l \| P) \xrightarrow{\tau}{}^* ([C'_{der}]_l \| P_{der}) \quad \Rightarrow \quad \begin{cases} \forall a_{l'} \in O(C') - O(C). C'_{der} \xrightarrow{\overline{a}_{l'}} \\ \forall a \in I(C') - I(C). P_{der} \xrightarrow{\overline{a}_l} \end{cases}$$

The following propositions permit to conclude that the set of potential inputs and outputs of the other contracts in the system (as long as it includes those needed to interact with the contract) is an information that does not influence the subcontract relation. The other way around, this allows us to characterize, in the following Sect 3.3, the general subcontract relation "$\preceq$" in terms of a subcontract relation which considers a reduced number of contexts.

Proposition 6. *Let $C \in \mathcal{P}_{con}$ be contracts, $O \subseteq \mathcal{N}_{loc}$ be a set of located output names and $I, I' \subseteq \mathcal{N}_{loc}$ be two sets of located input names such that $O(C) \subseteq I, I'$. We have that for every contract $C' \in \mathcal{P}_{con}$,*

$$C' \preceq_{I,O} C \quad \Longleftrightarrow \quad C' \preceq_{I',O} C$$

Proposition 7. *Let $C \in \mathcal{P}_{con}$ be contracts, $O, O' \subseteq \mathcal{N}_{loc}$ be two sets of located output names such that for every $l \in Loc$ we have $I(C) \subseteq O_l, O'_l$, and $I \subseteq \mathcal{N}_{loc}$ be a set of located input names. We have that for every contract $C' \in \mathcal{P}_{con}$,*

$$C' \preceq_{I,O} C \quad \Longleftrightarrow \quad C' \preceq_{I,O'} C$$

3.3   Resorting to Should Testing

The remainder of this Section is devoted to the definition of an actual procedure for determining that two contracts are in subcontract relation. This is achieved resorting to the theory of *should-testing* [RV05].

First, we need a preliminary result that is a direct consequence of the fact that $C' \preceq_{\mathcal{N}_{loc}, \bigcup_{l \in Loc} I([C]_l)} C$ if and only if $C' \preceq C$.

Lemma 1. *Let $C, C' \in \mathcal{P}_{con}$ be contracts. We have*

$$C' \backslash \! \backslash (I(C') - I(C)) \preceq C \quad \Rightarrow \quad C' \preceq C$$

Note that the opposite implication trivially holds (by taking $O = \mathcal{N}_{loc}$ and $I = \mathcal{N}_{loc}$ in Proposition 4).

In the following we denote with $\preceq_{test}$ the *should-testing* pre-order defined in [RV05] where we consider the set of actions used by terms as being $\mathcal{L} \cup \{\overline{a} \mid$

$a \in \mathcal{N}$} (i.e. we consider located and unlocated input and output actions and $\sqrt{}$ is included in the set of actions of terms under testing as any other action). We denote here with $\sqrt{}'$ the special action for the success of the test (denoted by $\sqrt{}$ in [RV05]). In the following we consider λ to range over $\mathcal{L} \cup \{\bar{a} \mid a \in \mathcal{N}\}$.

In order to resort to the theory defined in [RV05], we define a normal form for contracts of our calculus that corresponds to terms of the language in [RV05]. The normal form of the system P (denoted with $\mathcal{NF}(\mathcal{P})$) is defined as follows, by using the operator $rec_X\theta$ (defined in [RV05]) that represents the value of X in the solution of the minimum fixpoint of the finite set of equations θ,

$$\mathcal{NF}(\mathcal{P}) = rec_{X_1}\theta \quad \text{where } \theta \text{ is the set of equations}$$
$$X_i = \sum_j \lambda_{i,j}; X_{der(i,j)}$$

where, assuming to enumerate the states in the labeled transition system of P starting from X_1, each variable X_i corresponds to the i-th state of the labeled transition system of P, $\lambda_{i,j}$ is the label of the j-th outgoing transition from X_i, and $der(i,j)$ is the index of the state reached with the j-th outgoing transition from X_i. We assume empty sums to be equal to $\mathbf{0}$, i.e. if there are no outgoing transitions from X_i, we have $X_i = \mathbf{0}$.

Theorem 3. *Let $C, C' \in \mathcal{P}_{con}$ be two contracts. We have*

$$\mathcal{NF}(C' \backslash\!\!\backslash I(C') - I(C)) \preceq_{test} \mathcal{NF}(C) \quad \Rightarrow \quad C' \preceq C$$

In [BZ06a] you can find counter examples that prove that the opposite implication $C' \preceq C \Rightarrow \mathcal{NF}(C' \backslash\!\!\backslash I(C') - I(C)) \preceq_{test} \mathcal{NF}(C)$ does not hold in general.

4   Contract-Based Choreography Conformance

In this section we discuss how to exploit the choreography and the contract calculus in order to define a procedure that checks whether a service exposing a specific contract C can play the role r within a given choreography.

First of all we need to uniform the choreography and the contract calculus. From a syntactical viewpoint, we have to map the operation names used for choreographies with the names used for contracts assuming $Operations = \mathcal{N}$. We do the same also for the role names that are mapped into the location names, i.e., $Roles = Loc$. From the point of view of the operational semantics, we need to slightly modify the labels in the operational semantics of the contract calculus in order to have labels comparable to those used in the choreography calculus. To this aim we have to add the auxiliary set of labels $\{a_{r \to s}, \bar{a}_{rs} \mid a \in Operations, r, s, \in Roles\}$ and replace the second and the fourth rules in Table 3 with the following ones:

$$\frac{C \xrightarrow{\bar{a}_s} C'}{[C]_r \xrightarrow{\bar{a}_{rs}} [C']_r} \qquad \frac{P \xrightarrow{a_s} P' \quad Q \xrightarrow{\bar{a}_{rs}} Q'}{P\|Q \xrightarrow{a_{r \to s}} P'\|Q'}$$

With $P \xrightarrow{\tau^*} P'$ we denote the existence of a (possibly empty) sequence of τ-labeled transitions starting from the system P and leading to P'. Given the sequence of labels $w = \lambda_1 \cdots \lambda_n$, we write $P \xRightarrow{w} P'$ if there exist $P_1, \cdots, P_m$ such that $P \xrightarrow{\tau^*} P_1 \xrightarrow{\lambda_1} P_2 \xrightarrow{\tau^*} \cdots \xrightarrow{\tau^*} P_{m-1} \xrightarrow{\lambda_n} P_m \xrightarrow{\tau^*} P'$.

We are now ready to formalize the notion of correct implementation of a choreography. Intuitively, a system implements a choreography if it is a correct composition of contracts and all of its conversations (i.e. the possible sequences of message exchanges), are admitted by the choreography.

Definition 9 (Choreography implementation). *Given the choreography H and the system P, we say that P implements H (written $P \propto H$) if*

- *P is a correct contract composition and*
- *given a sequence w of labels of the kind $a_{r \to s}$, if $P \xRightarrow{w\checkmark} P'$ then there exists H' such that $H \xrightarrow{w\checkmark} H'$.*

Note that it is not necessary for an implementation to include all possible conversations admitted by a choreography.

Example 2. **(Implementation of the Travel Agency Choreography).** As an example, we present a possible implementation of the choreography reported in the Example 1.

$$[\tau; \overline{Reservation}_{TravelAgency}; Confirmation]_{Client} \parallel$$
$$[Reservation; (\tau; \overline{Reserve}_{AirCompany}; ConfirmFlight \mid$$
$$\tau; \overline{Hotel}_{AirCompany}; ConfirmRoom);$$
$$\tau; \overline{Confirmation}_{Client}]_{TravelAgency} \parallel$$
$$[Reserve; \tau; \overline{ConfirmFlight}_{TravelAgency}]_{AirCompany} \parallel$$
$$[Reserve; \tau; \overline{ConfirmRoom}_{TravelAgency}]_{Hotel}$$

Note that in this implementation we assume that the travel agency always replies positively to the request of the client sending the $Confirmation$ message.

We are now in place for the definition of the (family of) relations $C \lhd_H r$ indicating whether the contract C can play the role r in the choreography H.

Definition 10 (Conformance family). *Let $\lhd_H$ to denote relations between contracts and roles parameterized on the choreography H defined on the roles $r_1, \cdots, r_n$. A family of relations $\{\lhd_H \mid H \in Choreographies\}$ is a conformance family if we have that if $C_1 \lhd_H r_1, \cdots, C_n \lhd_H r_n$ then $[C_1]_{r_1} \parallel \cdots \parallel [C_n]_{r_n} \propto H$.*

It is interesting to observe that, differently from subcontract pre-order defined on contracts in the previous Section, there exists no maximal conformance family. For instance, consider the choreography $H = a_{r \to s} \mid b_{r \to s}$. We could have two different conformance families, the first one including $\lhd_H^1$ such that

$$(\tau; \overline{a}_s | \tau; \overline{b}_s) \lhd^1_H r \qquad\qquad (\tau; a; b \ + \ \tau; b; a) \lhd^1_H s$$

and the second one including $\lhd^2_H$ such that

$$(\tau; \overline{a}_s; \tau; \overline{b}_s + \tau; \overline{b}_s; \tau; \overline{a}_s) \lhd^2_H r \qquad\qquad (a|b) \lhd^2_H s$$

It is easy to see that it is not possible to have a conformance family that comprises the union of the two relations $\lhd^1_H$ and $\lhd^2_H$. In fact, the system

$$[\tau; \overline{a}_s; \tau; \overline{b}_s \ + \ \tau; \overline{b}_s; \tau; \overline{a}_s]_r \ \| \ [\tau; a; b \ + \ \tau; b; a]_s$$

is not a correct composition because the two contracts may internally select two incompatible orderings for the execution of the two message exchanges (and in this case they stuck).

The remainder of the paper is dedicated to the definition of a mechanism that, exploiting the notion of contract refinement defined in the previous section, permits to effectively characterize an interesting conformance family. The first step of this mechanism requires the definition of the projection of a choreography on a specific role.

Definition 11 (Choreography projection). *Given a choreography H, the projection H on the role r, denoted with $[\![H]\!]_r$, is defined inductively on the syntax of H in such a way that*

$$[\![a_{r \to s}]\!]_t \ = \ \begin{cases} \tau; \overline{a}_s & \text{if } t = r \\ a & \text{if } t = s \\ 1 & \text{otherwise} \end{cases}$$

and that it is a homomorphism with respect to all operators.

It is interesting to observe that given a choreography H, the system obtained composing its projections is not ensured to be an implementation of H. For instance, consider the choreography $a_{r \to s} \ ; \ b_{t \to u}$. The system obtained by projection is $[\overline{a}_s]_r \ \| \ [a]_s \ \| \ [\overline{b}_u]_t \ \| \ [b]_u$. Even if this is a correct composition of contracts, it is not an implementation of H because it comprises the conversation $b_{t \to u} a_{r \to s}$ which is not admitted by H.

The problem is not in the definition of the projection, but in the fact that the above choreography cannot be implemented preserving the message exchanges specified by the choreography. In fact, in order to guarantee that the communication between t and u is executed after the communication between r and s, it is necessary to add a further message exchange (for instance between s and r) which is not considered in the choreography. This problem has been already investigated in [CHY07] where a notion of well formed choreography is introduced, and it is proved that well formed choreographies admit a correct projection.[1]

Nevertheless, the notion of well formed choreography in [CHY07] is rather restrictive. In particular, after the execution of a message sent from the role v

---

[1] The projection defined in [CHY07] is more complex than ours as their choreography calculus comprises also an explicit notion of session.

to the role z, the subsequent message in the conversation should be mandatorily emitted by z. For instance, the choreography $a_{r \to s}; b_{r \to s}$ does not satisfy this constraint even if the system $[\tau; \overline{a}_s; \tau; \overline{b}_s]_r \parallel [a; b]_s$ obtained by projection is a correct implementation.

To be less restrictive than [CHY07], we consider as well formed all those choreographies for which the system obtained by projection is ensured to be a correct implementation.

Definition 12 (Well formed choreography). *A choreography H, defined on the roles $r_1, \cdots, r_n$, is well formed if $[\, [\![H]\!]_{r_1} \,]_{r_1} \parallel \cdots \parallel [\, [\![H]\!]_{r_n} \,]_{r_n} \propto H$.*

It is worthwhile to note that well formedness is decidable. In fact, given a choreography H, it is sufficient to take the corresponding system P obtained by projection, then consider P and H as finite state automata, and finally check whether the language of the first automaton is included in the language of the second one. Note that the terms P and H can be seen as finite state automata thanks to the fact that their infinite behaviours are defined using Kleene-star repetitions instead of general recursion.

Now, we define the notion of *consonance* between contracts and roles of a given choreography, and we prove that it is a conformance family.

Definition 13 (Consonance). *We say that the contract C is consonant with the role r of the well formed choreography H (written $C \bowtie_H r$) if*

$$\mathcal{NF}\big(C_r \backslash I([\![H]\!]_r) - I(C)\big) \preceq_{test} \mathcal{NF}\big([\![H]\!]_r\big)$$

where $\backslash$, defined in Section 3, is the restriction operator that acts independently on input and output actions; $I(\_)$, defined in Section 3.2, is the function that extracts from a contract the names used as inputs; $\mathcal{NF}(\_)$, defined in Section 3.3, is the function that returns the normal form of a contract; and $\preceq_{test}$, defined in Section 3.3, is the should-testing pre-order.

Theorem 4. *The family $\{\bowtie_H \mid H$ is a well formed choreography$\}$ of consonance relations is a conformance family.*

5 Related Work and Conclusion

We have addressed the problem of the deployment of service compositions via choreography specifications in the context of service oriented computing. In particular, we have formalized service choreographies and service contracts via process calculi and, exploiting the notion of choreography projection in combination with service contract refinement, we have defined a new relation called *consonance*. The consonance relation is parameterized on a given choreography H and relates service contracts to roles: if a contract C is consonant to a role r, then the services exposing contract C (or one of its refinements) correctly play role r in the considered choreography H.

Choreography languages have been already investigated in a process algebraic setting by Carbone et al. [CHY07] and by Busi et al. [BGG+05, BGG+06].

The paper [CHY07] is the first one, to the best out knowledge, in which the problem of ill-formed choreographies is considered: a choreography is ill-formed when it is not possible to achieve by projection a correct implementation that preserves the message exchanges specified by the choreography. The solution to this problem presented in [CHY07] is given by three basic principles that, when satisfied by a choreography, ensure to achieve a corresponding correct projection. On the one hand, the calculi proposed in [CHY07] are more expressive than the calculi we define in this paper because they comprise name passing and an explicit notion of session. On the other hand, the basic principles imposed in [CHY07] give rise to a more restrictive notion of well formed choreography with respect to the one proposed in this paper (this technical aspect is discussed in Section 4). In [BGG+05, BGG+06] a more general notion of conformance between a choreography and a corresponding implementation as a service system is defined. According to this more general notion of conformance the implementation does not necessarily follow from projection, but additional services (not included at the choreography level) can be added in order to synchronize the correct scheduling of the the message flow.

The theory of contracts that we discuss in Section 3 is an extension of the theory reported in our paper [BZ06a]. More precisely, Section 3 is a revisitation of that theory in a slightly different context. The main novelty here is that we associate a location to each contract, and we assume that output operations are specified by indicating, besides the name of the invoked operation, also its actual location. This difference has a very important consequence which is proved as an original result in this paper: contract refinement is no longer influenced by the set of output operations that can be executed by the other composed contracts. More precisely, contract refinement was defined in [BZ06a] with an associated parameter (the set of output operations available in the other composed contracts) while in the present paper we can define a new notion of contract refinement independently of this information. The details of this new results are discussed in Section 3.

The notion of contract refinement that we propose is achieved resorting to the theory of testing. There are some relevant differences between our form of testing and the traditional one proposed by De Nicola-Hennessy [DH84]. The most relevant difference is that, besides requiring the success of the test, we impose also that the tested process should successfully complete its execution. This further requirement has important consequences; for instance, we do not distinguish between the always unsuccessful process 0 and other processes, such as $a.1 + a.b.1$,[2] for which there are no guarantees of successful completion in any possible context. Another relevant difference is in the treatment of divergence: we do not follow the traditional catastrophic approach, but the fair approach introduced by the theory of should-testing of Rensink-Vogler [RV05]. In fact, we do not impose that all computations must succeed, but that all computations can always be extended in order to reach success.

---

[2] We use 0 to denote unsuccessful termination and 1 for successful completion.

Contracts have been investigated also by Fournet et al. [FHR$^+$04] and by Carpineti et al. [CCL$^+$06]. In [FHR$^+$04] contracts are CCS-like processes; a generic process P is defined as compliant to a contract C if, for every tuple of names $\tilde{a}$ and process Q, whenever $(\nu\tilde{a})(C|Q)$ is stuck-free then also $(\nu\tilde{a})(P|Q)$ is. Our notion of contract refinement differs from stuck-free conformance mainly because we consider a different notion of stuckness. In [FHR$^+$04] a process state is stuck (on a tuple of channel names $\tilde{a}$) if it has no internal moves (but it can execute at least one action on one of the channels in $\tilde{a}$). In our approach, an end-states different from successful termination is stuck (independently of any tuple $\tilde{a}$). Thus, we distinguish between internal deadlock and successful completion while this is not the case in [FHR$^+$04]. Another difference follows from the exploitation of the restriction $(\nu\tilde{a})$; this is used in [FHR$^+$04] to explicitly indicate the local channels of communication used between the contract C and the process Q. In our context we can make a stronger *closed-world* assumption (corresponding to a restriction on all channel names) because service contracts do not describe the entire behaviour of a service, but the flow of execution of its operations inside one session of communication.

The closed-world assumption is considered also in [CCL$^+$06] where, as in our case, a service oriented scenario is considered. In particular, in [CCL$^+$06] a theory of contracts is defined for investigating the compatibility between one client and one service. Our paper consider multi-party composition where several services are composed in a peer-to-peer manner. Moreover, we impose service substitutability as a mandatory property for our notion of refinement; this does not hold in [CCL$^+$06] where it is not in general possible to substitute a service exposing one contract with another one exposing a subcontract. Another relevant difference is that the contracts in [CCL$^+$06] comprises also choices guarded by both input and output actions.

References

[BZ06a]   Bravetti, M., Zavattaro, G.: Contract based Multi-party Service Composition. In: Roddick, J.F., Hornsby, K. (eds.) TSDM 2000. LNCS (LNAI), vol. 2007, Springer, Heidelberg (2001)

[BZ06b]   Bravetti, M., Zavattaro, G.: Towards a Unifying Theory for Choreography Conformance and Contract Compliance. Technical report available at http://cs.unibo.it/~bravetti

[BGG$^+$05] Busi, N., Gorrieri, R., Guidi, C., Lucchi, R., Zavattaro, G.: Choreography and orchestration: A synergic approach for system design. In: Benatallah, B., Casati, F., Traverso, P. (eds.) ICSOC 2005. LNCS, vol. 3826, pp. 228–240. Springer, Heidelberg (2005)

[BGG$^+$06] Busi, N., Gorrieri, R., Guidi, C., Lucchi, R., Zavattaro, G.: Choreography and orchestration conformance for system design. In: Ciancarini, P., Wiklicky, H. (eds.) COORDINATION 2006. LNCS, vol. 4038, pp. 63–81. Springer, Heidelberg (2006)

[CHY07]   Carbone, M., Honda, K., Yoshida, N.: Structured Communication-Centred Programming for Web Services. In: De Nicola, R. (ed.) ESOP 2007. LNCS, vol. 4421, Springer, Heidelberg (2007)

[CCL⁺06]   Carpineti, S., Castagna, G., Laneve, C., Padovani, L.: A Formal Account of Contracts for Web Services. In: Bravetti, M., Núñez, M., Zavattaro, G. (eds.) WS-FM 2006. LNCS, vol. 4184, pp. 148–162. Springer, Heidelberg (2006)

[CL06]   Carpineti, S., Laneve, C.: A Basic Contract Language for Web Services. In: Sestoft, P. (ed.) ESOP 2006 and ETAPS 2006. LNCS, vol. 3924, pp. 197–213. Springer, Heidelberg (2006)

[DH84]   Rocco De Nicola and Matthew Hennessy, Testing Equivalences for Processes. Theoretical Computer Science, volume 34: 83–133 (1984)

[FHR⁺04]   Fournet, C., Hoare, C.A.R., Rajamani, S.K., Rehof, J.: Stuck-Free Conformance. In: Alur, R., Peled, D.A. (eds.) CAV 2004. LNCS, vol. 3114, pp. 242–254. Springer, Heidelberg (2004)

[Ley01]   Leymann, F.: Web Services Flow Language (wsfl 1.0). Technical report, IBM Software Group (2001)

[RV05]   Rensink, A., Vogler, W.: Fair testing. CTIT Technical Report TR-CTIT-05-64, Department of Computer Science, University of Twente (December 2005)

[OAS]   OASIS. Web Services Business Process Execution Language Version 2.0

[Tha01]   Thatte, S.: XLANG: Web services for business process design. Microsoft Corporation (2001)

[W3C]   W3C. Web Services Choreography Description Language, http://www.w3.org/TR/2004/WD-ws-cdl-10-20041217

A Process-Algebraic Approach to Workflow Specification and Refinement

Peter Y.H. Wong and Jeremy Gibbons

Oxford University Computing Laboratory, United Kingdom
{peter.wong,jeremy.gibbons}@comlab.ox.ac.uk

Abstract. This paper describes a process-algebraic approach to specification and refinement of workflow processes. In particular, we model both specification and implementation of workflows as CSP processes. CSP's behavioural models and their respective refinement relations not only enable us to prove correctness properties of an individual workflow process against its behavioural specification but also allows us to design and develop workflow processes compositionally. Moreover, coupled with CSP is an industrial strength automated model checker FDR, which allows behavioural properties of workflow models to be proved automatically. This paper details some CSP models of van der Aalst et al.'s control flow workflow patterns, and illustrates behavioural specification and refinement of workflow systems with a business process scenario.

1 Introduction

Since van der Aalst published his short note [18] comparing Petri nets and π-calculus with respect to his workflow patterns [19], some attempts have been made to express these patterns in π-calculus [12,13] and its variants [11,15]. In this paper, we demonstrate how the process algebra CSP also can be applied to model complex workflow systems; more importantly, we can exploit CSP's notion of *process refinement* [6,14] to specify and compare these workflow systems. Furthermore, CSP is supported by the automated model checker FDR [4], which has been used extensively in industrial applications [10,2]. The combination of the mathematics of refinement and the model checker is crucial in the development process of workflow systems, especially when designers do not want to be concerned with the underlying mathematics. To complement the work described in this paper, we have given a formal semantics for BPMN in CSP [23], allowing workflow process designers to construct specifications using BPMN, and to formally compare BPMN diagrams.

We first detail CSP models of some of van der Aalst et al.'s control flow workflow patterns [19], which serve as "jigsaw" pieces for workflow construction. We then present a case study of a business process to illustrate the composition of some of the workflow pattern models and the use of process refinement in specification and verification.

The rest of this paper is structured as follows. Section 2 gives a brief introduction to CSP, its syntax and semantics. Section 3 describes the CSP models of

M. Lumpe and W. Vanderperren (Eds.): SC 2007, LNCS 4829, pp. 51–65, 2007.
© Springer-Verlag Berlin Heidelberg 2007

workflow patterns. Section 4 details the business process case study. Sections 5 and 6 discuss the related work and directions for future work respectively.

2   Communicating Sequential Processes

In CSP [6], a process is defined as a pattern of possible behaviour; a behaviour consists of events which are atomic and synchronous between the environment and the process. The environment in this case can be another process. Events can be compound, constructed using '.' the dot operator; often these compound events behave as channels communicating data objects synchronously between the process and the environment. For example $a.b$ is a compound event which communicates object b through channel a. Below is the grammar of a simplied version of CSP in BNF.

$$P, Q ::= \quad P \parallel\!\parallel Q \quad | \quad P \,[\![A]\!]\, Q \quad | \quad P \setminus A \quad | \quad P \triangle Q \quad |$$
$$P \,\square\, Q \quad | \quad P \sqcap Q \quad | \quad P \,\fatsemi\, Q \quad | \quad e \rightarrow P \quad | \quad Skip \quad | \quad Stop$$
$$e ::= \quad x \quad | \quad x.e$$

Process $P \parallel\!\parallel Q$ denotes the interleaved parallel composition of processes P and Q. Process $P \,[\![A]\!]\, Q$ denotes the partial interleaving of processes P and Q sharing events in set A. Process $P \setminus A$ is obtained by hiding all occurrences of events in set A from the environment of P. Process $P \triangle Q$ denotes a process initially behaving as P, but which may be interrupted by Q. Process $P \,\square\, Q$ denotes the external choice between processes P and Q; the process is ready to behave as either P or Q. Process $P \sqcap Q$ denotes the internal choice between processes P or Q, ready to behave at least one of P and Q but not necessarily offer either of them. Process $P \,\fatsemi\, Q$ denotes a process ready to behave as P; after P has successfully terminated, the process is ready to behave as Q. Our syntactic notation for process sequential composition follows Davies' style [3]. Process $e \rightarrow P$ denotes a process capable of performing event e, after which it will behave like process P. The process $Stop$ is a deadlocked process and the process $Skip$ is a successful termination. We write $\square \, a : \{ x_0 \ldots x_i \} \bullet P(a)$ to denote external choice over the set of processes $\{ P(x_0) \ldots P(x_i) \}$ and similarly for CSP operators $\sqcap$ and $\parallel\!\parallel$.

CSP has three denotational semantic models: traces ($\mathcal{T}$), stable failures ($\mathcal{F}$) and failures-divergences ($\mathcal{N}$) models, in order of increasing precision. In this paper our process definitions are divergence-free, so we will concentrate on the stable failures model. The traces model is insufficient because it does not record the availability of events and hence only models what a process *can* do and nothing about what it *must* do [14]. Notable is the semantic equivalence of processes $P \,\square\, Q$ and $P \sqcap Q$ under the traces model. Their trace semantics are defined below where $\mathcal{T}[\cdot]$ is a semantic function which maps a CSP expression to its set of possible traces $\mathbb{P}(\text{seq} \, \Sigma)$ and Σ is the set of all possible events.

$$\mathcal{T}[P \,\square\, Q] = \mathcal{T}[P \sqcap Q] = \mathcal{T}[P] \cup \mathcal{T}[Q]$$

In order to distinguish these processes, it is necessary to record not only what a process can do, but also what it can *refuse* to do. This information is preserved in *refusal sets*, sets of events from which a process in a stable state can refuse to communicate anything no matter how long it is offered. A (stable) *failure* is a pair in which the first element is the trace of a process and the second is a refusal set of the process after the given trace. Below is the stable failures semantics of both choice operators where $\mathcal{F}[\cdot]$ is a semantic function that maps a CSP expression to its set of failures $\mathbb{P}(\text{seq }\Sigma \times \mathbb{P}\,\Sigma)$.

$$\mathcal{F}[P \,\square\, Q] = \{ref : \mathbb{P}\,\Sigma \mid (\langle\rangle, ref) \in \mathcal{F}[P] \cap \mathcal{F}[Q] \bullet (\langle\rangle, ref)\}$$
$$\cup \{tr : \text{seq }\Sigma;\; ref : \mathbb{P}\,\Sigma \mid tr \neq \langle\rangle \wedge (tr, ref) \in \mathcal{F}[P] \cup \mathcal{F}[Q] \bullet (tr, ref)\}$$
$$\mathcal{F}[P \,\sqcap\, Q] = \mathcal{F}[P] \cup \mathcal{F}[Q]$$

Each CSP process hence is characterised by its pattern of behaviour; the type of specification we are concerned with is termed *behavioural specification*. In CSP's behavioural models ($\mathcal{T}, \mathcal{F}$ and $\mathcal{N}$) a specification R is expressed by constructing the most non-deterministic process satisfying it, called the *characteristic process* P_R. Any process Q that satisfies specification R has to refine P_R; this is denoted by $P_R \sqsubseteq Q$. In the stable failures model, we say process Q *failure-refines* process P if and only if every failure of Q is also a failure of P.

$$P \sqsubseteq_F Q \Leftrightarrow \mathcal{F}[Q] \subseteq \mathcal{F}[P]$$

Similarly, we say P is *failure-equivalent* to Q if and only if they have the same set of failures.

$$P \equiv_F Q \Leftrightarrow P \sqsubseteq_F Q \wedge Q \sqsubseteq_F P \Leftrightarrow \mathcal{F}[P] = \mathcal{F}[Q]$$

While traces only carries information about *safety* conditions, refinement under the stable failures model allows one to make assertions about a system's *safety* and *availability* properties. These assertions can be automatically proved using CSP's model checker FDR [4]. FDR stands for "Failures-Divergence Refinement"; Model checkers exhaustively explore the state space of a system, either returning one or more counterexamples to a stated property or guaranteeing that no counterexample exists. FDR is among the most powerful explicit exhaustive finite-state exploration tools and has been used extensively in industrial applications [10,2].

3   Patterns

Van der Aalst et al. introduced workflow patterns as the "gold standard" benchmark of workflow languages [19]. These patterns range from simple constructs to complex routing primitives. Their scope is limited to static control flow.

We model each of these control flow patterns in CSP, adhering to the interpretation of a process instance given by WfMC Reference Model [7] and van der Aalst et al.'s description of workflow activity [19]. We define set $\mathcal{A}$ as the set of workflow activities, and define set of compound events $\{\, n : \mathcal{A} \bullet init.n \,\}$ as the set of events representing workflow triggers and $\{\, n : \mathcal{A} \bullet work.n \,\}$ as the set of events representing the execution of workflow activities. We can then define the CSP process $P(a, X)$ where $a,b,c,...$ range over $\mathcal{A}$. This process models basic workflow activity a. We use $X, Y,...$ to range over $\mathbb{P}\,\mathcal{A}$.

$$P(a, X) = init.a \rightarrow work.a \rightarrow \;||| \; b : X \bullet init.b \rightarrow Skip$$

The process description $P(a, X)$ first performs the event $init.a$ with the co-operation of the environment. This event represents an external trigger to the start of the activity a; after the trigger has occurred, the event $work.a$, which represents some activity a, will be ready to perform. After $work.a$ has occurred, the process is ready to perform the set of events $\{\, b : X \mid init.b \,\}$ which trigger a set of workflow activities $X \subseteq \mathcal{A}$. A workflow activity which only triggers one subsequent activity can hence be defined.

$$SP(a, b) = P(a, \{b\})$$

Each CSP description of the workflow pattern represents an abstracted view of a workflow process. In this paper we only concern ourselves with the modelling of flow of control between activities and external to them. Each CSP process Q modelling some workflow activities hence has a corresponding process Q' which has the execution of its workflow activities internalised via the hiding operation.

$$Q' = Q \setminus \{\!| work |\!\}$$

The hiding operation reflects independent execution of individual workflow activities and allows us to model workflow processes with different levels of abstraction. As these workflow models are refined, more implementation details about individual activities might be added such as their internal data flow information. We use the event $init.acts$ to denote a general trigger for the workflow activity $acts$ which is outside the scope of the workflow process in which $init.acts$ occurs. It represents the completion of the relevant activities defined with the process. We use the event $init.null$ to denote a general trigger to some workflow activity $null$ that is outside the scope of the workflow process in which $init.null$ occurs and $null$ is ignored.

The rest of this section is devoted to a detailed description of the CSP model of these patterns based on the definitions above and the semantics of CSP. Due to page restriction, we have only included in this paper the CSP model of the workflow patterns which are relevant in the subsequent case study. A complete presentation of the CSP models of workflow patterns can be sought elsewhere [22].

3.1 Basic Control Flow Patterns

In this section the workflow patterns capture the basic control flows of workflow activities. They form the basis of more advanced patterns.

Sequence - An activity b in the workflow process is triggered after the completion of the activity a. This pattern is modelled by the CSP process $SEQ(S)$ where S is a non empty sequence of activities to be executed sequentially. For example, in the example given, S would be $\langle a, b \rangle$. (The symbol $^\frown$ denotes sequence concatenation.)

$$SEQ(\langle \rangle) = Skip$$
$$SEQ(\langle s \rangle) = SP(x, acts)$$
$$SEQ(\langle s, t \rangle ^\frown S) = SP(s, t) \, [\![\, \{init.t\} \,]\!] \, SEQ(\langle t \rangle ^\frown S)$$

Parallel Split (AND-split) - Both activities b and c are triggered after the completion of the activity a. The execution of b and c is concurrent. This pattern can be modelled by the CSP process $ASP(a, X)$ where a is some activity; set $X \subseteq \mathcal{A}$ is a non empty set of activities to be triggered in parallel after a has completed; in the example given, X would be $\{b, c\}$.

$$ASP(a, X) = P(a, X) \, [\![\, \{ \, k : X \bullet init.k \, \} \,]\!] \, \underset{k : X}{|||} \bullet SP(k, acts)$$

Synchronisation (AND-join) - An activity a is triggered after *both* activities b and c have completed execution, The execution of b and c is concurrent. This pattern may be modelled by the CSP process $AJP(X, y)$ where $X \subseteq \mathcal{A}$ is a non empty set of concurrent activities. In the example given, X would be $\{b, c\}$.

$$AJP(X, a) = \underset{k : X}{|||} \bullet SP(k, a) \, [\![\, \{init.a\} \,]\!] \, SP(a, acts)$$

Exclusive Choice (XOR-split) - Either activities b or c is triggered after the completion of the activity a. The choice between b and c is internally (demonically) nondeterministic since such decision is part of the implementation detail. This pattern is modelled by the CSP process $XS(a, X)$ where in the example given, X is $\{b, c\}$.

$$
\begin{aligned}
XS(a, X) = \\
\textsf{let} \quad & XSP(a, X) = init.a \rightarrow work.a \rightarrow \sqcap k : X \bullet init.k \rightarrow Skip \\
\textsf{within} \quad & XSP(a, X) \, [\![\, \{ \, k : X \bullet init.k \, \} \,]\!] \, \square k : X \bullet SP(k, acts)
\end{aligned}
$$

3.2   Multiple Instance Patterns

These patterns allow an activity in a workflow process to have more than one running, active instance at the same time. In our process descriptions we model a maximum of N instances of an activity running in any workflow process where N ranges over the strictly positive naturals $\mathbb{N}_1$. We define events $trig$, $done$ and $ntrig$ to denote the triggering, the completion and the cancelling of activity instances.

In this section we first define some CSP processes common to all multiple instance patterns described this paper. Each multiple instance pattern triggers multiple instances of some activity. We define process $SR(a, n)$ to model the triggering of n out of N instances of activity a.

$$SR(a, n) = (\underset{k : \{1 \,..\, n\}}{|||} \bullet init.a \rightarrow done \rightarrow Skip) \, \fatsemi \, (\underset{k : \{1 \,..\, N - n\}}{|||} \bullet end \rightarrow Skip)$$

We define process $RP1(a)$ to model the N instances of activity a; standard CSP does not allow unbounded nondeterminism, as its semantics raises deep issues.

$$RP1(a) = \left\| \left\| \, k : \{1 .. N\} \bullet (SP(a, null) \, [init.null \leftarrow done] \; \Box \; end \rightarrow Skip) \right.$$

Multiple Instances with a priori Design Time Knowledge - In this pattern multiple instances of activity b are triggered after activity a has completed execution. The number of instances is known at design time which means static within the model. Once all instances are completed, activity c is triggered. This pattern is modelled by the CSP process $DES(a, n, b, c)$ where n is the number of instances of activity b determined at design time. Process $DP(a, n, b, c)$ sets the number of instances of activity b before execution.

$$DES(a, n, b, c) =$$
$$\text{let} \quad DP(a, n, b, c) = init.a \rightarrow work.a \rightarrow SR(b, n) \, \mathring{9} \, init.c \rightarrow Skip$$
$$\text{within} \quad DP(a, n, b, c) \, [\![\, \{init.b, end, done\} \,]\!] \, RP1(b)) \setminus \{end, done\}$$
$$[\![\{init.c\}]\!] \, SP(c, acts)$$

Multiple Instances with a priori Runtime Knowledge - The semantics of this pattern is somewhat ambiguous as it offers two patterns of behaviour. According to van der Aalst et al.'s original work [19], multiple instances of activities may be triggered in parallel with the correct synchronisation or the execution of these activities may be routed sequentially. In this paper, both cases are considered. Note in CSP b & P denotes the conditional expression **if** b **then** P **else** $Stop$.

First case: we define CSP process $PAR(a, b, c)$ to model multiple instances of activity b being triggered in parallel after activity a has completed execution. Activity c is triggered after instances of activity b have completed execution. The number of instances is not determined until runtime.

$$SR1(a, b, c) =$$
$$\text{let} \quad IT1(a, n) = exec \rightarrow (n \geq N \; \& \; SR(a, n) \; \Box \; n < N \; \& \; IT1(a, n+1) \sqcap SR(a, n))$$
$$\text{within} \quad init.a \rightarrow work.a \rightarrow (IT1(b, 1) \, \mathring{9} \, init.c \rightarrow Skip \sqcap SR(b, 0) \, \mathring{9} \, init.c \rightarrow Skip)$$

$$PAR(a, b, c) = (SR1(a, b, c) \, [\![\, \{init.y, end, done\} \,]\!] \, RP1(y)) \setminus \{exec, done, end\}$$
$$[\![\{init.z\}]\!] \, SP(z, acts)$$

Second case: we define process $SR21(a, n)$ to model sequential triggering of n instances of activity a. Process $IT21(a, n)$ models a non-deterministic counter deciding upto N instances of a to be triggered.

$$SR21(a, n) =$$
$$\text{let} \quad SR(a, n) = (n = 0) \; \& \; Skip \; \Box \; n > 0 \; \& \; init.a \rightarrow done \rightarrow SR(a, n-1)$$
$$\text{within} \quad (\left\| \left\| \, k : \{1 .. N - n\} \bullet end \rightarrow Skip) \, \mathring{9} \, SR(x, n) \right.$$
$$IT21(a, n) =$$
$$exec \rightarrow (n \geq N \; \& \; SR21(a, n) \; \Box \; n < N \; \& \; IT21(a, n+1) \sqcap SR21(a, n))$$

We model the second case by defining the process $MSEQ(a, b, c)$.

$$SR2(a, b, c) = init.a \rightarrow work.a \rightarrow (IT21(b, 1) \, \S \, init.c \rightarrow Skip$$
$$\sqcap \, SR(b, 0) \, \S \, init.c \rightarrow Skip)$$
$$MSEQ(a, b, c) = (SR2(a, b, c) \, [\![\, \{init.b, end, done\} \,]\!] \, RP1(b)) \setminus \{exec, done, end\}$$
$$[\![\{init.c\}]\!] \, SP(c, acts)$$

It is easy to see that the sequential triggering of multiple instances, defined by the CSP model $MSEQ'(a, b, c)$, *failure-refines* the parallel triggering defined by the model $PAR'(a, b, c)$.

$$PAR'(a, b, c) \sqsubseteq_F MSEQ'(a, b, c)$$

Multiple Instances without a priori Runtime Knowledge - This is a generalisation of the pattern "Multiple Instances with a priori Runtime Knowledge". After the completion of activity a, some instances of activity b are triggered. The number of instances is not decided at runtime, rather it is decided during the execution of instances. Activity c will only be triggered after all triggered instances of activity b have completed execution. We define the CSP process $NPAR(a, b, c)$ to model this pattern.

$$SR31(a, n) = |\!|\!| \, k : \{1 \, .. \, N - n\} \bullet end \rightarrow Skip$$
$$IT31(a, n) = n \geq N \, \& \, Skip$$
$$\square \, n < N \, \& \, (init.a \rightarrow done \rightarrow IT31(a, n + 1)) \sqcap SR31(a, n)$$
$$SR3(a, b, c) = init.a \rightarrow work.a \rightarrow (IT31(b, 0) \, \S \, init.c \rightarrow Skip$$
$$\sqcap \, SR31(b, 0) \, \S \, init.c \rightarrow Skip)$$
$$NPAR(a, b, c) = (SR3(a, b, c) \, [\![\, \{init.b, end, done\} \,]\!] \, RP1(b)) \setminus \{exec, done, end\}$$
$$[\![\{init.c\}]\!] \, SP(c, acts)$$

3.3 State Based Patterns

This type of pattern captures external decisions at certain "states" within a workflow process. In previous patterns decisions on branching and looping are made a-priori and their semantics has been represented by the CSP internal choice operator. However, it is possible that these decisions are offered to the environment.

Deferred Choice - This is similar to "Multi-choice" pattern formalised above in which *either or both* activities b or c will be triggered after activity a has completed execution. However, in this pattern the choice is made by the environment. The semantics of this behaviour can be expressed by the CSP external choice operator. This pattern is modelled by the CSP process $DEF(a, X)$ where $X = \{b, c\}$.

$$DEF(a, X) = \text{let}$$
$$DC(a, X) = init.a \rightarrow work.a \rightarrow \square \, y : X \bullet init.y \rightarrow Skip$$
$$\text{within}$$
$$DC(a, X) \, [\![\, \{ \, y : X \bullet init.y \, \} \,]\!] \, \square \, y : X \bullet SP(y, acts)$$

4   Case Study

In this section we study a realistic complex business process of a traveller re-
serving and booking airline tickets, adapted from the Web Service Choreography
Interface (WSCI) specification [20]. A BPMN (Business Process Modelling Notation) diagram of the airline ticket reservation workflow is shown in Figure 1.

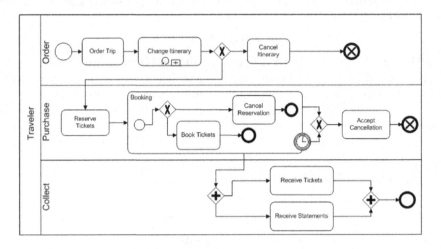

Fig. 1. Making an airline ticket reservation

4.1   Airline Ticket Reservation

We observe that the traveller can initiate the business process by ordering a trip.
She may change her travel itinerary or cancel it. She may make a reservation
with her chosen itinerary and before she confirms her booking she may at any
time cancel her reservation or be notified of a cancellation by the airline due to
the reservation period elapsing. After the traveller has confirmed her booking,
she will receive the booked tickets and the statement for them.

The textual description given in the previous paragraph is somewhat ambiguous and a graphical representation like Figure 1 becomes difficult to read as the
complexity of the control flow of the business process increases. Furthermore
both of these specifications lack a formal semantics and hence do not support
checking *behavioural* properties like deadlock and livelock freedom at the implementation level. By modelling such business process in a process algebra like
CSP, we can explore properties such as deadlock freedom by proving assertion
(1). The notion of process refinement allows us to prove such assertion by model
checking if P refines the *characteristic process* of the property we are interested
in proving. For deadlock freedom we can model check the refinement assertion
(2) where $DF = \bigsqcap x : \Sigma \bullet x \rightarrow DF$ is the most non-deterministic deadlock-free
process.

$$\forall\, tr : \mathcal{T}(P) \quad \bullet \quad (tr, \Sigma) \notin \mathcal{F}(P) \tag{1}$$

$$DF \sqsubseteq_F P \tag{2}$$

We now turn to the definition of the CSP model for this workflow process. We use TL to denote the CSP process describing control flow of the workflow model and define the set $\mathcal{W}_{tl}$ as the set of workflow activities performed by TL. The set $\mathcal{S}_{tl}$ is defined as the set of CSP processes to represent the states of control flow of the workflow model.

$\mathcal{W}_{tl} = \{order, change, cancelit, reserve, cancelres, timeout, accept, book, ticket, statemt\}$

$\mathcal{S}_{tl} = \{ORDER, CHANGE, CANCEL, RESERVE, CANRES, ACCEPT, BOOK, TIME,$
$\qquad TICKET, STATE\}$

We use the events *start*, *complete* and *fail* to denote the start, the completion and the abortion of the business process. We define αTL as the set of all events performed by process TL. We use the event *init.fault* to denote a fault has occurred and to represent an unsuccessful completion of the business process. We use the event *init.succ* to denote a successful completion of the business process; we use *init.fault* to denote an occurrence of cancellation during reservation; we use *init.itinfault* to denote an occurrence of cancellation before reservation. The events *init.null* and *init.acts* denote the triggering of out of scope activities as defined in Section 3.

$\alpha TL = \{\, a : \mathcal{W}_{tl} \bullet init.a, work.a\, \}$

$\qquad \cup\{\, start, complete, fail, init.null, init.acts, init.fault, init.itnfault, init.succ\, \}$

Here we specify some behavioural properties that the CSP process TL must satisfy. These properties are specified by the following assertions (3)–(6). Property (3) asserts TL to be a deadlock-free process; property (4) asserts that the business process must issue tickets if a booking has been made; here,

$$HB = init.book \rightarrow init.ticket \rightarrow HB$$

Property (5) asserts that the business process either aborts due to cancellation or completes successfully; here,

$$CSet = \{\, cancelres, cancelit, timeout\, \}$$
$$CC = (\sqcap x : CSet \bullet init.x \rightarrow fail \rightarrow CC)$$
$$\sqcap\; complete \rightarrow CC$$

Property (6) asserts that traveller can change her itinerary until she decides to make her reservation or to cancel her itinerary; here,

$$ITIN = init.change \rightarrow ITIN$$
$$\sqcap\; init.reserve \rightarrow (complete \rightarrow ITIN \sqcap fail \rightarrow ITIN)$$
$$\sqcap\; init.cancelit \rightarrow fail \rightarrow ITIN$$

$$DF \sqsubseteq_F TL \tag{3}$$

$$HB \sqsubseteq_F TL \setminus (\Sigma \setminus \alpha HB) \tag{4}$$

$$CC \sqsubseteq_F TL \setminus (\Sigma \setminus \alpha CC) \tag{5}$$

$$ITIN \sqsubseteq_F TL \setminus (\Sigma \setminus \alpha ITIN) \tag{6}$$

By employing the CSP models of the workflow patterns described in Section 3, we define each CSP process in $\mathcal{S}_{tl}$ as shown in Figure 2. Processes $SR4(a, b, X)$ and $DC1(a, X, Y)$ are defined in Figure 3. Process $SR4(a, b, X)$ is a combination of the processes $SR3(a, b, c)$ and $XSP(a, X)$ defined in Section 3's *Multiple Instances without a priori Runtime Knowledge* and *Exclusive Choice* patterns. Process $DC1(a, X, Y)$ is a combination of the processes $XSP(a, X)$ and $DEF(a, X)$ defined in Section 3's *Exclusive Choice* and *Deferred Choice* patterns.

$$ORDER = SR4'(order, change, \{cancelit, reserve\})$$
$$CHANGE = RP1'(change)$$
$$CANCEL = SP'(cancelit, fault)$$
$$RESERVE = DC1'(reserve, \{cancelres, book\}, \{timeout\})$$
$$CANRES = SEQ'(cancelres, accept)[init.acts \leftarrow init.fault]$$
$$BOOK = P'(book, \{ticket, statemt\})$$
$$TIME = SP'(timeout, fault)$$
$$TICKET = SP'(ticket, succ)$$
$$STATE = SP'(statemt, succ)$$

Fig. 2. The definition of CSP processes in $\mathcal{S}_{tl}$

$$SR4(a, b, X) = \mathsf{let} \ \ SR41(a, X) = (IT31(a, 0) \mathbin{{}_9^\circ} \sqcap b : X \bullet init.b \to Skip)$$
$$\sqcap (\sqcap b : X \bullet init.b \to Skip)$$
$$\mathsf{within} \ \ init.a \to work.a \to SR41(b, X)$$
$$DC1(a, Y, Z) = \mathsf{let} \ \ CHO(X, Y) = \sqcap b : X \bullet init.b \to Skip$$
$$\square (\square c : Y \bullet init.c \to Skip)$$
$$\mathsf{within} \ \ init.a \to work.a \to CHO(Y, Z)$$

Fig. 3. The definition of processes $SR4(x, y, X)$ and $DC1(x, Y, Z)$

Figure 4 is the definition of the CSP process TL which models the semantics of the control flows of the airline ticket reservation business process model by parallel composition of processes from set $\mathcal{S}_{tl}$.

$TL_c =$
  let
    $final = \{init.cancelres, init.book, init.timeout\}$
    $RECEIVE = TICKET \;|\!|\!|\; STATE$
  within
    $((ORDER \;|\![\;\{init.change, end, done\}\;]\!|\; CHANGE) \setminus \{end, done, exec\})$
    $|\![\;\{init.cancelit, init.reserve\}\;]\!|\; (CANCEL \;\Box\; (RESERVE \;|\![\;\{\,x : final \bullet init.x\,\}\;]\!|$
    $(TIME \;\Box\; (CANRES \;\Box\; (BOOK \;|\![\;\{init.ticket, init.statemt\}\;]\!|\; RECEIVE)))))$
$TL =$
  let
    $decision = \{init.succ, init.fault, init.itinfault\}$
    $COM = start \rightarrow init.order \rightarrow Skip$
    $FIN = init.succ \rightarrow init.succ \rightarrow complete \rightarrow Skip$
    $FAULT = init.fault \rightarrow cancel \rightarrow Skip \;\Box\; init.itinfault \rightarrow cancel \rightarrow Skip$
  within
    $(COM \;|\![\;\{init.order\}\;]\!|\; (TL_c \;|\![\;decision\;]\!|\; (FIN \;\Box\; FAULT))) \;\mathring{,}\; TL$

Fig. 4. The definition of processes TL

4.2   Composition and Refinement

Behavioural properties specified by assertions (3)–(6) can be readily checked by asking the FDR model checker about refinement assertions. Alternatively behavioural specifications can be composed to give a composite specification in which many of the assertions can be proved under a single refinement check. Property (7) asserts that the traveller may change her itinerary or cancellations may happen, otherwise she must commit to her itinerary and completes her transaction.

$$COMP = init.change \rightarrow COMP$$
$$\sqcap (\sqcap x : CSet \bullet init.x \rightarrow fail \rightarrow COMP)$$
$$\sqcap init.book \rightarrow init.ticket \rightarrow complete \rightarrow COMP$$

$$COMP \sqsubseteq_F TL (\Sigma \setminus \alpha COMP) \qquad\qquad (7)$$

A CSP model of the business process like the one described in this paper can be placed in parallel with CSP models of other business processes to describe their collaboration where each business process interacts by communicating. The term *service choreography* has been coined for such collaboration description. In our airline ticket reservation example we can define a global business collaboration protocol between the traveller's workflow, the airline reservation system and the travel agent models. We use process names AL and TA to denote the control flow description of the airline reservation system and the travel agent workflow models. An example collaboration between these business processes is depicted as a BPMN diagram in Figure 5. In this paper we do not define AL and TA, a complete description of their models can be found elsewhere [22].

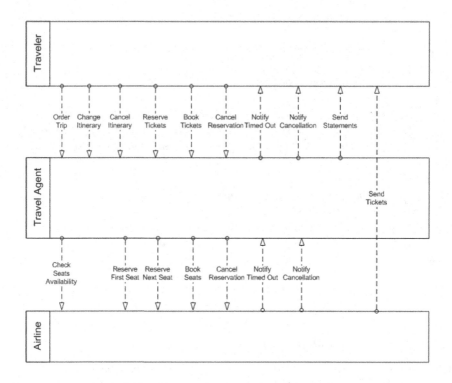

Fig. 5. Airline Ticket Reservation Choreography

One effect that can be anticipated when composing complex process definitions like *TL* in parallel is an exponential state explosion. For example given that i ranges over $\{1 .. N\}$ for some positive integer $N > 0$, if each process P_i has just two states, then the expression $\||\, i : \{1 .. N\} \bullet P_i$ has 2^N. By compositionality and monotonicity of refinement, we can reduce individual component processes' state space by abstracting them into sequential processes. For simplicity suppose the process *GB* is the model of the choreography by composing individual participating business process in parallel where X is a set of some events. We denote sequential process by subscript s.

$$GB = (TA \,[\![\, X \,]\!]\, AL) \,[\![\, X \,]\!]\, TL$$

We abstract *GB* into process GB_s then if the refinement assertions (8)–(10) hold, by monotonicity of refinement we prove assertion (11).

$$GB_s = (TA_s \,[\![\, X \,]\!]\, AL_s) \,[\![\, X \,]\!]\, TL_s$$

$$AL_s \sqsubseteq_F AL \tag{8}$$

$$TL_s \sqsubseteq_F TL \tag{9}$$

$$TA_s \sqsubseteq_F TA \tag{10}$$

$$GB_s \sqsubseteq_F GB \tag{11}$$

if GB_s refines some property defined by the characteristic process $SPEC$, by transitivity of refinement we prove GB also refines $SPEC$.

$$SPEC \sqsubseteq_F GB_s \wedge GB_s \sqsubseteq_F GB \Rightarrow SPEC \sqsubseteq_F GB$$

5 Related Work

Little research has been done to date into the application of CSP to workflow specification and verification. We have recently defined a process semantics for BPMN in CSP [23], which allows formal comparison between workflow processes described in BPMN and encourages automated tool support for the notation. The only other approach that has applied CSP in workflow process [16] did so as an extension of abstract machine notation for process specification within the domain of compositional information systems.

Other process algebras used to model workflow patterns include π-calculus [13] and CCS [15], a subset of π-calculus. These formalisations did not focus on process-based behavioural specification, and they did not demonstrate the applications of their models in workflow design. Moreover, the operational semantics of π-calculus and CCS do not provide a refinement relation; we have demonstrated in this paper that refinement is useful in the development of workflow processes, because it allows formal comparisons between workflows. A similar observation applies to the work of van der Aalst et al. [9,17] using Petri nets. Despite Puhlmann et al.'s advocacy of mobility in workflow modelling, our CSP models suggest it is not necessary when modelling static control flow interactions. However, it is still possible to introduce mobility into standard CSP semantics if needed; an attempt has been made by Welch et al. [21].

Although Stefansen [15] mentioned a model checker called Zing which bears some similarities with FDR, implementing a conformance checker based on stuck-freedom [5], it is more discriminative and only resembles the CSP concept of deadlock-freedom.

6 Conclusion

In this paper we described some CSP models of van der Aalst et al.'s workflow patterns to construct workflow processes. We then modelled a realistic workflow process by using models of workflow patterns and subsequently demonstrated the use of process refinement for asserting behavioural properties about the workflow process. These properties were described by process-based specifications defined in CSP and assertions were then proved automatically using the CSP model checker FDR. Like any development of a complex system, the application of refinement in workflow design means that development of a workflow design into an implementation becomes incremental. Due to monotonicity and transitivity of process refinement, it is possible to minimise exponential state explosion when model checking complex process by abstracting its individual component processes into corresponding sequential processes.

Future work will include the following:

- extend the CSP model described in this paper into a global domain, hence allowing a unified treatment of workflow orchestration and choreography;
- augment our current CSP model with a well-defined exception and compensation semantics, perhaps building on Butler's compensating CSP [1];
- combine our CSP control flow model with a dataflow semantics to allow a unified treatment of the semantics of workflow processes, perhaps building on Josephs' CSP dataflow model [8].
- automate the translation from workflow descriptions in BPMN to CSP processes, based on our recent work on BPMN semantics [23].

Acknowledgements

We would like to thank anonymous referees for useful suggestions and comments. This work is supported by a grant from Microsoft Research.

References

1. Butler, M., Hoare, T., Ferreira, C.: A trace semantics for long-running transactions. In: Abdallah, A.E., Jones, C.B., Sanders, J.W. (eds.) Communicating Sequential Processes. LNCS, vol. 3525, pp. 133–150. Springer, Heidelberg (2005)
2. Creese, S.: Industrial Strength CSP: Opportunities and Challenges in Model-Checking. In: Abdallah, A.E., Jones, C.B., Sanders, J.W. (eds.) Communicating Sequential Processes. LNCS, vol. 3525, p. 292. Springer, Heidelberg (2005)
3. Davies, J.: The CSP Package (March 2001),
   ftp://ftp.comlab.ox.ac.uk/pub/CSP/LaTeX/csp.sty
4. Formal Systems (Europe) Ltd. Failures-Divergences Refinement, FDR2 User Manual (1998), www.fsel.com
5. Fournet, C., Hoare, T., Rajamani, S.K., Rehof, J.: Stuck-Free Conformance. In: Alur, R., Peled, D.A. (eds.) CAV 2004. LNCS, vol. 3114, pp. 242–254. Springer, Heidelberg (2004)
6. Hoare, C.A.R.: Communicating Sequential Processes. Prentice-Hall, Englewood Cliffs (1985)
7. Hollingsworth, D.: The Workflow Reference Model. Technical Report WFMC-TC-1003, Workflow Management Coalition (January 1995)
8. Josephs, M.: Models for Data-Flow Sequential Processes. In: Abdallah, A.E., Jones, C.B., Sanders, J.W. (eds.) Communicating Sequential Processes. LNCS, vol. 3525, pp. 85–97. Springer, Heidelberg (2005)
9. Kiepuszewski, B.: Expressiveness and Suitability of languages for Control Flow Modelling in Workflows. PhD thesis, Queensland University of Technology, Brisbane, Australia (2002)
10. Lawrence, J.: Practical Application of CSP and FDR to Software Design. In: Abdallah, A.E., Jones, C.B., Sanders, J.W. (eds.) Communicating Sequential Processes. LNCS, vol. 3525, pp. 151–174. Springer, Heidelberg (2005)
11. Milner, R.: Communication and Concurrency. Prentice-Hall, Englewood Cliffs (1989)

12. Milner, R.: Communicating and Mobile Systems: the π-calculus. Cambridge University Press, Cambridge (1999)
13. Puhlmann, F., Weske, M.: Using the π-Calculus for Formalizing Workflow Patterns. In: van der Aalst, W.M.P., Benatallah, B., Casati, F., Curbera, F. (eds.) BPM 2005. LNCS, vol. 3649, pp. 153–168. Springer, Heidelberg (2005)
14. Roscoe, A.W.: The Theory and Practice of Concurrency. Prentice-Hall, Englewood Cliffs (1998)
15. Stefansen, C.: SMAWL: A SMAll workflow language based on CCS. Technical Report TR-06-05, Harvard University, Mar (2005)
16. Stupnikov, S.A., Kalinichenko, L.A., Dong, J.S.: Applying CSP-like Workflow Process Specifications for their Refinement in AMN by Pre-existing Workflows. In: Manolopoulos, Y., Návrat, P. (eds.) ADBIS 2002. LNCS, vol. 2435, Springer, Heidelberg (2002)
17. van der Aalst, W.M.P.: Verification of Workflow Nets. In: Azéma, P., Balbo, G. (eds.) ICATPN 1997. LNCS, vol. 1248, pp. 407–426. Springer, Heidelberg (1997)
18. van der Aalst, W.M.P.: Pi Calculus Versus Petri Nets: Let Us Eat Humble Pie Rather Than Further Inflate the Pi Hype. BPTrends 3(5), 1–11 (2005)
19. van der Aalst, W.M.P., ter Hofstede, A.H.M., Kiepuszewski, B., Barros, A.P.: Workflow Patterns. Distributed and Parallel Databases 14(3), 5–51 (2003)
20. W3C. Web Service Choreography Interface 1.0 (2002), www.w3.org/TR/wsci/
21. Welch, P.H., Barnes, F.R.M.: Mobile Barriers for occam-pi: Semantics, Implementation and Application. In: Communicating Process Architectures 2005. Concurrent Systems Engineering Series, vol. 63, pp. 289–316 (2005)
22. Wong, P.Y.H.: Towards a unified model for workflow orchestration and choreography, Transfer dissertation, Oxford University Computing Laboratory (2006)
23. Wong, P.Y.H., Gibbons, J.: A Process Semantics for BPMN, submitted for publication. Extended version (2007), available at http://web.comlab.ox.ac.uk/oucl/work/peter.wong/pub/bpmn-extended.pdf

Generic Feature-Based Software Composition

Tijs van der Storm

Centrum voor Wiskunde en Informatica
P.O. Box 94079, 1090 GB Amsterdam
The Netherlands
storm@cwi.nl

Abstract. Bridging problem domain and solution in product line engineering is a time-consuming and error-prone process. Since both domains are structured differently (features vs. artifacts), there is no natural way to map one to the other. Using an explicit and formal mapping creates opportunities for consistency checking and automation. This way both the configuration and the composition of product instances can be more robust, support more product variants and be performed more often.

1 Introduction

In product line engineering, automatic configuration of product line instances still remains a challenge [1]. Product configuration consists of selecting the required features and subsequently instantiating a software product from a set of implementation artifacts. Because features capture elements of the problem domain, automatic product composition requires the explicit mapping of features to elements of the solution domain. From a feature model we can then generate tool support to drive the configuration process.

However, successful configuration requires consistent specifications. For instance, a feature specification can be inconsistent if selecting one feature would require another feature that excludes the feature itself. Because of the possibly exponential size of the configuration space, maintaining consistency manually is no option.

We investigate how to bridge the "white-board distance" between problem space and solution space [15] by combining both domains in a single formalism based on feature descriptions [20]. White-board distance pertains to the different levels of abstraction in describing problem domain on the one hand, and solution domain on the other hand. In this paper, feature descriptions are used to formally describe the configuration space in terms of the problem domain. The solution domain is modeled by a dependency graph between artifacts.

By mapping features to one or more solution space artifacts, configurations resulting from the configuration task map to compositions in the solution domain. Thus it becomes possible to derive a configuration user interface from the feature model to automatically instantiate valid product line variants.

M. Lumpe and W. Vanderperren (Eds.): SC 2007, LNCS 4829, pp. 66–80, 2007.
© Springer-Verlag Berlin Heidelberg 2007

1.1   Problem-Solution Space Impedance Mismatch

The motivation for feature-based software composition is based on the following observations: solution space artifacts are unsuitable candidates for reasoning about the configurability in a product line. Configuration in terms of the problem domain, however, must stand in a meaningful relation to those very artifacts if it should be generally useful. Let's discuss each observation in turn.

First, if software artifacts can be composed or configured in different ways to produce different product variants it is often desirable to have a high-level view on which compositions are actually meaningful product instances. That is, the *configuration space* should be described at a high level of abstraction. If such configuration spaces are expressed in terms of problem space concepts, it is easier to choose which variant a particular consumer of the software actually needs. Finally, such a model should preferably be a formal model in order to prevent inconsistencies and configuration mistakes.

The second observation concerns the value of relating the configuration model to the solution space. The mental gap between problem space and solution space complicates keeping the configuration model consistent with the artifacts. Every time one or more artifacts change, the configuration model may become invalid. Synchronizing both realms without any form of tool support is a time-consuming and error-prone process. In addition, even if the configuration model is used to guide the configuration task, there is the possibility of inconsistencies in both the models and their interplay.

From these observations follows that in order to reduce the effort of configuring product lines and subsequently instantiating product variants tool support is needed that helps detecting inconsistencies and automates the manual, error-prone task of collecting the artifacts for every configuration. This leads to the requirements for realizing automatic software composition based on features.

- The configuration interface should be specified in a language that allows *formal* consistency checking. If a configuration interface is consistent then this means there are valid configurations. Only valid configurations must be used to instantiate products. Such configurations can be mapped to elements of the solution domain.
- A model is needed that relates features to artifacts in the solution space, so that if a certain feature is selected, all relevant artifacts are collected in the final product. Such a mapping should respect the (semantic) relations that exist between the artifacts. For the mapping to be as applicable as possible no assumptions should be made about programming language or software development methodology.

1.2   Related Work

This work is directly inspired by the technique proposed in [9]. In that position paper feature diagrams are compared to grammars, and parsing is used to check the consistency of feature diagrams. Features are mapped to software packages. Based on the selection of features and the dependencies between packages, the product variant is derived. Our approach generalizes this technique on two accounts: first we allow arbitrary constraints between features, and not only structural ones that can be verified by parsing. Second, in our approach *combinations* of features are mapped to artifacts, allowing more control over which artifact is required when.

There is related work on feature oriented programming that provides features with a direct solution space semantics. For instance, in AHEAD [2] features form elements in an algebra that can be synthesized into software components. Although this leaves open the choice of programming language it assumes that it is class-based. Czarnecki describes a method of mapping features to model elements in an model driven architecture (MDA) setting [7]. By "superimposing" *all* variants on top of UML models, a product can be instantiated by selectively disabling variation points.

An even more fine grained approach is presented in [17] where features become first-class citizens of the programming language. Finally, a direct mapping of features to a component role model is described in [12].

These approaches all, one way or the other, merge the problem domain and the solution domain in a single software development paradigm. In our approach we keep both domains separate and instead relate them through an explicit modeling step. Thus our approach does not enforce any programming language, methodology or architecture beforehand, but instead focuses on the possibility of automatic configuration and flexibility.

Checking feature diagrams for consistency is an active area of research [20, 6, 16] but the level of formality varies. The problem is that checking the consistency is equivalent to propositional satisfiability, and therefore it is often practically infeasible. Our approach is based on BDDs [19], a proven technique from model checking, which often makes the exponential configuration space practically manageable.

1.3   Contributions

The contributions of this paper can be summarized as follows:

- Using an example we analyze the challenges of bridging the gap between problem space and solution space. We identify the requirements for the explicit and controlled mapping of features to software artifacts.
- We propose a formal model that allows both worlds to be bridged in order to achieve (solution space) composition based on (problem space) configuration. Instances of the model are checked for consistency using scalable techniques widely used in model-checking.
- The model is unique in that it does not dictate programming language, is independent of software development methodology or architectural style, and does not require up-front design. The latter in turn allows the approach to be adopted late in the development process or in the context of legacy software.

Organization of this paper In the following section, Sect. 2, feature diagrams [13] are introduced as a model for the configuration space of product lines. Feature diagrams are commonly used to elicit commonality and variability of software systems during domain analysis [21]. They can be formally analyzed so they are a viable option for the first requirement.

Next, in Sect. 2.3 we present an abstract model of the solution space. Because we aim for a generic solution, this model is extremely simple: it is based on the generic notion of *dependency*. Thus, the solution space is modeled by a dependency graph between artifacts. Artifacts include any kind of file that shapes the final software product. This includes source files, build files, property files, locale files etc.

Then, in Sect. 3 we discuss how feature diagrams and dependency graphs should be related in order to allow automatic composition. The formalization of feature diagrams is described in Sect. 3.2, thus enabling the application of model-checking techniques for the detection of inconsistencies. How both models are combined is described in Sect. 4. This combined model is then used to derive product instances. Finally we present some conclusions and provide directions for future work.

2 Problem and Solution Space Models

2.1 Introduction

To be able to reason about the interaction between problem space an solution space, models are required that accurately represent the domains in a sufficiently formal way. In this section we introduce feature diagrams as a model for the problem space, and dependency graphs for the solution space.

2.2 Problem Space: Feature Diagrams

Figure 1 shows a graphical model of a small example's problem space using feature diagrams [13]. Feature diagrams have been used to elicit commonality and

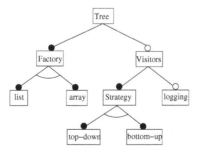

Fig. 1. Problem space of a small example visualized as a feature diagram

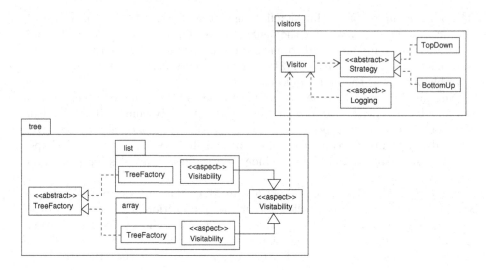

Fig. 2. UML view of an example product line

variability in domain engineering. A feature diagram can be seen as a specification of the configuration space of a product line.

In this example, the top feature, Tree, represents the application, in this case a small application for transforming tree-structured documents, such as parse trees. The Tree feature is further divided in two sub features: Factory and Visitors. The Visitors feature is optional (indicated by the open bullet), but if it is chosen, a choice must be made between the top-down or bottom-up alternatives of the Strategy feature and optionally there is the choice of enabling logging support when traversing trees. Finally, the left sub-feature of Tree, named Factory, captures a mandatory choice between two, mutually exclusive, implementations of trees: one based on lists and the other based on arrays.

Often these diagrams are extended with arbitrary constraints between features. For instance one could state that the array feature *requires* the logging feature. Such constraints make visually reasoning about the consistency of feature selection with respect to a feature diagram much harder. In order to automate such reasoning a semantics is needed. Many approaches exist, see e.g. [16, 3, 4]. In earlier work we interpreted the configuration problem as satisfiability problem and we will use that approach here too [19]. The description consistency checking of feature diagrams is deferred to Sect. 3.2.

2.3   Solution Space: Implementation Artifacts

The implementation of the example application consists of a number of Java classes and AspectJ files [14]. Figure 2 shows a tentative design in UML. The implementation of the transformation product line is divided over two components: a tree component and visitors component. Within the tree component the Abstract Factory design pattern is employed to facilitate the choice among list- and array-based trees. In addition to the choice between different implementations, trees can optionally be enhanced with a `Visitable` interface by weaving an aspect. This enables that clients of the tree component are able to traverse the trees by using the visitors component. So weaving in the Visitability aspect causes a dependency on the visitors component.

2.4 Artifact Dependency Graphs

What is a suitable model of the solution space? In this paper we take a an abstract stance and model the solution space by a directed acyclic dependency graph. In a dependency graph nodes represent artifacts and the edges represent dependencies between them. These dependencies may be specified explicitly or induced by the semantics of the source. As an example of the latter: a Java class file has a dependency on the class file of its superclass. Another example are aspects that depend on the classes they will be weaved in. For the example the dependencies are shown in Fig. 3. The figure shows dependencies of three kinds: subtype dependency (e.g. between list.Tree and Tree), aspect dependency (between Visitability and Tree), collaboration dependency (between Visitor and Strategy).

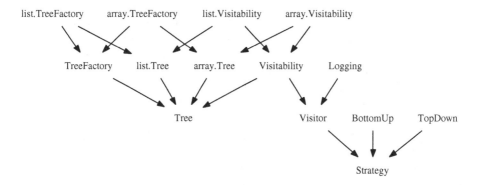

Fig. 3. Solution space model of the example: dependency graph between artifacts

Dependency graphs are consistent, provided that the dependency relation conforms to the semantics of the artifacts involved and provided that every node in the graph has a corresponding artifact. A set of artifacts is consistent with respect to a dependency graph if it is closed under the dependency relation induced by that graph.

A nice property of these graphs is that, in theory, every node in it represents a valid product variant (albeit a useless one most of the time). If we, for instance, take the Visitability node as an example, then we could release this 'product' by composing every artifact reachable from the Visitability node. So, similar to the problem space of the previous section, the solution space is also a kind of configuration space. It concisely captures the possibilities of delivery.

3   Mapping Features to Artifacts

3.1   Introduction

Now that the problem space is modeled by a feature diagram and the solution space by a dependency graph how can we bridge the gap between them? Intuitively one can map each feature of the feature diagram to one or more artifacts in the dependency graph. Such an approach is graphically depicted in Fig. 4.

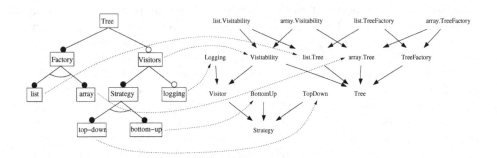

Fig. 4. Partial mapping of features to artifacts

The figure shows the feature diagram together with the dependency graph of the previous section. Arrows from features to the artifacts indicate which artifact should be included if a feature is selected. For instance, if the top-down strategy is chosen to visit trees, then the TopDown implementation will be delivered together with all its dependencies (i.e. the Strategy interface). Note that the feature mapping is incomplete: selecting the Visitors feature includes the Visitability aspect, but it is unspecified which concrete implementation (list.Visitability or array.Visitability) should be used. The graphical depiction thus is too weak to express the fact that if *both* array/list and Visitors is chosen, both the array.Visitability/list.Visitability and Visitability artifacts are required. In Sect. 4 this problem will be addressed by expressing mapping as constraints between features and artifacts.

3.2   Feature Diagram Semantics

This section describes how feature diagrams can be checked for consistency. We take a logic based approach that exploits the correspondence between feature diagrams and propositional logic (see Table 1). Since graphical formalisms are less practical for building tool support, we use a textual version of feature diagrams, called Feature Description Language (FDL) [20]. The textual analog of feature diagram in Fig. 1 is displayed in Fig. 5. Composite features start with an upper-case letter whereas atomic feature start in lower-case. Composing features is specified using connectives, such as, **all** (mandatory), **one-of** (alternative), ? (optional), and **more-of** (non-exclusive choice). In addition to representing the feature diagram, FDL allows arbitrary constraints between features.

Table 1. Feature descriptions as boolean formulas

Features	Logic
feature	boolean formula
atomic and composite features	atoms
configurability	satisfiability
configuration	valuation
validity of a configuration	satisfaction

Tree   : **all**(Factory, Visitors?)
Factory : **one-of**(list, array)
Visitors : **all**(Strategy, logging?)
Strategy : **one-of**(top-down, bottom-up)

Fig. 5. Textual FDL feature description of the example

For instance, in the example one could declare the constraint "array **requires** logging". This constraint has the straightforward meaning that selecting the array feature should involve selecting the logging feature. Because of these and other kinds of constraints a formal semantics of feature diagrams is needed, because constraints may introduce inconsistencies not visible in the diagram, and they may cause the invalidity of certain configurations, which is also not easily discerned in the diagram.

3.3   Configuration Consistency

The primary consistency requirement is internal consistency of the feature description. An inconsistent feature description cannot be configured, and thus it would not be possible to instantiate the corresponding product. An example of an inconsistent feature description would be the following:

A : **all**(b, c)
b **excludes** c

Feature b excludes feature c, but they are defined to be mandatory for A. This is a contradiction if A represents the product. Using the correspondence between feature descriptions and boolean formulas (cf. Table 1), we can check the consistency of a description by solving the satisfiability problem of the corresponding formula.

Configuration spaces of larger product lines quickly grow to exponential size. It is therefore essential that scalable techniques are employed for the verification and validation of feature descriptions and feature selections respectively. Elsewhere, we have described a method to check the logical consistency requirements of component-based feature diagrams [19]. That technique is based on translating component descriptions to logical formulas called binary decision diagrams (BDDs) [5]. BDDs are logical if-then-else expressions in which common subexpressions are shared; they are frequently used in model-checking applications because they often represent large search spaces in a feasible way. Any propositional formula can be translated to a BDD. A BDD that is different from falsum ($\perp$) means that the formula is satisfiable.

A slightly different mapping is used here to obtain the satisfiability result. The boolean formula derived from the example feature description is as follows:

$(Tree \rightarrow Factory) \wedge$

$(Factory \rightarrow ((list \wedge \neg array) \vee (\neg list \wedge array))) \wedge$

$(Visitors \rightarrow Strategy) \wedge$

$(Strategy \rightarrow ((top\text{-}down \wedge \neg bottom\text{-}up) \vee (\neg top\text{-}down \wedge bottom\text{-}up))))$

Note how all feature names become logical atoms in the translation. Feature definitions of the form $Name : Expression$ become implications, just like "requires" constraints. The translation of the connectives is straightforward. Such a boolean formula can be converted to a BDD using standard techniques (see for instance [11] for an elegant approach).

The resulting BDD can be displayed as a directed graph where each node represents an atom and has two outcoming edges corresponding to the two branches of the if-then-else expression. Figure 6 shows the BDD for the Visitors feature bot as a graph and if-then-else expression. As one can see from the paths in the graph, selecting the Visitors feature means enabling the Strategy feature. This in turn induces a choice between the top-down and bottom-up features. Note that the optional logging feature is absent from the BDD because it is not constrained by any of the other variables.

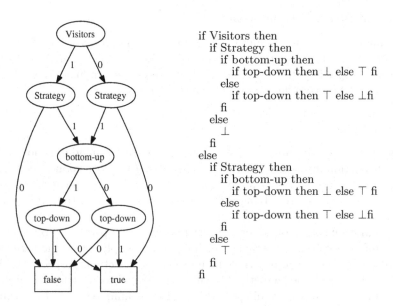

Fig. 6. BDD for the Visitors feature

4   Selection and Composition of Artifacts

4.1   Introduction

If a feature description is found to be consistent, it can be used to generate a configuration user interface. Using this user interface, an application engineer would select features declared in the feature description. Selections are then checked for validity using the BDD. The selection of features, called the configuration, is then used to instantiate the product. Sets of selected features correspond to a sets of artifacts. Let's call these the (configuration) induced artifacts. The induced artifacts form the initial composition of the product. Then, every artifact that is reachable from any of the induced artifacts in the dependency graph, is added to the composition.

4.2   Configuration and Selection

In Sect. 3 we indicated that mapping single features to sets of artifacts was not strong enough to respect certain constraints among the artifacts. The example was that the concrete Visitability aspects (array.Visitability and list.Visitability) were not selected if the Visitors feature were only mapped to the abstract aspect Visitability. To account for this problem we extend the logical framework introduced in Sect. 3.2 with constraints between features and artifacts. Thus, mappings become requires constraints (implications) that allow us to include artifacts when certain *combinations* of features are selected. The complete mapping of the example would then be specified as displayed in Fig. 7.

list **and** Visitors **requires** *list.Visitability*
array **and** Visitors **requires** *array.Visitability*
list **requires** *list.TreeFactory*
array **requires** *array.TreeFactory*
top-down **requires** *TopDown*
bottom-up **requires** *BottomUp*
logging **requires** *Logging*

Fig. 7. Mapping features to artifacts

The constraints in the figure – basically a conjunction of implications – are added to the feature description. Using the process described in the previous section, this hybrid 'feature' description is translated to a BDD. The set of required artifacts can then be found by partially evaluating the BDD with the selection of features. This results in a, possibly partial, truth-assignment for the atoms representing artifacts. Any artifact atom that gets assigned $\top$ will be included in the composition together with the artifacts reachable from it in the dependency graph. Every artifact that gets assigned $\bot$ will not be included. Finally, any artifact that did not get an implied assignment may or may not be included, but at least is not required by the selection of features.

Figure 8 shows all possible configurations for the example product line. The configurations are shown as a nested tree map. Every box represents a valid sub composition induced by the feature at left-hand side, upper corner. The artifacts contained in each composition are shown in italics. The figure shows that even this very small product line already exposes 12 product variants.

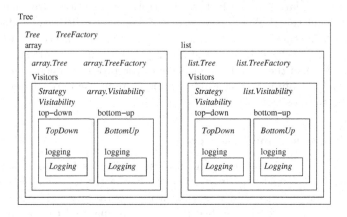

Fig. 8. All configurations/compositions of the example as a nested tree-map

4.3   Composition Methods

In the previous subsection we described how the combination of problem space feature models can be linked to solution space dependency graphs. For every valid configuration of the feature description we can derive the artifacts that should be included in the final composition. However, how to enact the composition was left unspecified. Here we discuss several options for composing the artifacts according to the dependency graph.

In the case of the example composing the Java source files entails collecting them in a directory an compiling the source files using `javac` and AspectJ. However, this presumes that the artifacts are actually Java source files, which may be a too fine granularity. Next we describe three approaches to composition that support different levels of granularity:

– Source tree Composition [8]
– Generation of a build scripts [22]
– Container-based dependency injection [10]

Source Tree Composition. Source tree composition is based on *source packages*. Source packages contain source code and have an abstract build interface. Each source package explicitly declares which other packages it requires during build, deployment and/or operation. The source trees contained in these packages can be composed to obtain a composite package. This package has a build interface that is used to build the composition by building every sub-packages in the right order with the right configuration parameters.

Applying this to our configuration approach this would mean that artifacts would correspond to source packages. Every valid selection of features would map to a set of root packages. From these root packages every transitively required packages can be found and subsequently be composed into a composite package, ready for distribution.

Build Script Generation. An approach taken in the KOALA framework [22] is similar to source tree composition but works at the level of C-files. In KOALA a distinction is made between *requires* interfaces (specifying dependencies of a component) and *provides* interfaces (declaring the function that a component has to offer). The composition algorithm of KOALA takes these interfaces and the component definitions (describing part-of hierarchies) and subsequently generates a `Makefile` that specifies how a particular composition should be built.

Again, this could be naturally applied in our context of dependency graphs. The artifacts would be represented by the interfaces and the providing components. The dependency graph then follows from the requires interfaces.

Dependency Injection. Another approach to creating the composition based on feature selections would consist of generating configuration files (or configuration code) for a dependency injection container implementation [10]. Dependency injection is a object-oriented design principle that states that every class should only reference interfaces in its code. Concrete implementations of these interfaces are then "injected" into a class via the constructor of via setter methods. How component classes are connected together ("wiring") is specified separately from the components.

In the case of Java components, we could easily derive the dependencies of those clasess by looking at the interface parameters of their constructors and setters. Moreover, we can statically derive which classes implement those interfaces (which also induces a dependency). Features would then be linked to these implementation classes. Based on the dependencies between the interfaces and classes one could then generate the wiring code.

5   Conclusions

5.1   Discussion: Maintaining the Mapping

Since problem space and solution space are structured differently, bridging the two may induce a high maintenance penalty if changes in either of the two invalidate the mapping. It is therefore important that the mapping of feature to artifacts is explicit, but not tangled.

The mapping of features to artifacts presented in this paper allows the automatic derivation of product instances based on dependency graphs, but the mapping itself must be maintained by hand. Maintaining the dependency relation manually is no option since it continually co-evolves with the code base itself, but often these relations can be derived from artifacts automatically (e.g., by static analysis).

It is precisely the separation of feature models and dependency graphs makes maintaining the mapping manageable if the dependency graphs are available automatically. For certain nodes in the graph we can compute the transitive closure, yielding all artifacts transitively required from the initial set of nodes. This means that a feature has to be mapped only to the *essential* (root) artifact; all other artifacts follow from the dependency graph.

Additionally, changes in the dependencies between artifacts (as follows from the code base) have less severe consequences on such mappings. On other words, the coevolution between feature model and mapping on the one hand, and the code base on the other is much less severe. This reduces the cost of keeping problem space and solution space in sync.

5.2   Conclusion and Future Work

The relation between problem space and solution space in the presence of variability poses both conceptual and technical challenges. We have shown that both worlds can be brought together by importing solution space artifacts into the domain of feature descriptions. By modeling the relations among software artifacts explicitly and interpreting the mapping of combinations of features to artifacts as constraints on the hybrid configuration space, we obtain a coherent formalism that can be used for generating configuration user interfaces. On the technical level we have proposed the use BDDs to make automatic consistency checking of feature descriptions and mapping feasible in practice. Configurations are input to the composition process which takes into account the complex dependencies between software artifacts.

This work, however, is by no means finished. The formal model, as discussed in this paper, is still immature and needs to be investigated in more detail. More analyses could be useful. For instance, one would like to know which configurations a certain artifact participates in order to better assess the impact of certain modifications to the code-base. Another direction we will explore is the implementation of a feature evolution environement that would help in maintaining feature models and their relation to the solution space.

A case-study must be performed to see how the approach would work in practice. This would involve building a tool set that allows the interactive editing, checking and testing of feature descriptions, which are subsequently fed into a product configurator, similar to the CML2 tool used for the Linux kernel [18]. The Linux kernel itself would provide a suitable case to test our approach.

References

1. Batory, D., Benavides, D., Ruiz-Cortés, A.: Automated analyses of feature models: Challenges ahead. Communications of the ACM (to appear, December 2006)
2. Batory, D., Sarvela, J.N., Rauschmayer, A.: Scaling step-wise refinement. In: ICSE 2003. Proceedings of the 25th International Conf. on Software Engineering, Piscataway, NJ, may 3–10, 2003, pp. 187–197. IEEE Computer Society Press, Los Alamitos (2003)

3. Benavides, D., Martín-Arroyo, P.T., Cortés, A.R.: Automated reasoning on feature models. In: Pastor, Ó., Falcão e Cunha, J. (eds.) CAiSE 2005. LNCS, vol. 3520, pp. 491–503. Springer, Heidelberg (2005)
4. Bontemps, Y., Heymans, P., Schobbens, P.-Y., Trigaux, J.-C.: Semantics of feature diagrams. In: Tomi, M., Bosch, J. (eds.) Proc. of Workshop on Software Variability Management for Product Derivation (Towards Tool Support), Boston (August 2004)
5. Bryant, R.E.: Symbolic Boolean manipulation with ordered binary-decision diagrams. ACM Computing Surveys 24(3), 293–318 (1992)
6. Cao, F., Bryant, B.R., Burt, C.C., Huang, Z., Raje, R.R., Olson, A.M., Auguston, M.: Automating feature-oriented domain analysis. In: SERP 2003. Proc. of the International Conf. on Software Engineering Research and Practice (2003)
7. Czarnecki, K., Antkiewicz, M.: Mapping features to models: A template approach based on superimposed variants. In: Glück, R., Lowry, M. (eds.) GPCE 2005. LNCS, vol. 3676, pp. 422–437. Springer, Heidelberg (2005)
8. de Jonge, M.: Source tree composition. In: Gacek, C. (ed.) Software Reuse: Methods, Techniques, and Tools. LNCS, vol. 2319, pp. 17–32. Springer, Heidelberg (2002)
9. de Jonge, M., Visser, J.: Grammars as feature diagrams. draft (April 2002)
10. Fowler, M.: Inversion of control containers and the dependency injection pattern. Online (February 2006), http://www.martinfowler.com/articles/injection.html
11. Groote, J.F., van de Pol, J.C.: Equational binary decision diagrams. Technical Report SEN-R0006, Centre for Mathematics and Computer Science (CWI), Amsterdam (2000)
12. Jansen, A.: Feature based composition. Master's thesis, Rijksuniversiteit Groning (2002)
13. Kang, K., Cohen, S., Hess, J., Novak, W., Peterson, A.: Feature-oriented domain analysis (FODA) feasibility study. Technical Report CMU/SEI-90-TR-21, SEI, CMU, Pittsburgh, PA (November 1990)
14. Kiczales, G., Hilsdale, E., Hugunin, J., Kersten, M., Palm, J., Griswold, W.G.: An overview of aspectj. In: Proceedings of the 15th European Conference on Object-Oriented Programming, pp. 327–353. Springer, Heidelberg (2001)
15. Klint, P., van der Storm, T.: Reflections on feature-oriented software engineering. In: Schwanninger, C. (ed.) OOPSLA 2004. Workshop on Managing Variabilities Consistently in Design and Code held at the 19th Annual ACM SIGPLAN Conference on Object-Oriented Programming, Systems, Languages, and Applications, ACM Press, New York (2004), Available from http://www.cwi.nl/~storm
16. Mannion, M.: Using first-order logic for product line model validation. In: Chastek, G.J. (ed.) Software Product Lines. LNCS, vol. 2379, pp. 176–187. Springer, Heidelberg (2002)
17. Prehofer, C.: Feature-oriented programming: A fresh look at objects. In: Aksit, M., Matsuoka, S. (eds.) ECOOP 1997. LNCS, vol. 1241, pp. 419–443. Springer, Heidelberg (1997)
18. Eric, S.: Raymond. The CML2 language. In: 9th International Python Conference (accessed October 2006), Available at http://www.catb.org/~esr/cml2/cml2-paper.html
19. van der Storm, T.: Variability and component composition. In: Bosch, J., Krueger, C. (eds.) ICOIN 2004 and ICSR 2004. LNCS, vol. 3107, pp. 86–100. Springer, Heidelberg (2004)

20. van Deursen, A., Klint, P.: Domain-specific language design requires feature descriptions. Journal of Computing and Information Technology 10(1), 1–18 (2002)
21. van Gurp, J., Bosch, J., Svahnberg, M.: On the Notion of Variability in Software Product Lines. In: WICSA 2001. Proceedings of the Working IEEE/IFIP Conf. on Software Architecture (2001)
22. van Ommering, R., Bosch, J.: Widening the scope of software product lines: from variation to composition. In: Chastek, G. (ed.) Software Product Lines. LNCS, vol. 2379, Springer, Heidelberg (2002)

Composition Management Interfaces for a Predictable Assembly

Xabier Aretxandieta[1], Goiuria Sagardui[1], and Franck Barbier[2]

[1] Mondragon Goi Eskola Politeknikoa, Informatika Saila, 20500 Mondragon, Spain
{xaretxandieta,gsagardui}@.eps.mondragon.edu,
www.eps.mondragon.edu
[2] PauWare Research Group, UPPA, BP 1155, 64031 Pau CEDEX, France
Franck.Barbier@FranckBarbier.com
http://www.PauWare.com

Abstract. Software system construction based on the reuse of software components has to be done with flexibility enough to control the desired behavior of the resulting assemblies. Applications created by component composition usually depend on a strict method of construction in which COTS or in-house components are only integrated with great difficulty. Actually, reliable assemblies result from being able to observe the inner workings of components and from getting an in-depth understanding of them. The need for fine-grained tailoring and adequate setups is also therefore essential. To enhance the usability, the interoperability and the runtime adaptability of components, composition management interfaces are proposed. They aim at preparing and guiding composition by exposing information about components' inners (states and transitions), which in turn allow for the making of rules that formalize appropriate composition conditions. Finally, state-based expressions for composition are built on a set of primitives discussed in the paper.

1 Introduction

Assembling software components is among others challenges [1] one of the key problems of Component-Based Software Engineering (CBSE). Nowadays, it is difficult to find compatible software components due to the diversity of sources of commercial components. Indeed, many of the COTS components currently on the market have not been developed with varied collaboration potentialities. As well as for in-house components, their compositionality must be anticipated, at design time especially. So, when designing components, one has to equip them with special interfaces and internal mechanisms to support runtime monitoring and mechanisms for adjusting composition [2]. This supposes that, at design time, such adjustment capabilities have been instrumented and transferred to the executable component for a component composition validation like in [3] but almost with different orientation. In this scope, this paper promotes composition primitives which are members of what we call "Composition Management Interface" (CMI). These primitives create a visibility on selected internal mechanisms of components in order to formalize composition in general. This paper

M. Lumpe and W. Vanderperren (Eds.): SC 2007, LNCS 4829, pp. 81–96, 2007.
© Springer-Verlag Berlin Heidelberg 2007

also discusses two different points of view on the use of these primitives. These two points of view are:

- the fact that a designer of a software system uses information gathered by the offered primitives to simulate component compositions in general. In this case, she/he carries out a verification/validation process. For instance, the resulting assembly may function while some QoS attributes may be deficient (e.g., performance);
- the fact that a designer of a software system calls the said primitives in its application, i.e. at runtime, to avoid composition failures. For instance, forcing a component to be in a given state before interacting with another one. Normally, this is an uncommon action since a component aims at, in general, encapsulating such internal features.

So, the necessity of controlling a system of collaborating components requires the assessment of the system's functional behavior and the possibility of managing abnormal situations, such as defects for instance. These often not only result from a single component deficiency but from the global collaboration itself. Since several collaborating components may come from different sources, composition may either fail or be unreliable if designers (COTS providers, in-house component developers) do not organize and offer composition monitoring/control capabilities for their products. In this paper, it is envisaged and proposed a notion of CMI which encompasses the ideas of component configurability, component observability and component controllability to support composition capabilities. This notion is based on the modeling of explicit states of components. Moreover, the consistent call sequences of primitives in CMI correspond to state-based design contracts that are both checked at model time and at runtime. Finally, assembly predictability in terms of an assembly's expected functional behavior and the analysis of unsatisfactory QoS properties (essentially failures) are first-class concerns resulting from the use of CMI. Instead of only having provided interfaces that document or instrument syntactical compositions (callable services [12]), there are described rules which provide a safer composition framework. For example, forcing a component for being into a given state is often a strict constraint which has to be satisfied before the component may begin collaborating with another component. Such a primary operation is typically a basic service of a CMI. As demonstrated in [21], the syntax of interfaces does not offer information enough for making a component execution adapt to unanticipated collaborations.

We show in [4] that COTS components benefit from having tangible states [9] which are accessible in management-based interfaces. From the point of view of component acquisition, this creates a support for evaluation, selection and adoption. From the viewpoint of component use and integration, in this paper, it is explained and illustrated through an example, an appropriate set of state-based composition primitives. In [5], we describe a software library and explain how to use this library in order to organize and implement the inner workings of components based on complex states and complex state dependencies. We also apply it to Enterprise JavaBeans[TM](EJBs), a widespread and well-known technological component framework.

In this paper, the notion of component is more open and not limited to EJBs. A case study in the field of Ambient Intelligence is presented. It is especially show how to construct components that encapsulate sensor and actuator operations. Since such components have states and state-based dependencies, it is explained how to master composition contract disruptions by means of state-based actions offered in CMI.

In section 2, we review the general kinds of composition, in which only the provided and required interfaces of components are used for expressing collaborations. In section 3, we define the notion of a State-Based Contract (SBC) and we state in further details the composition primitives which are grounded on component states. Section 3 also exposes what constitutes CMI and how they may be put into practice with an example. Finally, we conclude in section 4.

2   Composition Types

"Components are for composition" [7]. Our vision of components resides in the understanding of the component paradigm, not as an architectural abstraction related to an ADL but as an implementation as stated in [15]. To that extent, in [13] and in [14], they offer composition languages to create a composition in a correct way. In these two contributions, formal languages are provided to statically verify and validate the correctness of composition.

Two general-purpose means of composition are here considered: vertical and horizontal. Vertical composition (Fig.1a) refers to a whole-part relationship, in which a composite governs all of its compounds. Horizontal composition (Fig.1b) is defined as the cooperation of a set of distributed/non distributed components which do not create a bigger component. In a vertical composition, the assembly is itself a component, while within a horizontal composition the resulting

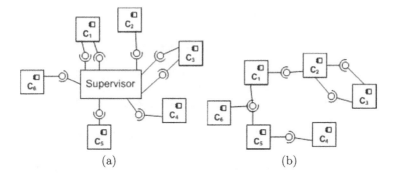

(a)   (b)

Fig. 1. a) Vertical composition, the assembly named "Supervisor" is the only way for clients to request services. b) Horizontal composition, one or more components may play the role of entry when clients request services.

assembly is simply a functional collaboration or scenario derived from the requirements. This is composition by interaction where the created message circuit corresponds to a composition topology with emergent properties. In vertical compositions, component states are shared between composites and compounds. In horizontal compositions, no coercive assumption can be made since composition conditions are more open than those within the context of vertical composition. Vertical composition indeed imposes in most cases coincident lifetimes of components [20].

Realizing horizontal component composition is either based on wrappers or glue code. This is the notion of exogenous composition [6]. This technique isolates components from their close environment, so that composition is accomplished through intermediate adapters: wrappers, glue code, containers, etc. If such brokers partially or totally hide components from their expected component clients, this creates a mixing of vertical and horizontal composition, as shown in Fig.2. The counterpart of exogenous composition is endogenous composition. This refers to the direct composition of components without any intermediary "broker" or "proxy" components where the composition primitives reside internally in the codification of the component. With this second type of composition, one may notice that technological component models (such as Enterprise JavaBeans for instance) enable the setup of deployment parameters for components in order to clearly show the linking of required interfaces with provided interfaces. This creates a direct and effective composition whose nature is safe[1] but limited in scope.

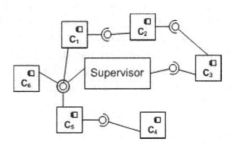

Fig. 2. Hybrid composition mixing the models in Fig.1a and in Fig.1b

In all cases, component composition stumbles over unknown or unpredictable execution contexts if key states of components have not been modeled. For instance, the reliable integration of a component requiring a database connection imposes, as a minimal requirement, the identification of two macroscopic states for a connection object: open and closed. Additional parallel states may also exist for states that embody other stable and well-identified contexts: Busy, Idle, Listening ... So, a connection object can be shared by more than one client, or

---

[1] The underlying composition model of EJBs predefines the numbers of composition forms and thus creates reliable compositions.

it may be unshared (only one client is served at a given time), or no client at all are served, etc. In this example, forcing the state of this component to be "unshared" or guarantying such a context, permits safer specialized collaborations which are often required if one expects to combine this component with others. Moreover, this decreases the risk of failures. For COTS components especially, they have not been specifically prepared for working together; the possibility of expressing composition pre-conditions as sketched above, is therefore useful.

3   State-Based Contracts

The notion of state-based contract relies on the implementation of the body (i.e. its inside) of a software component by means of a UML 2 state machine diagram [8] (Fig.3). For a system in which several components are assembled, there will be so many UML 2 state machine diagrams as existing individual components in the system.

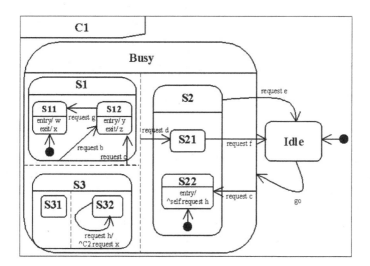

Fig. 3. C1 component specification

This way of working allows the creation of instances of components in two different abstraction levels. The high abstraction level is the level in which the behavior of a software component is modeled in terms of states and transitions. As for the low abstraction level, the component itself is the one that is implemented. The exercised design method leads to having events labeling transitions as services in the provided interfaces of the C1 component (Fig.4).

Composition capability limitation. The expression $^\wedge$C2.request x in C1 (Fig.3) corresponds to a composition or a required service of the component. More precisely, it amounts to the sending of an event to another component

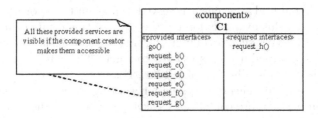

Fig. 4. Component C1 (Fig.3) provided services

instance, in this case C2. This C2 component by definition owns in its state machine a transition labeled by the request x event. Such an approach (i.e. expression $^\wedge$C2.request x inside C1) makes component composition immutable at runtime. It creates a high coupling and contradicts the black-box nature of components especially for COTS components whose future compositions are undefined. This kind of composition is rigid and looses the sense of independent component execution. It also makes difficult component composition prediction activity. In our opinion such composition style should be avoided. Furthermore, strong mechanisms to create a composition and a prediction-enabled technology which aims not only at operating at runtime but also managing it are needed (see section 3.1 and 3.2). In order to create a more flexible and open composition support, the possibility to express state based contracts is offered. For instance, a state-based contract has the following shape:

$$C2.exeTrans(requestx) \tag{1}$$

This expression represents that inside a component C1 it is defined such an expression to send an event (request x for this example) to C2, that has the capability to assume this request.

Our rationale is to externalize (or to avoid at modeling time) the business rules that require composition from the inside of components. Namely, to create a lower coupling, the $^\wedge$C2.request x composition expression must be removed from the behavior specification of C1. Following such a strategy, components gain autonomous capabilities. This component is a very flexible and useful component that the system designer can configure for a component composition. Now that composition it is externalized (out from the inners of the component) the system designer configures the component to assume the defined business rules of the system. The system designer materializes such business rules by expressions (state-based contract expressions) corresponding to a composition. In this case $^\wedge$C2.request x is replaced by C2.exeTrans(request x) that it is externally inserted by the designer and it is based on the availability of predefined primitives which make up a fixed composition management interface (Fig.5).

So, more generally, state-based contracts correspond to an expression of a business rule (or more simply a requirement of the global application to be built) using the primitives in the prefabricated Composition Management Interface. So for each defined business rule in the system there will exist state-based expressions

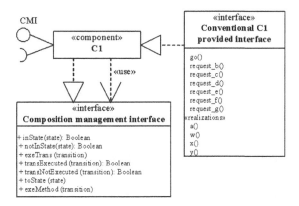

Fig. 5. C1 component realizes CMI interface services, but also uses this interface for the realization of the requested internal actions for a component composition. C1 defines its conventional interface for being used with CMI.

inside the components. And why? Because the components themselves do not cover all the system requirements directly and it is necessary an operation among components to cover those requirements. We are referring to composition.

The CMI just introduces behavior constraints into the component in order to adapt its behavior to the required and defined global system behavior. The component can run as expected. But due to the insertion of state based contract expressions hypothetical malfunction of the component can occur. In this case the responsible for the malfunctioning of the system is the system designer. From a logical viewpoint, a state-based contract can be evaluated at runtime: it holds or leads to a composition failure (see Section 3.2).

For such an intention, components may then be equipped with enhanced composition capabilities as depicted in Fig.5. In this figure, primitives are specified and executed by the CMI that are used to formalize the composition between components in state-base contract formalization.

The composition primitives are defined separately from the component implementation but together with it. The composition primitive's container has deployment descriptors that capture requester intentions for composition that are externally attached to the component. In our case we have created an XML (Fig.6) schema with all the necessary information to establish composition.

Through this XML source, we want to demonstrate that the inside of C1 is not again polluted by composition code (black box nature of the component) but compositions rules exist and occur externally.

The component diagram in Fig.5 imposes for C1 an implementation of the offered CMI. In this case C1 component uses the CMI to execute the business rules by means of a state based contract expression. C2 uses the CMI to execute inside the components the state based expressions from other components.

The way of working is the following: the system designer based on the state machines design of the individual components defines in the XML file the

```xml
<?xml version="1.0" encoding="utf-8" ?>
<!-- Composition Setup file  -->
- <composition>
    <!-- All the composed objects are defined here  -->
  - <assemblies>
    - <assembly>
        <name />
        <ip />
        <port />
      </assembly>
      ...
    </assemblies>
    <!-- All the events the actions and events that can have  -->
    <!-- associated composition primitives are defined here  -->
  - <events>
    - <event>
        <name />
        <state />
        <primitive />
        <remoteObject />
        <remoteAction />
        <remoteState />
      </event>
      ...
    </events>
  </composition>
```

Fig. 6. Composition specification XML schema

composition primitives that corresponds to a defined business rule. When an event occurs inside a component Cx the XML file is looked up in order to find some defined primitive for such event. In the case that primitives are defined for such event a primitive launcher function executes the related action with the necessary information. Once the primitive launcher executes the composition requirement the requested component performs the requested action (Fig.7).

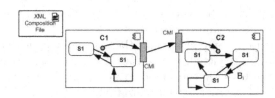

Fig. 7. CMI works for creating monitoring and composition facilities

Finally the prediction activity is defined. [19] Defines prediction as "the ability to effectively predict properties from the system". Our composition mechanism ensures that the design is analyzable, due to the state machine construction and the CMI facilities) and the resulting system will therefore be predictable. In our case we will execute all of the models and component coded using PauWare (statecharts execution engine [16]). Activity into the components will be simulated. And then for each activated business rule the states of all of the models will be studied. The combination of all of the component states will be the information used against the system requirements. If the result of the composition is not satisfactory the CMI can be used to define some failure actions (see section 3.2).

3.1   Composition Primitives

Next the composition primitives are described to define business rules among components. These components will create an assembly through the CMI. For the description of the composition primitives they are divided into two categories, action coordination and action enforced.

Action Coordination. Here are presented a set of composition primitives to establish some functional dependency among several components. These composition primitives enables the designer to, establish such as synchronization, more generally orchestration or a coordination dependency among components. This orchestration it is transferred to conditional actions-dependency used as guards or it is transferred to the action-accomplishment. For such intention the following primitives have been defined:

inState, notInState: These composition management functions are used to create a composition rule to specify a guard expression in the execution of some given action or a given event inside the component. To create coordinated actions, even synchronized actions between components, the specification of these actions have to be grounded on *inState* and *notInState*. These two primitives act as a Boolean guard (a pre-condition in fact) for the execution of some behavior activity inside the component. This activity can be the execution of an action related to a transition, or the entry/exit actions to be done when arriving in a given state or do activity during the presence in a state.

These primitives can play different roles to define a composition rule. "If"-sense expression or "While"-sense expression. With the first meaning the rule created using the primitive is that if in a given C_x component an e_x event causes an internal transition, this will be completed if another C_y component resides in the specified S_y state. With the second meaning a given component accomplishes some actions while another component resides in an specified state (Fig.10).

exeTrans: This primitive controls the interaction of many components. It sends a signal to another component to execute some desired action. The meaning of the rule is related to an event sending action that a component sends to another one or just a notification for an occurrence. This action, because of the nature of the codification of the component, is the execution of a method. The sending action by the petitioner will be served depending on the state of the receiver component. When possible, the sending transition execution action will be completed and the rule will be fulfilled otherwise the petition of the rule-completion will be ignored.

transExecuted, transNotExecuted: These primitives are used for detecting if some given transition has been occurred in a component. The utility of this rule resides on the creation of an action dependency among components involved in an assembly. It is used as the *inState* and *notInState* rules but in this case *transExecuted* and *transNotExecuted* is related to a transition-dependency.

Action enforced. This category amounts to a kind of duty-based composition. These are a set of primitives for a designer to try to correct the behavior of an undesired situation. The aim of these primitives is the initialization of the component or the definition of a new stable situation. These primitives are used for:

- The requirement for a component for being in a concrete state
- The requirement for a component to force the execution of a concrete method (in this case a transition).

These two rules are defined to force a component to act in a desired way. The *toState* and the *exeMethod* rules are proposed for this situation. These rules should be under the strict control of the constructor of the component because of the dangerousness of them.

toState: This primitive forces the component to change its current state to the specified one. By the use of this primitive the designer can specify the obligation for a component to be in a concrete and known state in order to ensure the component collaboration. The meaning of this primitive is that "it is mandatory for a component being in a known and concrete state or situation in order to guarantee the safeness and correctness of the system".

In Fig.9 an example is defined that uses the *toState* primitive. In this case the presence detector component uses the alarm component to activate the alarm, if the detected and identified person it is a non trustworthy person.

exeMethod: This primitive almost forces the component to execute a method (i.e. a transition) in any case although theoretically it is not possible to give a response from its current state. In this case this method is related to an execution of a transition that is not programmed. Like the previous mentioned primitive (i.e. *toState*) it is focused on getting the component into shape.

A very important issue in these two primitives is that both of them should be clearly specified by the constructor of the component, to guarantee the safeness of the component and the extensibility of the safeness and the stability of the system. It must also guarantee the controlled means of execution of the rules, to avoid anarchical executions or security faults, where every state and every part of the component is accessible. The use of these primitives can be secured by the use of the invariant state contract.

3.2 Composition Exception Capture

Individual behavior differs from group behavior as has been stated above. In all cases where composition primitives referred to business rules are used, a global behavior is defined. Using the CMI, an exception capture mechanism is used in parallel to govern these global behaviors. In a compound, due to the individual evolution of the composed components, some coordination faults can occur. The component can run correctly, as the vendor or the developer of the component has promised. It can have the correct or expected behavior, but because of the introduced composition primitives an error can be produced. The reason for using this exception capture is the possible non completion of a composition primitive. In these cases, the non compliance of the business rule should be captured to give the desired response to the abnormal situation. Formally speaking, this is not an error, since it is an uncoordinated action or a bad global state combination result of the composition primitive execution. In this case an unstable status of the system can be produced. Therefore instructions/actions should be proposed by the designer to act in consequence.

This abnormal situation must be captured by the system designer that has introduced the composition primitives. This is the part of the contract that the designer of the system establishes in order to guarantee the desired behavior of the whole system. Similar to [10] if the component does not accomplish with the defined global action the exception capture mechanism is where the composition primitives can be corrected. So for every defined composition rule, a composition exception capture mechanism must be defined to ensure the consistency of the system. This does not guarantee that the anomaly that originated the error is the last executed instruction. The latter is generated due to the occurrence of a coordination fault or cooperation faults. So this can be located where a composition rule has been used. In this case although something not desired has occurred, it is captured and the system is analyzed by trying to predict where the coordination fault has occurred.

3.3   Case Study

In order to put into practice the previous ideas, an ambient intelligence application (domotics system) is proposed and developed in the field of embedded systems. In this domotic system case study built on the top of PauWare [16], the identified collaborating components are:

- presence detector: this component detects the presence of somebody and tracks this presence in the house;
- preferences selector: a preferences manager in which the preferences of the states of the rooms are described in order to control them (sensors and actuators);
- illumination manager: direct actuator on the illumination of a room;
- alarm: this component detects an intrusion in the house and alerts the external security company.

A syntactical composition of all of these business components leads to the UML2 Component Diagram in Fig.8.

As can be seen in Fig.8 no one of the component connectors (provided and required interfaces assembly) have any name. This represents the specification of the composition necessities of the components that later will be created using the CMI. Here only the relations between the components are specified.

For each use case scenario (i.e. business rules) where there are several components, compositions primitives are defined. For example when a person enters the house, she/he is recognized by the Presence Detector (PD) as being a secure or non secure person. Next, preferences for the identified person in the house

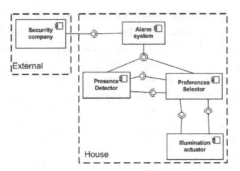

Fig. 8. Component diagram for the domotics system

are loaded and executed. This is the specification of the relationship between the two components in Fig.8. Then this business rule must be formalized in the XML composition specification file to declare explicitly which are the primitives for covering the business rule.

Once the preferences are loaded the illumination manager is the actuator that places the desired illumination level for a room taking the control over the lights and the blinds to graduate the amount of illumination desired.

In the next example (Fig.9) the utility of the CMI is demonstrated for the *exeTtrans* and *toState* primitives.

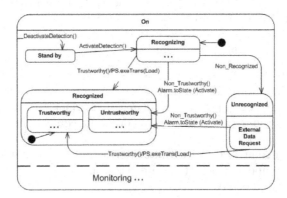

Fig. 9. Use of the *exeTrans* and *toState* primitives for the presence detector (PD) component

In Fig.9 the PD component functionality is explained. This component identifies the person who has entered the house. If the identified person is a trustworthy person (biometric information capture), the PD notifies preferences selector (PS) to load the preferences of that person. The *exeTrans* primitive specified by the signature PS.exeTrans(Load) it is used to send a signal to the PS component trying to execute the load method.

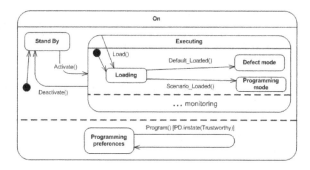

Fig. 10. Use of *inState* for the preferences selector (PS) component

If the detected person is a non trustworthy person, the PD component uses the alarm composed component to activate the sound of the alarm whatever this component is doing (`Alarm.toState(Activate)`).

In Fig.10 example the PS component and the *inState* primitive are shown. In this case the preferences for the actuators, only can be programmed by an identified and trustworthy person. By the use of Set Preferences [`PD.inState (Trustworthy)`] an scenario can be specified and programmed by users if the PD component resides in the trustworthy state (Fig.10).

It has been shown briefly the functioning of the CMI interface with the above exposition. In an ambient intelligence environment many components collaborate together in order to fulfill system requirements. Those components have been reconfigured in order to adapt their functionality to the desired one through the CMI. Their reconfiguration has been done respecting the nature of the components themselves as black box elements. Finally a prediction of the functionality has been done and conclusions can be obtained.

4   Conclusions

Due to the increasing complexity of systems, which results from the deferred necessary component adaptation to environmental constraints, composition has to be carried out through the latter, even for the dynamic (not static like in [17]) fixing of parameters of the involved components for a correct composition. Composition based on wrappers or glue code is nowadays no longer sufficient. SBC provides the system integrator with the necessary tools in order to introduce a component into a system in a controlled way. The CMI provides flexibility enough to create a component composition due to the common interface and in a predictable way because the SBC externalizes the internal visibility of the components.

The SBC's aim is to tackle composition difficulties due to interface incompatibilities and composition predictability. SBC proposes a unique and common interface that allows component composition based on defined composition primitive's actions. These primitives are also used to check properties of the components.

If a composition among components is carried out the SBC has an advantage over the mere component linkage technique. The SBC allows introducing norms of behavior for the components aside from the individual component behavior. This way the composition among components is more flexible. The component is an autonomous element which behavior's is refined to correspond to the desired one. The SBC defines a desired global behavior strategy that each component must comply in order to act together with other components trying to cover system requirements. Like this, components choreography can be laid down for a compound. It is important to notice that such approach does not use the source code of the components for establishing composition. The composition management functions offered by the CMI are used to adapt the component to its close environment.

Two key aspects are related to the CMI. The first one corresponds to the inclusion of the syntactic part of the component creation. However, the CMI must be added to the components construction in order to be composed (interoperability). The second one corresponds to the semantic part. The required information from the COTS supplier or in-house component developer should be based on the information of the components behavior, mainly the state attribute that depicts behavior. Thus, by extension, state machine diagrams define the behavior of the whole component. This information neither reveals the essence for example of the COTS (more problematic than in-house component), nor any crucial information about the component. It only describes the functionality of the component on a high level of abstraction to be used at design time. The description of the component must at least make reference to the previously mentioned information to avoid misinterpretations about the behavior of the component. If this information is not provided, it is very difficult to select an appropriate component for the specific necessities. The construction based on State Machines depicts control over the behavior.

It is important to realize that the inclusion of these composition primitives into the components depicts their nature of required services. The provided "services" of the components must be configured in such a way that those "services" are usable for the rest of the components involved into a composition. Because of that, the meaning of this "service" configuration for possible component collaboration and action coordination among components is understood as components required "services" or action dependency. Obviously the components provided "services" are the ones that are used to shape the behavior interface and its composition primitives.

The CMI must be ready to use the afore mentioned information in order to be used by the system integrator to define a global behavior with predictable consequences. This allows the insertion of composition rules to the individual components to preserve the global behavior. As a consequence the SBC has the advantage of a predictable composition. This is because the provided rules monitor the desired and undesired states in an effective way and they use this information in early steps of the system creation.

This interface also has monitoring capabilities so that the system constructor may analyze the properties of the system (for COTS for example often the documentation associated is not the most adequate). This feature reinforces the prediction capabilities of the CMI for the system's behavior.

From the CBSE viewpoint the proposal of this paper corresponds with the reality of the component concerned from other mature engineering. In this paper the component has been presented as an autonomous element which execution is not related to other components avoiding high component coupling. This way the component operating capacities are higher and can be used in many heterogeneous applications. It also has been presented the component as an executable unit independent [18] from its close environment. Consequently for component composition the system designer must use the CMI to adapt the component to all requirements.

References

1. Crnkovic, I., Larsson, M.: Building Reliable Component-Based Software Systems. Artech House publisher (2002) ISBN1-58053-327-2
2. Becker, S., Brogi, A., Gorton, I., Overhage, S., Romanovsky, A., Tivoli, M.: Towards an Engineering Approach to Component Adaptation. In: Reussner, R., Stafford, J.A., Szyperski, C.A. (eds.) Architecting Systems with Trustworthy Components. LNCS, vol. 3938, pp. 193–215. Springer, Heidelberg (2006)
3. Speck, A., Pulvermuller, E., Jerger, M., Franczyk, B.: Component composition validation. Int. J. Appl. Math. Comput. Sci. 12(4), 581–589 (2002)
4. Barbier, F.: Web-Based COTS Component Evaluation, proceedings of The 3rd International Conference on COTS-Based Software Systems. In: Kazman, R., Port, D. (eds.) ICCBSS 2004. LNCS, vol. 2959, pp. 2–4. Springer, Heidelberg (2004)
5. Barbier, F.: An Enhanced Composition Model for Conversational Enterprise JavaBeans. In: Gorton, I., Heineman, G.T., Crnkovic, I., Schmidt, H.W., Stafford, J.A., Szyperski, C.A., Wallnau, K. (eds.) CBSE 2006. LNCS, vol. 4063, Springer, Heidelberg (2006)
6. Lau, K.-K., Elizondo, P.V., ZhengWang,: Exogenous Connectors for Software Components. In: Heineman, G.T., Crnković, I., Schmidt, H.W., Stafford, J.A., Szyperski, C.A., Wallnau, K. (eds.) CBSE 2005. LNCS, vol. 3489, pp. 90–106. Springer, Heidelberg (2005)
7. Szyperski, C., Gruntz, D., Murer, S.: Component Software - Beyond Object-Oriented Programming, 2nd edn. Addison-Wesley, Reading (2002)
8. OMG Unified Modeling Language: Superstructure, version 2.0, Final Adopted specification, ptc/03-08-02 (2007), http://www.omg.org/uml/
9. Gamma, E., Helm, R., Johnson, R., Vlissides, J.: Design Patterns: Element of Reusable Object-Oriented Software. Addison-Wesley, Reading (1995)
10. Meyer, B.: Object-Oriented Software Construction, 1st edn. Prentice-Hall, Englewood Cliffs (1988) ISBN: 0-13-629031-0
11. Wallnau, K.C., PECT: Volume III: A Technology for Predictable Assembly from Certifiable Components (PACC). Technical Report CMY/SEI-, TR-009 ESC-TR-2003-009 (2003)
12. Zhang, S., Goddard, S.: xSADL: An Architecture Description Language to Specify Component-Based Systems. ITCC (2) 443–448 (2005)

13. Sofware Compositon Group (2007), http://www.iam.unibe.ch/~scg/
14. Assmann, U.: Invasive Software Composition. Springer, Heidelberg (2003) ISBN:3-540-44385-1
15. Bachmann, F., Bass, L., Buhman, C., Comella-Dorda, S., Long, F., Robert, J., Seacord, R., Wallnau, K.: Volume II: Technical Concepts of Component-Based Software Engineering, 2nd ed (CMU/SEI-2000-TR-008, ADA379930). Pittsburgh, PA: Software Engineering Institute, Carnegie Mellon University (2000)
16. (2007), http://www.PauWare.com
17. Inverardi, P., Wolf, A., Yankelevich, D.: Static checking of system behaviors using derived component assumptions. ACM Transactions on Software Engineering and Methodology 9(3), 239–272 (2000)
18. Nierstrasz, O., Tsichritzis, D.: Object-Oriented Software Composition. Prentice Hall, Englewood Cliffs (1995) ISBN: 0-13-220674-9
19. Hamlet, D.: Defining "Predictable Assembly". In: Gorton, I., Heineman, G.T., Crnkovic, I., Schmidt, H.W., Stafford, J.A., Szyperski, C.A., Wallnau, K. (eds.) CBSE 2006. LNCS, vol. 4063, pp. 3–540. Springer, Heidelberg (2006)
20. Barbier, F., Aretxandieta, X.: State-based Composition in UML 2, submitted to IJSEKE
21. Sagardui, G., Aretxandieta, X.: Leire Etxeberria Components Behaviour Specification and Validation with Abstract State Machines. In: IBIMA 2005 Conference on Theory and Practice of Software Engineering (TPSE), El Cairo, December 13-15, 2005 (2005)

Path-Based Error Propagation Analysis in Composition of Software Services[*]

Vittorio Cortellessa[1] and Pasqualina Potena[2]

[1] Dipartimento di Informatica
Università di L'Aquila
Via Vetoio 1, 67010 Coppito (AQ), Italy
cortelle@di.univaq.it
[2] Dipartimento di Scienze
Università "G.D'Annunzio"
Viale Pindaro, 42, Pescara, 65127 Italy
potena@sci.unich.it

Abstract. In Service-Oriented Architectures (SOA) composed services provide functionalities with certain non-functional properties that depend on the properties of the basic services. Models that represent dependencies among these properties are necessary to analyze non-functional properties of composed services. In this paper we focus on the reliability of a SOA. Most reliability models for software that is assembled from basic elements (e.g. objects, components or services) assume that the elements are independent, namely they do not take into account the dependencies that may exist between basic elements. We relax this assumption here and propose a reliability model for a SOA that embeds the "error propagation" property. We present a path-based model that generates the possible execution paths within a SOA from a set of scenarios. The reliability of the whole system is then obtained as a combination of the reliability of all generated paths. On the basis of our model, we show on an example that the error propagation analysis may be a key factor for a trustworthy prediction of the reliability of a SOA. Such a reliability model for a SOA may support, during the system development, the allocation of testing effort among services and, at run time, the selection of functionally equivalent services offered by different providers.

1 Introduction

"Service Oriented Architecture (SOA) is a paradigm for organizing and utilizing distributed capabilities that may be under the control of different ownership domains" [23]. A software system based on the SOA paradigm is developed by assembling software services. Services are offered by providers that hide to users their internal implementation. The users are only aware of a certain behavior that is specified by the service description. Given a set of services $\{s_1; ...; s_n\}$, the functional composition of services can be expressed by the following three operators:

---

[*] This work has been partially supported by the PLASTIC project: Providing Lightweight and Adaptable Service Technology for pervasive Information and Communication. EC - 6th Framework Programme. http://www.ist-plastic.org

M. Lumpe and W. Vanderperren (Eds.): SC 2007, LNCS 4829, pp. 97–112, 2007.
© Springer-Verlag Berlin Heidelberg 2007

$$C ::= (s_1; ...; s_n)|(s_1|...|s_n)|(s_1 + ... + s_n)$$

$(s_1; ...; s_n)$ represents the sequential execution of the services, $(s_1|...|s_n)$ represents the parallel execution and $(s_1 + ... + s_n)$ the possible execution of some services [12]. However, the composition of their non-functional properties, such as the reliability, is not so easy to represent.

In order to keep as simple as possible the modeling aspects of our work, we only consider here the sequential execution of services ([1]). The interactions within this type of composition can be implemented in several ways [23], and we assume that the services communicate by exchanging synchronous messages. In agreement with Parnas [17], sequentially executed services S_i and S_j may undergo two different relations, that are the *Uses* and the *Invokes* relations. The *Uses* relation (here represented as $USES(S_i; S_j)$) means that the service S_i uses S_j for providing its functionality, i.e. as soon as S_i receives a request of service it provides a request of service to S_j. Then, after received an answer from S_j, S_i can elaborate the answer and provide its functionality. The *Invokes* relation (here represented as $INV(S_i; S_j)$) means that the service S_i, at the end of its execution, gives the execution control to S_j. These types of relations will be used in our model for appropriately composing the reliability of services.

Most reliability models for software that is assembled from basic elements (e.g. objects, components or services [9] [12]) assume that the elements are independent, namely the models do not take into account the dependencies that may exist between elements. They assume that the failure of a certain element provokes the failure of the whole system. This assumption is not realistic, for example, in cases of distributed systems where a service interacts with remote services that could run on different operating systems. In this case the services are not independent each other, in fact the middleware that connects them could propagate an error from a service to another one. To some extent, applications that include service wrappers ensuring that a failure is caught in time and close to its source make this assumption more realistic [5].

The independence assumption implies a complete propagation between the services along a path, in the sense that if a service returns an erroneous message then the latter is certainly propagated along the path and the whole system always returns an erroneous message. Goal of this paper is to relax this assumption and consider a wider "error propagation" scenario. We introduce the probability that a service may not produce an erroneous message (i.e. it may "mask" an error to the output, therefore no complete propagation) whether it gets as input value an erroneous message [2].

Our model is based on the composition of scenarios that describe the dynamics of a SOA. Assuming that, for each service provided by the system, we dispose of a scenario represented by a collaboration diagram UML, we provide a technique to generate, for each scenario, all possible execution paths. The reliability of a service is then obtained as the composition of the reliability of all the paths based on the stochastic distribution of the runtime execution of the system, also known as operational profile [16]. The latter consists, on one hand, of the probability that the user executes a certain system service

---

[1] Being, at the best of our knowledge, the first paper that embeds error propagation in a SOA reliability model, we prefer to focus on this aspect rather than coping with all the above execution operators.

and, on the other hand, of the probability that a service interacts with another one. From the solution of our model, we show that the error propagation analysis may be a key factor for a trustworthy prediction of the reliability of service-based systems.

Information on the SOA may be incomplete. However, if (some) scenarios are not available, then the approach in [22] can be adopted to generate them. Besides, if the operational profile of the system is not (fully) available, then the technique described in [16] can be used to estimate it.

The paper is organized as follows: in section 2 we summarize the reliability estimation models presented in literature and we outline the novelty of our approach; in section 3.1 we introduce a model for SOA reliability that embeds the error propagation factor; in section 4 we provide an example of application of our model, and finally in section 5 we give concluding remarks.

2   Related Work and Novelty of Our Approach

In the last few years many reliability models for software that is assembled from basic elements (e.g. objects, components or services) have been introduced. They can be partitioned in path-based models and state-based models [9]. The former ones represent the architecture of the system as a combination of the possible execution paths, the latter ones as a combination of the possible states of the system. The formulation of the path-based model presented in [21] for component-based systems is the closest one to our approach. From the scenarios of the system, in [21] a *Component Dependency Graph* (CDG) that summarizes all possible execution paths of the system is built.

Inspired by the Yacoub's approach, we introduce in the service domain a model that allows to generate, with a different methodology, the possible execution paths of each scenario representing a service provided by the system. We obtain then the reliability of a service as a composition of the reliability of each generated path. In [21], as in most models for software that is assembled from basic elements (e.g. objects, components or services), it is assumed that the elements are independent, namely the model does not take into account the dependencies that may exist between elements. We relax this assumption here and consider the "error propagation" property in the reliability model for SOA that we propose. This property expresses the probability that a service may propagate an erroneous message when it receives as input an erroneous message. In all the current reliability model this probability is implicitly assumed to be 1, that is complete propagation of errors. In [1] this property has been defined for component-based systems and a formula for its estimation has been provided.

The following aspects characterize the novelty of our approach:

– Our model for SOAs could be adopted to estimate the reliability of software that is assembled from other basic elements (e.g objects or components), but some modifications should be made in order to adapt to other development paradigms. For example, we estimate the reliability of a SOA by partitioning the input domain of the services in equivalence classes. In order to adapt the model to a component-based system, it is necessary to take into account that a component could offer several services within a scenario. Therefore it is necessary to introduce a new criterion to partition its input domain.

- Our reliability model for SOA is not tied to any particular architectural style or to any particular service-based development process. It can be adopted to obtain a trustworthy prediction of the reliability whether a SOA is completely defined at the design time or certain services are discovered at runtime.
- In our reliability model for SOA we take into account the dependencies that may exist among services. In fact, in order to consider the failures that spread between services, we have embedded the "error propagation" property in the model.
- We model the behavior at runtime of the system by combining the behavior of the system (modelled by a SDG) with the operational profile and the probability of interaction between services. In particular, we consider this probability at the level of input equivalence classes of services.
- Our reliability model is independent from the methodology adopted to represent the scenarios and from the strategy used to generate the possible execution paths. In fact, we assume that each scenario of a service offered by the system is represented by an UML Collaboration Diagram. From the scenario of a service we generate the possible execution paths of the system and we apply to each path the reliability model. However, a scenario could be represented with whatever notation that permits to describe the system scenarios (e.g. the Message Sequence Charts (MSCs) [13] or the UML Sequence Diagrams).

3   Modeling the Reliability of a SOA

In this section we present our approach to build a reliability model of a SOA. We assume that a scenario is available for each functionality that the SOA offers to the users. Each scenario describes the internal dynamics of the functionality, in terms of paths of invoked services. We generate all the possible execution paths, then we estimate the reliability of each path and we obtain the SOA reliability as a composition of its path reliabilities.

At a coarse grain, we can classify the failures that could occur during the execution of a service-based system as follows:

- *crash failures*, that provoke the crash of the whole system, namely the system straightforwardly stops its execution.
- *no − crash failures*, that do not provoke the immediate termination of the whole system, but they manifest themselves by returning an erroneous message. This message may either propagate to the system output (thus generating a failure) or it can be masked along its path to the output (thus without actual effects on the system reliability). A finer grain classification of *no − crash failures* can be made, but it is out of the scope of this paper.

We focus our attention only on *no − crash failures*. Let us assume that, when a service is executed in a path, if it receives as input a correct message then it can fail and introduce an error in the path with a certain probability (i.e. probability of failure on demand, see section 3.2). Instead, if the service receives as input an erroneous message, then we assume that it may correct the erroneous message that it has received thus masking the internal error to the external outputs.

In the remainder of this section we first describe how to obtain all the execution paths from scenarios, then we introduce our model for the reliability of a single path, and finally we compose those reliabilities to model the whole SOA reliability.

3.1   Generating Execution Paths from Scenarios

Let S be a service oriented architecture composed by n elementary services. Let els_k be the name of the k-th service $(1 \leq k \leq n)$. Let us assume that the input domain of els_k is partitioned in ncl_k disjoint equivalence classes, and that erroneous messages in input that are out of the service domain can be automatically detected and discarded (e.g. with a service harness that filters them), therefore we deal only with erroneous messages that fall within the service domain. The input equivalence classes of each service can be determined in various ways, e.g. using the outlines of the domain testing [11].

Through the composition of its n elementary services, the SOA offers m external services $exts_k$ (i.e. system functionalities) to users, as illustrated in Figure 1.

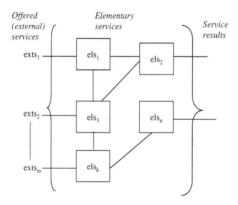

Fig. 1. A schematic representation of elementary and external services in a SOA

Let us assume that for each offered service we dispose of a scenario describing its dynamics (e.g. as an UML Collaboration Diagram) in terms of interactions that take place between elementary services to achieve the goal of the external service ([2]).

Basing on the structure of the Component Dependency Graph (CDG) in [21], we associate a Service Dependency Graph (SDG_k) for each external service $exts_k$, starting from its Collaboration Diagram. SDG_k is a directed graph that describes the behaviour

---

[2] Note that if the diagrams are incomplete or inconsistent, then the approach in [4] can be adopted to define a reasonably complete and consistent set of diagrams.

of the system (in terms of its possible execution paths) when the external service $exts_k$ is executed.

Another strategy can be used to generate the possible execution paths from each scenario. In [20] Uchitel et. al. synthesize the behaviour of the system from a set of scenarios. This can be done without changing the structure of our reliability model because it gets as input only the possible execution paths.

Definition 1: Service Dependency Graph "SDG_k" -   A Service Dependency Graph is defined by $SDG_k = \langle N, E, s, t \rangle$, where:

- $\langle N, E \rangle$ is a directed graph,
- s is the start node, t the termination node,
- N is a set of nodes in the graph,
- E is a set of edges in the graph.

In Figure 2 we show an example of SDG, whose details are given in the following.

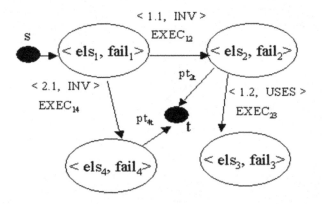

Fig. 2. An example of SDG

Definition 2: Nodes in a SDG -   A node i in a SDG represents an elementary service els_i. It is defined by the pair $< els_i, fail_i >$ where $fail_i$ is a vector of ncl_i elements. Each element of $fail_i$, here defined as $fail_i(c)$, $1 \leq c \leq ncl_i$, represents the probability of failure on demand of the service els_i with respect to the c-th equivalence class of its input domain. In other words, $fail_i(c)$ represents the probability that els_i produces an erroneous output given that it has received an input within the equivalence class c.

Definition 3: Directed Edges in a SDG -   For each pair of nodes i and j, a directed edge represents the invocation of the service els_j from the service els_i. The invocation is stochastically ruled by the matrix $EXEC_{ij} = [exec_{cd}]$, made of $ncl_i \cdot ncl_j$ elements, where an element $exec_{cd}$ ($1 \leq c \leq ncl_i$, $1 \leq d \leq ncl_j$) represents the probability that the service els_i maps an element of its c-th input equivalence class into an element of the d-th input class of els_j. In other words, the $EXEC_{ij}$ matrices represent the operational profile of the SOA at the level of input equivalence classes([3])).

Each edge is also labeled with a pair $< p.num, MODE >$. $p.num$ is a composed label, where p identifies the p-th path of execution of the system, and num is a progressive number that determines the sequence of the messages along the p-th path ([4]). $MODE$ is a label that may assume the values "USES" or "INV" if, with respect to the message $p.num$, the service els_i is tied to the service els_j through, respectively, the *Uses* or the *Invokes* relation (see section 1).

3.2 Modeling the Reliability of an External Service

After built the SDG_k for the external service $exts_k$, its reliability on demand ROD_k can be trivially formulated as a function of its probability of failure on demand $POFOD_k$, as follows:

$$ROD_k = 1 - POFOD_k \tag{1}$$

Let I be the event "the input of the service $exts_k$ is correct", and O the event "the output of the service $exts_k$ is erroneous (i.e. the returned result is not the expected one)". Then the probability of failure on demand $POFOD_k$ can be expressed as follows:

$$POFOD_k = P(I \cap O) = P(I)P(O|I) \tag{2}$$

where $P(I)$ is assumed to be equal to 1, because the reliability on demand of a system is always modelled under the hypothesis that the input of the system is correct (namely as defined by its specifications) [2].

Let nep_k be the number of execution paths of the system generated from the execution of the service $exts_k$, $1 \leq k \leq n$. Under our assumptions, the p-th path ($1 \leq p \leq nep_k$) will be made of a pipeline of n_p elementary services $< s_1, ..., s_{n_p} >$. Following the previous notation, ncl_j represents the number of equivalence classes of the j-th service in the p-th path ($1 \leq j \leq n_p$).

Then $P(I \cap O)$ for the k-th external service can be formulated as follows:

$$P(I \cap O) = P(O|I) = \sum_{p=1}^{nep_k} \left(\sum_{c=1}^{ncl_1} P(O|I_c) \right) \tag{3}$$

where I_c is the event "the input of the service $exts_k$ belongs to the c-th equivalence class of the service s_1 of the pipeline of services of the p-th path". This formula holds under the assumption that the equivalence classes are disjoint (see section 3.1).

---

[3] Note that input classes have no meaning for the end point t, thus in Figure 2 scalar probabilities pt_{it} label the transitions from each els_i service to t. Analogous scalar probabilities could label transitions from the start node s in case an SDG represents multiple paths with different initial nodes.

[4] Recall that we consider only the sequential composition of the services (see section 1).

The probability $P(O|I_c)$ that the output of the service $exts_k$ is erroneous, given that the input of the service $exts_k$ belongs to the c-th equivalence class of the service s_1 of the pipeline of services of the p-th path, can be reformulated by summing over $1 \leq cn \leq ncl_n$ the probabilities of the events "the last service of the pipeline of services of the p-th path produces an error given that the input of the last service of the pipeline of services of the p-th path belongs to its cn-th equivalence class and that the input of the service $exts_k$ belongs to the its c-th equivalence class". Then we have:

$$P(O|I_c) = \sum_{cn=1}^{ncl_n} P(E_n|I_{cn} \cap I_c) \tag{4}$$

where I_{cn} is the event "the input of the service s_{n_p} belongs to its cn-th equivalence class", E_n is the event "the service s_{n_p} produces an error".

In general, for the j-th service of the pipeline of services in the path we can write the following expression:

$$P(E_j) = P(CI_j) * P(F_j) + (1 - P(CI_j)) * P(NM_j) \tag{5}$$

where CI_j is the event "the input of the service s_j is correct", F_j is the event "the service s_j fails and returns an erroneous result", and NM_j is the event "the service s_j does not mask an error".

For two adjacent services i and j in a pipeline of services (where i precedes j) we can write the following formula based on (5):

$$P(E_j|I_{cj}) = \sum_{ci=1}^{ncl_i} P(T_{cicj}) * [(P(CI_j|I_{cj} \cap I_{ci}) * P(F_j|I_{cj}) + \tag{6}$$
$$+ (1 - (P(CI_j|I_{cj} \cap I_{ci})) * P(NM_j|I_{cj})]$$

We can separately obtain each term of the right-side of (6) as follows:

- $P(T_{cicj})$ represents the probability of the event T_{cicj} "the service s_i maps an element of its ci-th equivalence class to an element of the cj-th equivalence class of s_j"(see section 3.1).
- $P(CI_j|I_{cj} \cap I_{ci}) = (1 - P(E_i|I_{ci}))$,
  $P(CI_j|I_{cj} \cap I_{ci})$ can be recursively estimated. The probability that the service s_j receives a correct input depends on the probability that the services that precede it in the pipeline ($< s_1, ..., s_{j-1} >$) have not produced an error.

  $P(E_i|I_{ci})$ that represents the probability of the event "the service s_i produces an error given that the input of s_i belongs to its ci-th equivalence class" should be estimated by supposing that the input of the service s_j belongs to a certain equivalence class cj of its input domain. In order to keep our model as simple as possible, we assume that the service s_i, given an input in one of its equivalence classes ci, has the same probability to produce an error for each equivalence class of s_j.

– $P(F_j|I_{cj}) = fail_j(cj)$,

where $fail_j(cj)$ is the probability of failure on demand of service s_j with respect to the cj-th equivalence class of its input domain (see section 3.1). $P(F_j|I_{cj})$ should be estimated by supposing that the input of the service s_i belongs to a certain equivalence class ci of its input domain. In order to keep our model as simple as possible, we assume that the service s_j, with respect to an its equivalence class cj, has the same probability to produce an error for each equivalence class of s_i.

– $P(NM_j|I_{cj}) = P(s_j[x] \neq s_j[x']|x \neq x' \cap x, x' \, belong \, to \, the$
$$cj - th \quad equivalence \quad class),$$

$P(NM_j|I_{cj})$ should be estimated by supposing that the input of the service s_i belongs to a certain equivalence class ci of its input domain. In order to keep our model as simple as possible, we assume that the service s_j, with respect to an its equivalence class cj, has the same probability to not mask an error for each equivalence class of s_i.

Upon estimating the formula (6) for each equivalence class of the last service of the pipeline of services of a path, we substitute this estimation in formula (4). In turn, by back substituting in formulas (3), (2) and (1), we obtain an expression for ROD_k. Summarizing, the input parameters of ROD_k are:

– Transition Probability $P(T_{cicj})$;
– Probability of failure on demand $fail_j(cj)$;
– Probability that the service does not mask an error with respect to one of its equivalence classes $P(NM_j \cap I_{cj})$.

These parameters may be characterized by a not negligible uncertainty. The propagation of this uncertainty should be analyzed, but it is outside the scope of this paper. Several methods to perform this type of analysis can be found, e.g. it has been done in [8] for a reliability model. However, in Appendix we discuss how to estimate these parameters.

In order to provide an operational support to the model that we have introduced here, we have plugged the previous formulas into an algorithm that estimates the reliability on demand ROD of the p-th path of execution of the service $exts_k$ using the SDG_k graph. The *RelEval* algorithm is illustrated below.

We assume that the first node of the path models the service els_1 that is tied trough the *Invokes* relation with the service els_k, $1 < k \leq n$. $PEvet_{c1}$ is a global variable that we use to store, for each service that we find in the graph and that belongs to the pipeline of the path, the probability that it produces an error given that the input of the system (i.e. that one of the service els_1) belongs to its $c1$-th equivalence class. For each equivalence class of the j-th service of the pipeline of services, we evaluate the formula (6) ($\forall c1 = 1, ..., ncl_1$) and we store the results in $PEvet_{c1}$. $MODE$ is the edge label that specifies *Invokes* or *Uses* relations (see section 1). For sake of simplicity, and without loosing generality, we assume that in a path two adjacent edges with the *Uses* relation cannot be found and that the last node of the path is tied to the path with the *Uses* relation. $POFOD_p$ is a structure that we use to store the probability of failure on demand of the p-th path.

RelEval Algorithm

Parameters

consumes the $p-th$ *path of* SDG_k

produces $POFOD_p$

Algorithm

$push$ $(< els_1, fail_1 >,$

$\forall c1 = 1, ..., ncl_1$ *determine* $PEvet_{c1}$ *using* $(6))$

while Stack not EMPTY do

pop $(< els_i, fail_i >)$

if $els_i = t$ *(terminating node)*

$\forall c1 = 1, ..., ncl_1$ *determine* $PEvet_{c1}$

$$POFOD_p = \sum_{c1=1}^{ncl1} \sum_{ci=1}^{ncli} PEvet_{c1}[ci]$$

else

$push$ $(< els_j, fail_j > | els_j$ *is the   service represented in*

the successive node of the path)

if $(MODE \equiv USES)$

$\forall c1 = 1, ..., ncl_1$ *determine* $PEvet_{c1}$

using (6) *with respect to* els_j

$\forall c1 = 1, ..., ncl_1$ *determine* $PEvet_{c1}$

using (6) *with respect to* els_i

end while

On the loop problem. In the SGD_k graph there can exist some loop. This is a frequent problem of the path-based reliability models. The problem can be solved either by simplifying the number of paths with the ones observed experimentally during the testing [9], or by introducing the average time of execution of the system and of each service [21]. In the latter case the termination of a path is determined if its average execution time (obtained by summing up the average execution time of each component found along the path) is larger than the average execution time of the system. The average execution time of each service and the average execution time of the system can be estimated with monitoring techniques [3]. The *RelEval* algorithm can be easily modified to embed this termination criterion.

3.3 Modeling the System Reliability

It is easy to understand that the reliability of the whole system ROD can be modeled as follows:

$$ROD = \sum_{k=1}^{m} ROD_k \tag{7}$$

where we recall that ROD_k represents the reliability of the k-th service offered by the system

4 An Application Example

In order to show the practical usage of our reliability model, and the relevance of error propagation, in this section we apply it to an example. We have considered the "bank account example" used by McGovern et al. in [15], thus readers interested to the application details, that we do not provide here, can refer to [15]. We have taken into account two scenarios of the system, illustrated respectively in Figures 3 and 4. Each scenario models the dynamics of an external service provided from the system. After estimated the reliability of both services, the reliability of the whole system has been obtained as their algebraic mean, under the hypothesis of uniform probability for their invocation.

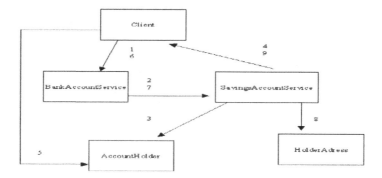

Fig. 3. First scenario of the bank account example

We have conducted two experiments that differ for probabilities of failures and error propagation probabilities of services. We describe the experiments in the following subsections.

4.1 First Configuration: Varying All Error Propagation Probabilities

We have observed the probability of failure on demand of the system while varying, at the same rate, the probability that all services do not mask an erroneous message $P(NM_j)$ (i.e. a measure of the error propagation property), for different values of the probability of failure on demand $fail_j$ of the service $BankAccountService$. So, we have assumed that only one service can introduce an error. The error may or may not be masked by the services in the pipeline of the path that follow the erroneous service, and this depends on their probability of error propagation.

In Figure 5 we report the results obtained in this configuration. Each curve represents the probability of failure on demand of the system while varying from 0.1 to 1 the error

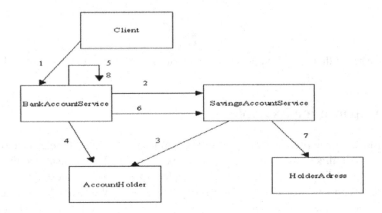

Fig. 4. Second scenario of the bank account example

propagation probability of all services. Curves differ because a different fixed value of the probability of failure of the service *BankAccountService* has been assigned for each curve. We have obtained the curves by varying this last value from 0.1 to 0.9.

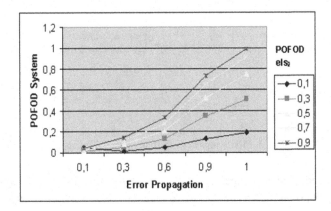

Fig. 5. Model solutions

As expected, for a given value of the probability of failure on demand of the service *BankAccountService* (i.e. for a given curve), the probability of failure on demand of the system increases while increasing the error propagation of each service of the path (i.e. the probability that an erroneous message produced by the service *BankAccountService* is not masked by other services that follows it in the pipeline).

This provides a first evidence of the relevance of the error propagation property in a SOA reliability model. In fact, the assumption of independence between failures of services, like in the model presented in [21], corresponds in Figure 5 to the points of the curves where the error propagation on the x-axis equals 1. They are, for each curve, the maximum values of the system $POFOD$. This means, as expected, that the independence between failures brings to an overpessimistic prediction of the probability of failure on demand of the system. This result confirms that the error propagation analysis is a key factor for a trustworthy prediction of the reliability of service-based systems, and its estimation leads in our model a more precise (and less pessimistic) estimation of the SOA reliability.

On the other hand, for the same value of error propagation probability of the services, the probability of failure on demand of the system decreases while decreasing the probability of failure of $BankAccountService$. This can be observed by fixing a value on the x-axis and observing the values on the curves while growing $POFOD$ of els_2.

4.2 Second Experiment: Varying One Error Propagation Probability

We have observed the probability of failure on demand of the system while varying the probability that the service $HolderAdress$ does not mask an erroneous message $P(NM_j)$, and varying the probability of failure on demand $fail_j$ of the service $BankAccountService$. So, we assume that only one service can introduce an error in the path, and that only one service can correct the error. Furthermore, we have partitioned the domain of the $HolderAdress$ service in two equivalence classes, and we have assumed that the first class is more used than the second one and that the following relation ties the two classes:

$$P(NM_j|I_2) = 1 - P(NM_j|I_1) \qquad (8)$$

In Figure 6 we report the results. Each curve represents the probability of failure on demand of the system while varying the error propagation of the first equivalence class of the domain of $HolderAdress$, and with the value of the probability of failure of the $BankAccountService$ service fixed. We have obtained the curves by varying this last

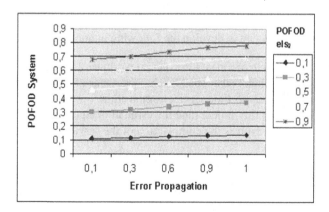

Fig. 6. Model solutions

one from 0.1 to 0.9 and the error propagation of the first class of equivalence of the service *HolderAdress* from 0.1 to 1.

The partition of the input domain of *HolderAdress* in two equivalence classes allows to obtain a better estimation of the probability of failure on demand of the system. In fact, basing on (8), for higher values of the error propagation probability of the first class we have lower probability of the error propagation of the second class that it could not be evidenced without domain partition.

A relevant observation is that, for corresponding values of curves in the two experiments, the probability of system failure is higher in the second experiment than in the first one. This is because in the first experiment we assume that all services in the path have the ability to correct an error, whereas in the second experiment we consider an error marking ability only for the service *HolderAdress* with all the other services always propagating errors.

5   Concluding Remarks and Future Work

In this paper we have introduced a model for the estimation of the reliability of a SOA, based on the reliability of each service and the operational profile, that embeds the error propagation property. The first results that we have obtained supports our intuition that the error propagation may be a key factor for a trustworthy estimation of a SOA reliability.

Our approach can be used at development time to appropriately allocate testing effort. For example, if the SOA reliability is too low, then several alternatives can be easily evaluated to study the sensitivity of the reliability to the SOA modifications, such as replacing a service with a more reliable one. Our approach can be also used at runtime, for example, as a basis for Service Level Agreement negotiation process. Providers may use this model to estimate the Quality of Service that they can provide, given the current status of the system.

The problem of service selection on the basis of their reliability has been widely investigated in the last few year, and it is not easy to solve. In fact, in [7] the authors demonstrate that the problem of service allocation for a composite Web service (i.e. a possible implementation of SOA [24]) is NP-complete.

As future work, we intend to develop the following major aspects of our approach:

- Widening the model experimentation on real world case studies.
- Embedding in our model other specific characteristics of the SOA domain, such as service discovery and run-time service composition.
- Enhancing our reliability model (and the estimation algorithm) by considering the other operators that express the composition of the services, such as parallel operators (see section 1).
- Introducing in our reliability model the probability of failure of a transition between services, that is modelled by an arc in an SDG graph.
- Introducing in our reliability model the *crash failures* (see section 3).
- Embedding our reliability model into a decision support automated framework.

References

1. Abdelmoez, W., et al.: Error Propagation in Software Architectures. In: Proc. of METRICS (2004)
2. Avizienis, A., Laprie, J.C., Randell, B., Landwehr, C.: Basic Concepts and Taxonomy of Dependable and Secure Computing. IEEE Trans. on Dependable and Secure Computing 1(1) (January-March 2004)
3. Baresi, L., Ghezzi, C., Guinea, S.: Smart Monitors for Composed Services. In: Proc. of the 2nd International Conference on Service Oriented Computing, pp. 193–202 (November 2004)
4. Bertolino, A., Marchetti, E., Muccini, H.: Introducing a Reasonably Complete and Coherent Approach for Model-based Testing. In: Garavel, H., Hatcliff, J. (eds.) ETAPS 2003 and TACAS 2003. LNCS, vol. 2619, Springer, Heidelberg (2003)
5. Cortellessa, V., Singh, H., Cukic, B.: Early reliability assessment of UML based software models. In: Proc. of WOSP 2002, Rome, Italy, July 24-26, 2002 (2002)
6. Diaconescu, A., Murphy, J.: Quality of Service in Wide Area Distributed Systems. In: Proc. of Information Technology and Telecommunications, Waterford, Ireland, pp. 39–47 (October 2002)
7. Esmaeilsabzali, S., Larson, K.: Service Allocation for Composite Web Services Based on Quality Attributes. In: SoS4CO. the First IEEE International Workshop on Service Oriented Solutions for Cooperative Organizations, pp. 71–79. IEEE Computer Society Press, Los Alamitos (2005)
8. Goseva-Popstojanova, K., Kamavaram, S.: Uncertainty Analysis of Software Reliability Based on Method of Moments, FastAbstract ISSRE (2002)
9. Goseva-Popstojanova, K., Trivedi, K.S.: Architecture based-approach to reliability assessment of software systems. Performance Evaluation 45, 179–204 (2001)
10. Hamlet, D., Mason, D., Woit, D.: Theory of Software Reliability Based on Components. In: ICSE 2001 (2001)
11. Kaner, C.: Teaching Domain Testing: A Status Report. In: CSEET 2004. Proc. of 17th Conference on Software Engineering Education and Training (2004)
12. Kokash, N.: A Service Selection Model to Improve Composition Reliability. In: ECAI 2006. Proc. of International Workshop on AI for Service Composition, in conjunction, Riva del Garda, Italy (August 2006)
13. ITU. ITU-T Recommendation Z.120 Message Sequence Charts (MSC99). Technical report, ITU Telecommunication Standardization Sector (1996)
14. Li, J., et al.: An Empirical Study of Variations in COTS-based Software Development Processes in Norwegian IT Industry. In: Proc. of METRICS 2004 (2004)
15. McGovern, J., Tyagi, S., Stevens, M., Mathew, S.: Java Web Services Architecture. published by Elsevier Science, Amsterdam, ch. 2 (July 2003)
16. Musa, J.D.: Operational profiles in software-reliability engineering. IEEE Software, 14–32 (1993)
17. Parnas, D.: On a "Buzzword": Hierarchical structure. In: Proc. of IFIP Congress (1974)
18. Rodrigues, G.N., Rosenblum, D.S., Uchitel, S.: Using Scenarios to Predict the Reliability of Concurrent Component-Based Software Systems. In: Cerioli, M. (ed.) FASE 2005. LNCS, vol. 3442, Springer, Heidelberg (2005)
19. Trivedi, K.: Probability and Statistics with Reliability, Queuing, and Computer Science Applications. J. Wiley and S., Chichester (2001)
20. Uchitel, S., Kramer, J., Magee, J.: Synthesis of Behavioral Models from Scenarios. IEEE Transactions on Software Engineering 29(2) (2003)

21. Yacoub, S., Cukic, B., Ammar, H.: Scenario-Based Reliability Analysis of Component-Based Software. In: ISSRE 1999. Proc. of the 10th International Symposium on Software Reliability Engineering, pp. 22–31 (1999)
22. Yue, K.: Generating interesting scenarios from system descriptions. In: Proc. the 1st international conference on Industrial and engineering applications of artificial intelligence and expert systems, pp. 212 - 218 (1988)
23. http://www.oasis-open.org/
24. www.w3.org/2002/ws/

Appendix: Parameters Estimation

Transition Probability "$P(T_{cicj})$" $P(T_{cicj})$ represents the probability that the service s_i maps an element of its ci-th equivalence class to an element of the cj-th equivalence class of s_j (see section 3).

The literature reports formulas for the estimation of the probability of transition between basic elements (e.g. objects, components or services). For example, in [10] Hamlet et al. have defined a formula for the probability of transition from a component to another one, on the basis of the input domain partition of a component into a set of functional subdomains (i.e. a subdomain for each functionality of the system). In [21] the authors have defined this probability with respect to each pair of components, on the basis of a CDG.

Probability of failure on demand "$fail_j(cj)$" $fail_j(cj)$ represents the probability for the service s_j to fail in one execution [19] with respect to its cj-th equivalence class (see section 3). We assume that it can be estimated by supposing that the operational profile of the service with respect to its equivalence classes is uniform. The estimate of $fail_j(cj)$ is outside the scope of this paper, however a rough upper bound $1/N_{nf}$ can be obtained by monitoring the service [3] and observing it being executed for a N_{nf} number of times with no failures. Besides, several empirical methods to estimate COTS failure rates [14] could be also used.

Probability that the service does not mask an error "$P(NM_j \cap I_{c_j})$" Since we assume that a service could fail only if it does not receive an erroneous message (see section 3) $P(NM_j \cap I_{c_j})$ can be easily estimated with the formula introduced by Abdelmoez et al. in [1]. Their formula does not embed the probability of failure on demand of a component. In fact, in [1] the error propagation probability from component A to component B, that are tied trough the connector X, is defined by the function Prob $Prob([B](x) \neq [B](x')|x \neq x')$, where $[B]$ denotes the function of component B, and x is an element of the connector X from A to B.

Dynamically Adaptable Applications with iPOJO Service Components

Clement Escoffier[1] and Richard S. Hall[2]

LSR, 220 Rue de la Chimie, BP 53
38041 Grenoble Cedex 9, France
{clement.escoffier,richard.hall}@imag.fr

Abstract. Traditional component models and frameworks simplified software system development by enabling developers to break software systems into independent pieces with well-defined interfaces. This approach led to looser coupling among the system pieces and enhanced possibilities for reuse. While the component-based approach led to advancements in the software development process, it still has its limitations. In particular, after a component-based application is developed and deployed it typically is a monolithic and static configuration of components. The advent of service-oriented component (SOC), the rise in popularity of consumer devices, and the ubiquity of connectivity have fostered a growing interest in applications that react dynamically to changes in the availability of various services. To simplify the creation of such dynamic software systems, it is possible to borrow concepts from SOC and include them into a component model, resulting in a service-oriented component model that specifically supports dynamically adaptable applications. This paper presents iPOJO, a service-oriented component framework to help developers implement dynamically adaptable software systems.

Keywords: Service Orientation, Component Orientation, Dynamic Adaptable Software, Software Composition.

1 Introduction

Traditional component models and frameworks simplified software system development by enabling developers to break software systems into independent pieces with well-defined interfaces. This approach led to looser coupling among the system pieces and enhanced possibilities for reuse. Component-based applications are constructed by developing, selecting, and assembling the individual system components. The components in the application are typically bound together with standard connectors and/or custom glue code. While the component-based approach led to advancements in the software development process, it still has its limitations. In particular, after a component-based application is developed and deployed it typically is a monolithic and static configuration of components. The characteristics of the component-based approach (i.e., loose coupling, third-party component selection, and reuse) only extend to the development portion of the

M. Lumpe and W. Vanderperren (Eds.): SC 2007, LNCS 4829, pp. 113–128, 2007.
© Springer-Verlag Berlin Heidelberg 2007

software life cycle, not to the run-time portion. While there are some exceptions to this characterization, such as the use of plugins, these exceptions tend to be low scale and coarse grained. The advent of service-oriented computing (SOC), the rise in popularity of devices such as cell phones, PDAs, and MP3 players, and the ubiquity of both wired and wireless connectivity (e.g., WiFi, Bluetooth) have fostered a growing interest in applications that react dynamically to changes in the availability of various services. For example, software systems may dynamically react to the presence of a Bluetooth-enabled mobile phone or printer in order to offer related services to the end user. While such dynamic capabilities are feasible in most component models and frameworks, there is no direct support for dynamic component composition. As a result, the developer must manage this non-functional aspect by hand. To simplify the creation of software systems that react dynamically to the changing availability of services, it is possible to borrow concepts from SOC and include them into a component model, resulting in a service-oriented component model that specifically supports dynamically adaptable applications. This paper presents iPOJO, a service-oriented component framework to help developers implement dynamically adaptable software systems. The rest of the paper is organized as follows. The next section presents SOC concepts and how they are useful in supporting dynamic composition. Section 3 describes the general principles of a service-oriented component model. Section 4 describes the approach of the iPOJO service-oriented component framework. Section 5 describes the iPOJO framework and how to design and implement dynamically adaptable applications, while section 6 describes iPOJO implementation details and experimentation. Section 7 presents related work, followed by a discussion of current and future work in section 8. Lastly, section 9 presents the conclusions.

2   Service-Oriented Computing Concepts

Service-oriented computing (SOC) [9][17] is a paradigm that utilizes services as fundamental elements for application design. The central objective of the service-oriented approach is to reduce dependencies among software islands, where an island is typically some remote piece of functionality accessed by clients. By reducing such dependencies, each element can evolve separately, so the resulting application is more flexible than monolithic applications. SOC is based on three actors:

- A service provider offers a service.
- A service consumer uses a service.
- A service broker contains references to available services.

Another central concept to SOC is the service specification, which is a description of the functionality provided by a service. Service providers implement a specific service specification and service consumers know how to interact with services implementing the specifications they require. Among these three actors are three kinds of interactions: service publication between the provider and the broker to offer services for use, service discovery between the consumer and broker to find desired services, and service invocation between the consumer and provider to actually use the service. From these concepts, SOC applications can exhibit interesting characteristics, such as:

- Loose coupling: a consumer does not need to know anything about the service implementation.
- Late binding: a consumer uses a broker to find desired services at run time.
- Dynamic resilience: a service consumer cannot rely on the same service implementation being returned by the broker between uses.
- Location transparent: providers and consumers are oblivious to the underlying communication infrastructure (e.g., local versus remote, specific protocols, etc.).

To design complex service-oriented applications, it is necessary to compose services to provide higher-level services, which means that providers may require other services to provide their own service. Current approaches to SOC, specifically in web services, offer process-oriented solutions to this issue; however, service-oriented applications can be difficult to develop since the mechanisms tend to require a lot of developer effort. Indeed, developers need to manage service publication/revocation, required service discovery, and run-time tracking of services. The SOC paradigm facilitates the implementation of dynamically adaptable software systems by supporting loose coupling and late binding, but is not sufficient in itself. The next section describes how SOC concepts can be merged into a component model to provide a more complete solution for dynamically adaptable software systems.

3   Service-Oriented Component Model

In[6], the general principles of a service-oriented component model were introduced, which are:

- A service is provided functionality.
- A service is characterized by a service specification, which describes some combination of a service's syntax, behavior, and semantics as well as dependencies on other services.
- Components implement service specifications, which may exhibit implementation-specific dependencies on services.
- The service-oriented interaction pattern is used to resolve service dependencies at run time.
- Compositions are described in terms of service specifications.
- Service specifications provide a basis for substitutability.

The model that results from these principles is rather flexible and powerful. It promotes service substitutability since compositions are defined in terms of specifications, not specific implementations. This notion of service substitutability is strengthen by recognizing two levels of dependencies, both specification and implementation levels. Traditional component orientation only recognizes implementation dependencies, hindering substitutability. Service orientation does not typically describe service dependencies as part of the service specification, which eliminates forms of behavior parameterization and structural service composition. Dependency description also simplifies composition because explicit wiring of constituent service specifications is not necessary since it can be inferred. Lastly, the service-oriented architecture and interaction pattern make it possible to defer service implementation selection until run time, which enables the creation of sophisticated adaptable applications. When using a service-oriented component approach to build an application, the application is decomposed into a collection of interacting services. The semantics and behavior of these services are carefully described independently of any implementation. By doing so, it is possible to develop the constituent services independently of each other as well as to have variant implementations that are easily interchangeable. Variant implementations can be used, for example, to support different platforms or different non-functional requirements. Once the application's services have been defined, it is possible to define a mapping to a set of components for implementation. A component may implement zero or more services and there is no requirement on how the mapping from service specification to component implementation occurs. For example, if certain services are related, then it might make sense from a cohesion or performance point of view to implement them using a single component; however, it is not required. Additionally, whether a service represents local or remote functionality is largely irrelevant. If a service does represent remote functionality, then the resulting component implementation is merely a proxy stub for the remote service, which can be treated like any other component implementing a local service. As pointed out in [7], one of the set of components that comprise a service-oriented component application is typically a core component that contains the main service composition or process that guides the application's execution. Other component instances provide the services used by the core component and these instances can themselves require services provided by other instances. This approach is similar to the exogenous connector approach promoted in [13]. In traditional component-oriented composition, the component selection process for a composition occurs at design time. The selection process for a service-oriented composition occurs at run time as component instances are created inside the execution environment. The execution of the application starts the moment the main component instance's dependencies are satisfied. The application composition is thus an abstract descriptor that could be used, for example, by a deployment system to deploy components that satisfy the service specifications required by the composition. The resulting application configuration depends on the specific set of deployed components, which may vary per platform or even dynamically at run time.

4   iPOJO Approach

iPOJO is a service-oriented component framework supporting the service-oriented component model concepts of section 3. One of the main goals of iPOJO is to keep service-oriented component development as simple as possible, which means keeping the component as close to a plain old Java object (POJO) as possible. The code of a component should focus on business logic, not on SOC mechanisms or non-functional requirements. To achieve this goal, iPOJO provides a component container that manages all SOC aspects, such as service publication, service object creation, and required service discovery and selection. The component developer only focuses on two tasks:

– Implementing the business logic.
– Configuring the component container.

The business logic is domain specific, but implementing it is simplified since it need not contain code that is component model specific. The POJO component is connected to iPOJO by configuring the component container, which consists of declaring component metadata that will be used by the container for run-time management. Component metadata declares information such as provided services, required services, and configurable properties. Figure 1 illustrates how the container automatically manages SOC activities, such as providing or requiring services. The container of C2 publishes its provided service. C1 also provides a service, but it has a dependency on the service that C2 provides. At run time the container of C1 tries to select a service implementation to resolve the dependency. If the dependency is not resolvable, the container will not publish C1's provided service. On other hand, if the dependency is resolvable, then the container will publish the service and manage component instance creation, not creating the component instance until its service is actually used.

The container for each component must be configured by declaring the metadata to provide and require the appropriate services. It should also be noted that the container manages the ongoing dynamic availability of services, which

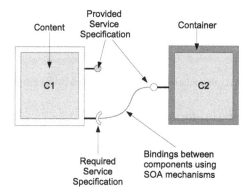

Fig. 1. Service component binding

means that it automatically deals with publishing and revoking services as dependencies are resolved and broken at run time if new component instances are introduced or existing ones are removed.

5   iPOJO Framework and Component Composition

iPOJO's approach to composition is very similar to traditional component composition, except that iPOJO compositions are in terms of service specifications rather than component instances, which allows for late selection and binding of component instances and substitutability. An iPOJO component declares its required services in its metadata and the iPOJO component container uses this information at runtime to automatically manage any necessary bindings between the component instance and any required services. The following subsections discuss how to implement iPOJO service components and the run-time support available to them.

5.1   Service Component Implementation and Description

To design an application with service components, developers need to describe which services a component requires (service dependency) and provides (provided service). With this information, iPOJO can create a composition at runtime. iPOJO tracks required services at runtime and injects required services into the component when they become available. The component in figure 2 illustrates a service component. This component exposes a multimedia message service (MMS) that allows clients to send an MMS message containing pictures from any number of attached cameras. To achieve this, the component requires two services: the first required service is MmsService, which allows a client to send an MMS message, and the second service is Camera, which allows a client to take a digital photograph. The metadata for the component's camera service dependency indicates that it is an aggregate dependency, meaning that it can be bound to one or more camera services.

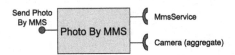

Fig. 2. Architecture of the Photo By MMS component

Service Component Implementation
The iPOJO approach is based on POJOs. Developers should only manage the logic of the component, forgetting service discovery and service publication. The code snippet in figure 3 shows a possible implementation of the above example component.

The component implementation is very simple. Service dependencies are simply coded with the assumption that the services are available as member fields

```
package fr.imag.adele.escoffier;
...
public class PhotoByMMS implement PhotoSender {
    private MmsSender sender;
    private Camera[] cameras;

    public void send() {
        MMS mms = new MMS();
        synchronized (cameras) {
          for (int i = 0; i < cameras.length; i++) {
              mms.add(cameras[i].getPhoto());
          }
        }
        sender.send("1234567890", mms);
    }
}
```

Fig. 3. Photo By MMS implementation

(e.g., sender and cameras); the one caveat is for aggregate dependencies, which require a synchronized block to avoid run-time list modification during the loop. The component provides the PhotoSender service by simply implementing the service interface.

Service Component Description

When a component is implemented, it needs metadata to describe which services are required and provided. Figure 4 shows the description of the previous component. The metadata declares two service dependencies and a provided service. At a minimum, a service dependency must specify the needed service specification name (the fully qualified Java type), but may also contain optionality, cardinality, and filter information.

In the example, the first service dependency is for MmsService. The declared dependency contains only the component's member field name to which the dependency will be associated; it is not necessary to specify the service specification

```
<iPOJO>
<component className="fr.imag.adele.escoffier.PhotoByMMS">
    <dependency field="sender"/>
    <dependency field="cameras"/>
    <provides/>
</component>
<instance component="fr.imag.adele.escoffier.PhotoByMMS"
 name=Sender/>
</iPOJO>
```

Fig. 4. iPOJO Metadata for the PhotoByMMS component

type since it can be identified from the member field type using reflection. By default, service dependencies are assumed to be mandatory. If a dependency is declared as optional, then the nullable object pattern is used to avoid null-case testing by the component developer. The second dependency is for Camera services; it is an aggregate dependency. All Camera services will be tracked. The metadata does not have to express the cardinality explicitly. Instead, reflection can determine that the field type in the component class is an array, which iPOJO interprets as an aggregate dependency. Aggregate dependencies can also be optional. An empty array is returned if no consistent providers are available. The component declares that it provides a service by explicitly declaring it in its metadata. However, the service type need not be mentioned explicitly since it can also be inferred using reflection. The metadata can also contain properties to attach to a published service, which can then be used for service filtering; the current example does not include any service properties.

Composition Binding Description

iPOJO components declare their dependencies on other service specifications. As a result, composition bindings do not need to be explicitly declared since they can be inferred from the individual component metadata. At runtime, iPOJO injects the final bindings into the components and also manages the dynamic availability of the services associated with the bindings and consequently the life cycle of the component instances.

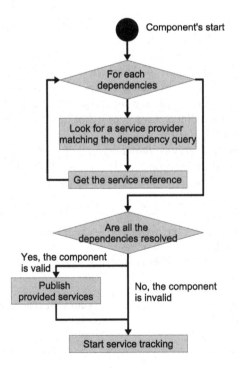

Fig. 5. Component initialization process

5.2   Dynamic Run-Time Composition Management

Managing the dynamic availability of services is difficult to do manually and it results in code that mixes business and non-functional logic. By separating the component class and the component metadata, iPOJO is able to externally manage service dynamics on behalf of the component; figures 5 and 6 depict this process.

When a component starts, for each service dependency iPOJO discovers all matching providers and injects one or more references to them as necessary into the component instance (see figure 5). If the component provides a service, iPOJO manages service publication according to the state of the component. A service component is valid if all service dependencies are resolved (i.e., at least one service provider exists for each mandatory dependency). In all other

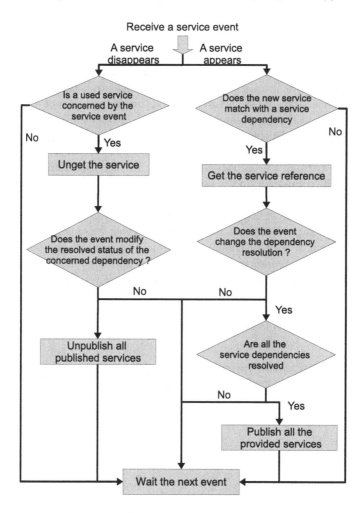

Fig. 6. Service event processing

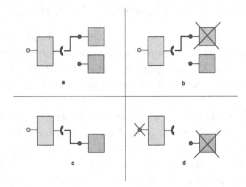

Fig. 7. Run-time composition and dynamics management

cases, the service component is invalid. An invalid component cannot have its service published, since its requirements are not met. As soon as the component becomes valid, its services can be published. A a component is initialized and enters the valid or invalid state, iPOJO continues to listen for service events indicating service arrival or departure and updates the component's state accordingly (see figure 6).For aggregate dependencies, iPOJO looks for all matching service providers and injects them as a list of service references. A mandatory aggregate service dependency is resolved if it at least one service is available.

Figure 7 illustrates the impact of dynamic service availability on a service component. The component in the figure requires a service and provides another. The environment contains two providers matching with the required service. In (a) the service component is bound to the first service provider. Consequently, its provided service is published because all of its service dependencies are resolved. In (b) the bound service provider goes away. The original component can no longer use the departed service and must find another one. iPOJO looks for and finds another provider and creates a binding to it (c). During this time the instance is frozen. When the second provider goes away in (d), iPOJO is unable to find a replacement. As a result, the original component becomes invalid and iPOJO revokes its provided service.

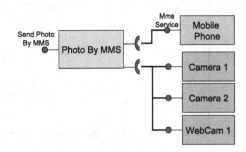

Fig. 8. Bindings for the Photo By MMS component

For aggregate dependencies, such as the example in the previous section, iPOJO needs to track all matching services and inject this set into the component instance. This set is automatically updated when a new service arrives or an existing one disappears; figure 8 depicts this behavior. An aggregate dependency is unresolved when no service implementation can be found at run time.

6   Implementation and Experimentation

iPOJO is implemented for the OSGi Service Platform [15] and is available as a subproject of the Apache Incubator Felix[1] project. iPOJO has been used in an industrial prototype for an European project named ANSO. This section briefly describes how iPOJO is implemented and how it is used in the ANSO project.

6.1   iPOJO Implementation

iPOJO is implemented on top of the OSGi Service Platform, which defines a framework to dynamically deploy services in a centralized (i.e., non-distributed) environment. The core OSGi framework automatically manages aspects of local service deployment, such as Java package dependency resolution, but leaves service dependency management as a manual task for component developers. iPOJO is built on top of the OSGi service platform for three main reasons:

- It is service-oriented platform,
- It is applicable to a large range of use cases (from mobile phones to application servers), and
- It is a dynamic platform, which is particularly interesting from a research perspective.

Although iPOJO is built on top of the OSGi Service Platform, the concepts it embodies are applicable to any service-oriented platform. The name iPOJO is derived from the phrase injected POJO, since the general approach of iPOJO is to inject POJOs with byte code to perform the management of non-functional behavior. Specifically, at component packaging time iPOJO instruments the component byte code to intercept all member field accesses. With this simple modification, iPOJO is able to inject member field values inside of the component when needed. At runtime, iPOJO uses the OSGi service registry to discover, track, and publish services. iPOJO also manages component property configuration, dynamic service properties, and publication of component factory services.

6.2   Experimentation

The ANSO project, supported by ITEA, is an European project attempting to design a residential gateway. The gateway is intended to manage devices

---

[1] http://incubator.apache.org/felix/

available in the home and provide higher-level services like alarm management and video-on-demand. A prototype of the ANSO gateway [1][2] was developed using iPOJO to manage available services. The motivation for using iPOJO was due to the fact that residential environments are very dynamic: devices (e.g., mobile phones, PDAs) appear and disappear dynamically and device state may change often as well as the end user context. iPOJO is used to aide developers in creating applications in such an environment; developers do not need to manage service events, device discovery, and invocation protocols. Additionally, iPOJO is used by EDF (French electricity company) to manage multi-modal interactions. In this context, iPOJO is used to manage dynamic availability of interactive devices (e.g., a mouse or joystick) in order to find the best configuration for disabled people [18].

7   Related Work

Component models and frameworks are not new. Numerous well-known examples exist, such as Common Object Model (COM) [3], JavaBeans [19], Enterprise JavaBeans [20], Fractal [4], and CORBA Component Model [14]. These component models and frameworks target various application domains. These approaches typically have a significant developer cost associated with them, such as the need to implement specific interfaces, extend specific base classes, and use specific application programming interfaces. A newer trend for component models is appearing that promotes the notion of POJOs, like EJB 3.0 [21] and Spring [12]. In these approaches, like in iPOJO, developers program POJOs and then configure a container that contains the POJO. Despite these similarities, these component models do not tackle the issues of dynamic availability and dynamic run-time composition. Using components to implement services is becoming relatively popular [22][23]. Some service-oriented component models exist, like Jini, Service Component Architecture (SCA) [10], Service Binder [5], Declarative Services [16], and Spring-OSGi [11]. Jini is a Java-based distributed middleware platform that supports the existence of multiple service registries. Jini uses the concept of service leasing as a mechanism to limit the time a client can access a service. However, Jini does not support a composition model and is intimately tied to Java remote method invocation (RMI). SCA provides a service-oriented component model mainly designed for web services. SCA defines an assembly model for loosely coupled web services. SCA components can support several kinds of implementation languages, e.g., Java, C++, and BPEL [8] processes. The SCA programming model uses Java annotations and is close to POJOs. SCA does not address dynamic availability and does not manage dynamic composition. Declarative Services in the OSGi Service Platform Release 4 specification was inspired by the work on Service Binder. Both address building component-based applications from dynamically available services. The approach taken by these component frameworks is somewhat complex since it involves using stylized programming and specific application programming interfaces. iPOJO is actually a continuation of the Service Binder work and attempts to rectify the shortcomings of that approach. Moreover, iPOJO provides an extensibility mechanisms away from Declarative Service. Spring-OSGi is the integration of the Spring framework with the OSGi framework. As with iPOJO, this new service component model uses POJOs and tries to address dynamic availability. Spring-OSGi uses an aspect framework to inject service dependencies. However, the developer need to explicitly manage exceptions when an unavailable service is used. Spring-OSGi also does not manage dynamic service properties and component factories.

8 Current and Future Work

This section explores current and future work that is being investigated as part of the overall research strategy of iPOJO. These issues can be divided into two main categories: service specification description and hierarchical composition.

8.1 Service Specification Description

Typically, service description is limited to the service interface definition and a set of properties. In order to automatically compose services, it is necessary to have a richer description of services. One simple example is the need for service-level dependencies. iPOJO's approach is to define compositions in terms of services, but without service-level dependencies then all composition must occur in glue code or within component implementations, which limits reusability and substitutability. The iPOJO approach allows developers to expose service-level dependencies at design time (see figure 9). The benefit is that these dependencies enable simple structural composition purely in terms of services so that management and verification of these dependencies can be offloaded to the component framework. This is different than web service composition, where services merely provide functionality and do not exposes any structural information. Additionally, service specifications become richer since it is now possible to parameterize service behavior in a well-defined way and create service specifications that follow patterns like model-view-controller. The service consumer is not impacted by this increased richness and continues to use the service as a black box.

It is also necessary to investigate forms of semantic, behavioral, and contextual description of services. Such additional richness will further improve the

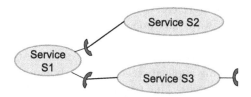

Fig. 9. An example of structural service composition

component framework's ability to determine when a service is appropriate for a given composition or which service to choose when many potential candidates exist.

8.2 Hierarchical Service Composition

Generally, service compositions are created using orchestration, like BPEL. In such a case, an orchestration engine manages the service invocation sequence and the information exchange among services.

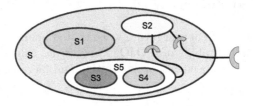

Fig. 10. Composite service

Another way to create service compositions is following a more component-oriented approach using hierarchical compositions to create composite services. Unlike traditional component-oriented approaches, these composite services are expressed in term of services instead of component instances to enable late selection and binding, which enables dynamic adaptability through substitutability. Figure 10 depicts an example of hierarchical service composition. As service-oriented component applications grow in size and complexity, composite services also provide a way to mitigate this complexity by further subdividing the application. A composite service creates a scope that encapsulates the constituent services from external services and vice versa. A composite service can import and export services from/to its parent composite. The service bindings among components inside a composite service are resolved only with services available in the composite or those which are imported.

9 Conclusion

Traditional component models and frameworks simplified software system development by enabling developers to break software systems into independent pieces with well-defined interfaces. While the component-based approach led to advancements in the software development process, it still has its limitations. In particular, after a component-based application is developed and deployed it typically is a monolithic and static configuration of components. This contrasts the growing interest in creating applications that react dynamically to changes in the availability of various services. This paper presented iPOJO, a service-oriented component framework that is trying to simplify creating dynamically adaptable software systems. The iPOJO approach is based on a model that combines concepts from service-oriented computing with component orientation. iPOJO implements its component model using byte code instrumentation, enabling the use of simple POJOs as components. From this foundation, iPOJO is able to manage all service-oriented aspects of its model on behalf of the components (e.g., service dependency resolution, service publication, dynamic service properties, and ongoing service availability tracking). The result is applications that are dynamically adaptable to changing service availability. iPOJO has demonstrated its usefulness in various prototypes and is available as part of the Apache Incubator Felix project. Work continues on enriching iPOJO and evaluating its usefulness after its initial successes.

References

[1] Bourcier, J., Escoffier, C., Desertot, M., Marin, C., Chazalet, A.: A Dynamic SOA Home Control Gateway. In: International Service Computing Conference (September 2006)
[2] Bourcier, J., Escoffier, C., Lalanda, P.: Implementing Home-Control Applications on Service Platform. In: Proceedings of the IEEE Consumer Communications and Networking Conference (January 2007)
[3] Box, D.: Essential COM. Addison-Wesley, Reading (January 1998)
[4] Bruneton, E., Coupaye, T., Stefani, J.B.: The Fractal Component Model Specification, Version 2.0-2 (September 2003),
    http://fractal.objectweb.org/specification/index.html
[5] Cervantes, H., Hall, R.S.: Automating Service Dependency Management in a Service-Oriented Component Model. In: CBSE 2006 (May 2003)
[6] Cervantes, H., Hall, R.S.: Autonomous Adaptation to Dynamic Availability Through a Service-Oriented Component Model. In: Proceedings of the International Conference on Software Engineering (May 2004)
[7] Cervantes, H., Hall, R.S.: A Framework for Constructing Adaptive Component-based Applications: Concepts and Experiences. In: CBSE 2007. Proceedings of the 7th International Symposium on Component-Based Software Engineering (May 2004)
[8] Curbera, F., Goland, Y., Klein, J., Leymann, F., Roller, D., Thatte, S., Weerawarana, S.: Business Process Execution Language (BPEL) for Web Services Version 1.0 (July 2002),
    ftp://www6.software.ibm.com/software/developer/library/ws-bpel1.pdf
[9] Huhns, M.N., Singh, M.P.: Service-Oriented Computing: Key Concepts and Principles. IEEE Internet Computing 9 (January 2005)
[10] IBM Corp. et al.: SCA Service Component Architecture Assembly Model Specification (November 2005),
    http://www-128.ibm.com/developerworks/library/specification/ws-sca/
[11] Interface21. Spring OSGi Specification (v0.7) (2006),
    http://www.springframework.org/osgi/specification
[12] Johnson, R., Hoeller, J., Arendsen, A., Risberg, T., Sampaleanu, C.: Professional Java Development with the Spring Framework. Wiley Publishing, Inc., Chichester (2005)
[13] Lau, K., Ukis, V.: Encapsulating Data in Component-based Systems. In: Proceedings of Ninth International Symposium on Component-based Software Engineering (June 2006)

[14] Object Management Group. CORBA Components Specification, Version 3.0, (June 2002)
[15] OSGi Alliance. OSGi Service Platform Core Specification Release 4 (August 2005), http://www.osgi.org
[16] OSGi Alliance. OSGi Service Platform Service Compendium Release 4 (August 2005), http://www.osgi.org
[17] Papazoglou, M.P., Georgakopoulos, D.: Service-Oriented Computing. Communications of the ACM 46(10) (October 2003)
[18] Renouard, S., Mokhtari, M., Menga, D., Brisson, G.: SCYLLA: A Toolkit for Document-Based Human Environment Interaction, Proceedings of the International Conference on Smart Homes and Health Telematics (June 2006)
[19] Sun Microsystems. JavaBeans Specification Version 1.01 (August 1997), http://java.sun.com/products/javabeans/docs/beans.101.pdf
[20] Sun Microsystems. Enterprise JavaBeans Specification, Version 2.1 (November 2003), http://java.sun.com/products/ejb/docs.html
[21] Sun Microsystems. Enterprise JavaBeans, Version 3.0, Simplified API (May 2006), http://java.sun.com/products/ejb/docs.html
[22] Yang, J.: Web Service Componentization. Communications of the ACM 46(10) (October 2003)
[23] Yang, J., Papazoglou, M.P.: Service Components for Managing the Life-Cycle of Service Compositions. Information Systems 29(2) (April 2004)

Dynamic Contextual Service Ranking*

André Bottaro[1,2] and Richard S. Hall[2]

[1] Francetelecom R&D, 28 Chemin du Vieux Chêne
38243 Meylan Cedex, France
`andre.bottaro@orange-ftgroup.com`
[2] LSR-IMAG, 220 rue de la Chimie - Domaine Universitaire, BP 53
38041 Grenoble, Cedex 9, France
`richard.hall@imag.fr`

Abstract. This paper explores service composition in pervasive environments with a focus on dynamic service selection. Service orientation offers the dynamism and loose coupling needed in pervasive applications. However, context-aware service composition is still a great challenge in pervasive computing. Service selection has to deal with dynamic contextual information to enable context-aware behaviors to emerge from the environment. This paper describes how to add dynamic contextual service ranking mechanisms to the service-oriented OSGi framework and further discusses service re-composition decisions.

1 Introduction

Pervasive environments emphasize the need for application dynamism and autonomic behaviors. These environments are characterized by the variability and mobility of acting entities on the network. Dynamically composing applications and guaranteeing service continuity to the users is a grand challenge in pervasive computing.

The home network is such an environment. Heterogeneous mobile and fixed devices join and leave the network. Numerous protocols coexist and provided interfaces need to be adapted. These devices offer various features to the users. Home context dynamism comes on the one hand from device mobility and evolving capacities and on the other hand from user mobility and activity.

Our previous work answered pragmatic problems related to dynamic service availability, distribution and interface heterogeneity [3]. In this work we also encountered other issues regarding dynamic adaptability. Context awareness is the key aspect in pervasive computing on which our present work focuses. Context awareness based on a context management system is a non-functional need that can be automatically dealt with in pervasive software composition.

Device self-organization and feature composition fulfilling the needs of the users are the ultimate goals for work in pervasive environments. Since service orientation is at the basis of much work in pervasive computing, many attempts

---

* This work is part of the ANSO project, which is partially supported by the French Ministry of Industry under the European ITEA program.

M. Lumpe and W. Vanderperren (Eds.): SC 2007, LNCS 4829, pp. 129–143, 2007.
© Springer-Verlag Berlin Heidelberg 2007

to reach "self-organization" focus on service composition. Available plug-n-play middleware relies on protocols for service discovery, service description, service control and address some other features from Quality of Service (QoS) to security [19].

Service selection and ranking, which consist of selecting the most appropriate service provider out of a list of discovered ones, is however not fully addressed by available service-oriented protocols today. The mechanisms are complex due to the complexity and dynamism of the home context. This task is often left to manual configuration. Automatic service selection is a difficult task that a lot of work tries to tackle. We propose a realistic approach in this domain and describe the implementation of our ideas on top of the OSGi framework [15].

This work is carried out within the ANSO project, which brings together major European actors interested in the development of pervasive home services, including telecommunication operators (France Telecom), video companies (Thomson) and home control solution providers (Schneider Electric). This work is demonstrated on a home application jointly developed by France Telecom and its ANSO partners [2].

The next section describes our vision of context management in service-oriented applications. The service selection problem is defined in section 3. The framework implementation on top of the OSGi platform [15] is detailed in section 4. The realization of a context-aware application on top of this framework is depicted in section 5. Comparisons with related work are found in section 6. The last section concludes on the use of this framework and discusses the opportunity to leverage this work to further design generic service rebinding mechanisms.

2   Vision

Application intelligence emerges from the behavior of its constituent components. In order to let the intelligence emerge from software composition, we strongly believe in a component-oriented vision where components are self-descriptive and self-adaptive. Autonomic mechanisms are to be implemented at the fine-grained level of the architecture. Our approach follows the grand challenge vision of autonomic computing [13].

Autonomic elements in our system are software components that provide and require services (see Figure 1). These services are distributed on the network or only locally visible on service platforms. Many works show how to reify distributed components on service platforms [3]. So the composition issue here is reduced to composition of local components on a unique service platform. Provided services and required services are declared at the component level in a specific component description. We leverage a service-oriented component architecture where service dependencies are dynamically resolved on every component thanks to a generic container dedicated to service publication, service discovery and service binding [4].

The target environment of our prototype is the home network [2]. In this environment, context-aware applications must adapt themselves according to

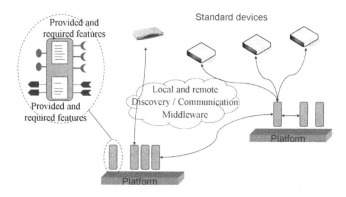

Fig. 1. Autonomic elements represented on service platforms

dynamic variables. The home context consists of (i) the user context comprised of location, preferences and activity, (ii) the device context comprised of location and capacities (iii) and external physical context such as place properties (weather parameters, physical location, etc.) [17].

This context is assessed by a context management system reasoning on information coming from sensors distributed in the environment. This system is visible on our service platform in the form of services identified as context sources. Based on reasoning techniques, context sources are able to identify, locate and assess the activity of users and devices in the home. Some context sources directly represent underlying sensors and some others provide treated and aggregated information from one or several context sources.

Context sources are the entities responsible for the contextualization of service trading. On the one hand, high-level context sources dynamically qualify provided services with contextual properties. On the other hand, they dynamically refine service requirements with contextual information.

We consider that the service platform is the smart dynamic receptacle of pervasive entities. This adaptable receptacle turns pervasive software composition into the composition of uniform contextualized service components. Service components are running on an adaptable executive environment, which we call a service platform. The main role of the platform is to adapt to the environment in locally representing all the relevant external entities with their context on the platform.

The contextualization of service trading in our platform-centric vision is discussed in the remainder of this paper.

3   Service Selection

3.1   Concepts

Service selection consists of selecting the most adequate service provider according to service requester needs. A service is described by a type (a.k.a. an abstract interface) that determines a set of operations (a.k.a. methods or actions) and by service metadata (e.g., properties) that qualifies the service. Service metadata is linked to contextual properties like location, features quality, current available capacities, etc.

Service metadata is often attribute-value pairs in various service architectures (OSGi [15], SLP [11], UPnP [8], Web Services [10] with ws-metadata-exchange and ws-policy). Services in the OSGi framework and in protocol middleware like SLP and UPnP can have an arbitrary set of attribute-value pairs attached to them. WS-Policy defines an extensible grammar to express capabilities for Web Service Provider and requirements for Web Service requester. Multiple attribute-value pairs with scoring functions are particularly common in e-commerce (see [14] for a list of technologies).

Many concepts are defined in existing middleware and in scientific literature to allow service selection:

- A **scope** defines the perimeter of a search request. Scopes are usually determined by network topology, user role or application context [19]. For instance, multicast communication methods naturally limit UPnP search requests to topological networks. Contextual scopes in SLP are freely assigned by service providers to their services at registration time and service requesters use scopes as a primary search filter. The use of hierarchical composition scopes is promoted in some component oriented architectures [4].
- A **filter** narrows the set of available services according to the service requester needs. It defines an acceptance threshold. In service-oriented architecture, the main filter concerns the service type. A service requester usually looks for precise service types. In models defining service properties as a set of attribute-value pairs [4], the equality operator and threshold operators are possible basic filter operators. We may distinguish mandatory and optional filters. A **mandatory filter** is always evaluated before service binding and eliminates the services that do not match from further evaluation. **Optional filters** are evaluated if the remaining number of services after the mandatory filter evaluation is greater than the number of services expected to be bound. They refine the first filter in order to narrow service selection (e.g., [9]).
- The objective of a **scoring function** (a.k.a. utility function, objective function, etc.) is to rank all the filtered services in a total order according to the adequacy of their ability to meet the service requirements. Many approaches on service ranking are based on the utility theory [12]. The latter defines properties as a set of attribute-value pairs qualifying resources, which may be services. A scoring function is a sum of weighted placeholders. Place-holders are attached to subscores evaluating property values of the potential services against the resource requester needs. The scoring function enables the service requester to rank available service providers. The service provider getting the best score is considered the one that optimizes service composition.

- **Policies** define ranking algorithms and may be implemented with scoring functions [14]. A policy has a very generic meaning. Some definitions embrace a more generic rule-based mechanism like Event-Condition-Action rules. For instance, reactive adaptation policies are defined in [7].

3.2 Problem Definition in Context-Aware Applications

Most of the service middleware only provides simple means to select services. Selection most often relies on scopes and filters due to the simplicity of these mechanisms. Scopes and filters narrow the set of possible bindings, but they make the service requester consider the remaining possibilities as identical. Service ambiguity occurs when several service providers fulfill the same service requirement. Therefore, these mechanisms do not avoid service ambiguity, which leads to composition unpredictability. This problem raises the need for the introduction of ranking algorithms in service composition mechanisms.

In context-aware applications, algorithms target the ranking of service providers against service contextual requirements at runtime. High-level mechanisms are required to separate the definition of contextual behavior from the core application. The problem can be decomposed into 4 subjects that are discussed in the next section:

- **Contextual service property management:** Service provider context may be acquired into the device itself or externally. This information has to be dynamically added in the description of the provided services.
- **Contextual service requirement management:** Static preferences and dynamic activity may be acquired through some internal inputs or external ones to the service requester. This information has to be dynamically added to the requirements of service requesters.
- **Dynamic service ranking:** Requirements can be designed into scopes, a mandatory filter, optional filters, and a sorting algorithm in order to dynamically rank the available services. A change in rankings generates rebinding actions.
- **(Re-)binding behaviors:** The designer has to map (un, re-)binding actions on ranking change events. Rebinding actions are connected to service continuity concerns, which lead to tasks that are difficult to automate and are often left to developers. Ranking change events are categorized in the next section.

4   Framework Implementation

Our contribution targets improving the OSGi Declarative Services model, which is based on early work described in [4]. This model is a service-oriented component model on top of the OSGi core framework. In this model, a component declares service requirements and provided services in a static file. A service dependency manager parses this declaration and manages the component life cycle with regard to service dependency resolution. The service dependency manager is responsible for service filter evaluation, service tracking according to this evaluation, service selection, service binding and service publication. On service arrival, service departure and service property change, service events are generated by the service registry. These events are received by the service dependency managers that are looking for matching services. Re-composition is triggered by these events at the component level.

Some features are missing in this model to fully adapt component life cycle to internal and external context dynamism:

- Component description dynamism: The description of the components service requirements and provided services is dynamically populated with contextual information in our architecture whereas Declarative Services only addresses static component description. Our contribution introduces writable service properties and writable service requirements at runtime.
- Enhanced service selection mechanisms: Optional filters and a ranking policy are added to the declaration of service requirements. Declarative Services only supports a unique mandatory filter.

In our extended framework, the service dependency manager enables service properties dynamic evolution, re-evaluates filters, adapts service tracking (active and passive service discovery), and adapts service selection. The dependency manager listens to service and contextual changes to dynamically bind the best subset of services. Thus, a specific view of the service registry is maintained for every service requester. Service requester bindings are dynamically changed by the dependency manager whenever a filtered unbound service gets a higher ranking than a bound one. Re-composition is then triggered by internal and external contextual events and is enhanced with complete service selection mechanisms.

4.1   Contextual Service Properties Management

Entities attaching scores and entities evaluating the scoring function must share the same context evaluation grid. It is possible to let every service provider declare their own contextual metadata and to let service requesters evaluate it. This is naturally done in most research work [14]. However, the fact that these entities share the same context semantics implies strong coupling between service providers and service requesters. This assumption goes against the loose coupling predicate of our service-oriented architecture.

In order to maintain loose coupling, we advocate that contextual property attachment be dealt with by the service context management layer itself. In our architecture, high-level context sources are capable of identifying software components and attaching the relevant contextual properties to the service specification at runtime.

Service providers are their own context sources for some contextual information (service state, service features, estimated QoS, etc.) and rely on external context sources for other contextual information (location, tested QoS, user rating, user immersion level, etc.).

In our framework, service provider metadata is populated with contextual properties by context source components. This feature makes use of the Configuration Admin model of the OSGi specification. In this model, the service provider has to additionally publish a *Managed Service* in the service registry. This enables external components, with the appropriate permission, to add, modify, and delete the properties of the provided service. Whenever the properties change, the service object (object representing the service provider) is directly called to make it aware of the update. The service object may internally react to this change.

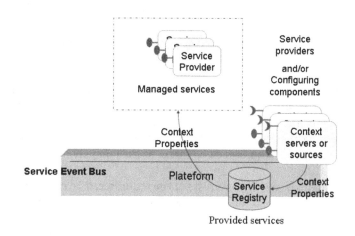

Fig. 2. Context sources populate services with contextual properties

In a service-oriented model, it is natural to design context sources as service providers. Some entities are responsible for aggregating context from context sources and assigning contextual properties to the relevant *managed services*. For instance, a location server may infer location information from context sources and attach location properties to *managed services* representing UPnP devices on the network. Another example could be a user preferences server that adds user rating information to *managed services*.

Thanks to this model, application components need not adhere to context management service interfaces. The only interface between application components is the shared service registry, which enables service properties to be writable (see Figure 2). The *Managed Service* interface is a neutral interface enabling the components to be aware of contextual changes and to declare the ability to accept property modification.

4.2   Contextual Service Requirements Management

Service requesters are also their own context sources for some contextual information (application state, user input through graphic interfaces, etc.) and rely on external context sources for other contextual information (user location, user activity, user preferences, desired QoS, etc.).

Service requesters follow the same pattern as service providers: High-level context sources attach contextual information to service requirement descriptions. Service requirements must then be accessible to components other than the service requester. We propose to register them in the service registry in our architecture with a simple interface which is defined below:

```
public interface ManagedRequester{
    ComponentInstance getInstance();
    void filterPartsUpdated(Filter f) throws ConfigurationException;
    addOptionalFilter(Filter f) throws ConfigurationException;
}
```

Every time a new component declared to have a context-aware behavior is instantiated, the service dependency manager associated with it registers a Managed Requester service for it. The *ComponentInstance* object mentioned in the interface provides the service requirements of the component. The method *filterPartsUpdated* enables context sources identifying the component to add some complementary contextual filters to the component filter. *addOptionalFilter* is a method enabling the allowed configuring components to add an optional filter to the managed service requester. The filters of the component are then writable in our architecture.

In order to show the specific interests of the requester, it is appropriate to allow placeholders to be added to the filter. These placeholders are interpreted by context sources, the configuring components in our model. For instance, an application looking for services in the room where a user called Maxandre is found would have the following filter part expression: *location=$location-room{Maxandre}* following the context-sensitive syntax of [5]. Location information sources would then be able to write the value of any property written this way.

Thanks to this model, the context management system is partly responsible for service binding decisions. In order to promote self-adaptability prior to manageability, components are responsible for property propagation: In our architecture, service providers and service requesters can ignore or modify the parameters which are submitted to them.

4.3   Dynamic Service Ranking

Scoring functions may be described in a complex language. The following examples are ranked from the easiest to the most complex. The first two functions are easily described with standard mathematical functions; the third one refers to a function attached to a specific semantic data model. It is noticeable that the last two also refer to a maximum value that is application-specific:

– Giving a score to a price, looking for a minimum, after having filtered the service with mandatory filter $(\&(price < 100)(currency = dollar))$:

$$(100 - price)/100 \qquad (1)$$

- Giving a score to the distance between a user and devices defined with geo-
metrical parameters in a basic model, looking for a minimum:

$$\frac{Max_{distance} - \sqrt{((x_{device} - x_{user})^2 + (y_{device} - y_{user})^2 + (z_{device} - z_{user})^2)}}{Max_{distance}}$$
$$(2)$$

- Giving a score to the distance between a user and devices defined in a semantic data model, looking for a minimum:

$$distance(room_{device}, room_{user})/Max_{distance} \qquad (3)$$

The examples show that scoring functions can be made of complex sub-
functions. Moreover, it shows that evaluating the adequacy of declared service
properties to service requirements is an application-specific task. We then consider the scoring function as a method in object-oriented programming.

From a component's perspective, service ranking may occur either internally
or externally depending on the circumstances. Service context management must
be able to support both. However, mixing complex ranking policies coming from
inside and outside of the component appears to be very complicated. Since components are self-adaptable we define the ranking policy in the component itself
in the present architecture. In our framework, it is called by the service dependency manager of the component. We are currently thinking about a more
generic ranking algorithm based on scores attached to service providers and cor-
respondent utility weights populating service requirements, but big issues are
raised with this approach. A generic utility function is also to be called on the
service dependency manager of the component.

Two selection mechanisms are added to the Declarative Services unique
mandatory filter:

- Optional filters are added to the first one. Optional filters enable further
selection when many service providers are fulfilling mandatory ones. DSCL
language [9] also defines mandatory and optional filters for better service
selection. Optional filters may be numerous and organized from the most
important to least important. This ordering enables progressive selection.
- A method name referring to a Java callback method in the component code
allows developers to program a complex ranking method in the component.
The ranking method is called with the remaining service references to be
ranked as input arguments in order to let the component sort them in a
total order. The component is then bound to the best available service (see
the mentioned *sort-method* in the XML description of the *user control factory*
of the application example in section 5).

The limitations of the Declarative Services model for service selection are
overcome in our model with writable filters, optional filters declaration, and the
addition of a method declaration in the XML component requirements description (see sort-method attribute in XML descriptions below). This way, filters
may be defined internally and externally at runtime and the sorting algorithm

is expressed by the developer of the service requester with the expressiveness of the Java programming language. A hook method is also given in order for the component to warn the component manager to evaluate this ranking method again on internal events.

4.4   (Re-)binding Behaviors

The component life cycle is affected by dynamic service ranking improvement (see Figure 3). Optional filters and the ranking method are only processed on components with a service requirement that is declared to be fulfilled with a limited number of service providers (i.e., a binding cardinality of $0..x$ and $1..x$ where x belongs to $]0, \infty[$; in standard OSGi Declarative Services x may only take the value 1). Otherwise, the component binds to all the available service providers fulfilling the mandatory filter - narrowing service selection seems useless in the case where $x = \infty$. Optional filters and the ranking method are called after mandatory filter processing and before calling the binding method. It is called in 3 types of situations:

- whenever a service is registered (or modified) and fulfills the service mandatory filter,
- whenever a current bound service is modified or unregistered,
- and whenever the component requirements change (mandatory filter, optional filters, or service ranking method).

5   Realization: A Context-Aware Application

Building a context-aware instant messaging application consists of dynamically binding to the adequate input/output services according to the user location and the user activity and interacting with the other devices that have an impact on this activity. When the user sits in front of the TV, the system may direct the communications to a part of the TV screen using the Picture In Picture system. If the user is having a nap on the couch, the state of the communications is viewed through colors and brightness on a lamp emitting a low-level light. When the user enters the kitchen to drink a soda, he may listen to the communications through a text-to-speech system if no display is available. When he arrives at his desk, the communications are set in an usual instant messaging user interface on the computer. Moreover, as the instant messaging application is informed about the user context, device context and physical context through the use of a context management infrastructure, user state usually typed by the user are inferred by the system and redirected on the current output interface.

The application is implemented as components in our extended model:

- A location server and a context server are simulated on a service platform of the network. Both simulated components require and configure all the *Managed Services* and the *Managed Requesters*, especially those which are qualified with a property querying the location of known users and devices

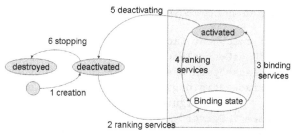

1. Creation
2. Ranking available filtered services with optional filters and ranking method
3. (Un,Re-) binding best services
4. Service ranking on following events: Bound service leaving or new service registered or requirements changed
5. Deactivation on following events: Mandatory service missing leading or stopping.
6. Stopping

Fig. 3. Service component life cycle

(e.g., see *user control component factory* description below). High-level key dynamic pieces of information are the willingness and the ability to communicate of every identified user [6].

- Some components represent physical devices (ambient lamp, computer, text-to-speech system) and are registered as delivering input/output user interfaces. These are dynamically categorized with location and contextual properties by the location server and the context server. Contextual properties are the user rating, the user willingness threshold and the necessary ability threshold.

```
<!-- Ambient lamp -->
<component name="AmbientLamp">
<implementation class="device.AmbientLamp" />
    <service>
        <provide interface="api.InstantMessagingUI,
                        org.osgi.service.cm.ManagedService"/>
    </service>
    <property name="location" value="living-room" type="string"/>
</component>
```

- A proxy representing a server of the instant messaging application located on the Internet.
- A user control component factory is responsible for instantiating as many user control components as the number of identified users. Every user control component is the instant messaging client for a particular user. This component links the instant messaging application server on the Internet and the input/output devices used by the user. It keeps control of the application state, i.e., maintaining the user contextual state in the instant messaging

application, maintaining the communication history and ensuring communication continuity at service re-composition time.

```
<!-- user control component factory -->
<component name="UserControlFactory">
<implementation class="pack.UserControlFactory" factory="true"/>
    <provide interface="org.osgi.service.component.ComponentFactory,
                        configuration.ManagedRequester" />
    <reference name="imServer"
      interface="api.InstantMessengerServer"
      cardinality="1..1" policy="dynamic"
      bind="bindServer" unbind="unbindServer" />
    <reference name="imUserInterface"
      interface="api. InstantMessagingUI"
      target="( & (location=$location-room{$user{unknown}} )
                  (willingness < willingness{$user{unknown}} )
                  (ability < ability{$user{unknown}} ))"
      optionalfilters="(sound.system=5.1)"
      cardinality="1..1" policy="dynamic"
      bind="bindUI" unbind="unbindUI"
      sort-method="sortUI"/>
</component>
```

The developer of the user control component factory defines three methods (*bindUI*, *unbindUI*, *sortUI*). *bindUI* and *unbindUI* are called respectively at binding and unbinding time. *sortUI* is called if service ranking is necessary. The service dependency manager is notified whenever new user interfaces are registered, modified or unregistered. Any time such an event occurs, it automatically updates the ranked list of filtered services. If the best available service has changed, the binding method is called and then the unbinding method is called to unbind the previous player.

As the user moves across rooms, the component instance attached to this user is notified by the location server through the use of writable filters when the user moves or begins a well-defined activity. Any time such an event occurs, service dependency tracking is reconfigured. The service ranking list is then updated and automatic re-binding behavior is triggered as mentioned before if the best service changes.

These components are packaged into bundles running on top of any OSGi platform implementation, e.g., Apache Felix. The implementation of the service dependency container (Declarative Services implementation) extends the one provided in the Apache Felix project.

6   Related Work

Our model on top of the OSGi framework fits a part of the architectural approach described by Steve White et al [18]. Our autonomic elements are self-described components able to classify provided services thanks to high-level internal policies. It *enables self-assembly without requiring central planning*. However, we are thinking of a more generic approach where internal policies can be mixed with external policies, which can be added at runtime in order to externally refine statically defined incomplete behaviors.

Among the described infrastructure elements described in [18], we make heavy use of the registry provided by the OSGi framework. The service registry offers the means to publish, find and bind services. It is the interface enabling the contextualization of software composition in our architecture.

David et al. [7] describe the implementation of self-adaptive mechanisms on top of the Fractal component model. The authors define reactive adaptation policies with Event-Condition-Reaction rules that are externally attached to the components. Internal and external events trigger the rule-based reactions. Reaction code is weaved into the base component implementation at runtime thanks to powerful aspect-oriented programming features. However, the architecture description language is made at a high level in the architecture whereas the components are self-descriptive in the model we chose. This aspect and the generic service trading mechanisms at the basis of our framework are more appropriate for representing the pervasive elements of the targeted environments. It lets software composition spontaneously emerge at runtime.

Chen et al. [5] introduce a context-sensitive model for resource discovery that uses INS (Intentional Naming Service) [1]. The proposed architecture enables distributed entities to publish and discover context attributes expressed in a simple syntax. This work could plug a complementary context management infrastructure into our design. Context sources could publish information through the use of *context-sensitive names*. Service requirements may be described with placeholders that the context management system could interpret as *context-sensitive name queries*. Context streams of Chen's architecture could then populate the service registry with contextual information.

A rich language dedicated to contextual service composition is described in [9]. It introduces a self-descriptive component model close to ours with service selection mechanisms based on attribute-value properties including mandatory and optional filters, contextual composition rules, and utility functions. Dynamic service availability and contextual service selection are clearly addressed by the work of Funk et al, nevertheless the definition of contextual behavior remains static.

The architectural design of a context-aware service discovery is described by participants in the European IST Amigo project [16]. The objective of the architecture is similar to ours: it links service discovery with a context management system and targets dynamic service composition in pervasive environments. The work carried out goes further in contextual information description in dealing with context ontology. It appears complementary to our work that targets clear component architecture in a software engineering study.

7 Conclusion

In this paper, we described a service-oriented component framework to structure the implementation of context-aware applications in pervasive environments. This framework enables dynamic service composition of pervasive entities in the network. The originality of the compositional approach relies on the contextualization made at the service registry level and on the automated decision-making mechanisms at the component level. Smart behaviors of the applications emerge from this autonomous composition of self-descriptive and self-adaptive components.

We strongly believe in a platform-centric vision where the execution environment reflects the pervasive aspects of the environment: Dynamic service availability, protocol heterogeneity, interface fragmentation and context dynamism. Every relevant entity on the network is reified on the platform and visible in the service registry. The registered services are also dynamically populated with contextual properties. In the described architecture, service requirements are declared at the component level and are also refined by dynamic contextual information with a similar model. The framework makes heavy use of the local dynamic service orientation of the component model.

Service selection mechanisms are needed in service-oriented architectures in order to overcome service ambiguity, which leads to composition unpredictability. Most service middleware defines scopes and filters to narrow unpredictability. Service ranking is another mechanism to achieve service selection. Moreover, service ranking is at the basis of self-optimization, which is one of the main design patterns in autonomic computing architectures [18].

In order to insert dynamic service ranking algorithms into service compositions, a compromise is made between the need to externally configure requirements and the need for powerful expressiveness in ranking algorithms. The algorithm is expressed in the programming language of the component and is called by an enveloping container.

In an attempt to further simplify the adoption of this architecture design, we are investigating using a POJO (Plain Old Java Object) programming paradigm. Existing implementations show that some non-functional needs are cleanly masked from the developer thanks to these techniques. This new trend is gaining momentum in the Java community, but it obviously raises other issues.

References

1. Adjie-Winoto, W., Schwartz, E., Balakrishnan, H., Lilley, J.: The de-sign and implementation of an intentional naming system. In: 17th ACM SOSP, Kiawah Island, SC, ACM Press, New York (December 1999)
2. Bottaro, A., Bourcier, J., Escoffier, C., Donsez, D., Lalanda, P.: A multi-protocol service-oriented platform for home control applications. In: CCNC 2007. Demonstration at IEEE Consumer Communications and Networking Conference, Las Vegas, Nevada, IEEE Computer Society Press, Los Alamitos (January 2007)

3. Bottaro, A., Gérodolle, A., Lalanda, P.: Pervasive spontaneous composition. In: SIPE 2006. Proceedings of the First IEEE International Workshop on Service Integration in Pervasive Environments, Lyon, France, IEEE Computer Society Press, Los Alamitos (June 2006)
4. Cervantes, H., Hall, R.S.: Autonomous adaptation to dynamic availability using a service-oriented component model. In: ICSE 2004. Proceedings of the International Conference on Software Engineering (May 2004)
5. Chen, G., Kotz, D.: Context-sensitive resource discovery. In: Proceedings of the First IEEE International Conference on Pervasive Computing and Communications, Fort Worth,Texas, pp. 243–252. IEEE Computer Society Press, Los Alamitos (March 2003)
6. Christensen, J., Sussman, J., Levy, S., Bennett, W.E., Wolf, T.V.-t., Kellogg, W.A.: Too much information.
7. David, P.-C., Ledoux, T.: An aspect-oriented approach for develop-ing self-adapting fractal components. In: Löwe, W., Südholt, M. (eds.) SC 2006. LNCS, vol. 4089, Springer, Heidelberg (2006)
8. Forum, U. Upnp av architecture v1.0 (June 2002)
9. Funk, C., Mitic, J., Kuhmuench, C.: Dscl: A language to support dynamic service composition. In: SIPE 2006. Proceedings of the First IEEE International Workshop on Service Integration in Pervasive Environments, Lyon, France, IEEE Computer Society Press, Los Alamitos (June 2006)
10. Graham, S., Davis, D., Simeonov, S., Daniels, G., Brittenham, P., Nakamura, Y., Fremantle, P., Koenig, D., Zentner, C.: Building Web Services with Java, 2nd edn. Sams Publishing (2004)
11. Guttman, E., Perkins, C., Veizades, J., Day, M.: Service location protocol (June 1999)
12. Keeney, R.L., Nair, K.: Decision analysis for the siting of nuclear power plants – the relevance of multiattribute utility theory. In: Proceedings of the IEEE, vol. 63(3), IEEE Computer Society Press, Los Alamitos (1975)
13. Kephart, J.O.: Research challenges of autonomic computing. In: Inverardi, P., Jazayeri, M. (eds.) ICSE 2005. LNCS, vol. 4309, Springer, Heidelberg (2006)
14. Lamparter, S., Ankolekar, A., Oberle, D., Studer, R., Weinhardt, C.: A policy framework for trading configurable goods and services in open electronic markets. In: Harper, R., Rauterberg, M., Combetto, M. (eds.) ICEC 2006. LNCS, vol. 4161, Springer, Heidelberg (2006)
15. OSGi Alliance. OSGi R4 Core Specification and Compendium (October 2005)
16. Pawar, P., Tomakoff, A.: Ontology-based context-aware service discovery for pervasive environments. In: SIPE 2006. Proceedings of the First IEEE International Workshop on Service Integration in Pervasive Environments, Lyon, France, June 2006, IEEE Computer Society Press, Los Alamitos (2006)
17. Ramparany, F., Euzenat, J., Broens, T., Pierson, J., Bottaro, A., Poortinga, R.: Context management and semantic modeling for ambient intelligence. In: FRCSS 2006. Proceedings of the First Workshop on Future Research Challenges for Software and Services, Vienna, Austria (April 2006)
18. White, S.R., Hanson, J.E., Whalley, I., Chess, D.M., Kephart, J.O.: An architectural approach to autonomic computing. In: ICAC 2004. Proceedings. International Conference on Autonomic Computing (May 2004)
19. Zhu, F., Mutka, M.W., Ni, L.M.: Service discovery in pervasive computing environments. IEEE Pervasive Computing 4, 81–90 (2005)

Measuring Reactability of Persistent Computing Systems

Takumi Endo, Yuichi Goto, and Jingde Cheng

Department of Information and Computer Sciences,
Saitama University, Saitama, 338-8570, Japan
{endo,gotoh,cheng}@aise.ics.saitama-u.ac.jp

Abstract. A persistent computing system is a reactive system that functions continuously anytime without stopping its reactions even when it needs to be maintained, upgraded, or reconfigured, it has some trouble, or it is attacked. However, the requirement that a computing system should run continuously and persistently is never taken into account as an essential and/or general requirement by traditional system design and development methodologies. As a result, there is no clearly defined standard to be used for measuring the reactability of a computing system. This paper proposes the first method to measure the reactability of a persistent computing system in a unified way. The paper introduces the notion of reactive processing path among components and shows that the reactive processing paths can be used to measure the reactability of a persistent computing system.

1 Introduction

Motivated by needs to provide continuously available, reliable, and secure computing systems, we have proposed a new type of advanced reactive systems, named *persistent computing systems* [1,2]. A persistent computing system is a reactive system that functions continuously anytime without stopping its reactions even when it needs to be maintained, upgraded, or reconfigured, it has some trouble, or it is attacked. From the viewpoint of reaction, all states of a computing system can be classified into three classes: *reactive state, partially reactive state,* and *dead state*. They mean, respectively, that the system can react completely, it can react partially but not completely, and it cannot react at all. Based on this definitions, a persistent computing system can be defined as a reactive system which will never be in the dead state [2].

The most fundamental issue towards implementation of a persistent computing system is how to measure the reactability of the system. Here we use the term *"reactability"* to represent the capability how many kinds of input data a running reactive system can react to at a certain time. Obviously the reactability of a persistent computing system is the most important property to characterize the system. However, the requirement that a computing system should run continuously and persistently is never taken into account as an essential and/or

M. Lumpe and W. Vanderperren (Eds.): SC 2007, LNCS 4829, pp. 144–151, 2007.
© Springer-Verlag Berlin Heidelberg 2007

general requirement by traditional system design and development methodologies. As a result, there is no clearly defined standard to be used for measuring the reactability of a computing system.

This paper proposes the first method to measure the reactability of a persistent computing system in a unified way. The paper introduces the notion of reactive processing path among components and shows that the reactive processing paths can be used to measure the reactability of a persistent computing system.

2   System Model

A persistent computing system can be built as a component-based system consisting of *control components* with self-measuring, self-monitoring, and self-controlling facilities to preserve reactability of the system and *functional components* to carry out special functionalities of the system [1,2]. In this context, almost all traditional component-based systems can be regarded as being constructed only by functional components.

We summarize some definitions about component-based systems as follows. The definition of a component proposed by Szyperski is "A software *component* is a unit of composition with contractually specified interfaces and explicit context dependencies only" [3]. An *interface* is an abstraction of the behavior of a component that consists of a subset of interactions that component together with a set of constraints describing when they may occur. A component can have one or more interfaces, and performs its operations via their interfaces. A system is constructed by components and binding their interfaces appropriately at the configuration level, and overall behavior of the system can be defined as sets of operations with partial orderings.

3   The Notion of Reactive Processing Path

A natural and simple way to measure the reactability of a persistent computing system may be to count the numbers of workable and unworkable components of the system in the following sense: reactability is a ratio of the number of workable components to the total of components in a system. The reactive state can be defined as the state where all components are workable, a partially reactive state can be defined as the state where there exists both workable components and unworkable components, and the dead state can be defined as the state where there is no workable components.

However, this method has two problems. First, it is too rough to a system with some components which have several interfaces because such a component may be partly workable even when it cannot perform some operations. Second, in general, reactions of a system should be behavior concerning all components of the system as the whole rather than individual components. Let us consider a simple system where all components interact each other in the pipe-and-filter style. The system must be in the dead state when one component is unworkable even if all other components are workable. This example shows that we cannot regard a system as being in a partially reactive state only based on the fact that there exist some workable components in the system. The two problems show that for measuring the reactability of a system it is not satisfactory to count the numbers of workable and unworkable components of the system.

Thus, we consider that operations and the order among them performed by component interfaces of a persistent computing system are the most primitive entities in the behavior of the system. Therefore, to measure the reactability of the system, the operations and the order among them have to be taken into account. Based on the fundamental consideration, we introduce the notion of reactive processing path to specify a series of operations.

Conceptually, a reactive processing path, RPP for short, is simply a directed acyclic graph which specifies operations and the processing order among them performed by component interfaces of a persistent computing system. By using this notion, a reaction of the system can be defined as an execution path from its start-operation to its end-operation.

Definition 1 (RPP). *A reactive processing path (RPP) is defined by a 7-tuple* $RPP = (\mathcal{O}, \mathcal{O}_{internal}, \mathcal{O}_{external}, s, e, \mathcal{C}, \mathcal{F})$:

- $\mathcal{O}$ *is a finite set of operations of a reaction,*
- $\mathcal{O}_{internal} \subseteq \mathcal{O}$ *is a finite set of internal operations that do not interact with the outside environment,*
- $\mathcal{O}_{external} \subseteq \mathcal{O}$ *is a finite set of external operations that interact with the outside environment,*
- $\mathcal{O}_{internal} \cap \mathcal{O}_{external} = \emptyset$ *and* $\mathcal{O}_{internal} \cup \mathcal{O}_{external} = \mathcal{O}$,
- $s \in \mathcal{O}$ *is the start-operation (origin of the path),*
- $e \in \mathcal{O}$ *is the end-operation (terminal of the path),*
- $\{s, e\} \cap \mathcal{O}_{external} \neq \emptyset$ *(One of or both of them are elements of* $\mathcal{O}_{external}$*),*
- $\mathcal{O} - \{s, e\} \subseteq \mathcal{O}_{internal}$,
- $\mathcal{C}$ *is a finite set of pre- and post- conditions to perform the operation.*
- $\mathcal{F} : \mathcal{C} \to \mathcal{O}$.

Pre- and post- conditions in operations $\mathcal{C}$ stands for control flow relations between operations and is used to build forks, and synchronizers of the path. A *fork* allows independent execution between concurrent paths within one RPP and a *synchronizer* is applied to synchronize such concurrent paths.

These two types of modeling objects have already been provided in workflow graph [4,5], and it can help to handle behavioral concurrency. On the other hand, the clear separation between $\mathcal{O}_{internal}$ and $\mathcal{O}_{external}$, the restrictions of $\{s, e\} \cap \mathcal{O}_{external} \neq \emptyset$ and $\mathcal{O} - \{s, e\} \subseteq \mathcal{O}_{internal}$, and the pre- and post- conditions have never been considered in their approach. We newly introduce these matters in order to acquire the compatibility with reactive systems. In addition, a workflow graph is not claim that nodes in the path must be operations performed by components whereas an RPP claims it explicitly in order to assure compatibility with component-based systems.

Note that all RPPs can be decidable statically in the sense that they can be uniquely decidable by giving the configuration from a certain specification.

Any RPP must provide reachability. To assure this constraint is possible because we can apply the two correctness criteria in a workflow graph [4,5] to an RPP as follows: one is *deadlock free*, i.e., an RPP does not generate an RPP that contains only a proper subset of the incoming operations of a synchronizer, and the other is *lack of synchronization free*, i.e., the summation of all RPPs does not generate an RPP that contains more than one incoming nodes of a merge node.

The *RPP map* means the directed acyclic graph to represent all RPP in a persistent computing system. The RPP map can be derived from all RPPs in the system, and vice versa.

Definition 2 (Checking states of RPPs)

- *An RPP is active if all operations that consist of the RPP are workable,*
- *An RPP is inactive if the RPP involves at least one unworkable operation.*

An RPP of a reaction is active iff the reaction is alive. An RPP of a reaction is inactive iff the reaction is dead. Therefore, we can know whether a reaction of a system is dead or alive by checking whether interfaces of components in an RPP of the reaction are workable or not.

Using the above-mentioned notions, we acquire ability to distinguish among the reactive state, a partially reactive state, and the dead state according to the following definition.

Definition 3 (States of a Persistent Computing System). *The states of a running persistent computing system at given time can be defined as follows:*

- *a system is in the reactive state if all RPPs are active in the system,*
- *a system is in a partially reactive state if both active RPPs and inactive RPPs exists in the system,*
- *a system is in the dead state if all RPPs are inactive in the system.*

If control component can grasp the number of active RPPs by measuring the running system itself permanently and provide the way to make inactive RPPs active before all active RPPs fall into inactive, the resulting system will keep the reactive state or a partially reactive state eternally. On the other hand, from the viewpoint of repairing, since control components can catch "what an RPP is inactive" and "what an interface of a component consisting of the RPP is problematic," we can get a sound basis "what an interface of a component should be repaired."

4   A Design of Reactability Measurement Facilities

To grasp the number of active RPPs, control components must be able to check conditions of every RPPs in such a way that the components can measure and monitor the behavior of the system.

We consider that targets to be measured (tracked) should be interactions among participating components whose operations consist of an RPP, such that control components can grasp the progress of operations on the relevant RPP and reason about whether the every operations from the start-point to the end-point can complete their executions or not, i.e., whether the RPP is active or inactive. Note we propose the most primitive design of reactability measurement facilities for persistent computing systems, in this paper, we do not consider reliability, security, and real-time properties.

When the start-operation of an RPP starts its execution, the context information can be informed to control components. Here context information contains a 4-tuple: $(S_C - ID, S_P - ID, D_C - ID, D_P - ID)$. They mean respectively, the ID of the source component, the operation ID performed by the source component, the ID of the destination component, and the operation ID performed by the destination component. Note that such context information never contain payload (body) of the message. Similarly, when a component executes an operation to interact with other components, only the tuple are sent to control components. Control components receive such context information and check the conditions of an RPP by analyzing them.

To decide whether the operation is workable or not, we use two context information: one to be used in the output operation of the source component (below S) and one to be used in the input operation of the destination component (below D). Control component first check whether $D_P - ID$ in S is equal to $S_P - ID$ in D or not, and then calculates the difference between compare time of receipt of them. An operation can be defined as unworkable if the difference differs vastly. As a result, control components can grasp the number of active RPPs.

However, by using such "reactive sensing", control components can not aware that an operation in the RPP is in unworkable state till the start-operation can be executed. Ideally, it is necessary for control components to awake soon after an operation is unworkable for some reasons (e.g., failures or attacks). As a practical scheme to solve this issue, we require "proactive sensing," meaning that control components send query to a component periodically and then receive the ACK from the component in such a way the responsible component receives and sends the messages via the contractually specified interfaces. Since the interfaces correspond operations consisting of RPP(s), control components can awake that the relevant operation is unworkable if the ACK can be sent to them in an allowable time.

5   Discussion

The work presented in this paper is still in progress and as such there remains many implementation issues to implement control components in a persistent computing system. From our perspective, we discuss such issues and suggest promising solutions.

5.1   How to Sense RPPs States

Gao et al. presented three tracking mechanisms for component-based systems [6]. One of them is *automatic component wrapping* that means adding tracking code to monitor the external interface and behaviors of components by wrapping them as black boxes. This must be more sound than others, because it does not require source code, it gains code separation and low overhead, and both in-house and COTS (commercial off-the-shelf) components can be applied to our approach. Due to these advantages, we will be able to gain a reasonable measuring and monitoring mechanism for all persistent computing systems in a language-independent and platform-independent manner.

5.2   How to Generate the RPP Map

Control components never understand the RPP map of a system without a specification defined by system developers. Therefore, it is a clearly issue to decide what languages can be used to specify the RPP map.

There can be two prominent types of such specifications: global ones for the whole system and local ones for individual components, both of which are basically application-dependent. A typical example of the former is one specified by an architecture description language (ADL), whereas an example of the latter specification is an interface definition of a component, which is usually specified by a interface definition language (IDL). Since neither ADLs nor IDLs purpose to describe an RPP map, an attractive way is to elicit the RPP map at run-time from an architecture or component interfaces automatically. To elicit the RPP map, we prefer component interfaces rather than an architecture description because of the following reasons. One is that up-front full precise description of the architecture of a system (in particular, a dynamically reconfigurable system) is somewhat restrictive and difficult for developers. The other reason is that ADLs typically subsume a formal semantic theory (e.g., π-calculus in Darwin), but developers may not be familiar with such theory.

If we select component interfaces to elicit the RPP map, we should mention the well-recognized problem: prevalent IDLs provide just the syntactic descriptions of the component's *signatures* (names and signatures of operations) and do not provide *protocols* (relative order between exchanged messages and blocking conditions) and *semantics* ("meaning" of operations). The lack of protocols or semantics causes compositional errors [7,8]. To overcome this problem, there are many well-established researches on extended interface definitions such as [7,8]. The protocols in such extended interfaces are information we just desire for control components to understand the RPP map. Hence, it is reasonable to use component interfaces with such protocol contracts as the specifications of the RPP map.

5.3   How to Repair Inactive RPPs

Some repairing (or recovering) mechanisms are indispensable for a persistent computing system in the sense that the system must eventually be in the dead state without any repairing mechanism even if the system can accurately measure reactability of itself.

The most simple way is a manual repair: control components report to an authorized developer or maintainer about what interfaces of components should be repaired, and he/she repairs the problematic interfaces. Although this is surely necessary, unfortunately there is no guarantee that he/she can help for the system to be recovered whenever the system have some troubles. Therefore, as more sophisticated ways, some automatic repairing mechanisms must also be necessary. To our knowledge, even though a number of researches on dynamic reconfiguration can partly support the repair of a component-based system by removing or upgrading some problematic interfaces, few researchers focus their attention on run-time repairing (or recovering) of such a system explicitly. We must closely investigate this issue and find a good solution. An attractive direction is to integrate several research areas: autonomic computing systems [9], recovery-oriented systems [10], or self-healing systems [11].

6   Concluding Remarks

In this paper, we have introduced the notion of reactive processing path for reactability measurement of a persistent computing system. We also presented how a persistent computing system with the facilities to measure the reactability can be constructed by a group of control components and a group of functional components, and discussed its implementation issues. Now we are developing of the prototype of control components with essential features presented in this paper.

We have not considered reliability, security, and real-time properties. There are many interesting issues if we consider those properties. In order to improve the reliability of persistent computing systems, it is natural that there are several interfaces which can perform same operation in a persistent computing system. In that case, we should discuss how to check whether an RPP which includes the several interfaces is active or not. Moreover, we should investigate how to measure whether an interface is workable or not if the interface behaves irregularly because of its bugs. From the viewpoint of security, even if there are several interfaces which can perform same operation in a persistent computing system, it may have to use only a particular interface of them. In that case, how do we measure and decide whether RPPs which include those interfaces are active or not? On the other hand, when a reaction of a persistent computing system must be finished until a certain time, how do we measure and decide the RPP of the reaction is active or not? In such case, control components to measure the reactability of the system may become a bottleneck of the performance of the system such that we should put several or more control components on the system. Thus, we should investigate how we keep the consistency of the RPP map of the system among those control components.

References

1. Cheng, J.: Connecting components with soft system buses: A new methodology for design, development, and maintenance of reconfigurable, ubiquitous, and persistent reactive systems. In: Proc. 19th International Conference on Advanced Information Networking and Applications, Taipei, Taiwan, vol. 1, pp. 667–672 (2005)
2. Cheng, J.: Persistent computing systems as continuously available, reliable, and secure systems. In: Proc. 1st International Conference on Availability, Reliability and Security, Vienna, Austria, pp. 631–638 (2006)
3. Szyperski, C.: Component Software: Beyond Object-Oriented Programming. Addison-Wesley, Reading (1997)
4. Sadiq, W., Orlowska, M.E.: Applying graph reduction techniques for identifying structural conflicts in process models. In: Jarke, M., Oberweis, A. (eds.) CAiSE 1999. LNCS, vol. 1626, pp. 195–209. Springer, Heidelberg (1999)
5. Sadiq, W., Orlowska, M.E.: Analyzing process models using graph reduction techniques. Information Systems 25, 117–134 (2000)
6. Gao, J., Zhu, E.Y., Shim, S., Chang, L.: Monitoring software components and component-based software. In: Proc. 24th International Computer Software and Applications Conference, IEEE Computer Society, pp. 403–412. IEEE Computer Society Press, Los Alamitos (2000)
7. Canal, C., Fuentes, L., Troya, J., Vallecillo, A.: Extending CORBA interfaces with π-calculus for protocol compatibility. In: Proc. Technology of Object-Oriented Languages and Systems, pp. 208–225 (2000)
8. Han, J.: A comprehensive interface definition framework for software components. In: Proc. 1998 Asia-Pacific Software Engineering Conference, pp. 110–117 (1998)
9. Kephart, J.O., Chess, D.M.: The vision of autonomic computing. IEEE Computer 36, 41–50 (2003)
10. Patterson, D., et al.: Recovery oriented computing (ROC): Motivation, definition, techniques, and case studies. Technical report, UC Berkeley Computer Science UCB//CSD-02-1175 (2002)
11. Shaw, M.: "self-healing": softening precision to avoid brittleness (position paper). In: Proc. the First Workshop on Self-Healing Systems, pp. 111–114 (2002)

Requirements for Applying Aspect-Oriented Techniques in Web Service Composition Languages

Mathieu Braem and Niels Joncheere

System and Software Engineering Lab (SSEL)
Vrije Universiteit Brussel
Pleinlaan 2, 1050 Brussels, Belgium
mbraem@vub.ac.be, njonchee@vub.ac.be

Abstract. In current composition languages for web services, there is insufficient support to explicitly separate crosscutting concerns, which leads to compositions that are hard to maintain or evolve. A similar problem in object-oriented languages is being tackled by aspect-oriented programming, and some work has been started to apply these techniques to web service composition languages as well. We identified some problems with these approaches. This short paper lists these limitations and offers a number of requirements to apply aspect-oriented techniques to workflow languages.

1 Introduction

Web services [1] are a popular way of making existing software available as external services over a network, through standardized protocols. In recent years, workflow languages [2] are used to express these web service compositions. One of the most popular languages today, is WS-BPEL [3].

Even though WS-BPEL, and other workflow languages, are very well suited to express these kind of compositions, its abstraction model doesn't explicitly support a good separation of concerns [4]. WS-BPEL processes are coded according to the requirements of the core functionality, which means that concerns other from the main concern, do not fit the decomposition, and end up scattered in the process.

A typical example of a non-core concern, is a business rule such as "billing" [5], which keeps some data during the execution of the process, e.g. the duration of invocations of external services, and charges the user proportionally. Without explicit support for separation of concerns, the billing concern cannot be cleanly separated from the base process, and is scattered in and tangled with the other concerns.

The same problem was originally identified in object-oriented systems, and aspect-oriented software development (AOSD) proves to be a valid solution [6]. The research community acknowledges this problem for workflow languages, and understands AOSD has potential in this context too [7]. There already have

M. Lumpe and W. Vanderperren (Eds.): SC 2007, LNCS 4829, pp. 152–159, 2007.
© Springer-Verlag Berlin Heidelberg 2007

been proposals to approach the problem with AOSD solutions. However, they literally translate the existing AOSD approaches for object-oriented languages to workflow languages, without much regards for the specific needs of these workflow languages.

In this short paper the requirements for applying aspect-oriented techniques, to separate crosscutting concerns in web service composition languages, are outlined. Section 2 details the problem with current workflow languages. Section 3 gives an overview of the current approaches and their limitations. In section 4 we layout the directions for our future research, and list the features and requirements that we deem necessary in an AOSD approach to the problem. Section 5 concludes the paper with a short summary of the problem and our envisioned solution.

2   Crosscutting Concerns in Web Service Compositions

Web services are a relatively new standard that allow communication between distributed processes, based on existing internet protocols (e.g. http), with the addition of some required "middleware"-enabling protocols, e.g. WS-Security. Web services are of use in two different settings. They can be used to offer certain paid services on the internet, or they can realize the integration between several business processes. A web service is an interface, describing a number of operations that can be called by sending messages over a network. They are the foundation of the service oriented architecture (SOA). In this approach, applications use services that offer a certain function on the network. The clients are unaware of the specific implementation of the service, and only rely on its interface. This kind of loose coupling allows independent evolution of services, while maintaining compatibility with client applications.

2.1   Web Service Compositions

Web service composition is a powerful mechanism to create new web services. Imagine, for example, a travelling agent that offers separate services to book airplane tickets and hotel reservations. By composing these two services, we obtain a new service with which customers can book all-in trips. This kind of reuse removes a lot of complexity in designing advanced web services, as large parts of the service are handled by external services. They offer an added value over regular web services.

We can distinct two large families of web service composition languages. On one side, there are languages that define executable processes by means of web service orchestrations. They do so by fixing a well-defined order of interaction between web services. On the other side, web service choreographies only define the publicly visible behavior of the messages that are exchanged between services. They do not define the internal logic of a process, and as a result, they are not executable.

Choreographies are useful to verify the communication protocol of services, the specific order of messages that are to be exchanged. Consider for example a web service where a user has to log himself in and out with the service, before and after further interaction. This protocol can be enforced with a choreography specification, without detailing the internal logic of the services. A number of high level composition languages exist that support web services standards. Most notably, there are WSCL [8], YAWL [9], en WS-BPEL [3]. However, none of these languages offers a way to separate crosscutting concerns.

2.2 Crosscutting Concerns

One important principle in programming languages, is that of separation of concerns, which states that properties of software systems must be dealt with separately. Doing so, those parts of the system can be more easily specified, changed, removed or reused.

In object-oriented programming, programs are built by making a class hierarchy of the problem domain. Properties that do not fit this modularization, end up scattered in the application, and entangled with each other. These properties, are the so-called cross-cutting concerns, and are a direct result of the tyranny of this dominant decomposition [10]. As noticed by Arsanjani et al. [7] and others [11,12,13], this problem also applies to web service composition languages.

In our example of the travelling agent, this could be a "Billing" concern, that measures the time it took to talk to the several web services, and charges the user accordingly. Coding this in the web service composition using the traditional mechanisms, leads to scattered and entangled code. An approach to this general problem is proposed under the form of aspect-oriented programming, and while most research is focused on its application to object-oriented programming, a few approaches for web service composition languages have come forward as well. The following section gives more details on these approaches.

3   Current Approaches

Current approaches to achieve better separation of concerns in web service compositions are designed to use aspect-oriented technology. This section starts with an overview of this relatively new programming paradigm, and continues to describe the current approaches and their shortcomings.

3.1   Aspect-Oriented Software Development

To support a better separation of concerns, aspect-oriented software programming (AOP) is proposed. Kiczales et al. note that with the existing methods, certain properties of an application have to be implemented in multiple modules of the system. The same logic is repeated over several modules, which means there is an amount of code duplication. This gives the typical problems that it is hard to add or remove these concerns, to change or even reuse them. AOP wants to achieve a better separation of concerns by moving these crosscutting concerns into separate modules, named aspects. Changing, adding or removing concerns that are specified in aspects, no longer require changes in the rest of the system.

Several approaches to AOP exist. AspectJ is the first, and also the most well known, approach. This language is an extension to Java and allows programming of concerns in modules (aspects), separate from the classes of the base system. AspectJ introduces a few new concepts to achieve this goal. An aspect describes when it applies, by selecting a number of "join points". These join points are well-defined events during the execution of a program, e.g. the execution of a method. The expression that selects these join points is called a "pointcut". The aspect specifies in the "advice" what should happen on those selected join points. An "aspect weaver" activates the aspects on the places specified by the pointcuts.

3.2   Current Approaches Using AOSD on Web Services

- *AO4BPEL.* In [11], Charfi presents AO4BPEL, an aspect-oriented extension to WS-BPEL. It is a dynamic approach, meaning that aspects can be added to or removed from a composition at runtime, while the process is being executed. This approach requires a modified WS-BPEL engine, and is not compatible with existing software. In AO4BPEL each activity is a possible join point. Pointcuts capturing these join points are written in the low-level XPath language.
- *AdaptiveBPEL.* Another dynamic approach is AdaptiveBPEL [14]. This is a framework that allows managing dynamic aspects. In this approach it is possible to plug in and remove aspects into a core service composition to address quality-of-service concerns and adapt to changes in business rules. AdaptiveBPEL also relies on a modified WS-BPEL engine which applies aspects at runtime.
- *Courbis and Finkelstein.* An aspect-oriented extension resembling AO4BPEL is proposed by Courbis and Finkelstein [15]. In their approach they use XPath as a pointcut language and a modified WS-BPEL engine to allow dynamic addition and removal of aspects. Their advice language is Java.

3.3   Limitations of the Current Approaches

A first observation we made in studying the current approaches, is that they are all quite literal, direct translations of aspect-oriented solutions of object-oriented systems to the web service composition context. A result of this, is that these approaches suffer from a number of shortcomings. Some problems arise with the application of AOSD to the web service composition domain (problems 1 and 2). Others stem from the difficulties in object-oriented AOSD research (problems 3, 4 and 5). The issues there are also appearant in the web service composition domain, and it is worthwhile to investigate the application of the current techniques in this new context.

1. *Confused layers of abstraction.* It is important to stay on the same level of abstraction as the base WS-BPEL process. In more recent versions of AO4BPEL it is possible to alter SOAP messages on the engine level, which allows expressing concerns that can not (easily) be written in a WS-BPEL process. But doing so, this is no longer an approach to separate concerns on workflow level. This extension is also specific to implementation details, by being only applicable on WS-BPEL engines that uses SOAP as the transport protocol. In the approach of Courbis and Finkelstein, the abstraction layers also fade. Their advice code is written in Java, and, unfortunately, is not only used to obtain a clean separation of concerns, but also to execute arbitrary Java code in WS-BPEL processes. Code expressed in the Java language is of a lower abstraction-level than WS-BPEL.
2. *Missing workflow-specific concepts.* The current approaches lack concepts that are specific to web service composition languages. The advice model should support workflow specific concepts, such as synchronization, skipping activities, etc.
3. *Limited pointcut language*
   (a) The pointcut language in AO4BPEL and the approach of Courbis and Finkelstein is XPath, which is a language to navigate an XML structure. The pointcuts in these approaches are no more than XPath expressions that point to a direct path in a WS-BPEL XML document. Being tied so closely to the structure of an XML file, limits the reusability of the pointcuts. They are very fragile, and easily break when the process would evolve.
   (b) None of the approaches support quantification of the join points based on protocol. If we for instance want to express that an aspect can only activate on the third execution of a certain action, we should be able to express this in the pointcut language.
4. *Reusability.* One of the most appealing advantages of aspects is that they are reusable. A concern implemented in an aspect, should be applicable to multiple compositions. However, current approaches require the aspect to be changed to the specifics of the composition it is applied to. Some techniques to solve this are proposed in current research in the AOSD field, but are not considered in the approaches for composition languages.
5. *Aspect interaction.* When multiple aspects are applicable on a single join point, the so called "feature interaction" problem occurs. Aspects are not necessarily orthogonal, and as such, the order of execution matters. It is furthermore desirable to express more advanced aspect compositions than a simple ordering. Current approaches for composition languages either do not consider this problem, or try to tackle it in a very limited way.

4   Towards Better Separation of Concerns in Web Service Compositions

In this section we list the requirements for a better aspect-oriented approach to separation of concerns in web service composition languages. The list is based on the limitations we identified in existing approaches and introduces some novel ideas.

1. *Workflow-specific advice.* We extend the advice language with concepts that are specific for workflow languages. Examples of these specific concepts are listed here.

   (a) *Advice without order.* In advising web service compositions it occurs that a branch has to be added in a construction where the order is not of importance. For example, an extra activity to be executed in a parallel split, or an extra condition in a merge activity. This kind of advice is named "in" advice [16]. Another kind of workflow specific advice is the "while" advice, that specifies that a certain activity is to be executed during the execution of the selected join point.

   (b) *Skipping advice.* Aspects can specify that certain activities are no longer to be executed. Consider for example an aspect that specifies that a certain part of a web service composition is no longer of use, because some decisions are made by the client beforehand.

   (c) *Synchronize activities.* Aspects can alter workflows in such a way, that new synchronization points are to be introduced in the composition. In future research we plan to look into how this can be easily expressed, and how this can be efficiently implemented.

2. *Declarative pointcut language.* Using a pointcut language based on logic programming offers advantages over traditional pointcut languages. Pointcuts are no more than logic rules that select join points. It is very easy to create new pointcuts by reusing the old ones. Furthermore, it is possible to write recursive pointcuts. Introducing an expressive pointcut language, addresses problem 3a.

3. *Protocol based quantification.* Web service compositions express processes, and precisely in such program specifications it is interesting to express the applicability based on a sequence or a protocol of events (problem 3b). Consider for instance a workflow where a user has three chances to complete a password request before he is denied further access to the service. This can be encoded in a separate aspect, if there is support for remembering prior events in the execution of a workflow. This is also known as "statefull aspects" [17,18].

4. *Deployment constructs.* Aspects are often applicable on more than a single web service composition, and therefore we want them to be as reusable as possible. As shown in problem 4, current approaches have little support for this. In order to achieve this, we plan to use a dedicated layer between the aspects and the compositions to which they apply. In this layer deployment specifications are made. In the deployment constructions we also express the aspect composition specifications that address the feature interaction problem (as shown in problem 5). Lastly, the deployment construct is a good place to specify how the aspects are to be deployed: e.g. one per workflow instance, globally, etc.

5   Conclusion

Current web service composition languages lack support to explicitly separate crosscutting concerns from each other and the base workflow. This problem was already found in object-oriented programming language, and the solution that is proposed for these languages can be applied to workflow languages as well. However, this approach can not be literally translated to this other paradigm, as workflow languages have their own specific needs. Current approaches approaches do not take this into account, and as such suffer from some shortcomings.

In this short paper we identified these limitations of the current approaches. We also listed a number of requirements for future work to tackle these problems. We already started the development of an aspect-oriented extension to WS-BPEL, which we named Padus [16]. This approach strives to a better reusability of aspects and uses several techniques to accomplish this. Padus uses a declarative pointcut language, based on logic programming. In this pointcut language, it is possible to select join points in a describing way, rather than explicitly listing the points. Padus also supports explicit aspect deployments for further reuse. In addition to the regular before-, after- and around advice, the advice model of this language already supports "in" advice to allow including new branches in orderless structures like parallel splits (flow activities). Padus, however does not yet support some of the requirements listed in the previous section, e.g. the "while" advice and support for protocol based quantification in the pointcut language.

References

1. Alonso, G., Casati, F., Kuno, H., Machiraju, V. (eds.): Web Services: Concepts, Architectures and Applications. Springer-Verlag, Heidelberg, Germany (2004)
2. Du, W., Elmagarmid, A.: Workflow management: State of the art vs. state of the products. Technical Report HPL-97-90, Hewlett-Packard Labs, Palo Alto, CA, USA (1997)
3. Andrews, T., Curbera, F., Dholakia, H., Goland, Y., Klein, J., Leymann, F., Liu, K., Roller, D., Smith, D., Thatte, S., Trickovic, I., Weerawarana, S.: Business Process Execution Language for Web Services, version 1.1 (2003)
4. Parnas, D.L.: On the criteria to be used in decomposing systems into modules. Comm. ACM 15(12), 1053–1058 (1972)
5. D'Hondt, M., Jonckers, V.: Hybrid aspects for weaving object-oriented functionality and rule-based knowledge. [19] 132–140
6. Kiczales, G., Lamping, J., Mendhekar, A., Maeda, C., Lopes, C., Loingtier, J.M., Irwin, J.: Aspect-oriented programming. Technical Report SPL97-008 P9710042, Xerox PARC (1997)
7. Arsanjani, A., Hailpern, B., Martin, J., Tarr, P.: Web services: Promises and compromises. Queue 1(1), 48–58 (2003)
8. Banerji, A., Bartolini, C., Beringer, D., Chopella, V., Govindarajan, K., Karp, A., Kuno, H., Lemon, M., Pogossiants, G., Sharma, S., Williams, S.: Web Services Conversation Language (WSCL) 1.0. W3C Note 14 March, 2002, World Wide Web Consortium(2002), http://www.w3.org/TR/2002/NOTE-wscl10-20020314/

9. van der Aalst, W.M.P., ter Hofstede, A.H.M.: YAWL: Yet Another Workflow Language (revised version). QUT Technical Report FIT-TR-2003-04, Queensland University of Technology, Brisbane, Australia (2003)
10. Ossher, H., Tarr, P.: Using subject-oriented programming to overcome common problems in object-oriented software development/evolution. In: Proc. 21st Int'l Conf. Software Engineering, pp. 687–688. IEEE Computer Society Press, Los Alamitos (1999)
11. Charfi, A., Mezini, M.: Aspect-oriented web service composition with AO4BPEL. In: Zhang, L.-J, Jeckle, M. (eds.) ECOWS 2004. LNCS, vol. 3250, pp. 168–182. Springer, Heidelberg (2004)
12. Cottenier, T., Elrad, T.: Dynamic and decentralized service composition with Contextual Aspect-Sensitive Services. In: WEBIST 2005. Proceedings of the 1st International Conference on Web Information Systems and Technologies, Miami, FL, USA, pp. 56–63 (2005)
13. Verheecke, B., Vanderperren, W., Jonckers, V.: Unraveling crosscutting concerns in web services middleware. IEEE Software 23(1), 42–50 (2006)
14. Erradi, A., Maheshwari, P.: AdaptiveBPEL: A policy-driven middleware for flexible web services composition. In: MWS 2005. Proc. of the EDOC Middleware for Web Services Workshop, Enschede, The Netherlands (2005)
15. Courbis, C., Finkelstein, A.: Towards aspect weaving applications. In: Inverardi, P., Jazayeri, M. (eds.) ICSE 2005. LNCS, vol. 4309, pp. 69–77. Springer, Heidelberg (2006)
16. Braem, M., Verlaenen, K., Joncheere, N., Vanderperren, W., Van Der Straeten, R., Truyen, E., Joosen, W., Jonckers, V.: Isolating process-level concerns using Padus. In: Dustdar, S., Fiadeiro, J.L., Sheth, A. (eds.) BPM 2006. LNCS, vol. 4102, pp. 113–128. Springer, Heidelberg (2006)
17. Douence, R., Fradet, P., Südholt, M.: Composition, reuse and interaction analysis of stateful aspects. In: [19] pp. 141–150.
18. Vanderperren, W., Suvée, D., Cibrán, M.A., De Fraine, B.: Stateful aspects in JAsCo. In: Gschwind, T., Aßmann, U., Nierstrasz, O. (eds.) SC 2005. LNCS, vol. 3628, pp. 167–181. Springer, Heidelberg (2005)
19. Lieberherr, K. (ed.): AOSD 2004. Proc. 3rd Int' Conf. on Aspect-Oriented Software Development. ACM Press, New York (2004)

Synthesizing Communication Middleware from Explicit Connectors in Component Based Distributed Architectures

Dietmar Schreiner[1,2] and Karl M. Göschka[1]

[1] Vienna University of Technology
Institute of Information Systems, Distributed Systems Group
Argentinierstrasse 8 / 184-1, A-1040 Vienna, Austria
{d.schreiner,k.goeschka}@infosys.tuwien.ac.at
[2] University of Applied Sciences Technikum Vienna
Department of Embedded Systems
Höchstädtplatz 5, A-1200 Vienna, Austria

Abstract. In component based software engineering, an application is build by composing trusted and reusable units of execution, the components. A composition is formed by connecting the components' related interfaces. The point of connection, namely the connector, is an abstract representation of their interaction. Most component models' implementations rely on extensive middleware, which handles component interaction and hides matters of heterogeneity and distribution from the application components. In resource constrained embedded systems this middleware and its resource demands are a key factor for the acceptance and usability of component based software. By addressing connectors as first class architectural entities at model level, all application logic related to interaction can be located within them. Therefore, the set of all explicit connectors of a component architecture denotes the exact requirements of that application's communication and interaction needs. We contribute by demonstrating how to use explicit connectors in model driven development to synthesize a custom tailored, component based communication middleware. This synthesis is achieved by model transformations and optimizations using prefabricated basic building blocks for communication primitives.

1 Introduction

Driven by market demands, the application of embedded systems experienced a significant upturn over the last years. A wide variety of new fields of application as well as more demanding requirements in established ones lead to a tremendous boost in complexity of embedded systems software. Today's embedded applications are no longer simple programs executed on one single electronic control unit (ECU). In fact, they are heterogeneous software systems in distributed and often safety or mission critical environments and hence have to be small, efficient but also extremely reliable.

M. Lumpe and W. Vanderperren (Eds.): SC 2007, LNCS 4829, pp. 160–167, 2007.
© Springer-Verlag Berlin Heidelberg 2007

1.1 State of the Art

A well accepted approach in developing cost-efficient and sound embedded systems software is that of component based software engineering (CBSE): applications are built by assembling small, well defined and trusted building blocks, so called components.

In accordance to the work of [1,2,3,4] a component is a (i) trusted architectural element, an element of execution, representing (ii) software or hardware functionality, with a (iii) well defined usage description. It conforms to a (iv) component model and can be independently composed and deployed without modification according to the model's composition standard. At run-time components interact through their provided and required interfaces conforming to the component model's interaction standard. Therefore, components are reusable and exchangeable.

The process of interaction may become rather complex especially in distributed heterogeneous systems. As it is good practice to keep application components simple and focused on their primary purpose, any program code related to interaction handling has to be separated from the application component's implementation. This is typically done by introducing communication middleware handling all types of interaction in a transparent way. Interacting application components utilize that middleware and therefore face their distribution and deployment scenario as configuration issue only.

1.2 Contribution

Using a general purpose communication middleware seems to be a great advantage at first glance, but turns out to be rather cumbersome in resource constrained systems. As such middleware has to cope with all possible types of interaction, implementations tend to be rather heavy-weight pieces of monolithic software. Since resource consumption is a key factor in embedded systems software development, we provide an overview on how application specific communication middleware can be synthesized from software models containing explicit connectors within a model driven development process. This custom tailored middleware exactly covers the application's communication needs and therefore helps in building a light-weight component middleware for embedded systems. In addition the proposed approach leads to component based middleware, so available mechanisms and tools from the domain of CBSE (e.g. model verification techniques) can be applied to the middleware itself.

1.3 Overview

Section 2 describes the types of connectors in component models. It gives a detailed view on explicit connectors, as they are used to generate communication middleware in our approach. The general structure of component middleware feasible for embedded systems is described in Section 3. Section 4 finally gives an overview on how communication middleware can be synthesized in model driven development by transforming and optimizing application models, utilizing prefabricated basic communication primitives.

2 Implicit and Explicit Connectors

Two components may interact at runtime if their related *provided-* and *required interfaces* are validly associated at composition time. This association, namely the connector, is an abstract representation of any interaction occurring between the connected components. As mentioned before, in most component models the process of interaction is covered within middleware, therefore we consider these connectors to be implicit.

An explicit connector is an architectural entity, that is used to represent component composition and interaction and owns its own implementation of interaction operators. Therefore an explicit connector encapsulates all communication logic for one specific type of interaction. In addition, it specifies properties of the connected components' interaction and provides contracts regarding communication channels and resource requirements.

Modeling component based applications using explicit connectors in UML 2.0 requires the UML component syntax to be extended. UML 2.0 specifies two types of connectors: (i) the assembly connector and (ii) the delegation connector. When talking about connectors within this paper, we refer to assembly connectors and their extensions.

To keep explicit connectors small in size, they have to be highly specialized in type and target platform.

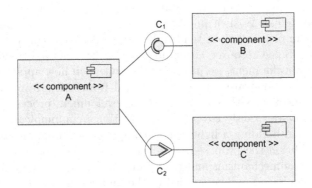

Fig. 1. Client-Server and Sender-Receiver Connector

Explicit connectors fall into two main classes:

Client-Server Connectors: A component providing a service is called server, a component using that service is called client. The client-server connector connects components of this type. Typical client-server connectors are those connecting procedural interfaces. Figure 1 shows a client-server connector labeled C_1 where component A is the client and component B is the server.

Sender-Receiver Connectors: These connectors provide means of non-blocking, one-to-many and many-to-one data distribution. Sender-receiver connectors typically implement a "last-is-best" semantic—only the last received data value is valid and accessible—and are used to connect components emitting and collecting data. Figure 1 also shows a sender-receiver connector labeled C_2 where component A is the sender and component C is the receiver.

A detailed classification of explicit connectors for the domain of automotive embedded systems according to the *AUTOSAR* [5] standard was provided within the project *COMPASS* [6], but is out of the scope of this paper.

Although explicit connectors have a great similarity to components, they differ in many aspects: In contrary to components, a connector changes its appearance during its life-cycle due to model transformations. (i) In platform independent models the explicit connector is an abstract representation of component interconnection, specifying properties of the interaction type. (ii) In platform specific models the explicit connector is transformed into a set of distributed fragments, which in total implement the functionality of that specific explicit connector. Connector fragments are deployed along with their associated components and are themselves composed structures made up of basic components. Any connectors that remain at the platform specific level after applying all transformations are implicit connectors, typically local procedure calls. (iii) At deployment- and finally at run-time the explicit connector is no longer visible. True components, representing the explicit connectors functionality, are deployed and executed.

Figure 2 depicts a connector fragment of connector C_2 from Figure 1 in a platform specific model. It consists of a (generated) interface adapter

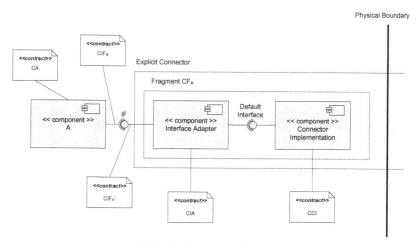

Fig. 2. Connector Fragment

component and a generic sender component. The two client-server connectors left over in this model are implicit local procedure calls and do not have to be transformed any further. In addition, Figure 2 shows various contracts associated with components and interfaces. These contracts can be used for a more detailed model verification of the constructed component architecture [7,8,9].

3   Middleware

As described in Section 1, the process of interaction in component architectures is typically handled by middleware. Middleware is an additional software layer, that is located between an application and the operating system and its communication stack. Component middleware additionally manages the life-cycle of components, handles their interaction, no matter if local or distributed, and provides infrastructural services for the components.

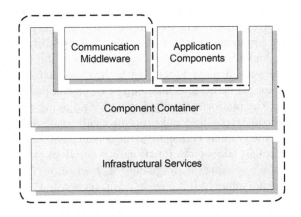

Fig. 3. Component Middleware

Figure 3 shows a simplified version of component middleware (encircled by the dashed line) that meets the requirements of distributed embedded systems applications. In safety critical applications of that domain, components have to be bound statically, instantiation occurs only at initialization time and communication channels are statically predefined. The component middleware therefore consists only of a (i) *component container* that hosts all components and manages their life-cycle and instantiation and of (ii) *infrastructural services* that are required by the container but may also be provided for the components. All components residing within the container may interact locally. To enable remote interaction with a distributed system, the component middleware finally includes (iii) *communication middleware*.

As one can see, we located the communication middleware inside the component container. This is because we synthesize communication middleware from the application model and basic building blocks, that are simple components themselves. This process of synthesis is presented within the next section.

4   Middleware Synthesis

Explicit connectors as introduced in Section 2 encapsulate the implementation of the specific interaction process of the connectors' type. Application components interact via their interfaces, that are linked by explicit connectors. No other means of interaction are allowed within component models. This consequently implies, that the set of all explicit connectors of a component architecture covers the architecture's communication requirements. By transforming the application's models, explicit connectors are transformed into connector fragments, that themselves are transformed into various components like senders, receivers, protocol handlers or interface adapters. By eliminating redundant building blocks within the transformed architecture, the total set of required communication related components, the component middleware, can be calculated and deployed.

We are going to demonstrate the synthesis of communication middleware with a simplified example. This is no real world application but it will show the basic idea of our approach without exceeding this paper's page limit.

4.1   Application Specification

As first step in creating an application with a model driven process we define the component architecture in a platform independent model by assembling all application components within a UML 2.0 component diagram. All *required interfaces* are connected to the corresponding *provided interfaces* by specifying explicit connectors.

Figure 1 depicts the platform independent model of our demonstrator application. Component A requires services provided by component B by a procedural interface and provides data to component C by a sender-receiver interface.

The second step in developing our application is to specify the deployment scenario. For our example we deploy the application components on two distinct ECUs. Component A will be deployed on the first ECU while components B and C will be deployed on the second one. Note that explicit connectors at this stage of development are considered to be abstract entities, consisting of fragments, and therefore must not be included in the deployment specification.

4.2   Connector Transformation

By defining the component architecture and its deployment, all information required to transform the connectors into components becomes available. The so called *connector transformation* selects the proper connector implementations (e.g. a remote procedure call connector) from a connector library. It connects identified connector fragments to the application components. To do so, it generates interface adapter components to match all interfaces and modifies the

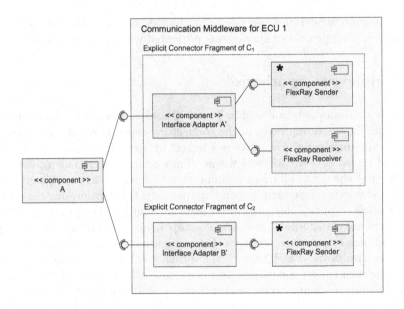

Fig. 4. Example Transformation for ECU 1

deployment specification to cover the inserted components, that in total represent the connectors' functionality.

Figure 4 depicts the result of the *connector transformation* for the example application part deployed on ECU 1. One can see, that the application component A now is connected to two connector fragments, fragment C_1 for a procedure call connector to component B and fragment C_2 for a data emitter connector to component C. Generated interface adapters map the application component's interface to the generic building blocks from the connector library. The used procedure call connector is a remote one, as the connected application components do not reside within the same address space—remember that we deployed them on two distinct ECUs)—and uses a receiver to get results back from component B.

All five components within the outer box are not application components and deal with interaction related issues only. Together, they assemble the custom tailored communication middleware for ECU 1.

4.3   Architectural Optimization

In a final step, the generated component architectures have to be optimized to eliminate redundant elements and meet additional system constraints like contractually specified uniqueness of specific components (e.g. singletons).

In our example, the sender components, both labeled with (*), redundantly exist within our middleware. To optimize the middleware's size these redundancy can be eliminated by sharing the sender between both connector fragments.

4.4 Summary

Component based software engineering is a well established engineering paradigm for distributed embedded systems. However, state-of-the-art component models often rely on heavy-weight component- and communication middleware to keep application components small and simple. The middleware's resource usage is a crucial factor in resource constrained systems. We provided an overview on how to synthesize the communication part of a component middleware from application models in order to keep it small. To enable this approach, we introduced explicit connectors as first class architectural entities at model level. In addition, we described how their implementation is performed by composing basic building blocks, stored within a connector library. By following our approach, the set of all explicit connectors within the application's platform independent model will be transformed into a custom tailored, light-weight communication middleware for each deployment node. Moreover, methods of verification for component architectures can be applied not only to the application but also to parts of its middleware.

Acknowledgements

This work has been partially funded by the FIT-IT [embedded systems initiative of the Austrian Federal Ministry of Transport, Innovation, and Technology] and managed by Eutema and the Austrian Research Agency FFG within project COMPASS [6] under contract 809444.

References

1. Szyperski, C.: Component Software: Beyond Object-Oriented Programming. Addison-Wesley, Reading (1998)
2. Meyer, B.: The grand challenge of trusted components. In: ICSE 2003, pp. 660–667 (2003)
3. Heineman, G.T., Councill, W.T. (eds.): Component-Based Software Engineering. Addison-Wesley, Reading (2001)
4. Nierstrasz, O., Tsichritzis, D. (eds.): Object-Oriented Software Composition. Object-Oriented Series. Prentice-Hall, Englewood Cliffs (1995)
5. AUTOSAR (Automotive Open System Architecture), http://www.autosar.org/
6. COMPASS (Component Based Automotive System Software), http://www.infosys.tuwien.ac.at/compass.
7. Schreiner, D., Göschka, K.M.: Explicit connectors in component based software engineering for distributed embedded systems. In: van Leeuwen, J., Italiano, G.F., van der Hoek, W., Meinel, C., Sack, H., Plášil, F. (eds.) SOFSEM 2007. LNCS, vol. 4362, pp. 923–934. Springer, Heidelberg (2007)
8. Reussner, R.H., Schmidt, H.W.: Using parameterised contracts to predict properties of component based software architectures. In: Ivica Crnkovic, S.L., Stafford, J. (eds.) Workshop on Component-based Software Engineering Proceedings (2002)
9. Plasil, F., Visnovsky, S.: Behavior protocols for software components. IEEE Trans. Software Eng. 28(11), 1056–1076 (2002)

Streamlining Feature-Oriented Designs

Martin Kuhlemann, Sven Apel, and Thomas Leich

School of Computer Science, University of Magdeburg, Germany
{kuhlemann,apel,leich}@iti.cs.uni-magdeburg.de

Abstract. Software development for embedded systems gains momentum but faces many challenges. Especially the constraints of deeply embedded systems, i.e., extreme resource and performance constraints, seem to prohibit the successful application of modern and approved programming and modularization techniques. In this paper we indicate that this objection is not necessarily justified. We propose to use refinement chain optimization to tailor and streamline feature-oriented designs to satisfy the resource constraints of (deeply) embedded systems. By means of a quantitative analysis of a case study we show that our proposal leads to a performance and footprint improvement significant for (deeply) embedded systems.

1 Introduction

Software engineering for embedded systems is an emerging but challenging area. Embedded systems are characterized by strict resource constraints and a high demand for variability and customizability. Since it is reasonable to expect that embedded systems will gain further momentum, it is crucial to adopt modern programming techniques that suffice in other domains. In this paper we focus on the level of code synthesis to deal with the strict resource constraints of deeply embedded systems and to enforce modularity at the same time. Previous attempts failed with respect to the specific resource constraints of deeply embedded systems [1, 2], e.g., micro-controlers in ubiquitous computing or cars [3, 4, 5]. Hence, low-level languages as C or assembly languages are still used to develop embedded software [6].

To overcome this handicap we propose to use feature-oriented programming (FOP) [7] to build modular system product lines. FOP decomposes software into features that are increments in program functionality. Features are applied to a program in an incremental fashion representing development steps. This way, a conceptually layered design is created. FOP has the potential to improve modularity and thus reusability and customizability of product lines [7, 8, 9, 10] – both are important for the domain of embedded systems.

Unfortunately, an FOP design imposes an overhead in execution time and code size due to its layered structure. That is, the control flow is passed from layer to layer, which causes performance penalties. The layered structure demands more program code, which results in larger binaries. Both – performance and footprint penalties – are not acceptable for deeply embedded systems.

M. Lumpe and W. Vanderperren (Eds.): SC 2007, LNCS 4829, pp. 168–175, 2007.
© Springer-Verlag Berlin Heidelberg 2007

To be able to employ feature-oriented techniques without any penalties in performance and footprint, we suggest to streamline feature-oriented designs, i.e., the layered structure to minimize runtime and footprint overhead. Specifically, we show how refinement chain optimization of FOP designs (by super-imposing refinements) leads in the best case to a performance improvement of 40% and a footprint saving of 59%, compared to the unoptimized variants; the worst case still results in 5% footprint reduction and acceptable performance characteristics. Streamlining FOP designs makes them suitable for the specific constraints of embedded systems, without sacrificing their benefits in modularity and structuring.

Compared to inlining techniques, that have been used for years, we argue that streamlining of feature-oriented designs does not rely on heuristics but it exploits the stepwise development methodology of FOP.

2   Feature-Oriented Programming

FOP studies the modularity of features in product lines, where a feature is an increment in program functionality [7]. *Feature modules* realize features at design and implementation levels. The idea of FOP is to synthesize software (individual programs) by composing feature modules developed for a whole family of programs. Typically, features modules refine the content of other features modules in an incremental fashion. Hence, the term refinement refers to the set of changes a feature applies to others. Stepwise refinement leads to conceptually layered software designs.

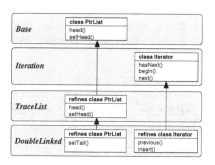

Fig. 1. A stack of feature modules for a linked list product line

The key point of FOP is the observation that features are seldomly implemented by single classes; often a whole set of *collaborating* classes defines and contributes to a feature [7, 11, 12, 13, 14, 9, 10]. Classes play different *roles* in different *collaborations* [14]. FOP aims at abstracting and explicitly representing these collaborations.

A feature module is a static component encapsulating fragments (roles) of multiple classes so that all related fragments are composed consistently. Figure 1 depicts a stack of four feature modules of a product line of linked lists (*Base, Iteration, TraceList, DoubleLinked*) in top down order. Typically, a feature crosscuts multiple classes (e.g., *PtrList, Iterator*). White boxes represent classes and their refinements; on the code level refinements are prefixed by the *refines* keyword; gray boxes denote feature modules; filled arrows refer to refinement.

3 Synthesizing Programs

In this section we explain two ways to synthesize programs out of a given FOP design, *mixin layers* and *jampacks*.

Mixin Layers. Mixin layers transform refinement chains inside an FOP design *one-to-one* to class hierarchies [13]. Each refinement is implemented as sub-class to a base-class. Thus, for n features there are potentially n sub-classes for a given class. For our list example, the mixin layer approach results in three generated classes for *PtrList* and in two classes for *Iterator* (Fig. 2) – all named based on the features they belong to and on their base-class.

Methods are extended by overriding. An extended method is invoked by an explicit *super*-call. For example, the method *setHead* of class *PtrList_Base* is overridden by the method *setHead* of class *PtrList_Trace*. The latter calls the former by using *super*. This way, the base method is extended (refined) instead of being replaced (Fig. 3).

Client code is aware only of the most specialized refinement, that is the final class, which appears due to inheritance as super-imposition of the overall refinement chain (e.g., *PtrList* in Fig. 2). It embodies all methods defined in its super-classes.

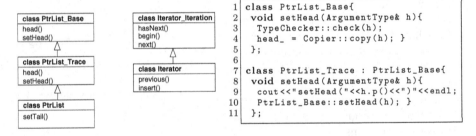

Fig. 2. Mixin layer implementation of the linked list product line

Fig. 3. Method extension in mixin layers through inheritance and overriding

It is reasonable to expect that the high number of generated classes as well as the additional level of indirection for all extended methods impose a performance and footprint overhead, significant for embedded systems. Therefore, it seems that mixin layers confirm the objections against modern software engineering practices (cf. Sec. 4).

Jampacks. Jampacks are a generative programming technique, which flattens the refinement chains of FOP architectures [7]. Classes are merged with all their refinements. That is, all fields and methods of a class and its associated refinements are merged into *one* final class. Fields with the same names are considered errors; methods with the same name are merged preserving their overriding semantics; the position of the *super*-call in the refining method defines how to merge both method bodies.

Figure 4 shows the flattened refinement chains of our list example. The methods and fields of *PtrList* and *Iterator* and their refinements are merged into two final classes. The body of the method *setHead* is a composition of the original method of layer *Base* and a refining method of layer *TraceList* (Fig. 5).

class PtrList
head()
setHead()
setTail()

class Iterator
hasNext()
begin()
next()
previous()
insert()

```
1  class PtrList{
2    void setHead(ArgumentType& h){
3    cout<<"setHead("<<h.p()<<")"<<endl;
4    TypeChecker::check(h);
5    head_ = Copier::copy(h); }
6  };
```

Fig. 4. Jampack composition of a list   **Fig. 5.** Method extension in jampacks

With respect to embedded systems it is reasonable to expect that jampacks reduce the overhead of FOP's layered designs. This conjecture has never been examined since FOP was intended for large-scale program synthesis where the assumed positive effects do not carry weight. Since jampacks decrease the number of classes by factor n for $n-1$ refinements (in our example, 2 instead of 5) and avoid additional call indirections and virtual methods (since there is no inheritance hierarchy and no method overriding), they may improve the runtime and footprint characteristics significantly for deeply embedded systems.

4   Evaluation

4.1   Experimental Setup

We implemented and analyzed a product line of linked lists, borrowed from [15, 16]. The product line consists of 26 features (containing 12 classes and 27 refinements), that can be combined in numerous ways.

For our experimental evaluation we used FEATUREC++[1] (v.0.3), a C++ language extension and a compiler for FOP [17]. FEATUREC++ supports mixin layer and jampack composition.[2]

FEATUREC++ transforms FOP code into native C++ code. As underlying C++ compiler we used the Microsoft[TM]C/C++ compiler (13.10.3077 for 80x86) with different optimization levels: no optimization (/Od), minimal space (/O1) and maximum optimization (/Ox). The footprint measurements were obtained from the object files to minimize side effects of wrapper and loader code. We used *strip* to cut the symbol tables and *size* to determine the footprint (GNU

---

[1] http://wwwiti.cs.uni-magdeburg.de/iti_db/fcc/
[2] Merging method bodies automatically is under development.

strip/size 2.17.50 20060817). As platform we used an AMD Athlon™64x2 Dual Core Processor 3800+. The performance measurements were obtained using assembler instrumentation code[3] and a small application that instantiated and used the generated lists. For each experiment we warmed up the cache by several dummy runs preceding the actual measurement. The results are given in averaged and rounded numbers over 100 runs each.

4.2 Mixin Layers vs. Jampacks

The footprint and performance measurements were performed for ten distinct list configurations with different sets of features: 3, 4, 5, and 13 to 19 features. These ten configurations were synthesized by mixin layer and jampack composition.

Footprint Measurements. The results of the footprint measurements are shown in Table 1. The footprint is proportional to the number of included features. Figure 6 depicts the footprints for the ten configurations (ten pairs of bars), each implemented by jampack (respective left bar) and mixin layers (respective right bar). Each bar shows the results for three optimization levels (superimposed bars).

It is remarkable that the maximally optimized jampack configuration (/Ox) with 19 features has a smaller footprint than the mixin-based configuration with 3 features. In the best case (19 features), jampacks achieve a footprint reduction of up to 59%; in the worst case (3 features) of about 5% after all.

Figure 7 reveals that jampack composition performs best at optimization level /O1. The overhead of adding individual features using jampacks is significantly smaller than for mixin layers.

A dummy implementation that includes 100 features all forwarding a request to its super layer induces a footprint benefit of 96% by using jampacks (not depicted).

Table 1. Footprints (*byte*) of ten configurations using different optimization levels

# features	/Od		/O1		/Ox	
	mixin	jampack	mixin	jampack	mixin	jampack
3	1400	1336	563	517	1096	1016
4	1592	1464	667	584	1032	888
5	1704	1528	717	586	1176	920
13	2024	1560	1073	599	1800	936
14	2136	1608	1114	606	1864	952
15	2440	1752	1141	637	2168	984
16	2524	1788	1186	659	2252	1004
17	2588	1788	1223	659	2348	1004
18	2732	1852	1277	676	2492	1052
19	2860	1916	1337	673	2636	1068

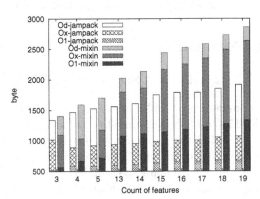

Fig. 6. Footprints (# features)

---

[3] Basically, we read out the *rdtsc* register.

Performance Measurements.
Figure 8 depicts the results
of the performance measurements for three composed methods (*insert, setID, setTail*). In
all but one case the mixin
layer variants are slower than
their jampack counterparts –
once they are equal. In the
ideal case jampacks reduce the
execution time by 40% (19
features, method *insert*). Furthermore, the runtime overhead
increases as the number of fea-

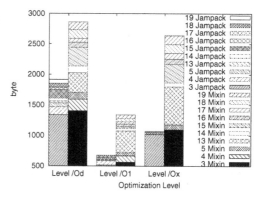

Fig. 7. Footprints (optimization level)

tures increases. Figure 9 visualizes the data of Table 8. It bares the conjecture
that the difference between jampacks and mixin layers is proportional to the
number of features. The runtime overhead of mixin layers induced by additional
features is caused by indirections in the program control flow and newly introduced members, such as constructors for every refined class. By using jampacks
we merged classes and their refinements and thus we removed several steps of
computation.

# features	insert		setID		setTail	
	mixin	jampack	mixin	jampack	mixin	jampack
3	396	381			91	91
4	495	448			118	111
5	495	463			145	119
13	664	487			140	122
14	703	536			139	119
15	809	590			187	149
16	827	570	97	91	185	148
17	859	571	102	91	185	146
18	925	571	144	126	185	146
19	945	561	165	139	189	146

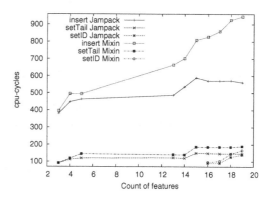

Fig. 8. Average runtime measurements (*cpu-cycles*) of three
methods

Fig. 9. Average execution time (*cpu-cycles*) of 100
iterations for jampack and mixin variants

Our dummy implementation of 100 features performs with runtime benefits
of 95% by using jampacks (not depicted).

5 Related Work

Several studies have shown the penalties of advanced programming techniques
such as C++ [18, 19, 20]. Different approaches, e.g., Embedded C++, omit

expensive language features to cope with the extreme resource constraints of deeply embedded systems. But this limits the programmer structuring software appropriately.

Reducing the cost of indirect or virtual function calls generated by a C++ compiler is addressed in [18, 21, 22]. In [23] a source code transformation based on aspect-oriented programming is proposed that uses domain-specific information for optimizing object-oriented design patterns, e.g., the replacement of dynamic casts by static code. Class hierarchy analysis and optimization of object-oriented programs aim in eliminating dynamically-dispatched message sends automatically [20].

Our approach of streamlining FOP designs does not limit the programmer in modularizing software in terms of OOP. It introduces a domain-independent, automatic optimization step. This way, the programmer profits from the advanced capabilities of FOP (cf. [9, 10]) without scarifying performance or a minimal footprint.

Martin et al. and others aim to use a mapping to model constraint resources in UML [24, 6]. This is orthogonal to our approach of optimizing code since it is possible to model FOP using UML. Thus, their proposals can be integrated into FOP implementations as well.

Lee et al. analyzed the OSGi framework to manage different software components [25]. They propose to use an architecture based on services to compose different embedded devices, i.e., software components, but do not focus mainly on the development of the single embedded system.

6   Conclusion

By means of a case study, we have shown how FOP can be tailored to the domain of embedded systems. While FOP is known to improve modularity, reusability, and customizability of product lines, we demonstrate how to streamline FOP's layered designs to minimize footprint and maximize performance.

We observed that jampack composition outperforms mixin layers with regard to performance (40%) and footprint (59%). The worst case still results in 5% footprint improvement and does not burden the execution time. We believe that the reduction of footprint and runtime overhead opens the door to adopt FOP to the domain of embedded systems.

References

[1] Driesen, K., Hölzle, U.: The Direct Cost of Virtual Function Calls in C++. In: OOPSLA (1996)

[2] Calder, B., Grunwald, D., Zorn, B.: Quantifying Behavioral Differences Between C and C++ Programs. Journal of Programming Languages 2(4) (1994)

[3] Lohmann, D., Schröder-Preikschat, W., Spinczyk, O.: On the Design and Development of a Customizable Embedded Operating System. In: Proceedings of the International Workshop on Dependable Embedded Systems (2004)

[4] Beuche, D., Guerrouat, A., Papajewski, H., Schröder-Preikschat, W., Spinczyk, O., Spinczyk, U.: The PURE Family of Object-Oriented Operating Systems for Deeply Embedded Systems. In: ISORC (1999)

[5] Beuche, D., Meyer, R., Schröder-Preikschat, W., Spinczyk, O., Spinczyk, U.: Streamlined PURE Systems. In: Bertino, E. (ed.) ECOOP 2000. LNCS, vol. 1850, Springer, Heidelberg (2000)

[6] Sangiovanni-Vincentelli, A., Martin, G.: Platform-Based Design and Software Design Methodology for Embedded Systems. IEEE Design & Test of Computers 18(6), 23–33 (2001)

[7] Batory, D., Sarvela, J., Rauschmayer, A.: Scaling Stepwise Refinement. IEEE Transactions on Software Engineering 30(6) (2004)

[8] Prehofer, C.: Feature-Oriented Programming: A Fresh Look at Objects. In: ECOOP (1997)

[9] Apel, S., Leich, T., Saake, G.: Aspectual Mixin Layers: Aspects and Features in Concert. In: ICSE (2006)

[10] Apel, S., Batory, D.: When to Use Features and Aspects? A Case Study. In: GPCE (2006)

[11] Mezini, M., Ostermann, K.: Variability Management with Feature-Oriented Programming and Aspects. In: ACM SIGSOFT FSE, ACM Press, New York (2004)

[12] Lieberherr, K., Lorenz, D.H., Ovlinger, J.: Aspectual Collaborations: Combining Modules and Aspects. The Computer Journal 46(5) (2003)

[13] Smaragdakis, Y., Batory, D.: Mixin Layers: An Object-Oriented Implementation Technique for Refinements and Collaboration-Based Designs. ACM Transactions on Software Engineering and Methodology 11(2) (2002)

[14] VanHilst, M., Notkin, D.: Using Role Components in Implement Collaboration-based Designs. In: OOPSLA (1996)

[15] Czarnecki, K., Eisenecker, U.W.: Generative Programming: Methods, Tools, and Applications. Addison-Wesley, Reading (2000)

[16] Apel, S., Kuhlemann, M., Leich, T.: Generic Feature Modules: Two-Dimensional Program Customization. In: ICSOFT (2006)

[17] Apel, S., et al.: FeatureC++: On the Symbiosis of Feature-Oriented and Aspect-Oriented Programming. In: GPCE (2005)

[18] Calder, B., Grunwald, D.: Reducing Indirect Function Call Overhead in C++ Programs. In: POPL (1994)

[19] Calder, B., Grunwald, D., Zorn, B.: Quantifying Behavioral Differences Between C and C+ + Programs. Journal of Programming Languages 2(4) (1994)

[20] Dean, J., Grove, D., Chambers, C.: Optimization of Object-Oriented Programs Using Static Class Hierarchy Analysis. In: ECOOP (1995)

[21] Pande, H.D., Ryder, B.G.: Static Type Determination for C++. In: C++ Conference (1994)

[22] Aigner, G., Hölzle, U.: Eliminating Virtual Function Calls in C++ Programs. In: ECCOP (1996)

[23] Friedrich, M., et al.: Efficient Object-Oriented Software with Design Patterns. In: GCSE (2000)

[24] Martin, G., Lavagno, L., Louis-Guerin, J.: Embedded UML: a merger of real-time UML and co-design. In: Proceedings of the ninth international symposium on Hardware/software codesign (CODES) (2001)

[25] Lee, C., Nordstedt, D., Helal, S.: Enabling Smart Spaces with OSGi. IEEE Pervasive Computing 2(3), 89–94 (2003)

Requirements for Reusable Aspect Deployment

Bruno De Fraine and Mathieu Braem

System and Software Engineering Lab, Vrije Universiteit Brussel
Pleinlaan 2, 1050 Brussels, Belgium

Abstract. The aspect-oriented paradigm aims to modularize concerns that crosscut traditional abstraction boundaries. In the AOSD community, there is an increasing interest in the development of reusable implementations of typical crosscutting concerns, such as security, synchronization, profiling, etc. To employ a reusable aspect in a concrete application, deployment logic has to be written that specifies where and how to apply the new behavior, and how the interaction with the base application and the other aspects in the system is organized. We have analyzed the means for the specification of such deployment logic in current aspect-oriented technologies and have identified a number of issues regarding its reuse, its dynamic invocation and its integration with the rest of the system. With the knowledge gained, we propose important first steps towards better support for the specification of deployment logic.

1 Introduction

Aspect-Oriented Software Development [1] is a recent software engineering paradigm that aims at providing a better separation of concerns. One of the most popular mechanisms offered by AOSD approaches is that of *pointcuts* that define points in the execution of the program (called *join points*), and *advices* that specify additional behavior to apply at these join points. As such the implementation of so-called *crosscutting concerns* can be specified in a modular way; a *weaver* will automatically integrate the behavior with the rest of the application.

In the AOSD community there is an increasing interest in the development of reusable aspect implementations. Some approaches such as Aspectual Components [2] and JAsCo [3] explore the integration with Component-Based Software Development (CBSD) [4], a paradigm that aims at constructing software by combining highly-reusable components in a plug-and-play fashion. To develop aspects according to this view, it must be possible to specify aspects as reusable and independent entities. Additionally, aspect reuse is also gaining interest in the context of more traditional AOP approaches, in order to provide *aspect libraries* with reusable implementations of recurring crosscutting concerns, e.g. [5,6,7,8].

The usage of reusable aspects necessarily involves a separate deployment step during which the aspects are configured for a concrete application at hand. The deployment logic specified to this end can take various forms, e.g. explicit

M. Lumpe and W. Vanderperren (Eds.): SC 2007, LNCS 4829, pp. 176–183, 2007.
© Springer-Verlag Berlin Heidelberg 2007

or implicit *connector* entities, or XML deployment descriptors. As aspects are used more fundamentally in the development of an application, we observe that the current means for the specification of deployment logic become insufficient. Compared to the general programming language, they do not offer a comparable level of reusability, flexibility and expressiveness, even though the deployment might specify logic that is equally crucial to the application.

The main contribution of this paper is an in-depth analysis of the different functions that constitute the deployment of a reusable aspect, and of the deployment specification properties pressed for by the intensive usage of reusable aspects throughout the implementation of a software application. In addition, we present important first steps towards AOP language facilities that meet the identified requirements.

We proceed as follows. Section 2 introduces a small case study and identifies the different responsibilities of deployment logic in the context of this example. The case is also used as a running example in section 3, where we analyze the requirements for deployments in detail and demonstrate current shortcomings. Section 4 outlines first steps towards a solution and section 5 compares with related work in this area. Section 6 concludes the paper.

2   Representative Case Study

As a running example, we will use a small but representative case of functionality that prints an execution trace of the program on a given output handle. To present this example, we employ the AspectJ language [9], one of the first and best-known AOSD approaches. (The discussion is similar for other approaches, although a number of specific points are discussed in section 5.) An implementation of this tracing behavior as a reusable aspect in AspectJ is shown in listing 1. This aspect declares a pointcut that selects join points that expose an object as a context value (line 10), but no definition for this pointcut is given (i.e. the pointcut is left abstract). An advice (lines 12–14) specifies that, before entering these join points, a description of the exposed object has to be printed. The other members of the aspect manage the output stream to which the tracing messages can be sent. The aspect in listing 2 specifies a number of important pointcuts of the application. We place them in a separate aspect because we have the intention of sharing them between different aspects. The pointcut
selects the execution of *setter*-methods that belong to the class   . As the parameter, it exposes the   object on which the method is executed.

Listing 3 then provides an example of deployment logic for the
aspect. In the AspectJ language, deployment does not occur through a dedicated connector entity. Rather, a new aspect   is created that inherits from the generic aspect and provides an implementation for the abstract pointcut(s) from the parent to specify concrete program points. In our example, we employ the predefined pointcut   (line 2 in listing 3). Additionally, the deployment can control the creation and configuration of aspect instances. AspectJ stipulates that aspect instances cannot be created directly by the developer; they

Listing 1. AspectJ implementation of a generic tracing aspect

Listing 2. Independent specification of program pointcuts

are created implicitly by the runtime system, according to a number of predefined strategies. In this case, the declaration   (line 1) stipulates the creation of a single aspect instance[1]. To configure this instance with an appropriate output stream as it is created, we employ the argumentless constructor of the aspect (lines 4–6). Finally, the deployment also specifies a combination strategy that specifies how different aspects are to be combined when they advise the same join point. We specify that tracing should be executed before security checks (line 8), presumably deployed through the aspect   . AspectJ only supports ordering of advices; other approaches allow to express more advanced combinations of aspects such as exclusion or dependency.

In summary, the responsibilities of the deployment logic are: (i) it specifies the concrete program points where the behavior of a generic aspect has to be applied, (ii) it configures the (creation of) aspect instances and sets-up communication with the rest of the program, and (iii) it specifies an appropriate strategy for the combination with other aspects in the system, with whom the aspect might share join points. All of this logic is usually specific to the application where the

---

[1] Although singleton aspects are the default in AspectJ, we include the declaration here for clarity.

```
1
2
3
4
5
6
7
8
9
```

Listing 3. Logic for the deployment of tracing behavior

aspects are employed. It can therefore never be part of the specification of the reusable aspect.

3   Requirements and Identified Problems

In this section, we analyze the requirements for deployment facilities and present identified shortcomings in current approaches. We organize this discussion according to the possibilities for reuse, dynamic invocation and integration.

Reuse of Deployment Logic. Consider the case where we also want to add profiling behavior to the system in much the same way as we deployed the tracing behavior. We assume that a reusable profiling aspect similar to the tracing aspect of listing 1 is available. We want to apply it to the same program points as the tracing behavior, with the same instantiation, output stream and precedence order as was configured for that behavior. Although we can reuse the definition of the pointcut   from the aspect   , we have to duplicate the entire deployment logic from listing 3 in a new deployment aspect (presumably named   ). This code duplication is undesirable and impedes the maintenance of the software application, especially when one takes more complex deployments into account.

Dynamic Deployment. Most approaches only support the static deployment of aspects. In AspectJ for example, the application of a reusable aspect to a new set of program points requires the introduction of a (static) entity such as the   aspect, in which a concrete pointcut definition that selects these program points is provided. (This is the case even if we reuse an existing pointcut definition without modification, as in listing 3.) The dynamic deployment of aspectual behavior is prevented since the pointcut/advice pair must be provided statically. Imagine we identify a number of important sections in our program, for each of which we provide a pointcut in the   class to select it. If we want to enable and disable both tracing and profiling for each of these sections individually at runtime, we have to define an unwieldily large number of entities: for each of the sections one aspect that deploys tracing and one that deploys profiling. Each of these deployments would contain a pointcut with a dynamic condition that verifies whether that particular part is activated.

Although we imagine that it is possible to create a tool that assists the developer with the generation of these aspects, this remains a second-class solution. Furthermore, it still restricts some dynamic cases made possible by recent aspect-oriented implementation tools such as runtime weavers [10] or aspect-aware virtual machines [11,12]. For example, it remains impossible to refer to parts of the application whose concrete implementation is not known at compile-time, such as plugins that are dynamically loaded. Because the namespaces and type names of such plugins are only known at runtime, their code can only be influenced through very wide pointcuts that quantify over the entire application.

Base Program Integration. An aspect instance can store data between the different advice invocations that are triggered as join points are encountered while the program is executed. Within the context of one deployment, it is often desirable to set-up different aspect instances with separate state information. In AspectJ, aspect instances are always created automatically according to a number of pre-defined strategies, such as   ,   and   . However, as we argued in previous work [13], these predefined strategies cannot support even simple variations. Imagine that we want to deploy two instances of the tracing aspect instead of one: one that writes to the application log file and another one that writes to a personal log file of the user. To realize the creation of two aspect instances, we would have to write two singleton deployment aspects. Although the deployment logic of these two aspects could be shared in a common superaspect that inherits from   , the requirement to create a new entity for each instance is cumbersome and imposes static restrictions, as explained in the previous paragraph.

Furthermore, we often want the creation of aspect instances to be triggered by specific events in the execution. For example, writing tracing information to a user's personal log file is only relevant after a user has logged in. We would want an instance of the tracing aspect to be created on every login (and destroyed on logout), but predefined instantiation modes do not support this. In these cases the implicit instantiation also renders it very difficult to configure the aspect instances with appropriate program parameters. For example, in listing 3 we can obtain a reference to the (global) application log file with relative ease by accessing the static program members of the base program. However, in case of local information, such as the user's personal log file in a system where multiple users can be logged in simultaneously, this becomes significantly harder.

4   Towards Improved Facilities for Reusable Aspect Deployment

The deployment logic we have considered realizes aspectual behavior by employing reusable parts that specify different facets of the behavior. The main kinds of 'building blocks' are pointcuts, advices and combination strategies. As a basis for improved language facilities for reusable aspect deployment, we propose to organize deployment logic as procedures that employ these entities (or their instances) as *first-class values*. More concretely, this means that pointcuts, advices and combinations strategies are passable and returnable as parameters to and from pieces of deployment logic, and that the deployment logic can be dynamically invoked with these entities as runtime values.

We revisit each of the previously identified issues below, and discuss the implications of this solution in more detail.

Reuse of Deployment Logic. The ability to parametrize pieces of deployment logic enables to build abstractions that allow reuse of this logic. For example, when both tracing and profiling behavior have to be deployed in the same manner, we can define this common logic as a general deployment strategy that receives the aspect to deploy as a parameter. As such, it can be shared between the deployment of both concerns and implementation details can be hidden from their specifications. If pieces of deployment logic are also made extensible, individual variations can be specified in different deployment strategies that each extend the common case.

Dynamic Deployment. The required support for the dynamic deployment of aspects is met through the ability to invoke pieces of deployment logic with pointcuts, advices and combination strategies as runtime values. In case of our running example, the selective tracing of application parts could be realized by dynamically deploying combinations of predefined pointcuts and advices. Although a large number of combinations is possible, we can create them on demand. To further match the capabilities of recent weaver technology, it seems appropriate to also make pointcuts constructible at runtime, during the execution of the deployment logic. The reflective capabilities of the programming language could be employed to refer to specific program parts during the execution. As such, aspects can be deployed for program parts that are not known at compile-time.

One obvious difficulty of dynamic deployment, besides weaver technology, is that the treatment of a deployment by the compiler might provide certain static guarantees that we wish to uphold. For example, the AspectJ compiler will verify the compatibility between a pointcut and an advice in a deployment. We believe it is possible to maintain these static guarantees even when the deployment logic is executed dynamically, although this might require more advanced typing formalisms.

Base Program Integration. Because aspects often require a tight integration with the base program to realize their functionality, we propose to make it possible to link pieces of deployment logic to points in the execution of the main application. As such this logic is executed each time the execution of the application reaches one of these points. This makes it easier to accommodate for different variations in the instantiation of aspects, because aspect instances can be created explicitly by the developer, at the relevant events. It also greatly facilitates the configuration of these instances, because the relevant parameters for communication with the base program are often readily available at these points (e.g. a reference to the user and his log file is likely to be around in the code section that handles a login event).

5   Related Work

A number of existing approaches already address some of the issues regarding deployment logic that are raised in this paper.

On the one hand, the Caesar [14] language aims to provide better modularity on top of the pointcut/advice mechanism offered by AspectJ. It identifies reusable aspect bindings as one of its design goals and realizes this by installing a mixin-based inheritance mechanism between aspects. As such, reusable implementations and reusable bindings can be inherited independently by a deployment aspect. Furthermore, Caesar allows to instantiate aspects explicitly and the developer can combine the creation and configuration of aspect instances with the main program. The major drawback in comparison to our proposal however, is that every combination of an implementation and a binding must still be introduced statically; dynamic deployment (in the terminology of Caesar) refers to the ability to merely *activate* these combinations for a certain control flow, thread, etc. at runtime. Similarly, pointcuts are still static entities that cannot refer to parts of the application that are unknown at the time of compilation.

On the other hand, a number of aspect frameworks have been proposed both in an academic (e.g. Reflex [15], AspectS [16]) and industrial setting (e.g. JBoss AOP [17], AspectWerkz [18]). These approaches do not employ a dedicated language, and specify aspectual behavior through standard libraries (sometimes complemented with XML configuration files). Specifying deployment logic as regular code that employs a framework library has many potential advantages. E.g. the runtime APIs of JBoss AOP and AspectS allow changing pointcut and advice bindings, hence enabling dynamic deployment. By employing the already present abstraction mechanisms of the base programming language, reuse of deployment logic could be organized as well, however this possibility is seldom considered by most frameworks. Worse, pointcuts cannot always be separated from the deployment logic, hindering independent reuse. Another important problem is that frameworks do not offer the same static guarantees as the type systems of regular aspect languages that can depend on a dedicated compiler.

6   Conclusions

In this paper, we have analyzed the means for the specification of deployment logic for reusable aspects in current aspect-oriented approaches. When aspects are used for the implementation of fundamental parts of the application, we observe a number of issues regarding the reuse of deployment logic, its dynamic invocation and its integration with the rest of the system. We proposed a number of important steps towards a solution which is based on the notion of organizing deployment logic as procedures that employ reusable pointcuts, advices and combination strategies as first-class values. We are in the course of implementing this solution concretely as a part of the EcoSys [19] AOP framework. This framework specifically aims at providing the same static typing guarantees as provided by language-based approaches.

References

1. Kiczales, G., et al.: Aspect-oriented programming. In: Aksit, M., Matsuoka, S. (eds.) ECOOP 1997. LNCS, vol. 1241, pp. 220–242. Springer, Heidelberg (1997)
2. Lieberherr, K., Lorenz, D., Mezini, M.: Programming with Aspectual Components. Technical Report NU-CCS-99-01, CCS, Northeastern University, Boston, MA (1999)
3. Suvée, D., Vanderperren, W.: JAsCo: An aspect-oriented approach tailored for component based software development. In: [21] pp. 21–29
4. Szyperski, C.: Component Software: Beyond Object-Oriented Programming, 1st edn. Addison Wesley, Reading, Massachusetts, USA (1998)
5. Huang, M., Wang, C., Zhang, L.: Toward a reusable and generic security aspect library. In: De Win, B., Shah, V., Joosen, W., Bodkin, R. (eds.) AOSDSEC: AOSD Technology for Application-Level Security (2004)
6. Isberg, W.: AOP@Work: Check out library aspects with AspectJ 5. Technical report, IBM Developer Works (2006)
7. Pearce, D.J., Noble, J.: Relationship aspects. In: [20] pp. 75–86
8. Cunha, C.A.: Reusable aspect-oriented implementations of concurrency patterns and mechanisms. In: [20] pp. 134–145
9. Kiczales, G., et al.: An overview of AspectJ. In: Knudsen, J.L. (ed.) ECOOP 2001. LNCS, vol. 2072, pp. 327–353. Springer, Heidelberg (2001)
10. De Fraine, B., Vanderperren, W., Suvée, D., Brichau, J.: Jumping aspects revisited. In: Filman, R.E., Haupt, M., Hirschfeld, R. (eds.) Dynamic Aspects Workshop, pp. 77–86 (2005)
11. Bockisch, C., Haupt, M., Mezini, M., Ostermann, K.: Virtual machine support for dynamic join points. In: Lieberherr, K. (ed.) AOSD 2004. Proc. 3rd Int' Conf. on Aspect-Oriented Software Development, pp. 83–92. ACM Press, New York (2004)
12. Bonér, J., Vasseur, A., Dahlstedt, J.: JRockit JVM support for AOP, part 1. Technical report, BEA dev2dev (2005)
13. De Fraine, B., Vanderperren, W., Suvée, D.: Motivations for framework-based AOP. In: Open and Dynamic Aspect Languages Workshop (2006)
14. Ostermann, K., Mezini, M.: Conquering aspects with Caesar. In: [21] pp. 90–99
15. Tanter, É., Noyé, J.: A versatile kernel for multi-language AOP. In: Glück, R., Lowry, M. (eds.) GPCE 2005. LNCS, vol. 3676, pp. 173–188. Springer, Heidelberg (2005)
16. Hirschfeld, R.: Aspect-oriented programming with AspectS. In: Akşit, M., Mezini, M. (eds.) Net.Object Days 2002 (2002)
17. Burke, B., et al.: JBoss Aspect-Oriented Programming. Home page (2004), at
18. Bonér, J., Vasseur, A.: AspectWerkz: simple, high-performant, dynamic, lightweight and powerful AOP for Java. Home page (2004),
19. De Fraine, B., Vanderperren, W., Suvée, D.: Eco: A flexible, open and type-safe framework for aspect-oriented programming. Technical Report SSEL 01/2006 /a, VUB (2006),
20. Masuhara, H., Rashid, A. (eds.): Proc. 5th Int. Conf. on Aspect-Oriented Software Development AOSD 2006. ACM Press, New York (2006)
21. Akşit, M. (ed.): Proc. 2nd Int. Conf. on Aspect-Oriented Software Development AOSD 2003. ACM Press, New York (2003)

Aspect-Oriented Programming: Selecting and Exposing Object Paths

Mohammed Al-Mansari, Stefan Hanenberg, and Rainer Unland

University of Duisburg-Essen, Schützenbahn 70, 45117 Essen, Germany
{Mohammed.Al-Mansari,Stefan.Hanenberg,Rainer.Unland}
@icb.uni-due.de

Abstract. Aspects require access to the join point context in order to select and adapt join points. For this purpose, current aspect-oriented systems offer a large number of pointcut constructs that provide access to join point information that is *local* to the join point context, like parameters in method call join points. However, these systems are quite miserly with *non-local* information that cannot directly be derived from the local execution context. Recently, there have been some proposals that offer access to some kind of non-local information. One such proposal is the *path expression pointcut* that permits to abstract over *non-local object information*. Path pointcuts expose non-local objects that are specified in corresponding path expression patterns. In this paper, we show recurrent situations where developers need to access the whole *object paths*, and consequently, they add workarounds other than pointcut constructs to get the required accesses. Then, we present and study an extension to the path expression pointcuts to permit exposing the object paths and show how this extension overcomes the problem.

1 Introduction

Aspect-oriented programming aims to increase the modularity of software. This is achieved by features that are used to select points in the execution of the program and to adapt them. Pointcuts are the language constructs used for selecting these points, which are called *join points* [15]. The join point adaptation is achieved by the so-called advice. The selection and the adaptation of a join point depend on the characteristics of this join point.

These characteristics are called *join point properties* [1, 12] and are divided into two categories: Local and non-local join point properties depending on whether they are accessible and derivable from the join point context or not, respectively. For example, the current executing object at a method execution join point is considered a local join point property, which can be accessed with the this pointcut in AspectJ [15]. In general, current aspect-oriented systems offer several pointcut constructs that can be used to derive the local information of a join point. On the other hand, these systems provide only a small number of pointcut constructs that provide access to the non-local join points properties, like the call stack in languages such as Java and C++.

One intention of aspect-oriented systems is to provide pointcut languages that permit the developer to specify expressive pointcuts [26] where the join point selections

M. Lumpe and W. Vanderperren (Eds.): SC 2007, LNCS 4829, pp. 184–199, 2007.
© Springer-Verlag Berlin Heidelberg 2007

correspond to the developer's mental model [31]. This also implies that the available join point properties provided by an aspect-oriented system must suffice the developers' needs. In addition to that, the resulting aspects would be easier to maintain, more robust against changes, and contain no mixture between the pointcut and advice code. As a consequence, it has been pointed out by a number of researchers that there is a need for more pointcuts that offer abstractions over non-local properties [2, 22, 34]. However, none of these proposals provide abstractions over the non-local properties that are based on object information, for which we proposed the path expression pointcut [1] as an explicit construct.

In this paper we take a step forward by extending the path expression pointcut that allows aspects to access the whole object information in the matching paths. We motivate our proposal using two examples from the object persistence concern. These examples illustrate why we need to get not only object references from the whole path but also field information that establishes the relationships between these objects. This is achieved by exposing the whole non-local part of the object graph that is related to the join point to the aspect.

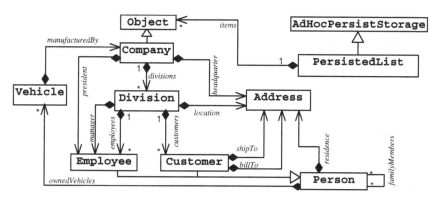

Fig. 1. Class diagram for the problem domain

The rest of the paper is organized as follows: In the rest of this section, we first describe the object model of an example that is used throughout the paper. Then for the purpose of self-containedness, we give a brief description on the current version of the path expression pointcut. In Sect. 2, we discuss two motivating examples and the problem statement. Section 3 presents the extension to the path expression pointcut. We talk about related works in Sect. 4. In Sect. 5 we discuss some issues regarding our proposal and its implementation. The paper is concluded in Sect. 6.

1.1 Example

Figure 1 shows a class hierarchy adopted from [16] for a company object model. The intention is to persist all company objects that are added to special containers called "persistent lists": Instances of PersistedList class that persist all contained objects. These objects are not prepared to be persistent; rather they become persistent at the time they are added to the lists. This persistence service is an ad-hoc functionality provided by the persistent lists in a similar way to *spontaneous containers* [28].

As Fig. 1 elaborates, each company has a number of divisions, a president and a headquarter address. Each division in turn has a manager, a number of employees, a number of customers and a location address. Customer (which we added) and Employee are subtypes of Person. Each person object is associated with a collection of vehicle objects. Finally, vehicle objects are associated with corresponding company objects by the relation manufacturedBy.

1.2 Path Expression Pointcut

The path pointcut traverses the current object graph in order to find paths that match a given path expression. A pointcut making use of a path pointcut picks out the join points where there exists at least one matching path. The general form is:

```
path(PathExpressionPattern);
```

For a detailed description of the syntax, please refer to Sect. 3.1 in [1]. Within path expression patterns may specify certain objects as source objects, target objects and intermediate objects of the paths. Moreover, the associations between objects can be specified by names. The path pointcut applies pattern matching mechanism by using the wildcards "*" and "/" to specify associations between objects along the path. The path pointcut is used to expose both local and non-local context from the join points and it can be used along with other pointcut designators by means of operators "&&", "||" and "!". For example, consider the following pointcut:

```
pointcut pc(Company c, Person p, Object o):
  path(c -*-> Employee p -/-> o) && set(* *) && target(o);
```

This pointcut picks out every set join point whose target is the object o and where there is at least one path between the objects c and o via p. The wildcard "*" in the path expression indicates that there is a direct relationship between c and p, whereas "/" indicates that there may be many objects on the path between these objects.

Like in AspectJ, the objects described in the path expression can be bound to the corresponding variables in the pointcut's header. Then the bounded objects are exposed from the join point context to the aspect context. According to the semantics of the path pointcut, the result of a path expression is a set of distinct valid parameter bindings rather than a set of matched paths.

For example, in Fig. 2, the path expression in the pointcut matches two paths: (com -headquarter-> addr) and (com -divisions-> div -location-> addr), however, the valid parameter bindings is only: (c=com, a=addr). Notice that there are two occurrences of the variable name a, once as a destination in the path expression and then it is used in the target pointcut. The path pointcut allows multiple occurrences of the same variable name in one or more path expressions and unifies these occurrences to be bound to the same value.

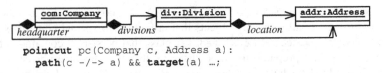

```
pointcut pc(Company c, Address a):
  path(c -/-> a) && target(a) ...;
```

Fig. 2. A Company instance has two references to the same Address instance

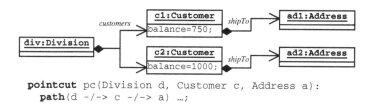

```
pointcut pc(Division d, Customer c, Address a):
   path(d -/-> c -/-> a) …;
```

Fig. 3. Two resulting paths between a division and an address are resolved to two bindings

A consequence of multiple parameter bindings is that the advice execution mechanism is modified to allow a single advice that is associated with the pointcut to be executed as many times as the size of the parameter bindings set.

For example, according to the pointcut of Fig. **3**, the resulting bindings are: (d=div, c=c1, a=ad1) and (d=div, c=c2, a=ad2). Hence, each single advice that is associated with this pointcut must be executed two times for each single binding. An important question is in which order these executions should be performed. For example, assume that there are two concurrent transactions, each updates one of the objects ad1 and ad2 and that the developer wants to run these concurrent changes in a descending order by customers balances. Since the balance of c2 is greater than that of c1, the advice must be executed first with the binding: (d=div, c=c2, a=ad2).

```
public boolean addrChg(Object[] o1, Object[] o2) {
   Customer cust1 = (Customer) o1[1];
   Customer cust2 = (Customer) o2[1];
   return cust1.getBalance() > cust2.getBalance();
}
pointcut pc(Div d, Customer c, Address a):
   set(* *)&& target(a)&& path(d -/-> c -/-> a) orderBy(this.addrChg);
```

Fig. 4. Possible ordering method specification

As a solution, we provide an extra construct, namely orderBy that is added to the path pointcut. It takes a name of the method containing the ordering code specified by the developer. The method is similar to the compare method of the Comparable interface in the Java API. For example, in the pointcut pc of Fig. **4**, the parameter of the orderBy is the name of the method addrchg whose signature has two array parameters of type Object each representing a single binding. The method extracts the second clement from both arrays, casts them to type Customer and returns the comparison result between their balance fields. When no orderBy clause is specified, then the order would be undefined.

2 Motivation

One of the important issues of object persistence is to ensure the isolation property of concurrently executing transactions by means of concurrency control approaches. The concept of locking data items is one of the main used techniques of the concurrency control. There are two main types of locks: Shared or exclusive, generally known as read and write lock respectively. In what follows, we will consider two locking policies in our motivating examples: The field-based locking policy and the cascading-version locking policy.

2.1 Example 1: Field-Based Locking

In the locking-based concurrency control of transactions literature, there is a large number of researchers discussing locking granularities [11], proposing techniques for fine-granularity locking [23, 27] and discussing the benefits and the effects of multiple locking granularities [29]. The granule of the data that can be locked is either the whole database, an extension of objects, an object or a field of an object [14]. Here, we focus on locking the fields of the object that are being changed so that multiple transactions can be executed on this object.

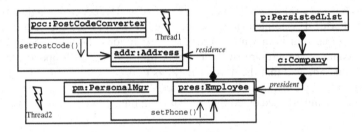

Fig. 5. Two separate concurrent transactions attempt to change the pres state

In Fig. 5, the Company instance c, which references the object pres, is added to the persistent list p. Hence, this company object and all objects in its closure are to be made persistent. Assume that we are interested in applying locking on the fields of the Employee object. Two separate concurrent threads attempt to update the state of the employee. Thread1 in pcc wants to change the postcode value of addr and Thread2 in pm attempts to change the phone field of the employee. In order to permit both threads to modify the employee object simultaneously, we should acquire separate write locks for the fields residence and phone rather than for the object pres.

In aspect-oriented terms, each update is a join point that should be selected since the employee object belongs to the persistent list p. The needed information is: the objects p and pres. The aspect then should acquire a write-lock for each field that is to be changed. Here, the needed information is the fields residence and phone.

The local relevant context at the join point in Thread1 is the object addr, and the local relevant context for Thread2 is the object pres. In Thread1, objects p and pres, in addition to the field name residence, are considered to be non-local, while in Thread2 the non-local relevant information is object p.

Consider the pointcut pc1 in Fig. 6, it selects all set join points where the target object e of type Employee is reachable from the persistent list p1. According to Fig. 5, pc1 selects the employee object pres due to the matching path: (p -> c -> pres), and the resulting bindings is: (p1=p, e=pres), which is exposed to the before advice. The advice gets the changed field by means of the reflective facilities in AspectJ and Java. Finally, the advice acquires the write-lock to the field phone of the object pres.

```
pointcut pc1(PersistedList pl, Employee e):
  set(* *) && target(e) && path(pl -/-> e);

pointcut pc2(PersistedList pl, Employee e, Object o):
  set(* *) && target(o) && path(pl -/-> e -/-> o);

before(PersistedList pl, Employee e): pc1(pl, e) {
  String fname = thisJoinPoint.getSignature().getName();
  Field field = ... // code to get the field by using its name and lock it
}
before(PersistedList pl, Employee e, Object o):
  pc2(pl, e, o) {
  // code for getting the field of e which is the beginning of the reference closure from e to o
}
```

Fig. 6. Using the path pointcut in the field locking example

The pointcut pc2 selects all set operations targeted to any object o that is reachable from the persistent list pl via object e. From Fig. 5, there is one matching path to the path expression pattern in pc2, i.e. (p -> c -> pres -> addr). Hence, this resulting binding is (pl=p, e=pres, o=addr), which provides the advice with the access to the non-local objects p and e in addition to the local object addr. The advice must acquire a write-lock for the dirty field residence, however, this field is not available for the advice since this information is non-local to the join point.

To get access to the non-local field information, developers implement work-arounds since this information cannot be accessed by using the available pointcut constructs. These solutions are complex, difficult to maintain and error-prone though. Moreover, the code does not reflect the join point selection and adaptation semantics.

2.2 Example 2: Cascading Version Locking

To solve the concurrency control problem, researchers also proposed a number of version-based locking policies [17, 21, 24]. In these policies, all transactions can grant shared read access to the object, and whenever a transaction attempts to update the state of the object, the application should check whether this update is performed on the right version of the object.

Version locking mechanisms use a so-called version (or write-lock) field that is added to every object and compare this field every time an update operation on the object is committed with the current value in the datastore. If they are equal, then the change is committed to the datastore, otherwise the change is disallowed and this indicates that the object must have been updated by another transaction. In the cascading version locking, the version field of all objects that reference the dirty object must be updated also.

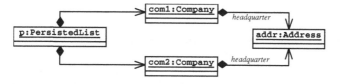

Fig. 7. A shared Address instance between two Company instances

As an example, consider the object graph in Fig. **7**. Two Company instances, com1 and com2, both referencing the same object addr. The Company instances are stored in the persistent list p. According to the version locking policy, any change to the addr will update the version field of addr as well as the version fields of its owner objects, i.e., com1 end com2. In our aspect, we want to be sure that the changed object is reachable from a persistent list. If so, the aspect should perform the dedicated version locking policy on the shared object. So, we use the following pointcut:

pointcut pc(PersistedList pl, Object o):

  set(* *) && **target**(o) && **path**(pl -/-> o);

A corresponding advice gets access to the binding (pl=p, o=addr), despite the fact that there are two different paths from p to addr. The advice will consider the changes in the Address object and update its version field. However, the corresponding version field of com1 and com2 are not modified yet. Such situations affect the data consistency. In order to overcome this problem, we must get access to all objects in each path from p to addr in order to modify their versions.

As mentioned in the first example, the only way currently available for the developer in conventional aspect-oriented systems is to apply introspective facilities of the language to traverse the entire reference path to get the required accesses. These kind of solutions are not trivial, error-prone and mostly not reusable.

In summary, both examples illustrate the need for more expressive path pointcuts. The first example motivates the need for exposing not only the non-local objects, but also the non-local field information. The second example motivates the need for exposing all objects in the matching paths instead of the distinct parameter bindings.

3   Extended Path Expression Pointcuts

In this section, we present an extension to the path expression pointcuts that overcomes the problems described above. We modified the syntax and the semantics of the pointcut construct so that the resulting paths are exposed to pointcuts and advice as a subgraph of the whole object graph. This subgraph is made local to the aspect and from its interface developers can extract the objects and their relationships.

3.1   Syntax and Semantics of the Path Pointcut

In order to get access to the resulting paths, we slightly modified the syntax of the path expression pointcut so that it has two parameters: The first parameter refers to an instance of type PEGraph (discussed in Sect. 3.2). The second parameter is the path expression pattern. The new syntax is:

path(PEGraph identifier, PathExpressionPattern).

The new model maintains the syntax specifications of the PathExpressionPattern discussed in [1]. The path pointcut calculates the path expression pattern against the current heap and adds all matching paths to a generated PEGraph object. When the evaluation process ends, the resulting PEGraph object is bound to the variable name identifier. The pointcut header must include this variable name as a parameter of type PEGraph. This parameter will be added to resulting parameter bindings being exposed to the pointcut and the associated advice.

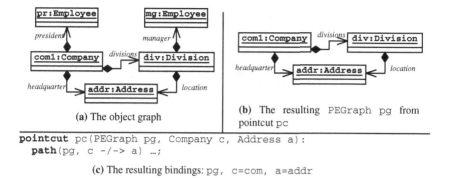

(a) The object graph

(b) The resulting PEGraph pg from pointcut pc

```
pointcut pc(PEGraph pg, Company c, Address a):
  path(pg, c -/-> a) …;
```

(c) The resulting bindings: pg, c=com, a=addr

Fig. 8. Two paths between a Company and an Address

As an example, consider the object graph in part (a) of Fig. **8**. There are two matching paths to the given expression in the path pointcut: (com -divisions-> div - location-> addr) and (com -headquarter-> addr). The evaluation of this path expression creates an object of PEGraph that consists of the subgraph in Fig. **8**-(b). This object is bound to the variable pg. Finally, as shown in part c), the pointcut pc resolves the parameter bindings (pg, c=com, a=addr).

The created PEGraph at a given join point depends also on the resolved bindings. That means each distinct parameter binding has its own corresponding PEGraph object, which ensures exposing only relevant information to the join point. The relevant information consists of the objects and their relationships that are included in the matching paths even if these paths contain cycles. Notice that in Fig. **8**-(b), the two Employee objects along with their referencing field information, i.e. president and manager, are excluded from the result of the path pointcut since this information is not relevant to the given path expression.

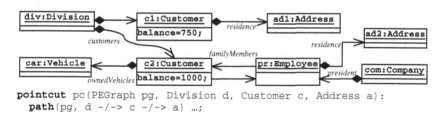

```
pointcut pc(PEGraph pg, Division d, Customer c, Address a):
  path(pg, d -/-> c -/-> a) …;
```

Fig. 9. Infinite number of paths between objects div and ad2

The presence of cycles in object graphs raises an important question regarding the termination of our pointcut construct. If a cycle appears in a matching path then it must be included in the resulting path graph. To guarantee the termination feature of the path pointcut, cycles should not be traversed more than once except when it is needed to traverse them again to fulfill the required set of bindings. Notice that we have to detect the cycles during the traversal of the object graph and have to add them to the resulting PEGraph if they occur in a matching path.

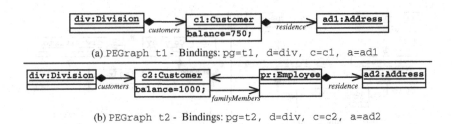

(a) PEGraph t1 - Bindings: pg=t1, d=div, c=c1, a=ad1

(b) PEGraph t2 - Bindings: pg=t2, d=div, c=c2, a=ad2

Fig. 10. Two PEGraph objects, each for a different bindings

Consider the collaboration diagram in Fig. **9**. According to the given path expression, there is one matching path from div to ad1 via c1, which constructs a temporary PEGraph object t1 that is bound to the variable pg. The resolved binding is: (pg=t1, d=div, c=c1, a=ad1) as shown in Fig. **10**–(a). On the other hand, there is an infinite number of matching paths from div to ad2 via c2 due to the presence of the cycle between the objects pr and c2. Suppose that the traversal algorithm visits div then c2 and finally reaches pr, if it selects to go through the edge labeled familyMembers then it will visit c2 again, detect the cycle, save all information (objects and relations) and finally will return back to pr and follow the other edge to the object ad2. At this point the traversal algorithm finds a matching path as well as a valid distinct bindings for d, c and a. The whole path along with the cycle will be put in a temporary PEGraph object t2 as in Fig. **10**–(b), and then the pointcut resolves the second binding: (pg=t2, d=div, c=c2, a=ad2). The pointcut evaluation stops afterwards since there are no more matching paths.

Last but not least, the new extension maintains the semantics of the advice execution in the first version of the path pointcut. Since the number of distinct resulting bindings is two in the last example, any advice associates with the pointcut pc executes two times. The ordering schema discussed in Sect. 1 also applies here. Hence, if the developer wants to run the advice first on the bindings that contains higher balance customers, then (s)he must define the same ordering method of Fig. **4** except that the index of the customer object in the binding is 2 instead of 1.

3.2 Path Expression Graph

As stated above, the result from the path pointcut is a subgraph of the whole object graph that contains only the information relevant to the selected join point. We said that this resulting graph will be assigned to an object of type PEGraph. The public interface of this data structure is illustrated in Fig. **11**.

Each node of the PEGraph is of type PENode and contains a reference to an object of a generic type, a list of outgoing edges and a list of incoming edges. The edge of the PEGraph is of type PEEdge, which has two methods: getRelatedNode to get the generic typed object that represents the related node to the owner node of this edge (i.e. the node at the other edge). The method getRelField returns the relation name. The graph object provides the ability to navigate from any given object either in a forward or in a backward manner. This is done by getting access to the current object of the PEGraph instance, and then accessing its related objects and referencing fields.

```
class PEGraph<Current, Next> {
  private Current current;
  private Next next;
  public Current getCurrent();
  public Next getNext();
  public List<PENode> getNextNodes();
  public List<PEEdge> getNextEdges();
  public boolean setCurrentObject(Current current);
}
class PENode<T> {
  public T getObject();
  public List<PEEdge> getOutEdges();
  public List<PEEdge> getInEdges();
}
class PEEdge<T> {
  public PENode<T> getRelatedNode();
  public String getRelField();
}
```

Fig. 11. The public interface of the PEGraph

The PEGraph interface cannot be mutated other than setting the current object field of the PEGraph class by using the method setCurrentObject. It is possible to set the current node by passing a reference to a specific object or a given PENode. The methods getNextNodes, getNextEdges and getNext are used to traverse through the PEGraph. It should be mentioned that the object and field information returned from these methods is obtained from the resulting path expression graph. Other object information from the whole object graph that is not related to the selected join point could be accessed from the object that is associated with the PENode. The method getCurrent returns the current object as a PENode, which can be used to get the object being associated with this node directly with the help of method getObject.

This representation is making use of generic types, which allow developers to use the type information they know, either directly or from the PEGraph object, without casting. For example, consider the following pointcut specification:

```
pointcut pc(PEGraph<PENode<Division>, PEGraph<PENode<Customer>>> pg,

            Division d, Customer c): path(pg, d -*-> c) ...;
```

Here, the source of any matching path is specified to be of type PENode<Division>. Hence the following is type-safe:

```
Division myDiv = pg.getCurrent().getObject();
```

We try to make it as easy as possible for the developer to query over the dynamic object information that is relevant to the join point. Of course, there is a complexity overhead in our representation of the PEGraph, however, this is significant from the developer's point of view since it needs less effort to reason about type information (as compared to performing reflective operations and casting operations).

3.3 Field-Based Locking Example Revisited

We use the new path pointcut in the pointcuts pc1 and pc2 as shown in Fig. **12**. According to the object graph in Fig. **5**, the path expression in pointcut pc1 matches the path: (p -items-> c -president-> pres). The PEGraph object pg will contain this path and it will be exposed to the advice along with the bindings

```
pointcut pc1(
   PEGraph<PENode<PersistedList>, PEGraph<Object, Object>> pg,
   PersistedList pl, Employee e):
   set(* *) && target(e) && path(pg, pl -/-> e);

pointcut pc2(
   PEGraph<PENode<PersistedList>, PEGraph<Object, Object>> pg,
   PersistedList pl, Employee e, Object o):
   set(* *) && target(o) && path(pg, pl -/-> e -/-> o);

before(
   PEGraph<PENode<PersistedList>, PEGraph<Object, Object>> pg,
   PersistedList pl, Employee e, Object o):
   pc2(pg, pl, e, o) {
   pg.setCurrentObject(e);
   List<String> dirtyFields = pg.getNextFields();
   for(String dfn: dirtyFields) {
      // get the field from the object e and acquire a write-lock for it ...
   }
}
```

Fig. 12. The PEGraph object is used in the path pointcut in pc1 and pc2

(pl=p, e=pres). The associated advice would adapt the join point as shown in the motivating example since the pres object and the field phone is local information to the join point. It must be noted that the aspect maintains the PersistedList objects from which the traversing process begins.

When applying the pointcut pc2 to the collaboration diagram in Fig. 5, the only matching path is: (p -items-> c -president-> pres -residence-> addr) that represents the resulting PEGraph object pg. This object along with the objects p, pres and addr are exposed to the associated before advice in the figure. The first line of the advice sets the current object of the pg to e, which is the variable bound to the Employee object pres. The second line gets all fields of the current object pres that are available in the pg graph and puts the result in the array dirtyFields. The rest of the advice is the code responsible for iterating through the list elements and acquiring a write-lock for each. The only available field according to the resulting path graph in pg is the field residence of the object pres.

3.4 Version-Based Locking Example Revisited

As in the last section, the extended path pointcut provides us with access to the required non-local information in the example: First, the persistent list object that contains the changed object, second, all objects in all reference paths from the persistent list to its contained changed object.

The following pointcut is making use of the path pointcut construct:

```
pointcut pc(PEGraph<PENode<PersistedList>, PEGraph<Object, Object>>
pg, PersistedList pl, Object o):
   set(* *) && target(o) && path(pg, pl -/-> o);
```

With respect to Fig. 7, the resulting paths from this pointcut are: (p -items-> com1 -headquarter-> addr) and (p -items-> com2 -headquarter-> addr). These paths construct the part of the object graph that will be exposed to the advice as illustrated in Fig. **7**. This subgraph contains the information relevant to the set join point on the address object, that is, all objects that are referencing the changed object addr. The pointcut pc resolves one parameter binding: (p1=p, o=addr), which is exposed to the advice, which will be executed just once.

Since the whole reference paths are exposed to the advice, performing the cascading version locking would be trivial. The only thing developers have to do inside the advice is backward traversing the nodes of the pg object after setting the current object of the pg to point to addr. They can easily update the version fields of all traversed objects in order to apply the cascading version locking. Note that although the paths in this example are of length 2, this algorithm is useful for any length of the reference path where there is a guarantee to get access to all owner objects of the current object.

4 Related Work

Path expressions, first introduced in [5] to synchronize the operations on data objects, then became central ingredient of object-oriented query languages such as [10, 16, 33]. The W3 Consortium introduced the XPath language [6] in order to address parts of an XML document [4]. In our work, we study the benefit of the application of path expressions in increasing the expressiveness of pointcut languages in addressing object relationships at runtime and providing aspects with access to this information.

Adaptive programming (AP) [19, 20] and strategic programming (SP) [18] provide interesting notions similar to the path expressions. They provide the developer with traversal control by the help of so-called traversal strategies and traversal schemes, respectively. The idea behind the aspect versions of AP and SP is that the advice is executed whenever the visitor component visits an object that belongs to a path that matches the given traversal. This is in contrast to the path pointcut that participates in the selection of the join point and exposes the matching object paths as well.

A lot of research effort is done to provide access to the non-local join point properties. Some works cover the importance of selecting and adapting the join points based on execution trace matching. Stateful aspects [8, 34] define conditions based on finite state transitions to trigger advice executions on a protocol sequence of join points. Other trace-based solutions have been discussed in [2, 9, 35]. Data flow pointcuts [22] solve the problem of non-locality of data flow information at the join point. The context-aware aspects [32] provide means to access information that is associated with certain contexts that are currently available or occur in the past. Another well-known example of accessing the non-local call stack at the join point is the cflow pointcut in AspectJ. However, all these proposals neither point to nor solve the problem of non-local join point properties that are based on object information.

Some works already discussed the need for expressive join point models that reflect the mental model of the developer [31]. Moreover, expressive pointcuts increase the modularity [26] and are robust to absorb any changes to the application features and compositions. The authors in [26] followed their previous remark about pointcuts that access dynamic properties of the program [3] by implementing the Alpha language whose pointcuts are Prolog queries over a database consisting of different semantic models of the program execution. In our proposal we have to keep small parts of the current heap at a given join point. In contrast to logic-based pointcuts, the path pointcut relies on traversing the heap to get relevant object information in a form of paths. Alpha predicates can be used to compose pointcuts that represent the notion of path pointcuts, however, these compositions may result in complex pointcut definitions that can be avoided by using the path pointcut. Moreover, one of the main goals of our proposal is to apply the path expressions technique to AOP as an explicit construct and to discuss the effects of this integration and how to resolve them.

In association aspects [30], a new pointcut designator is introduced to AspectJ, namely `associate`, which is used to associate extended per-object aspect instances to a group of objects. The authors point to the need for multiple executions of the advice in the associated aspect instances. This multiple advice execution corresponds to our approach, however, they do not give a clear specification of the order in which these executions run such as what we have proposed in this paper.

5 Discussion

Objects graphs are directed and may contain cycles, which is a source of complexity since there is a infinite number of matching paths to a given path expression in such structure. We can minimize this complexity by considering some restrictions, e.g., finding paths in the object graph that contain a cover to the needed bindings. This can be achieved using any of the efficient algorithms to detect cycles in directed object graphs and stop traversing through these cycles. For example, the time complexity of Floyd's cycle-finding algorithm [7] is $O(V)$, where V is the number of nodes in the graph. Moreover, this guarantees the termination of the path evaluation process.

Depending on the path expression, there are different situations of complexity. If the source and the target objects of the path expression are specified, then the problem is minimized to the single-pair shortest path, which is faster than the cases where one or both objects are not know. The running time is ranging from $O(V \lg V + E)$ to $O(V^2 \lg V + VE)$ or even to $O(V^3)$ in the worst case for finding all paths between any two objects [7], where V and E are the number of nodes and edges of the object graph respectively. In fact this complexity also depends on the algorithm being used and the type of the object graph. For example, in sparse graphs, where E is much less than V^2, Johnson's algorithm runs faster than the Floyd-Warshall algorithm.

The here proposed extension for the path pointcut maintains the same ordering schema of the multiple advice executions at a given join point. I.e., the developers are asked to define their own ordering rules in a separate method. Following our argument about the rationale behind this design choice in [1], we still believe that it is not difficult to define reasonable ordering methods that ensure the termination.

One important issue when dealing with the object graphs in persistence systems is how these systems manipulate the collection objects. Most persistence systems consider these objects as second-class objects, e.g., [13]. When two objects are sharing a second class object then each will have its own copy of this shared object so the changes in one copy will not be observed by the other owner object. Consequently, there must be a clear definition of how to represent these objects in the resulting PEGraph from a path pointcut. For simplicity purposes, we ignore this issue in this paper and treat items of the collection individually.

6 Conclusion

In this paper, we continue our argumentation about the need for abstractions in aspect-oriented systems that provide access to the non-local join point context. The motivating examples show the need to access non-local join point context that is not only based on objects but also on the relationships between these objects. Our examples cover some recurrent situations that occur when applying well-known locking policies in object persistence systems in an aspect-oriented manner. We have considered two such policies, field-based locking and cascading version locking mechanisms. For the first policy, we illustrate the need for accessing the non-local field information to apply the desired locking. In the second case, we show the need for getting the whole resulting paths instead of getting access to some objects in the path.

Then we describe our solution to such problems as an extension for the path expression pointcut [1]. The new extension provides access to the whole part of the object graph that is related to the join point and that is constructed from the matching paths. This subgraph is exposed then by the path pointcut to the aspect. Then we discuss some issues related to the extension. These include the public interface of the constructed subgraph that the developers can use to reason about objects and their relationships inside their aspects. We give our arguments about this representation. Then we discuss various aspect-oriented programming concepts and how the path pointcuts influence them with the help of some illustrative examples.

In the last section we present a general discussion about our proposal and some of its weaknesses. We suggest some possible ideas how to minimize the effects of these problems. These points are the focus of our future work.

Our experience with the path expression pointcuts shows a reasonable number of cases that require access to non-local object relationship information in persistence systems. However, we expect that path pointcuts have a large impact on increasing the expressiveness of pointcut languages. The reason for this is the flexibility of the path pointcut to express the mental model of the developers upon the role of object relationships in join point selection.

References

1. Al-Mansari, M., Hanenberg, S.: Path Expression Pointcuts: Abstracting over Non-Local Object Relationships in Aspect-Oriented Languages. In: NODe, Erfurt, Germany. LNI, vol. P-88, pp. 81–96 (2006)
2. Allan, C., Augustinov, P., Christensen, A.S., Hendren, L., Kuzins, S., Lhoták, O., de Moor, O., Sereni, D., Sittampalam, G., Tibble, J.: Adding Trace Matching with Free Variables to AspectJ. In: OOPSLA, San Diego, California, pp. 345–364. ACM Press, New York (2005)
3. Bockisch, C., Mezini, M., Ostermann, K.: Quantifying over dynamic properties of program execution. In: 2nd Dynamic Aspects Workshop, Chicago, Illinois, pp. 71–75 (March 2005)
4. Bray, T., Paoli, J., Sperberg-McQueen (eds.): Extensible Markup Language (1998), Available online http://www.w3.org/TR/REC-XML
5. Campbell, R., Habermann, A.: The Specification of Process Synchronization by Path Expressions. In: Goos, G., Hartmanls, J. (eds.). LNCS, vol. 16, pp. 89–102 (1974)

6. Clark, J., Derose, S. (eds.): XML Path Language (XPath), version 1.0 (1999), Available online http://www.w3.org/TR/Xpath
7. Cormen, T., Leiserson, C., Rivest, R., Stein, C.: Introduction to Algorithms, 2nd edn. The MIT Press and McGraw-Hill (2001)
8. Douence, R., Fradet, P., Südholt, M.: Composition, Reuse and Interaction Analysis of Stateful Aspects. In: AOSD, Lancaster, UK, pp. 141–150 (March 2004)
9. Douence, R., Fradet, P., Súdholt, M.: Trace-based aspects. In: Filman, R.E., Erlad, T., Clarke, S., Aksit, M. (eds.) Aspect-oriented Software Development, pp. 201–217. Addison-Wesley, Reading (2005)
10. Frohn, J., Lausen, G., Uphoff, H.: Access to Objects by Path Expressions and Rules. In: VLDB, Santiago, Chile, pp. 273–284 (September 1994)
11. Gray, J., Lorie, R., Putzolu, G., Traiger, I.: Granularity of Locks in a Large Shared Data Base. In: VLDB, pp. 428–451 (1975)
12. Hanenberg, S.: Design Dimensions of Aspect-Oriented Systems. PhD dissertation. Duisburg-Essen University (October 2005)
13. Jordan, D., Russell, C.: Java Data Objects, 1st edn., O'Reilly Media (2003)
14. Kemper, A., Moerkotte, G.: Object-Oriented Database Management: Applications in Engineering and Computer Science. Prentice-Hall, Englewood Cliffs (1994)
15. Kiczales, G., Hilsdale, E., Hugunin, J., Kersten, M., Palm, J., Griswold, W.G.: An overview of AspectJ. In: Knudsen, J.L. (ed.) ECOOP 2001. LNCS, vol. 2072, pp. 327–353. Springer, Heidelberg (2001)
16. Kifer, M., Kim, W., Sagiv, Y.: Querying Object-Oriented Databases. In: SIGMOD Conference 1992, pp. 393–402 (1992)
17. Kim, H., Park, S.: Two Version Concurrency Control Algorithm with Query Locking for Decision Support. In: ER Workshops 1998, pp. 157–168 (1998)
18. Lämmel, R., Visser, E., Visser, J.: Strategic Programming Meets Adaptive Programming. In: AOSD, Boston, USA, pp. 168–177. ACM Press, New York (2003)
19. Lieberherr, K., Lorenz, D.: Coupling Aspect-Oriented and Adaptive Programming. In: Filman, R.E., Erlad, T., Clarke, S., Aksit, M. (eds.) Aspect-oriented Software Development, pp. 145–164. Addison-Wesley, Reading (2005)
20. Lieberherr, K., Patt-Shamir, B., Orleans, D.: Traversals of Object Structures: Specification and Efficient Implementation. In: ACM TOPLAS, pp. 370–412 (2004)
21. Lin, W., Nolte, J.: Basic Timestamp, Multiple Version Timestamp, and Two-Phase Locking. In: VLDB, pp. 109–119 (1983)
22. Masuhara, H., Kawauchi, K.: Dataflow pointcut in aspect-oriented programming. In: Ohori, A. (ed.) APLAS 2003. LNCS, vol. 2895, pp. 105–121. Springer, Heidelberg (2003)
23. Mohan, C., Haderle, D.: Algorithms for Flexible Space Management in Transaction Systems Supporting Fine-Granularity Locking. In: Jarke, M., Bubenko, J., Jeffery, K.G. (eds.) EDBT 1994. LNCS, vol. 779, pp. 131–144. Springer, Heidelberg (1994)
24. Mohan, C., Pirahesh, H., Lorie, R.: Efficient and Flexible Methods for Transient Versioning of Records to Avoid Locking by Read-Only Transactions. In: SIGMOD Conf. 1992, pp. 124–133 (1992)
25. Orleans, D., Lieberherr, K.: DJ: Dynamic Adaptive Programming in Java. In: The 3rd Intel Conf on Metalevel Arch. and Separation of Crosscutting Concerns, pp. 73–80 (September 2001)
26. Ostermann, K., Mezini, M., Bockisch, C.: Expressive pointcuts for increased modularity. In: Black, A.P. (ed.) ECOOP 2005. LNCS, vol. 3586, pp. 214–240. Springer, Heidelberg (2005)

27. Panagos, E., Biliris, A., Jagadish, H., Rastogi, R.: Fine-granularity Locking and Client-Based Logging for Distributed Architectures. In: EDBT, pp. 388–402 (1996)
28. Popovici, A., Alonso, G., Gross, T.: Spontaneous Container Services. In: Cardelli, L. (ed.) ECOOP 2003. LNCS, vol. 2743, pp. 29–53. Springer, Heidelberg (2003)
29. Ries, D., Stonebraker, M.: Effects of Locking Granularity in a Database Management System. ACM Transaction of Database Systems 2(3), 233–246 (1977)
30. Sakurai, K., Masuhara, H., Ubayashi, N., Matsuura, S., Komiya, S.: Association aspects. In: AOSD, Lancaster, UK, pp. 16–25. ACM Press, New York (2004)
31. Stein, D., Hanenberg, S., Unland, R.: Expressing Different Conceptual Models of Join Point Selections in Aspect-Oriented Design. In: AOSD, Bonn, Germany, pp. 15–26. ACM Press, New York (2006)
32. Tanter, E., Gybels, K., Denker, M., Bergel, A.: Context-Aware Aspects. In ETAPS Software Composition, Vienna, Austria, LNCS, pp.227-242 (March 2006)
33. Van den Bussche, J., Vossen, G.: An Extension of Path Expressions to Simplify Navigation in Object-Oriented Queries. In: DOOD, pp. 276–282 (1993)
34. Vanderperren, W., Suvée, D., Cibrán, M.A., De Fraine, B.: Stateful aspects in JAsCo. In: ETAPS Software Composition, Edinburgh, Scotland. LNCS, pp. 167–181 (April 2005)
35. Walker, R., Viggers, K.: Implementing protocols via declarative event patterns. In: ACM SIGSOFT Intel. Sym. on Foundations of Soft. Eng., vol. FSE-12, pp. 159–169 (2004)

Debugging Aspect-Enabled Programs

Marc Eaddy[1], Alfred Aho[1], Weiping Hu[2], Paddy McDonald[2], and Julian Burger[2]

[1] Department of Computer Science
Columbia University
New York, NY 10027
{eaddy,aho}@cs.columbia.edu
[2] Microsoft Corporation
One Microsoft Way
Redmond, WA 98052
{weipingh,paddymcd,julianbu}@microsoft.com

Abstract. The ability to debug programs composed using aspect-oriented programming (AOP) techniques is critical to the adoption of AOP. Nevertheless, many AOP systems lack adequate support for debugging, making it difficult to diagnose faults and understand the program's composition and control flow. We present an *AOP debug model* that characterizes AOP-specific program composition techniques and AOP-specific program behaviors, and relates them to the AOP-specific faults they induce. We specify debugging criteria that we feel all AOP systems should support and compare how several AOP systems measure up to this ideal.

We explain why AOP composition techniques, particularly dynamic and binary weaving, hinder source-level debugging, and how results from related research on debugging optimized code help solve the problem. We also present Wicca, the first dynamic AOP system to support full source-level debugging. We demonstrate how Wicca's powerful interactive debugging features allow a programmer to quickly diagnose faults in the base program behavior or AOP-specific behavior.

1 Introduction

We use the term *debuggability* to mean the ability to diagnose faults in a software system, and to improve comprehension of a system, *by monitoring the execution of the system*. Many debugging techniques exist, including source-level debugging, *printf*-style debugging, assertions, tracing, logging, and runtime visualization.

The ability to debug aspect-enabled programs is important for many reasons. The interaction of aspects with a system introduces new fault types and complicates fault resolution [2]. Programmers rely on debugging to diagnose these faults and perform post-mortem analyses. Debugging is also an important tool for program comprehension. Aspect functionality can drastically change the behavior and control flow of the base program, leading to unexpected behavior [2] and resulting in the same complexity that multi-threaded programs are notorious for. Debugging provides a way to demystify these intricacies and better understand the composed program.

M. Lumpe and W. Vanderperren (Eds.): SC 2007, LNCS 4829, pp. 200–215, 2007.
© Springer-Verlag Berlin Heidelberg 2007

Aspect-oriented programming (AOP) [28] is still an emerging field with many different techniques for aspect specification, composition, and integration. Along with tool support, debugging support serves as an indicator of AOP maturity [17, 32]. Commercial software developers are hesitant to adopt aspect-oriented software development practices or ship AOP-enabled products that are difficult to debug and service [2, 17, 24, 25].

Debugging is no substitute for *aspect visualization* [17] and testing. Indeed they are complementary: aspect visualization provides the ability to predict aspect behavior; testing provides a process for automatically detecting anomalies; and debugging provides a way to manually detect, diagnose, and fix anomalies and to better understand program behavior.

The outline and contributions of this paper are as follows:

- We argue that debugging aspect-enabled programs is more difficult and possibly more important, than debugging conventionally composed programs.
- We present a general model for discussing debugging aspect-enabled programs. The model includes a classification of AOP-specific composition techniques and AOP-specific program behaviors, and a fault model. We define the properties of an ideal AOP debugging solution, including support for *debug obliviousness* and *debug intimacy*. (§2)
- We evaluate several current AOP systems as to how well they support AOP debugging. (§3)
- Since many AOP systems employ source or binary code transformations, we consider how this affects *source-level debugging*, and present solutions suggested by related research on debugging optimized code. (§4)
- We present Wicca, our dynamic AOP system that employs a novel weaving strategy to provide full source-level debugging, and is the first dynamic AOP system to do so (§5). We present the results of a debugging experiment using Wicca that demonstrates its unique AOP debugging capabilities. (§6)

2 A Debug Model for AOP

Our AOP debug model has five components: a classification of AOP-specific composition techniques (*weaving strategies*), a classification of AOP-specific program behaviors (*AOP activities*), a fault model, a definition for debug obliviousness, and a set of debugging criteria.

2.1 A Classification of Weaving Strategies

The AOP-specific composition technique, i.e., *weaving strategy*, used by an AOP system has a strong impact on its debuggability. Weaving is classified as either *invasive* or *noninvasive*, depending upon whether or not it performs a transformation of the base program code to enable aspect functionality. Invasive systems are further classified into *source weavers* and *binary (byte-code or machine-code) weavers*. Noninvasive systems are classified by whether they use a *custom runtime environment* or *interception*. Figure 1 depicts how the different dimensions of the weaving strategies are related.

During *source weaving* (the solid line in Figure 1), aspects are woven into the program by performing a source-to-source transformation, usually by transforming the abstract syntax tree representation of the program. The woven source is then compiled to create the final program. Because the aspect code is woven directly into the source code, it is possible to perform full source-level debugging on the aspect code using standard debuggers.

A downside of *binary weaving* (the dashed line in Figure 1) is that debug information may be invalidated by the weaving process or unavailable for injected code [2, 25]. Furthermore, companies like Microsoft have based their technical support on the assumption that an executable file and its associated attributes (date, size, checksum, and version) are fixed. Invasive weaving breaks that assumption.

Extensions to the runtime environment (the dotted line in Figure 1), e.g., AOP-enabled virtual machines and call interception plug-ins, enable aspect functionality noninvasively, i.e., without modifying the base program. Unfortunately, aspect-related behavior that is implemented in the extension may be difficult to debug.

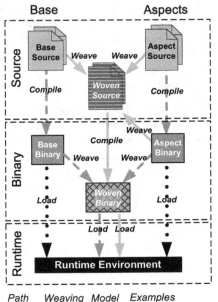

Path	Weaving Model	Examples
⟶	Source-level weaving	AspectJ,Wiccav1
⇢	Binary weaving	AspectJ, AspectWerkz, Wicca v1
⋯▶	Custom runtime or Interception	Steamloom

Fig. 1. The relationships between different AOP weaving strategies

2.2 A Classification of AOP Activities

An *AOP activity* is any program behavior that occurs either inside the base program or inside some AOP infrastructure in support of a concept from the AOP semantic model. We use the AspectJ semantic model [27] as our reference. Table 1 categorizes the AOP activities that we have gathered from studying a wide-variety of AOP systems. Some activities, such as advice execution, map naturally to AspectJ-like language semantics, while others are common implementation approaches for supporting those semantics. Different AOP systems may combine or omit some activities. For the purposes of this paper, to qualify as an AOP system the only required activity is *advice execution*, which corresponds with the definition in [13].

We do not attempt to classify all AOP-related behavior. The level of granularity chosen is designed to be widely applicable while at the same time able to differentiate AOP systems based on their varied debug capabilities. The terminology is general enough to apply to other advanced techniques for the separation of concerns, including multi-dimensional separation of concerns (Hyper/J), composition filters, adaptive programming, and subject-oriented programming.

Table 1. AOP activities that programmers would like to be able to debug

Activity	Purpose	Examples
Dynamic aspect selection	Determines at runtime which aspects apply and when.	Dynamic residue (if, instanceof, and cflow residue left over by dynamic cross-cuts) [4, 21]. Can involve runtime reflection or calls into the AOP system. Includes join point context reification [18].
Aspect instantiation	Instantiates or selects aspect instances to fulfill deployment/scoping semantics [21].	"Per" deployment semantics [21], instance-level advising, and aspect factories.
Aspect activation	Alters control flow to execute advice and provides access to join point context.	Advice method call, inlined advice code, runtime interception [31], dynamic proxies [7], and trampolines [29].
Advice execution	Execution of the advice body.	Inlined code, method call
Bookkeeping	Maintains additional AOP dynamic state.	Thread-local stack for cflow pointcuts [21].
Static scaffolding	Static modifications to the program's code, type system, or metadata.	Introductions needed to support intertype declarations, per-clause aspects, mixins, and closures. Code hoisting. [7, 21]

2.3 Fault Model

Each of the AOP activities in Table 1 introduces the possibility for new types of faults that were absent from the base program. Alexander et al. [2] specified a fault model for AOP that classified the new types of faults that AOP introduces that are distinct from the fault models of object-oriented and procedural programming languages. These AOP fault types were later extended by Ceccato et al. [8]. We build upon their work by generalizing and consolidating some of these fault types, by adding two of our own (*object identity errors* and *incorrect join point context*), and by associating the fault types with the AOP activities that may exhibit them.

Incorrect pointcut descriptor or advice declaration – A pointcut does not match a join point when expected, or the advice type (e.g., before, around), pointcut type (e.g., call, execution) or deployment type (e.g., "per" semantics) are incorrect. *Exhibited by activities*: dynamic aspect selection, aspect instantiation, and aspect activation.

Incorrect aspect composition – Multiple aspects that match the same join point are executed in the wrong order. *Exhibited by activities*: dynamic aspect selection, aspect instantiation, and aspect activation.

Failure to establish expected postconditions or preserve state invariants – Advice behavior or AOP activity causes a postcondition or state invariant of the base program to be violated. *Exhibited by activities*: advice execution. However, this fault can be caused by a faulty implementation of any AOP activity.

Incorrect focus of control flow – A pointcut that depends on dynamic context information, e.g., the call stack, does not match a join point when expected. The *cflow* and *if* pointcut types are examples. *Exhibited by activities*: dynamic aspect selection, aspect activation, and bookkeeping.

Incorrect changes in control dependencies – Advice changes the control flow in a way that causes the base program to malfunction. For example, adding a method override changes the dynamic target of a virtual method call. *Exhibited by activities*: aspect activation, advice execution, and static scaffolding.

Incorrect changes in exceptional control flow – Exceptions that are thrown or handled differently than they were in the base program may cause new unhandled exceptions to be thrown or prevent the original exception handlers from being called. *Exhibited by activities*: dynamic aspect selection, aspect activation, and bookkeeping.

Object identity errors – Type modifications (intertype declarations) or proxies break functionality related to object identity such as reflection, serialization, persistence, object equality, runtime type identification, self-calls, etc. *Exhibited by activities*: static scaffolding.

Incorrect join point context – The join point context available to a piece of advice is incorrect due to faulty context binding or reification. *Exhibited by activities*: dynamic aspect selection, aspect activation, and advice execution.

This list can be extended to include more fault types. The main idea is that AOP activity can introduce new types of faults that need to be debugged. We measure the debuggability of an AOP system by how easy it is to diagnose these faults. However, we will see in the next section that debuggability is at odds with the programmer's desire to remain oblivious of AOP activities.

2.4 Debug Obliviousness and Intimacy

When debugging an aspect-enabled program, the goal of *debug obliviousness* is to maintain a view of the program *as if no weaving has taken place*. Obliviousness is the primary goal for debugging optimized programs [20] as well as programs that use software dynamic translation [29] because these transformations preserve the semantics of the original program. Despite the relative importance attached to this goal [15], we are aware of no AOP system that fully supports obliviousness during debugging. The only alternative is to debug the original (non-aspect-enabled) program. However, the original program may not be available, or may require some aspects to function correctly.

Debug obliviousness is difficult to attain for invasive AOP systems because the debugger cannot distinguish between (untangle) the aspect and base program code [19]. Noninvasive systems, on the other hand, hide most aspect-related behavior by default. They still need to inform the debugging process, however, so that control flow changes related to aspect execution are also hidden. Otherwise, stepping through source code in the debugger results in unexpected jumps into aspect code. Complete obliviousness will not be possible in cases where the program's join points are entirely bypassed, for example, when *around* advice does not invoke the original join point.

Debug obliviousness becomes a liability when trying to diagnose a fault introduced by the AOP system. In this situation, we desire *debug intimacy*, the converse of debug obliviousness.

2.5 Properties of an Ideal Debugging Solution

An ideal AOP debugging solution will support debugging of all AOP activity when required or desired, and complete obliviousness otherwise. The properties of an ideal debugging solution for AOP are

(P1) *Idempotence* – Preservation of the base program's debug information. Idempotence ensures that whatever debug information was available before aspects were added to the base program is also available after. Noninvasive systems do not modify the original program at all. AspectJ and our Wicca system are examples of invasive systems that use source and binary weaving and ensure the debug information is maintained.

(P2) *Debug obliviousness* – The ability to hide AOP activity during debugging so programmers only see the base program's behavior and code.

(P3) *Debug intimacy* – The ability to debug all AOP activity including injected and synthesized code.

(P4) *Dynamism* – The ability to enable/disable aspects at runtime. When a fault occurs, the process of elimination can be used to rule out specific aspects.

(P5) *Aspect introduction* – The ability to introduce new aspects, e.g., debugging and testing aspects, in an unanticipated fashion. An example of this is *dynamic aspect introduction* that allows aspects to be introduced without restarting.

(P6) *Runtime modification* (also called *edit-and-continue*) – The ability to modify base or aspect code at runtime, e.g., to quickly add a *printf* statement, enable tracing, or try out a bug fix, without restarting. This is useful for interactive debugging and for diagnosing hard-to-reproduce bugs.

(P7) *Fault isolation* – The ability for the debugger to automatically determine if a fault lies within the base code, advice code, or some other AOP activity code. Invasive weavers may invalidate the traditional assumption that library boundaries establish ownership since AOP-related code or metadata, possibly written by a third party, is intermingled with the base program [19].

3 An Evaluation of the Debuggability of Existing AOP Systems

In Table 2, we show the results of our evaluation of a representative sample of AOP systems based on our ideal debugging properties.

Static AOP. All the Java byte-code weavers satisfy the idempotence property, because they maintain the debug information of the original program when weaving.

Table 2. AOP debuggability comparison matrix. Our system, Wicca, is shown in bold

AOP Tools & Systems	Idempotence	Debug intimacy	Debug obliviousness	Dynamism	Aspect introduction	Runtime modification	Fault isolat./repud.
AOP.NET	✓	O		✓			
AOP-Engine		O		✓	✓		
Arachne	✓			✓	✓		
AspectJ	✓	O					
AspectWerkz	✓	O	¤	✓			
Axon	✓	O	¤	✓			
CaesarJ	✓						
CAMEO	✓	✓					
CLAW		O		✓			
EAOP	✓	O	¤	✓	✓		
Handi-Wrap	✓			✓	✓		
Hyper/J	✓	✓					
JAsCo		O	¤	✓	✓		
nitrO		O		✓	✓		
Wicca v1	✓	✓		✓	✓	✓	
PROSE v2	✓	O	¤	✓	✓		
SourceWeave.NET	✓	✓					
Steamloom	✓	O	¤	✓	✓		
Wool	✓	O	¤	✓	✓		

✓- Fully supported
O- Partial *advice execution* debugging supported
¤- Partial obliviousness supported

Java stores debug information inside the class file, alongside the class definition and byte code. The debug information is co-located with the class file, and its format is well documented, improving the likelihood that byte-code rewriters will propagate it correctly.

For Windows executables, debug information is stored in a separate program database (PDB) file that becomes invalid when the executable is transformed. Ideally, the transformation process would update the debug information but this is a very complex process. Our Wicca system is the only .NET byte-code weaver (that we are aware of) that updates the debug information, which is made possible by the Microsoft Phoenix backend compiler framework[1].

Dynamic AOP. *Invasive* dynamic AOP systems transform the base program by using dynamic proxies [7] or by injecting join point stubs (also called hooks or trampolines)

---

[1] http://research.microsoft.com/phoenix

at all potential join points [6, 9, 16]. These systems typically support debugging of advice execution. Aspect selection, instantiation, or activation logic, however, may be implemented inside the *dynamic AOP infrastructure* [19] and may be difficult to debug. This difficulty makes it hard to understand the woven program's control flow and diagnose problems related to aspect ordering and selection ("Why didn't my aspect run?") [2]. In addition, hook injection may invalidate the base program's debug information (violating the idempotence property), which will result in a confusing or misleading debugging experience.

Noninvasive dynamic AOP systems use a custom runtime environment (e.g., JRockit[2], Steamloom [19], PROSE [31]) or take advantage of interception services (e.g., .NET Profiler API [16], Java debugger APIs [3, 31]), to provide AOP functionality without transforming the base program. These systems have the benefit that the base program's debug information is left intact (idempotence). They suffer from the drawback that any AOP activities that are implemented as part of the runtime or native library are not debuggable. Aspect-enabled programs can be confusing to debug at the source level because control flow appears to change mysteriously; e.g., stepping into a function in the debugger results in a different function being entered. In addition, use of the Java debugger APIs to implement dynamic AOP currently prevents the application from being debugged inside a standard debugger.

4 Source-Level Debugging

Source-level debuggers strive to maintain the illusion of a source-level view of program execution. They commonly allow the programmer to set location and data breakpoints, step through code, inspect the stack, inspect and modify variables and memory, and even change the running code. To enable this, the debugger requires a correspondence between the program's compiled code and source code. This *debug information* is generated during compilation and consists of file names, instruction-to-line number mappings, and the names and memory locations of symbols. The information is usually stored inside the program executable, library, or class file, or in a separate *debug information file*. It may be absent if the build process excluded it, to lower the memory footprint for example, or if it was stripped out for the purposes of compression or obfuscation.

When compilation involves a straightforward syntax-directed translation [1], the compiler can provide a one-to-one correspondence from byte code (or machine code) and memory locations to source. The correspondence becomes more complicated as transformations are applied at various stages of the pre-processing, compilation, linking, loading, just-in-time compilation, and runtime pipeline. This lack of correspondence between the source and compiled code makes it difficult for the debugger to match the *actual behavior* of the executing code with the *expected behavior* from the source-code perspective [34], and leads to the *code location* and *data-value problems* that have been studied extensively in the context of debugging optimized code

---

[2] http://dev2dev.bea.com/jrockit

[14, 20, 29, 34]. In the context of debugging aspect-enabled programs these problems have been mentioned but briefly [2, 7, 24, 25].

In the AOP context, we define *full source-level debugging* as the ability to perform source-level debugging on all the AOP activities listed in Table 1.

4.1 The Code Location Problem

The *code location problem* arises when transformations are applied that prevent a one-to-one correspondence between compiled code and source code. In the domain of optimizing compilers [1], the problem is caused by the removal, merging, duplication (in-lining), reordering, or interleaving of instructions. In the domain of AOP weaving, the code location problem is usually caused by the removal (e.g., hoisting [4]), insertion (e.g., code synthesis, dynamic residue, aspect method calls, aspect in-lining, closures), duplication (e.g., initialization in-lining), or reordering (e.g., due to around-advice) of instructions [21]. The problem causes the debugger to show the wrong source line or call stack, or show byte code (or machine code) instead of source code.

4.2 The Data-Value Problem

The *data-value problem* occurs when transformations obscure the correspondence between variables in the source code and locations in memory [20]. Optimizing compilers commonly fold constants, eliminate common subexpressions, and represent variables in registers instead of memory (sometimes the same storage location will represent different variables at different times). In the context of AOP, weavers may add fields to classes (*introduction*) and formal arguments and local variables to methods (e.g., for context exposure) [21]. This problem causes the debugger to show new variables or fields incorrectly, e.g., it may be missing or have the wrong name.

4.3 Possible Approaches for Supporting Source-Level Debugging

Below we have consolidated and generalized some common approaches to the problem of performing source-level debugging of aspect-enabled programs.

Source weaving [33] – Wicca, AspectJ, and SourceWeave.NET [25] are example AOP systems that use source weaving and support full source-level debugging.

Debugger-friendly weaving – Wicca, AspectJ, and AspectWerkz [7] are example AOP systems that use binary-level weaving but are able to preserve the original debug information, thus supporting the idempotence property (P1).

Annotation [5] – Refers to the ability to annotate aspect code to provide rich debug information, to allow the debugger to hide the code in support of debug obliviousness, and to support fault isolation. Although AspectJ and Steamloom [19] use byte code annotation, no AOP system that we are aware of currently uses annotation for debugging purposes.

Reverse engineering [2, 23] – When the debugger encounters byte or machine code that has no matching source information, it can hide the code if debug obliviousness is desired or synthesize the source code on-the-fly if debug intimacy is desired.

Static analysis [20] – Static analysis techniques can be used to detect injected aspect code, for example, and, similar to annotation, used to provide debug information or to support obliviousness.

To allow the programmer to be truly oblivious of the aspects composed with the program, source-level debugging must hide all AOP-related code and behavior. However, we are aware of no AOP system that fully supports this. In §6, we show how intimate source-level debugging is useful for debugging AOP-specific faults. This is akin to directing a C compiler to display preprocessed source files to diagnose problems with include files and macros. Furthermore, when the transformation technology is immature, as is the case for AOP, a source-level representation of the transformation helps implementers detect faults [29, 34].

Noninvasive AOP implementations may not weave code at all. For these implementations, the ability to debug AOP-related code at the source level is nonsensical. However, these systems can still provide support for debug obliviousness and intimacy. For example, intimacy can be supported by showing a runtime visualization of the base program and aspect behavior [17]. For obliviousness, only the base program behavior is shown.

5 Wicca

Most dynamic AOP solutions involve binary weaving, a custom runtime, dynamic proxies, or method call interception. To support full source-level debugging, Wicca takes a new approach—it performs *dynamic source weaving*.

5.1 Overview

Wicca[3] v1 is a prototype dynamic AOP system for C# applications that performs source weaving (the solid line in Figure 1) at runtime. The woven source code is compiled in the background and the running executable is patched on-the-fly [12]. The entire weave-compile-update process takes less than 2.5 seconds for a C# program with 14,531 source lines on a Pentium IV 3.6 GHz processor. Wicca v1 uses the .NET Profiler API to enable dynamic weaving and patching, which imposes a 5-7% runtime overhead on application performance when compared to running the program without aspects enabled. Wicca also supports static byte-code weaving. A more detailed description of Wicca including performance measurements can be found in the expanded version of this paper [11].

Because all AOP activities are represented in source code, the programmer can perform full source-level debugging on the woven program using *wdbg*, our custom debugger. In addition, several ancillary debugging activities are supported:

- Full source-level debugging (*idempotence* and *debug intimacy*)
- Aspects can be enabled/disabled at runtime (*dynamism*)

---

[3] Derived from the Old Norse word *vikja* meaning to turn, bend and shape.

- Aspect rules, located in an XML file, can be changed at runtime (*dynamism*)
- New aspects can be introduced at runtime (*aspect introduction*)
- Advice code can be modified at runtime (*runtime modification*)
- Base code can be modified at runtime (*runtime modification*)

To our knowledge, Wicca is the first dynamic AOP system to support full source-level debugging and modification of advice and base code at runtime. Although Wicca uses a radical approach, i.e., dynamic source weaving, this approach offers unique interactive source-level debugging capabilities. If the interactive capabilities are not needed, *static source weaving* [25] is a simple and sufficient alternative.

5.2 The Wicca Debugger (wdbg)

Wdbg is the first debugger we are aware of that supports source-level debugging of dynamically updated programs. It is an extension to the Microsoft cordbg command-line debugger. An extension was required because standard Windows debuggers do not support dynamically changing the debug information associated with the application being debugged. Without this extension, the source code and variables displayed in the debugger may be incorrect. Static weavers do not have to deal with this issue.

5.3 Limitations

Wicca v1 has limited AOP functionality. Only before and after advice, and method execution and field access join points, are supported. Introductions (inter-type declarations) are not supported. Wicca v1 also requires source code for both the base program and the aspects. While Wicca v1 does not support debug obliviousness, this could be achieved using our statement annotation technology [10].

Due to a limitation of the Profiler API, we are not able to update a function that is active on the stack. The function is updated the next time it is called. Unfortunately, wdbg will incorrectly show the woven source code instead of the original source code, if the function has been updated yet. We expect the fix for this to be straightforward.

6 Evaluation

In this section we present the results of an experiment to demonstrate the interactive debugging capabilities of Wicca.

6.1 Experimental Setup

We are given a buggy C# class that is supposed to implement a stack (see Listing 1) and a test driver for exercising the stack class. We will use Wicca to interactively diagnose and fix the bugs. To help diagnose the bug, we create an aspect that embodies the *design-by-contract* (DBC) [30] principle. DBC allows the programmer to make assertions [22] about the system, in the form of *preconditions*, *postconditions*, and *class invariants*. For example, the class invariant for the stack class is that the top element of a non-empty stack must not be null. Its push method has a precondition that the object being pushed is non-null, and a postcondition that the stack's size has been incremented.

Normally, the assertion checking and handling code is scattered throughout the system. By localizing the assertion code into a DBC aspect (Listing 2), we obtain many benefits including improved code clarity, the ability to easily change the assertion violation policy, to strengthen or weaken class invariants, to add assertions to a class after-the-fact, and to automate contract enforcement.

```
public class Stack {
    ArrayList elements = new ArrayList();
    public void push(object arg1) {
        elements.Add(arg1);
        elements.Add(arg1); // <-- Bug!
    }
    public object pop() {
        object popped = top();
        elements.RemoveAt(elements.Count-1);
        return popped;
    }
    public object top() {
        return elements[elements.Count-1];
    }
}
```

Listing 1. A stack class written in C# that contains a bug in the push() method

[26] Moreover, unlike normal assertions which are only checked for debug builds, or which require continuous checking at runtime, Wicca can inject these *test probes* [22] on demand, thus completely eliminating checking overhead when assertions are disabled.

6.2 Detecting Faults Using Test Probes

To test the stack class we create a test driver that pushes several items onto the stack and then pops each one while writing its value to the console. Shortly after launching the test driver, we notice a bug (see Listing 1) where every item in the stack is duplicated. While the driver is running, we enable the stack DBC aspect, which may already exist or which we may have introduced for this debugging task. Wicca detects this change and *rebuilds* (reparses, reweaves, and recompiles) the driver, taking a total of 610 ms on a Pentium IV 3.6 GHz processor.

```
public class StackDBCAspect {
    static int __savedCount;

    static void PostCond_push(Stack __this, object arg1) {
        if (__this.isEmpty())
            throw new InvalidOperationException(
                "Postcondition violated: Stack is empty after push");
        if (__this.top() != arg1)
            throw new InvalidOperationException(
                "Postcondition violated: Pushed item is not on top of stack");
        if (__this.count() != __savedCount + 1)
            throw new InvalidOperationException(
                "Postcondition violated: Stack size did not increase " +
                "by one after push");
    }
    ...pre and postconditions for pop, etc...
```

Listing 2. A design-by-contract aspect for the stack class. Variables that start with "__" are renamed during weaving.

```
<aspects enable="true">
 <aspect class="StackDBCAspect" sources="StackDBCAspect.cs">
  <advice name="PreCond_push" type="after">
   <pointcut expression="execution(Stack.push())" />
  </advice>
  <advice name="PostCond_push" type="before">
   <pointcut expression="execution(Stack.push())" />
  </advice>
```

Listing 3. Aspect rule file with erroneous before and after advice

Listing 3 shows the aspect rule file after we added the stack DBC aspect and enabled weaving. Immediately, the aspect code detects a postcondition violation and throws the exception: "Postcondition violated: Stack is empty after push." The exception message provides the file name and line number where the exception occurred.

6.3 Just-In-Time Debugging

We launch the Wicca debugger, wdbg, to debug the exception. After pointing wdbg to the debug information of the woven program, we can step into the push method and see the interwoven source code (see Figure 2). What is significant about this figure is that the base program and all AOP activities are debuggable at the source level.

Looking at the source code for the push method, it is obvious that there are actually *two* bugs: the precondition and postcondition are switched and the Add method is called twice. The first bug is a manifestation of an AOP-specific fault: *incorrect*

```
Command Prompt - wdbg                                  _ □ ✕
010:      public void push(object arg1)
011:      {
012:          int savedCount = this.count;
013:          if(this.isEmpty)
014:              throw(new InvalidOperationException("Post-condit
ion violated: Stack is empty after push"));
015:*         if(this.top != arg1)
016:              throw(new InvalidOperationException("Post-condit
ion violated: Pushed item is not on top of stack"));
017:          if(this.count != savedCount + 1)
018:              throw(new InvalidOperationException("Post-condit
ion violated: Stack size did not increase " + "by one after push"
));
019:          elements.Add(arg1);
020:          elements.Add(arg1);
021:          if(arg1 == null)
022:              throw(new ArgumentException("Argument cannot be
null", "arg1"));
023:          savedCount = this.count;
024:      }
(wdbg)
```

Fig. 2. A wdbg debugging session showing aspect code interwoven with the stack class. The asterisk (*) indicates the current line.

pointcut descriptor. This fault is difficult to diagnose without a source-level representation of the woven code. From the woven code it appears that the postcondition and precondition are switched. Looking closely at the aspect rules in Listing 3 reveals that the push precondition (PreCond_push) is erroneous because the advice type is "after" when it should actually be "before", and similarly for the postcondition.

A quick change to the aspect rules to fix this oversight causes Wicca to reparse, reweave, and recompile the driver. As expected, an exception is thrown immediately but this time with the correct message: "Postcondition violated: Stack size did not increase by one after push." After removing the extraneous Add method call, Wicca rebuilds the driver, and we immediately see the correct behavior. *At no time during the debugging session did we have to restart the test driver.*

7 Related Work

A few systems deserve further comment. SourceWeave.NET [25] employs a very similar source weaving strategy that is designed to improve source-level debugging. However, it weaves statically whereas Wicca weaves dynamically, enabling aspects to be introduced and reconfigured at runtime.

Few AOP systems support debug obliviousness or fault isolation, which requires a debugger to identify AOP activity code. AspectJ and Steamloom support byte-code annotations for identifying aspects to prevent recursion during weaving [21] and to facilitate aspect removal [19]. As far as we know, no AOP system uses byte-code annotations to support obliviousness or fault isolation.

8 Conclusion

We described the problem of debugging aspect-enabled programs and why it has become an important gating criterion for the adoption of AOP. We provided a debug model for AOP that classified all AOP activities, related them to the new type of faults they can introduce, outlined the properties of an ideal debugging solution, and surveyed the state of the art of AOP debugging. For source-level debugging, we explained how the nature of binary weavers gives rise to the *code location problem*, that originates from the field of optimizing compilers. We showed how results from that community apply to debugging aspect-enabled programs.

We demonstrated how our Wicca system offers a novel approach to debugging dynamically composed aspect-enabled programs. Wicca is the first dynamic AOP system to support full source-level debugging. It does this by employing a novel *dynamic source weaving* strategy that combines source weaving with online byte-code patching with relatively low overhead. Our future work will be to explore using byte-code annotations [10] to fully support debug obliviousness and fault isolation.

Acknowledgements

We thank Mike Stall, John Lefor, Chuck Mitchell, Jan Gray, Sonja Keserovic, and Andy Ayers from Microsoft for their support and feedback. We also thank Gregor

Kiczales, Hrvoje Benko, Rean Griffith, and our anonymous reviewers for their feedback. This research is funded in part by a grant from Microsoft Research.

References

[1] Aho, A., Lam, M., Sethi, R., Ullman, J.: Principles, Techniques, and Tools, 2nd edn. Addison-Wesley, Reading (2007)

[2] Alexander, R., Bieman, J.M., Andrews, A.: Towards the Systematic Testing of Aspect-Oriented Programs. Tech Rep CS-4-105. Dept. of CS, Colorado State Univ. (March 2004)

[3] Aussmann, S., Haupt, M.: Axon – Dynamic AOP through Runtime Inspection and Monitoring. In: ASARTI 2003. Proc. of the Wkshp. on Advancing the State-of-the-Art in Runtime Inspection (July 2003)

[4] Avgustinov, P., Christensen, A.S., Hendren, L., Kuzins, S., Lhoták, J., Lhoták, O., de Moor, O., Sereni, D., Sittampalam, G., Tibble, J.: Optimising AspectJ. In: PLDI 2005. Proc. of Prog. Language Design and Implementation (June 2005)

[5] Van Baalen, J., Robinson, P., Lowry, M., Pressburger, T.: Explaining Synthesized Software. In: ASE 1998. Proc. of Automated Software Eng. (October 1998)

[6] Baker, J., Hsieh, W.: Runtime aspect weaving through metaprogramming. In: AOSD 2002. Proc. of Aspect-Oriented Software Development (April 2002)

[7] Bonér, J.: AspectWerkz — dynamic AOP for Java. In: AOSD 2004. Invited talk at Aspect-Oriented Software Development (March 2004)

[8] Ceccato, M., Tonella, P., Ricca, F.: Is AOP code easier or harder to test than OOP code? In: WTAOP 2005. Proc. of the Wkshp. on Testing Aspect-Oriented Programs (March 2005)

[9] Douence, R., Fritz, T., Loriant, N., Menaud, J.-M., Segura-Devillechaise, M., Südholt, M.: An expressive aspect language for system applications with Arachne. In: AOSD 2005. Proc. of Aspect-Oriented Software Development (March 2005)

[10] Eaddy, M., Aho, A.: Statement Annotations for Fine-Grained Advising. In: RAM-SE 2006. Proc. of the Wkshp. on Reflection, AOP, and Meta-data for Software Evol. (July 2006)

[11] Eaddy, M., Aho, A., Hu, W., McDonald, P., Burger, J.: Debugging Woven Code. Tech Rep. CUCS-035-06. Dept. of CS, Columbia Univ. (September 2006)

[12] Eaddy, M., Feiner, S.: Multi-Language Edit-and-Continue for the Masses. Tech Rep CUCS-015-05. Dept. of CS, Columbia Univ. (April 2005)

[13] Elrad, T., Filman, R., Bader, A.: Aspect-oriented programming: Introduction. Communications of the ACM 44(10), 29–32 (2001)

[14] Faith, R.: Debugging Programs after Structure-Changing Transformation. Ph.D. dissertation, CS Dept., Univ. of North Carolina (December 1997)

[15] Filman, R., Friedman, D.: Aspect-Oriented Programming is Quantification and Obliviousness. In: OOPSLA Wkshp. on Advanced Separation of Concerns (October 2000)

[16] Grawehr, F.P., Alonso, G.: A Dynamic AOP-Engine for .NET. Tech Rep 445. Dept. of CS, ETH Zürich (March 2004)

[17] Griswold, W.G., Yuan, J., Kato, Y.: Exploiting the Map Metaphor in a Tool for Software Evolution. In: ICSE 2001. Proc. of the Intl. Conf. on Software Eng. (May 2001)

[18] Haupt, M., Mezini, M.: Micro-Measurements for Dynamic Aspect-Oriented Systems. In: Weske, M., Liggesmeyer, P. (eds.) NODe 2004. LNCS, vol. 3263, pp. 81–96. Springer, Heidelberg (2004)

[19] Haupt, M., Mezini, M., Bockisch, C., Dinkelaker, T., Eichberg, M., Krebs, M.: An Execution Layer for Aspect-Oriented Prog. Languages. In: VEE 2005. Proc. of Virtual Execution Environments (June 2005)

[20] Hennessy, J.: Symbolic Debugging of Optimized Code. ACM Transactions on Prog. Languages and Systems 4(3), 323–344 (1982)

[21] Hilsdale, E., Hugunin, J.: Advice weaving in AspectJ. In: AOSD 2004 (March 2004)

[22] Hoare, A.R.: Assertions: a personal perspective. In: Software pioneers: contributions to software engineering, pp. 356–366. Springer, Heidelberg (2002)

[23] Hölzle, U., Chambers, C., Ungar, D.: Debugging Optimized Code with Dynamic Deoptimization. In: PLDI 2005. Proc. of Prog. Language Design and Implementation (July 1992)

[24] Hugunin, J.: The next steps for aspect-oriented programming languages (in Java). In: Proc. of Wkshp. on New Visions for Software Design & Prod.: Research & Apps. (December 2001)

[25] Jackson, A., Clarke, S.: SourceWeave.NET: Source-level cross-language aspect-oriented programming. In: Karsai, G., Visser, E. (eds.) GPCE 2004. LNCS, vol. 3286, Springer, Heidelberg (2004)

[26] Lippert, M., Lopes, C.V.: A Study on Exception Detection and Handling Using Aspect-Oriented Programming. In: ICSE 2000. Proc. of the Intl. Conf. Software Eng. (June 2000)

[27] Kiczales, G., Hilsdale, E., Hugunin, J., Kersten, M., Palm, J., Griswold, W.G.: An overview of AspectJ. In: Knudsen, J.L. (ed.) ECOOP 2001. LNCS, vol. 2072, pp. 327–353. Springer, Heidelberg (2001)

[28] Kiczales, G., Lamping, J., Mendhekar, A., Maeda, C., Lopes, C.V., Loingtier, J.-M., Irwin, J.: Aspect-oriented programming. TR SPL97-008 P9710042, Xerox PARC (February 1997)

[29] Kumar, N., Childers, B., Soffa, M.L.: Tdb: a source-level debugger for dynamically translated programs. In: AADEBUG 2005. Proc. of the Intl. Symp. on Automated and Analysis-Driven Debugging (September 2005)

[30] Meyer, B.: Object-Oriented Software Construction. Prentice Hall, New Jersey (1997)

[31] Nicoara, A., Alonso, G.: Dynamic AOP with PROSE. In: ASMEA 2005. Proc. of the Wkshp. on Adaptive and Self-Managing Enterprise Applications (June 2005)

[32] Redwine, S., Riddle, W.: Software technology maturation. In: SE 1985. Proc. of Software Eng. (August 1985)

[33] Tice, C., Graham, S.: OPTVIEW: A New Approach for Examining Optimized Code. In: PASTE 1998. Wkshp. on Program Analysis for Software Tools and Eng. (June 1998)

[34] Zellweger, P.T.: Interactive Source-Level Debugging of Optimized Programs. Ph.D. dissertation, CS Dept., Univ. of California, Berkeley. Also published as Xerox PARC Tech. Rep. CSL-84-5 (May 1984)

Unification of Static and Dynamic AOP for Evolution in Embedded Software Systems

Wasif Gilani, Fabian Scheler, Daniel Lohman,
Olaf Spinczyk, and Wolfgang Schröder-Preikschat

Friedrich-Alexander University Erlangen-Nuremberg
{gilani,scheler,lohmann,spinczyk,wosch}@cs.fau.de

Abstract. This paper discusses how evolution in software systems can be supported by a unified application of both static as well as dynamic aspect-oriented technology. The support for evolution is required statically, where the applications could be taken offline and adapted, and dynamically where going offline is not an available option. While this is straightforward in the static case by taking the system offline and statically weaving the aspects, runtime evolution requires an additional dynamic aspect weaving infrastructure.

Our current implementation of the *family-based dynamic aspect weaving infrastructure* supports most of the features known from the static aspect weaving domain, offers a tailored dynamic aspect weaving support, and is able to target a wide range of applications including embedded systems with very small memory footprint. The availability of a *single language* both for static and dynamic aspects means that the decision whether an aspect is static or dynamic is postponed to the later stages of the deployment of aspects into the sytem, and is decided according to the requirements and available resources. As a case study, we will present our experiences with the static and runtime evolution of the embedded operating system eCos.

1 Introduction

Software evolution is the process of keeping the software up-to-date and bug-free by continuous enhancement, corrections, extensions and customizations as per the emerging requirements. This process involves either adapting the core functional behavior, or the insertion of new non-functional behavior. Lehman defined software evolution as the collection of programming activities intended to generate a new version from an older and operational version [9]. Currently, it is estimated that four out of seven software engineers work on repair and enhancement of existing software [26].

Software evolution can be classified into static and runtime evolution. Static evolution corresponds to compile time changes, and involves modification of the code by taking the system offline, reconfiguring, rapairing, and then recompiling as per the new requirements. Runtime evolution means that the system is upgraded and maintained dynamically at runtime, and is vital for long running systems. Traditionally, runtime evolution is handled with approaches like redundant systems, larger memories, increasing processing power, and feature-rich software. Such approaches noticeably bloat applications, reduce reusability, and increase complexity, costs, and further hinder the evolution of the system.

M. Lumpe and W. Vanderperren (Eds.): SC 2007, LNCS 4829, pp. 216–234, 2007.
© Springer-Verlag Berlin Heidelberg 2007

The evolution could be a continuous change, which happens with the maturity of the technology and involves an incremental adoption approach, or it may be radical and forces a system-wide change. When evolution requires changes to multiple modules, it is difficult to localize resulting in crosscutting. This crosscutting limits the offered levels of evolvability, variability, and granularity of the software. Some concerns like security, profiling, tracing, synchronization, etc., are typically reflected in many points of the code, and therefore difficult to implement as independent encapsulated entities. Aspect-oriented programming (AOP) allows encapsulating crosscutting concerns into completely isolated entities called *aspects,* and injection of the additional behavior, encapsulated by aspects, into multiple modules statically or at runtime by *advice.* With AOP, each and every crosscutting concern is well encapsulated in a separate module, thus, allowing evolution in the system in complete isolation without major redesign of the whole system.

This paper provides details and results about some radical improvements carried out in our dynamic aspect weaver family, which have contributed significantly to further bring down the dynamic weaving costs and making it viable even for embedded systems. We further propose the unification of static and dynamic AOP for the C++ domain, by providing a single language, for achieving static and runtime evolution of software systems. The availability of a *single language* means that the decision whether an aspect is to be deployed statically or dynamically is delayed till the deployment stage.

The remaining paper is organized as follows. We start with the motivation by describing an application scenario. This is followed by a discussion of the related work. The sections 4 and 5 describe the improved implementation of the *family-based dynamic weaver,* and the materialization of the *single language approach.* Section 6 presents a case study which was conducted with the embedded operating system eCos. Finally, section 7 concludes the paper.

2 Motivation: Evolvable Software Systems

While the process of static evolution requires the running system to be taken offline and adapted as per newly emerging requirements, runtime evolution requires that the system could be adapted and maintained on the fly. Such a requirement is vital for highly available systems where downtime could be a catastophe in terms of data loss, performance, revenue, etc. Examples of such highly available systems are mission critical space missions, air traffic control, telephone switching systems, business critical applications, etc. The importance of runtime evolution was demonstrated when NASA's Mars Pathfinder robot, which was launched to relay high-resolution pictures and valuable metereological data of the Martian surface back to Earth, experienced serious malfunctioning. A low priority job held a system-wide important resource. This resulted in repeated resets and thereby loss of important data. Fortunately, the limited runtime evolution capability integrated into the system turned out to be vital for the rescue of the multimillion dollar project which otherwise would had been a total failure. A detailed analysis of the problem with the Mars Pathfinder along with the handling of such runtime evolution problems with our unified static and dynamic aspect-based solution is provided in section 6.3.

2.1 Aspects for Evolution

With AOP, the concerns that are prone to evolution, and are crosscutting in nature, are neatly encapsulated in aspects. In static AOP, these aspects are woven at compile time onto the primary functionality in an additive manner without altering the existing architecture. The aspect code is inlined into classes, and therefore, does not induce any significant overhead into the system. Once woven, the static aspects cannot be removed or reconfigured later during runtime. For evolution, the system has to be taken offline to change aspects as per requirements, and the system has to be recompiled for the changes to be made available.

For long running systems, where going offline is not a choice, a runtime mechanism is needed to enable the system to evolve dynamically. Dynamic AOP provides mechanisms to modularize and thereby apply crosscutting policies encapsulated as aspects into the running system in complete isolation. With dynamic AOP, the runtime evolution involves the addition or replacement of aspects or components.

2.2 Unification of Static and Runtime Evolution

Static evolution with static AOP is more efficient as it incurs low overhead, improves start-up time, and reduces memory usage, but at the expense of flexibility. This option is best suited for devices with resource constraints but is limited because of the lack of the knowledge of execution environments. The solutions supporting exclusively dynamic evolution via dynamic weaving might not be acceptable for some domains due to considerable runtime overhead, and low efficiency. We advocate the principle of *static processing where possible and dynamic processing where needed* by a unified application of static and dynamic AOP. Such a unification demands a homogenous support in terms of the AOP features and a single description language for both static and dynamic aspects. This approach would result in the coexistence of both static as well as dynamic aspects in the system. An evolvable concern would be implemented as an aspect if it has a crosscutting behaviour. The decision whether the aspect is static or dynamic could be removed from the aspect implementation and decided purely as per the requirements and available resources.

2.3 Low-Cost Dynamic Weaving Support

For runtime evolution via dynamic AOP, the system has to be equipped with a dynamic aspect weaver. However, many of the available dynamic aspect weaving infrastructures provide fixed runtime support, are either architecture-specific (C-based weavers) or quite expensive (Java-based weaver) to be deployed on the systems with few kilobytes of memory. Another important motivation of our work is to provide a dynamic aspect weaving infrastructure, which should be efficient, low-cost, portable, and could be tailored down to become viable even for resource-constrained systems.

3 Related Work

Many different approaches have been proposed by the research community for runtime evolution. Some advocate using patterns in several features [7,25]. Other approaches suggest the use of reflection and component frameworks [20,8]. We are more interested in the approaches based on employing AOP for software evolution [21,19,17,11,13]. Most of the AOP-based evolution approaches proposed so far are restricted mainly to applying static AOP for static evolution [17,25,11].

For runtime evolution, there are many dynamic weavers available, but all provide fixed runtime support and suffer from various limitations like portability, memory and runtime overhead, limited AOP feature support, etc. The weavers in Java are based on bytecode manipulation via the JVM debugging interface, customized class loaders, or virtual machine extensions [15,3,18,5,24]. The current memory requirements of Java-based weavers are an order of magnitude too large for many embedded devices. Though the presence of JVM promises a very portable solution, the mere presence of JVM and core libraries require considerable memory. Furthermore, the Java based weavers typically offer slow execution speed as compared to their counterparts in the C or C++ language. This problem is further aggravated by the employment of the debugger interface in some dynamic weavers, which requires the application to be executed in the debug mode. To speed up applications, some weavers employ JIT compilers, but this requires additional resources.

In the C domain, binary code manipulation is generally employed to support dynamic aspect weaving. The availability of mechanisms to perform runtime hooking, precisely at the required join points, means there is no extra overhead due to unnecessary hooks. *Arachne* [14], *TOSKANA* [10] and *TinyC*^{2} [4] follow the binary code manipulation approach. The actual weaving positions in the binary code are determined with the help of symbol tables and/or debug information, generated by the C compiler. Code inlining or stripping of symbol information has to be disabled. All weavers in C provide fixed runtime supports, and their implementations are limited to specific processors and compilers. The platform dependence means they are not appropriate, especially, in the domain of embedded systems which employ a wide spectrum of CPU and hardware platforms. The performance overhead of these weavers [10,14] is significantly lower than the Java-based systems. The offered AOP features are, on the other hand, also limited.

Disabling of code inlining or stripping of symbol information might be acceptable for C, most C++ compilers implicitly perform such optimizations. Therefore, dynamic aspect weaving via binary code manipulation is not a viable option in the C++ domain. There is a very limited research in the C++ domain for supporting dynamic weaving. We are aware of only one approach in the C++ domain, called *DAO C++*[16], which is based on source code instrumentation. Since the instrumentation process does not depend on binary code, DAO C++ is independent of any architecture or compiler-specific restrictions, resulting in a portable solution. However, the absence of any filtration mechanism means that all join points of the target application are hooked leading to significant memory and runtime overhead.

4   A Family-Based Dynamic Weaving Infrastructure

None of the available weavers offer a tailorable dynamic weaving support. They follow the traditional one-size-fits all approach. For the development of our dynamic weaver infrastructure, we had two objectives. First, to provide a feature-rich dynamic aspect weaver that could be tailored according to specific requirements, and second, to bring down the cost of dynamic weaving and thereby, make dynamic weaving viable even for embedded devices. We applied the software product line (SPL) [2] approach to the dynamic aspect weaving domain and come up with the family-based weaver [22]. The tailored weavers are generated by selecting only the required set of AOP features from the weaver family. Variant management tools simplify and reduce the complexities associated with the configuration and the generation of variants from the software families. They provide graphical support to define application requirements in the form of feature selection in order to generate application-specific variants. We have employed a variant management tool called *pure::variants* to completely automate the generation process [1]. Besides enabling to generate tailored weavers, the availability of a powerful join point filtration mechanism, and additional mechanisms to exploit the "a-priori-knowledge" of the target application restricts the incurred dynamic weaving overhead due to actually affected joinpoints, actually woven aspects, and used AOP features [22]. The optimizations performed by the exploitation of "a-priori-knowledge" about the target application are comparable to the ones offered by static weavers, which basically exploit the same information for this purpose: actually affected joinpoints, aspects, and used AOP features. The main difference is that this information is implicitly available to static weavers, while it has to be explicitly provided for the generation of a tailored dynamic weaver. Overall, the family-based dynamic weaver infrastructure allows a fine-grained adjustment of the trade-off between flexibility and required resources. In conjunction with the single language approach (Section 5), this perfectly fulfills the goal of minimal overhead: For any kind of application, it is now possible to weave as much as possible statically, while providing as much runtime flexibility as necessary. Static versus dynamic weaving of aspects becomes a configurable and tailorable property.

4.1 Improvements in the Implementation

The architecture of the dynamic aspect weaver family consists of three main building blocks, namely, the weaver binding, the runtime monitor, and the build environment for dynamic aspects [22]. Due to significant improvements in the binding mode (AspectC++), and the general dynamic weaving infrastructure, we were able to further bring down the memory and runtime costs of dynamic weaving. The following subsections describe the various improvements carried out in each of these building blocks.

4.2 Weaver Binding

AspectC++ [12] is employed as a binding mode in our family-based weaver as shown in figure 1. Before describing the improvements, we would like to provide a brief overview of how AspectC++ works as a hooking platform in the weaver family.

As shown in Figure 2, hooks are encapsulated in the advice code of the static preparation aspect. Since only *before* and *after* advice are defined in this variant, the weaving of this aspect would result in a dynamic weaver variant, which supports only before and after advice. If an around advice is to be supported, then the preparation aspect is implemented accordingly. Furthermore, the required amount of context information

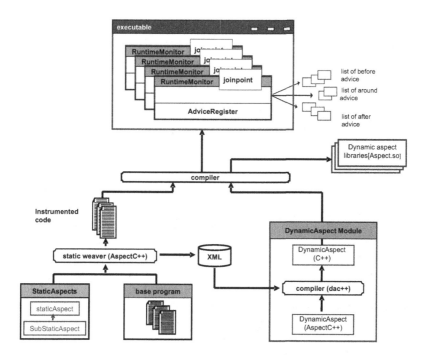

Fig. 1. Architecture of the family-based dynamic aspect weaver

about the join points is extracted from the static weaver binding mode, and passed to
the dynamic advice code. AspectC++ provides static as well as dynamic context information about the affected join points. The static information includes the join point
signature, the argument types, a unique ID, etc., whereas the dynamic information includes current argument values, result value, object instance, etc. It can be noticed that
in this particular case, only the join point signature information (*JoinPoint::signature()*)
is retrieved by the static advice code and parsed via the inserted hooks to the runtime
system. The aspect *instrument* defines a pure virtual pointcut named *dynamicJPS*. The
aspect *beforeafterExe* shown in the listing below derives from the *instrument* aspect,
and defines exact locations in the source code where hooks should be inserted. The
weaving of this aspect would result in the hooking of all execution join points, and all
call join points with the exclusion of the functions of the standard library which don't
generally contribute to the application's semantics.

```
pointcut std_function_calls() = call("% std::%(...)");
aspect beforeafterExe : public instrument {
  pointcut virtual dynamicJPS() = execution("% ...::%(...)") || call("% ...::%(...)"
                        && !std_function_calls();
```

The poincut mechanism in AspectC++, therefore, enables comprehensive filtering of
join points for dynamically woven aspects at a fine-grained level, and allows to implement complex hooking policies with ease. During the hooking process, the AspectC++
weaver outputs a project repository, which provides extensive information about the

```
aspect instrument {
  pointcut virtual dynamicJPS()=0;
  public:
    advice dynamicJPS():before(){
      ArgsJnPnt<JoinPoint::ARGS> jp;
      jp.jointpointName = JoinPoint::signature();
      monitor<JoinPoint::JPID,MONIT_>::BeforeAdvice(&jp);
    }
    advice dynamicJPS():before(){
      ArgsJnPnt<JoinPoint::ARGS> jp;
      jp.jointpointName = JoinPoint::signature();
      monitor<JoinPoint::JPID,MONIT_>::AfterAdvice(&jp);
    }
};
```

Fig. 2. A static preparation aspect for inserting hooks into the target application

hooked join points, for example their signatures, types, ids, etc. The information is exploited to resolve the pointcuts described in the dynamic aspect code.

We did some significant improvements in the AspectC++ weaver implementation since our last paper [22]. In the previous implementation, the cost of employing around advice for hooking was substantially higher than that of before and after advice. This was particularly problematic in the case of the generation of a variant, from the weaver family, which was required to support both before and after advice. As can be seen from Figure 2, the same context information had to be generated twice at both before and after advice, for each join point. We calculated that in the case of extracting only the signature of the join point, the extra overhead was 13 bytes of memory. In the case of big projects with thousands of join points, this resulted in a significant overhead. In the new version of the AspectC++ weaver, the generation of `tjp->proceed()` function, which is provided in the around advice to invoke the original method, is reimplemented so that `proceed()` can be inlined for small functions. This has resulted in around advice being as efficient as before and after advice in the AspectC++ weaver. Since the cost of the advice types in the weaver family is directly dependent on the cost of the corresponding advice types in AspectC++, this improvement resulted in reducing the cost associated with the dynamic "around advice" in the weaver family. Furthermore, the employment of static around advice helped to avoid extra overhead caused due to the duplicate generation of context information, since the same context information could be shared by different advice types as is shown in figure 3.

4.3 Runtime Monitor

All dynamic aspect weavers follow a centralized model where a single runtime monitor takes care of all interaction between the join points and aspects. Our old version of the dynamic weaver family followed the same design with a single centralized monitor controlling all coordination among the aspects and joinpoints [22]. However, this approach introduces significant runtime overhead as each time when the thread of control reaches a hooked join point, the list of join points registered with the runtime monitor is traversed to find out the matching join point. The associated complexity with this join point look-up operation is $O(\log N)$, where N is the number of join points registered with the monitor. Once the right join point is located, the advice stored

```
advice dynamicJPS():around(){
    ArgsJnPnt<JoinPoint::ARGS> jp;
    jp.jointpointName = JoinPoint::signature();
    jp._that = tjp->that();
    ...
    monitor<JoinPoint::JPID,MONIT_>::BeforeAdvice(&jp);
    tjp->proceed();
    monitor<JoinPoint::JPID,MONIT_>::AfterAdvice(&jp);
}
```

Fig. 3. Modified hooking mechanism employing around advice and templates

in the advice containers associated with the join point are executed. Even if there are just empty hooks with no advice registered, this model causes significant runtime overhead.

As a solution, we implemented a new version where each potential join point is provided with a unique runtime monitor. The allocation of unique monitor objects means that the involved complexity for join point look-up is effectively reduced to $O(1)$ in contrast to the $O(log\ N)$ complexity of the centralized model. Figure 1 shows the architecture of the weaver family with decentralized runtime monitors. It could have been quite a cumbersome and expensive process to assign each join point with a unique runtime monitor, but templates in C++ come to the rescue, as shown in Figure 3. AspectC++ weaver assigns unique numeric ids to all hooked join points, which are exploited to generate a unique monitor for each join point. It can be seen that the template takes an additional parameter ($MONIT\_$), which is used for module identification. This parameter is necessary in the case of "Extensible Systems" to be able to weave dynamic aspects even into the modules loaded later into the running system. The components employed in the old implementation that had the sole responsibility of registering and later identifying each of the module's monitor objects for the weaving and unweaving of aspects are no longer needed. This helped to save 5078 bytes of memory which was consumed by the Extensible Systems feature in the old implementation.

Furthermore, the memory cost of different AOP features, and hooking is brought down remarkably. This is due to significant optimizations and improvements carried out in the implementation of our static and family-based dynamic weaver. A comparison between the cost of some of the variants of our dynamic aspect weaver family with the old and new implementation are shown in figure 4. It can be seen that the variants with the new implementation consume significantly less memory as compared to the old implementation[22] while providing the same level of AOP feature support. In the new implementation, the variant with minimal AOP feature support consumes exactly 5707 bytes of memory, which is almost half to what it costed in our old implementation (12079 bytes). The variant with maximum AOP feature support (all types of advice, ordering, context, etc.) consumes 10020 bytes of memory which is also significantly lower as compared to previous implementation (23315 bytes). Additionally, the memory cost of each hook has been reduced to just 12 bytes as shown in figure 5. We cannot imagine any further reduction in this cost except moving to binary code manipulation approach which restricts our weaver to specific architectures.

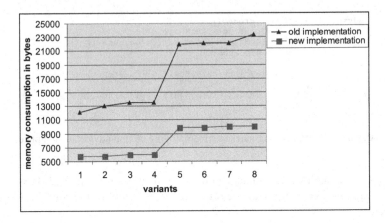

Fig. 4. Different variants of the family-based weaver as per their memory consumption

Without Instrumentation

```
void Foo::g( ) {
  puts ("g( )\n");
}

0000003c <Foo::g()>:

3c:  push  %ebp
3d:  mov   %esp,%ebp
3f:  movl  .rodata.str1.1,0x8(%ebp)
46:  pop   %ebp
47:  jmp   puts
```

With Instrumentation

```
aspect instrumentExe : public instrument {
  pointcut virtual dynamicJPS() =
    execution("void Foo1::g()");
};
00000098 <Foo1::g()>:

98:  push  %ebp
99:  mov   %esp,%ebp
9b:  pushl monitor<1,0>::advicebefore
a1:  call  Cont::trigAdvice(adviceCont_list*)
a6:  pop   %eax
a7:  movl  .rodata.str1.1,0x8(%ebp)
ae:  leave
af:  jmp   puts
```

Fig. 5. Cost of hook = 12 bytes

4.4   Build Environment for Dynamic Aspects

In the old implementation, the static aspects were implemented in AspectC++, whereas the dynamic aspects were implemented in C++. In the new implementation, the AspectC++ language has been adopted for the description of dynamic aspects as well (see section 5). Before the dynamic aspects could be loaded into the target application, they have to be transformed into the standard C++ code. A dynamic aspect compiler *dac++* has been developed that transforms the dynamic aspects defined in AspectC++ to standard C++ code. Once transformed, a standard C++ compiler is employed to compile the aspects into shared libraries. The dynamic aspect code itself can be linked either statically with the component code, or loaded at runtime by means of a dynamic aspect loader (Loader). As soon as a dynamic aspect is loaded into the target application, whenever a join point matched by the pointcut definition is reached, the unique monitor for the join point activates the advice code, and returns the control to the application.

5   The Single Language Approach

AspectC++ was designed primarily for the description of static aspects. The adoption of AspectC++ for dynamic aspects required the same level of AOP feature by the weaver family as is available in the static AspectC++ weaver. In our previous paper [23], we analyzed the possibility of supporting a single language, and discussed reasons for the absence of some of the AOP features in the dynamic aspect weavers in the C/C++ domain. We further suggested solutions that have been realized for the dynamic aspect weaver family.

Table 1. Status of the availability of various AOP features in our static and dynamic aspect weaving infrastructures

AOP Features	Static Weaving	Dynamic Weaving
before advice	√	√
after advice	√	√
around advice	√	√
exec join points	√	√
call join points	√	√
object construction	√	√
object destruction	√	√
get/set field	–	–
multiple aspects	√	√
context information	√	√
aspect ordering	√	√
introductions	√	√*

* Introductions of base classes and virtual functions are not yet supported

Table 1 gives an overview of the various AOP features currently supported by both our static weaver (AspectC++), and dynamic weaver family. Our dynamic weaver supports more AOP features than any of its counterpart in the C/C++ domain. The features not supported in the current implementation are get/set fields. This can be considered as challenging to impossible in languages that support C-style pointers[1].

The transformation process of dynamic aspects from AspectC++ to C++ is straightforward. The following listing shows an aspect *Hello* written with AspectC++:

```
aspect Hello {
    advice somePointCut() : before() {
        std::cout << "hello from dynamic aspect! " << std::endl;
    }
    advice somePointCut() : before() {
        std::cout << "hello from dynamic aspect! " << std::endl;
        std::cout << "signature " << tjp->signature() << std::endl;
```

---

[1] The support for get/set join points in existing weavers is quite limited, as it is restricted to direct access of global variables.

```
    }
};


class Hello {
  static void advice1_a0_before() {
    std::cout << "hello from dynamic aspect! " << std::endl;
  }
template<class ThisJoinPoint>
  static void advice1_a1_before(ThisJoinPoint *tjp) {
    std::cout << "hello from dynamic aspect! " << std::endl;
    std::cout << "signature " << tjp->signature() << std::endl;
  }
};


#include "monitor.h" // runtime monitor
void invoke_a0_before() {
  Hello::advice1_a0_before();
}
void invoke_a1_before(void *djp) {
  typedef DynamicJoinPoint<0> DJP;
  Hello::advice1_a1_before<DJP>((DJP*)djp);
}
/* module initialisation code */

__attribute__ ((constructor))
void __init_dynamic_aspects() {
  monitor<invoke_a0_before,0,0>::registerBeforeAdvice();
  monitor<invoke_a1_before,0,0>::registerBeforeAdvice();
}
__attribute__ ((destructor))
void __fini_dynamic_aspects() {
  monitor<invoke_a0_before,0,0>::unregisterBeforeAdvice();
  monitor<invoke_a1_before,0,0>::unregisterBeforeAdvice();
}
```

As seen from the above listing, *dac++* extracts ids of the join points matched by the pointcut from the project repository to translate pointcut descriptions into a sequence of template-based C++ statements, which use join point ids as parameters, to register the advice code. This template-based pointcut matching mechanism provides a very efficient solution in comparison to any mechanism based on signature matching at runtime.

The adoption of AspectC++ both for static and dynamic aspects has resulted in the merger of the static and dynamic AOP for C++, where the decision whether an aspect is static or dynamic is delayed till the deployment stages, and is purely driven by the available resources and the requirements. This type of flexibility is particularly crucial for resource-constrained systems, which follow the principle of static evolution where possible and runtime evolution where necessary.

6   Static and Runtime Evolution in the eCos Operating System

eCos is a small and highly configurable operating system targeted for the market of embedded systems. It is available for a broad variety of 16 and 32 bit microprocessor architectures (PPC, x86, H8/300, ARM7, ARM9, ...) and used in many different application domains (MP3 player, digital cameras, printers, routers, ...). The eCos system itself is provided as a congregation of various components, which are configured *statically* with a configuration tool called *eCosConfig*. The components are implemented in

Table 2. The left table shows the amount of CCCs in the source code of the kernel before and after refactoring, the right table shows the distribution of the cross cutting code over the different CCCs

	original LOC	original %	aspectized LOC	aspectized %
CCC Code	1069	20.54 %	290	6.41 %
Component Code	4136	79.46 %	4237	93.59 %
Total	5205	100 %	4527	100 %

	original	aspectized
Tracing	336	4
Assertions	384	286
Kernel Instrumentation	162	0
Interrupt Synchronization	187	0
Total	1069	290

a mixture of C++, C, C-preprocessor macros and assembly code. After the user selects an appropriate eCos configuration within *eCosConfig*, a configuration-specific system of headers and makefiles is generated, which is used to build the *eCos-library*. Against this library the final applications will be linked.

6.1 Analysis

In the context of a case study, we analyzed several parts of the eCos system (kernel, C library, POSIX subsystem, μITRON subsystem, Memory Management, Wallclock Driver, and Watchdog Driver) with respect to their evolvability. For the following discussion we will exemplarily concentrate on the eCos kernel.

For system software clean encapsulation of the different features is crucial in order to be evolvable. Therefore, our first goal was to figure out the positions and the amount of code that implements highly crosscutting concerns and locally crosscutting optional features. The analysis revealed that 20.54% of the kernel source code is needed to implement four highly crosscutting concerns: *Tracing*, *Assertion*, and *Kernel Instrumentation* (profiling) for development support and *Interrupt Synchronization*. Table 2 (column "original") presents the numbers for each of these concerns individually. Actually, these figures only reflect the number of call sites activating these CCCs, the functional parts of their implementations were not taken into account here.

The results of the analysis show that eCos indeed is configurable to a great extent, but certainly lacks evolvability. The high portion of crosscutting concerns and the amount of scattered configuration options in the eCos kernel indicate that complex correlations between different features exist on the level of the implementation. These correlations make it very hard to omit certain features or add new ones, in other words, these correlations hamper the evolution of the eCos kernel.

6.2 Static Evolution

During the case study, we enhanced the evolvability of eCos by "aspectizing" the highly crosscutting concerns and crosscutting optional features mentioned in the previous section. The necessary refactoring of the source code was straight forward, as the affected code was easy to spot. Highly crosscutting concerns such as *Tracing* are realized as macros to avoid code redundancy. Optional feature implementations are bracketed by preprocessor directives for conditional compilation.

The refactored code was also analyzed and the results are shown in the right columns of Table 2. These results clearly illustrate, that most of the crosscutting concerns and optional features could be modularized very well by aspects. However, we were not able to modularize assertions, due to their individual semantic, and features implemented in C, as our aspect weaver is not capable of weaving in pure C code.

6.3 Runtime Evolution

The Mars Pathfinder mission launched in 1996 is one of the most well-known space missions of the foregoing decade. On the one side, because it was the first mission to Mars that included a rover (robotic exploration vehicle). On the other side, because of the problems experienced during this mission [27]. After a few days of successful operation the spacecraft experienced total system resets and each of these resets caused a loss of valuable metereological data.

The absence of the tracing facility on the spacecraft forced the engineers to spend hours running the system on the exact spacecraft replica in their lab with tracing turned on, in an attempt to replicate the precise conditions under which they believed that the reset occurred. The traces finally revealed the priority inversion scenario. The problem was that while a low and a high priority task were competing for the same mutex, a middle priority task preempted the low priority task holding the mutex and, thus, prevented it from unlocking the mutex. The high priority task, thereby, was delayed too long and missed its deadline. This in turn, caused a watchdog to go off and reset the whole system. While such a scenario does not cause too much trouble in normal computing systems it is a serious problem in a real-time computing systems and known as uncontrolled priority inversion. Mutexes in VXWorks (the operating system used for this mission) could either be equipped with the priority inheritance protocol or not. Initially the mutex entailing the priority inversion was configured not to use the priority inheritance protocol. A C-interpreter, embedded into the computing system on the spacecraft, helped to fix the problem by uploading a C-program to the spacecraft with the purpose to enable the priority inheritance protocol for the particular mutex. From this point on, no priority inversion occurred any more. The problem was solved and the mission could be finished successfully.

Motivation. Both the tracing facility and the C-interpreter were absolutely crucial to solve the problem. However, the absence of the tracing facility in the actual system made it extremely hard and time consuming to locate the problem. Additionally, the support for the priority inheritance protocol was statically embedded in the computing system of the spacecraft, but what would had happened if it was not? Or if the C-interpreter was not a part of the computing system due to memory restrictions? The problem would have been unsolvable, the mission would have failed!

Furthermore, one should keep in mind that the scenario described above can not only be caused by design faults, but also in the context of runtime evolution. Consider you want to extend the functionality of a running system. Therefore, it might be necessary that additional threads have to be added which also have to lock a specific mutex. In such a scenario the conditions that enable priority inversion can easily be fulfilled by accident.

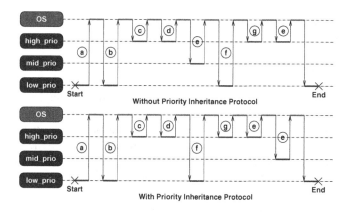

Fig. 6. Execution sequence without and with priority inheritance protocol

An alternative solution for such problems is provided by dynamic aspect weaving. Tracing and the priority inheritance protocol, both implemented as dynamic aspects, could then be uploaded to the spacecraft and woven into the running system. There is no need to embed the priority inheritance protocol from the very beginning, anymore, it would be loadable on demand. It would not be necessary to have a fully developed C-interpreter, only an infrastructure is needed that allows to weave aspects during runtime. In a former case study [23] we have already shown that tracing could be implemented by a dynamic aspect without suffering significant overhead in comparison to a static tracing aspect. Here we demonstrate that the eCos' priority inheritance protocol could also be implemented as dynamic aspect without having to put up with in-acceptable overhead in comparison to static aspects.

Implementation. We already re-factored eCos' priority inheritance protocol into a static aspect in previous work [6]. In the priority inheritance implementation of eCos the owner of a mutex inherits the priority of a thread trying to lock the same mutex and, thus, blocks. The owner's priority is set back to its original priority when it has unlocked all mutexes it owns, therefore, the count of mutexes locked by one thread has to be tracked. This variant of the priority inheritance protocol induces slightly longer blocking times when a thread holds more than one mutex, but simplifies the implementation a lot. The implementation as static aspect gives advice on the construction of a thread to initialize the number of mutexes locked and to the methods mutex_lock(), mutex_unlock() and mutex_trylock() of the mutex class to update the count of locked mutexes. Call advice on the activation site of the scheduler within method mutex_lock() transfers the priority of the blocking thread to the owner of the mutex while execution advice on the method mutex_unlock() checks whether all mutexes are unlocked again and the owner's original priority has to be restored.

The conversion from the static aspect to a dynamic version was very straight forward and demanded virtually no manual intervention. The dynamic advice transferring the blocking thread's priority to the owner of the mutex is shown below:

```
1   advice call("% Cyg_Scheduler::reschedule(...)")
2       && within("% Cyg_Mutex::lock_inner(...)")
3       : after() {
4   Cyg_Thread self = Cyg_Thread::self();
5   inherit_priority(tjp->that()->owner,self);
6   }
```

Evaluation Setup. In order to evaluate our implementation we implemented a small, synthetic eCos test application leading to a priority inversion scenario. At first, this scenario was executed with no priority inheritance protocol present. Then, the dynamic priority inheritance protocol aspect was woven into the system and the same scenario was executed again. The exact execution sequence of both scenarios is depicted in figure 6, the system calls used at each step of the execution sequence can be obtained from table 3.

Table 3. System calls used in the test application

	System Call	Description
a	mutex_lock(&mutex)	lock mutex, as it has not been locked before it can be successfully locked
b	thread_resume(high_prio)	activate thread high_prio, a context switch occurs
c	thread_resume(mid_prio)	activate thread mid_prio, no context switch occurs as mid_prio's priority is lower than high_prio's priority
d	mutex_lock(&mutex)	try to lock the mutex, as it has already been locked by low_prio, high_prio blocks
e	thread_exit()	the current thread finishes execution, a context switch occurs
f	mutex_unlock(&mutex)	thread low_prio unlocks the mutex, a context switch occurs as a thread with a higher priority is already awaiting the allocation of the mutex
g	cyg_mutex_unlock(&mutex)	thread high_prio unlocks the mutex

The test application was then linked against four different variants of eCos. Two variants contained support for the weaving of dynamic aspects. In the first of those two variants (variant *dynamic (perfect)*) only these join points needed to weave the dynamic priority inheritance aspect are hooked. This variant illustrates the overhead of the dynamic aspect itself. The second variant (variant *dynamic (flexible)*) hooks all methods of the classes Cyg_Thread and Cyg_Mutex for dynamic execution join points and all call sites within these classes for dynamic call join points. This variant also would allow to implement other synchronization mechanisms that affect more join points and illustrates the price one has to pay for dynamic evolution. The other variants use static aspects (variant *static*), only, and either contain the priority inheritance protocol or not.

The test application and the eCos operating system were compiled and linked using the GNU compiler collection and the GNU bintutils[2]. The testcase scenario was executed on a Pentium III (1 GHz) with caches turned on. The binary was downloaded onto the target machine using eCos Redboot[3] and gdb via the serial line and the gdb remote

---

[2] Gcc version 4.03, binutils version 2.16.1.
[3] The boot loader provided along with eCos.

protocol. The memory consumption of the eCos kernel was determined by analysing the memory map file generated by the GNU linker. For run time measurements the test application was executed for 4000 times and the average values of all these measurements obtained by the pentium's rdtsc instruction were computed.

Evaluation Results. The analysis of the memory consumption of the different variants of the test application is mainly restricted to the eCos kernel, the priority inheritance aspect and the dynamic weaver infrastructure. The results of the analysis are shown in table 4. For a perfect hooking (variant *dynamic (perfect)*) the memory overhead within the eCos kernel is very low, only 144 bytes of RAM and about 1.5 KB of ROM plus 52 bytes of ROM for the dynamic weaver infrastructure are additionally needed in comparison to the variant employing static aspects only (variant *static (prio. inh.)*). As soon as more join points are hooked (variant *dynamic (flexible)*), the memory requirements are noticeably increased by the dynamic weaver infrastructure, extra 628 Bytes of RAM and about 8 KB of ROM are needed in comparison to variant *static (prio. inh.)*. Keeping in mind that the complete test application consumes about 26 KB of RAM and between 18 KB and 27 KB of ROM, this is still a price that is affordable and should be definitely cheaper than embedding a fully developed C-interpreter. There is no RAM and only very little ROM consumption delcared for the dynamic weaver infrastructure, because a direct consequence of our dynamic weaver implementation is that the memory overhead caused by join point monitors is spread over the whole system (see section 4) and is already contained by the RAM and ROM demand of the kernel. The memory demand of the dynamic priority inheritance aspect looks quite large in contrast to the static aspect. This is because the static aspect uses introductions a lot, thus, this memory demand is assigned to the kernel itself, while the memory demand for the introductions of a dynamic aspects are fulfilled by the aspect itself.

Table 4. Memory consumption of the different eCos variants measured in bytes. *Kernel* subsumes the total memory consumption of the eCos kernel, *Priority Inh.* and *Weaver* refer to the memory consumption of the dynamic or the static aspect and the dynamic weaver infrastructure and are already contained in the kernel's memory demand. Column *Total* shows the memory consumption of the complete test application.

	Kernel		Priority Inh.		Weaver	Total	
	RAM	ROM	RAM	ROM	ROM	RAM	ROM
dynamic (flexible)	2834	13478	168	2562	52	27177	27738
dynamic (perfect)	2350	6800	136	1554	52	26721	21130
static (prio. inh.)	2206	5375	0	77	0	26495	18325
static (no. prio. inh.)	2194	4427	0	0	0	26445	17305

For the assessment of the runtime overhead imposed by the dynamic aspect and the dynamic weaver infrastructure we measured the execution time of the methods that are affected most by the priority inheritance protocol: these are mutex_lock() and mutex_unlock(), each with and without a subsequent context switch (refer to a,d,f,g in Table 3 and Figure 6). The results of these measurements are shown in Figure 4.

These results confirm the results of the memory measurement. Variant *dynamic (perfect)* only shows minimal decline of runtime performance in contrast to variant *static*, i.e. the runtime cost of one hook and the dynamic aspect is quite small in comparison to the static aspect. As soon as more join points are hooked (variant *dynamic (flexible)*) the runtime overhead increases and reaches a factor up to about two (mutex_lock (d), priority inheritance protocol enabled). The only figure not fostering this observation is the execution time of mutex_unlock() when no context switch follows and the priority inheritance protocol is enabled. Here the variant hooking more join points (*dynamic (flexible)*, 391 clock cycles) is faster than the variant that only hooks those join points that are really needed (*dynamic (perfect)*, 440 clock cycles). Actually, this system call even executes faster with the dynamic aspect woven (with priority inheritance protocol) than without the dynamic aspect (without priority inheritance protocol, 398 clock cylces). There are some explanations possible: caching effects, code alignment, DRAM refresh cycles, etc., but it is nearly impossible to identify the one of them that really causes the different execution times. The only thing that is almost sure is that there should be no relation to the code of the dynamic weaver infrastructure. In variant *dynamic (perfect)* the dynamic weaver infrastructure is activated twice during this system call, while it is activated for six times in variant *dynamic (flexible)*. The rest of this system call and the code of the dynamic weaver infrastructure are identical for both versions.

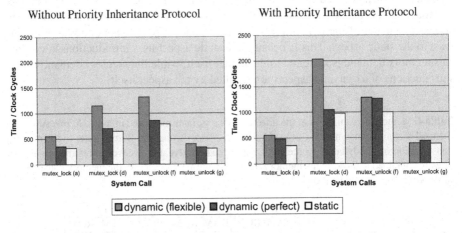

Fig. 7. Runtime performance comparison of different eCos variants. The left diagram shows the execution of the analysed system calls with the priority inheritance protocol, the right diagram the execution times without priority inheritance protocol.

6.4 Discussion

In general, this case study shows that for many concerns in embedded system software, aspect-oriented implementations and especially dynamically woven aspects are affordable. After the refactoring and the integration of the dynamic weaver infrastructure into eCos, the system now offers an even better static as well as runtime evolvability. Better static evolvability because crosscutting concerns and crosscutting optional features are now cleanly modularized and encapsulated. Better runtime evolvability because it is now possible to adapt to changing requirements at runtime. However, this case study also illustrates, that dynamic evolution is not for free, especially when many join points have to be instrumented the overhead increases sensibly.

7   Summary

In this paper, we have presented our improved version of the dynamic aspect weaver family, which has significantly reduced the memory and runtime overhead associated with the dynamic aspect weaving. Additionally, the availability of a single language for both static and dynamic aspects allowed to provide a unified mechanism for both static and runtime evolution. Such a unified mechanism results in an increased levels of flexibility and evolvability of software systems as the decision whether an aspect is a static or a dynamic one, is postponed to the later stages of deployement, and is decided as per the requirements and available resources. By virtue of our family-based dynamic weaver, even systems with very small memory footprint are able to afford some degree of dynamism to deal gracefully with the runtime evolution requirements they are subjected to.

References

1. Beuche, D.: Variant management with pure:variants. Technical report, pure-systems GmbH (2003), http://www.pure-systems.com/
2. Czarnecki, K., Eisenecker, U.W.: Generative Programming. Methods, Tools and Applications. Addison-Wesley, Reading (2000)
3. Popovici, A., et al.: Just in Time Aspects: efficient dynamic weaving for java. In: AOSD 2003, pp. 100–109. ACM Press, New York (2003)
4. Zhang, C., et al.: TinyC: Towards building a dynamic weaving aspect language for C. In: AOSD-FOAL 2003, Boston, USA (March 2003)
5. Bockisch, C., et al.: Virtual machine support for dynamic join points. In: AOSD 2004, Lancaster, UK, pp. 83–92. ACM Press, New York (2004)
6. Lohmann, D., et al.: A quantitative analysis of aspects in the eCos kernel. In: EuroSys 2006, pp. 191–204. ACM Press, New York (2006)
7. Schmidt, D.C., et al.: Pattern-Oriented Software Architecture: Patterns for Concurrent and Networked Objects (2000)
8. Kon, F., et al.: Monitoring, Security, and Dynamic Configuration with the DynamicTAO Reflective ORB. In: Middleware 2000. IFIP/ACM Distributed Systems Platforms and Open Distributed Processing (April 2000)
9. Lehman, M.M., et al.: Towards a theory of software evolution - and its practical impact. In: ISPSE 2000, pp. 2–11 (November 2000)
10. Engel, M., et al.: Supporting Autonomic Computing Functionality via Dynamic Operating System Kernel Aspects. In: AOSD 2005, pp. 51–62 (March 2005)
11. Loughran, N., et al.: Supporting Product Line Evolution With Framed Aspects. In: 3rd AOSD (AOSD-ACP4IS 2004) (March 2004)
12. Spinczyk, O., et al.: AspectC++: An aspect-oriented extension to C++. In: Field, T., Harrison, P.G., Bradley, J., Harder, U. (eds.) TOOLS 2002. LNCS, vol. 2324, pp. 53–60. Springer, Heidelberg (2002)

13. Greenwood, P., et al.: Dynamic framed aspects for dynamic software evolution. In: ECOOP-RAM-SE 2004 (June 2004)
14. Douence, R., et al.: An expressive aspect language for system applications with Arachne. In: AOSD 2005, pp. 27–38 (March 2005)
15. Pawlak, R., et al.: JAC: A flexible framework for AOP in Java. In: Yonezawa, A., Matsuoka, S. (eds.) Metalevel Architectures and Separation of Crosscutting Concerns. LNCS, vol. 2192, pp. 1–24. Springer, Heidelberg (2001)
16. Almajali, S., et al.: Dynamic Aspect Oriented C++ for Upgrading without Restarting. In: AITA 2004 (July 2004)
17. Apel, S., et al.: Combining Feature-Oriented and Aspect-Oriented Programming to Support Software Evolution. In: ECOOP-RAM-SE 2005, pp. 3–16 (July 2005)
18. Aussmann, S., et al.: Axon - Dynamic AOP through Runtime Inspection and Monitoring. In: ECOOP-ASARTI 2003, Darmstadt, Germany (July 2003)
19. Ishio, T., et al.: Program Slicing Tool for Effective Software Evolution Using Aspect-Oriented Technique. In: PSE 2003, pp. 3–12 (November 2003)
20. Ledoux, T., et al.: OpenCorba: A reflective open broker. In: Cointe, P. (ed.) Reflection 1999. LNCS, vol. 1616, pp. 197–214. Springer, Heidelberg (1999)
21. Cazzola, W., et al.: AOP for software evolution: a design oriented approach. In: Preneel, B., Tavares, S. (eds.) SAC 2005. LNCS, vol. 3897, pp. 1346–1350. Springer, Heidelberg (2006)
22. Gilani, W., et al.: Dynamic aspect weaver family for family-based adaptable systems. In: NODE 2005, pp. 94–109 (September 2005)
23. Schröder-Preikschat, W., et al.: Static and dynamic weaving in system software with As-pectC++. In: HICSS 2006 (2006)
24. Sato, Y., et al.: A selective, just-in-time aspect weaver. In: Pfenning, F., Smaragdakis, Y. (eds.) GPCE 2003. LNCS, vol. 2830, pp. 189–208. Springer, Heidelberg (2003)
25. Gomaa, H.: Architecture-centric evolution in software product lines. In: ECOOP-ACE 2005 (July 2005)
26. Verhoef, C.: Towards automated modification of legacy assets. Annals of Software Engineering 9(1-4), 315–336 (2000)
27. Wilner, D.: Vx-files: What really happened on mars? In: RTSS 1997. Keynote at the 18th IEEE Real-Time Systems Symposium (December 1997)

Patterns of Component Evolution

Rajesh Vasa[1], Markus Lumpe[2], and Jean-Guy Schneider[1]

[1] Faculty of Information & Communication Technologies
Swinburne University of Technology
P.O. Box 218
Hawthorn, VIC 3122, Australia
{rvasa,jschneider}@swin.edu.au
[2] Department of Computer Science
Iowa State University
Ames, IA 50011, USA
lumpe@cs.iastate.edu

Abstract. Contemporary software systems are composed of many components, which, in general, undergo phased and incremental development. In order to facilitate the corresponding construction process, it is important that the development team in charge has a good understanding of how individual software components typically evolve. Furthermore, software engineers need to be able to recognize abnormal patterns of growth with respect to size, structure, and complexity of the components and the resulting composite. Only if a development team understands the processes that underpin the evolution of software systems, will they be able to make better development choices. In this paper, we analyze recurring structural and evolutionary patterns that we have observed in public-domain software systems built using object-oriented programming languages. Based on our analysis, we discuss common growth patterns found in present-day component-based software systems and illustrate simple means to aid developers in achieving a better understanding of those patterns. As a consequence, we hope to raise the awareness level in the community on how component-based software systems tend to naturally evolve.

1 Introduction

The *Laws of Software Evolution*, as formulated by Lehman et al. [11], establish the fact that regardless of domain, size, or complexity, software systems evolve, they become more complex, and require more resources to preserve and simplify their structure. Software systems *must be continually adapted*, or else they become progressively less useful in a real-world environment. Many well-known techniques exist to facilitate system evolution in the presence of changing requirements. The key to a successful software evolution approach lies, however, not only in anticipating new requirements and adapting a system accordingly [7], but also in understanding of the nature and the dynamics of change.

Evolution is at the heart of component-based software engineering, which has become the major approach to develop modern, large-scale software systems [23, 22]. Component-based software technology has emerged from the object-oriented software

M. Lumpe and W. Vanderperren (Eds.): SC 2007, LNCS 4829, pp. 235–251, 2007.
© Springer-Verlag Berlin Heidelberg 2007

development approach, which is the predominant engineering method to build software systems today. Already a decade ago, Nierstrasz et al. [18] showed that objects provide a suitable organizational paradigm for both *decomposing* large applications into cooperating software entities and *composing* applications from pre-packaged software components. In addition, Dami [5] pointed out in his work that *extensibility* is another crucial aspect of software composition, which one must not underestimate. The desire to achieve substitutability and "plug-compatibility" of components imposes a certain discipline to structure, use, and connect component plugs that also impacts the overall design, architecture, and interaction patterns of an application.

Although we a have good grasp of the technological issues involving the evolution of class-based systems (e.g., the modular refinement of classes [3, 2, 13] and the injection of orthogonal behavior into classes [1, 3]), we have a less clear understanding of the nature and dynamics underlying change. So, how do software systems really evolve? How do components evolve? How does the interface of a component evolve? Can we provide a sufficient answer to those questions, while the definitive description of the term "component" is still elusive? In an attempt to offer some answers to these questions, the goal of this work is to provide a new perspective to the way software systems change over time. In particular, in this paper we shall (i) study selected recurring structural and evolutionary growth patterns that we have observed in present-day software systems and (ii) identify simple means that can help development teams improve the overall component-based product and process quality.

Our study focuses on *growth estimation*, an approach that offers a powerful means for proactive risk management [20]. In particular, we are interested in a *normalized ratio* of change in terms of size and complexity of component-based systems. Component-based software engineering emphasizes reuse rather than the creation of software artifacts. The evolution of a component-based system consequently involves the reuse and adaptation of existing *components off-the-shelf* (COTS) and naturally all of their embodied contextual relationships [23]. The size and complexity of these software artifacts is known and can be easily factored into the overall growth estimation of a system. However, a refined version of a system may also require new components and *partially-developed* software artifacts. The size and the complexity of these elements is largely unknown and, as a result, their development involves a fair degree of risk. However, this risk can be proactively assessed, as the growth value of these new elements is governed by a predefined and system-specific growth factor that is *unique* for each system and cultural environment within which the actual development is being carried out.

Precise assessment of the nature of how a software system evolves in the future is both an art and science [20]. The underlying development approach and utilized associated project metrics are invaluable assets that can provide a historical perspective to generate quantitative estimates on how a given system may evolve in the future. Common project metrics are, for example, the number of lines of code (LOC), the number of key classes, and the number of secondary classes. However, these metrics are based on absolute values, which can be misleading, as they only capture the absolute growth of a system. In order to achieve a better proactive risk management, we need to *normalize* the quantitative data to obtain a *relative* growth value that should be *constant* over the system's lifetime.

The rest of this paper is organized as follows: in Section 2, we introduce the concept of *software dependency graphs* and define a number of metrics based on such graphs used throughout our studies. In Section 3, we discuss our selection methodology and illustrate what techniques were used to extract information out of the software systems under investigation. Section 4 details our observations and presents the growth patterns identified. We discuss related work in Section 5 and conclude this paper in Section 6 with a summary of the main insights as well as directions for further work.

2   Understanding Software Structure

2.1   Software Metrics

Software systems exhibit two broad quantitative aspects that we can measure using a wide range of software metrics [6]: *size* and *complexity*. These measures provide an objective view for both the process being used to create the software system and its internal structure. By rigorously collecting and analyzing these measures over time, we can distill a temporal dimension, which is capable of revealing new, yet invaluable information like the rate of size growth [12, 11] and evolutionary jumps in the complexity of a software system [8], respectively. Moreover, recent results have shown that *evolution measures* can be used to detect architectural shifts automatically [26].

Numerous approaches have been proposed and verified (e.g., purely size-oriented measures like the number of lines of code (LOC) or function-oriented measures to analyze process aspects like costs and productivity) that can help us to understand the size as well as the complexity of a software system. For object-oriented systems, common *size* measures include, for example, the *number of classes*, the *number of methods*, and the *number of public methods*. Size measures provide an indication of the *volume of functionality* provided by a software system and can be used as a broad indicator of effort required to build that system, as it takes usually more effort to create a larger-size system than a smaller one.

Complexity is commonly captured by measuring structural attributes of a software system [10]. An attractive approach to measure the complexity of class-based systems is to analyze the *fan-in* and *fan-out* ratios for a given class [26]. Theses measures naturally capture the number of classes a given class X depends upon and the number of classes that depend on X. In combination, theses ratios provide a precise information about the degree of *coupling* of X with other classes in the system. For example, a class X with a high fan-in (relative to other classes in the system) is being considered "complex", since any changes made to X have the potential to significantly impact other classes that depend on X. Similarly, a class X that has a very high fan-out is also considered "complex", since X makes use of a large number of different functional aspects of the system in order to satisfy its responsibilities. As a consequence, developers cannot alter X in a meaningful way before they understand all classes that X uses.

2.2   Type Dependency Graphs

In order to measure fan-in and fan-out, we need to construct a *type dependency graph* of a software system [26]. For the purpose of this presentation, a type dependency graph

G^T is an ordered pair (V, E), where V is a finite, nonempty set of *types* (i.e., classes and interfaces) and E is a finite, possibly empty, set of *directed links* between types (i.e., $E \subseteq V \times V$). In addition, we shall use N to denote the number of nodes and L to denote the number of directed types links of a given type dependency graph G^T throughout the rest of this paper.

In order to capture both fan-in and fan-out of a given type, represented by node $n \in V$ in G^T, we use $l_{in}(n)$ to denote the *in-degree* and $l_{out}(n)$ to denote the *out-degree* of node n. More precisely, $l_{in}(n)$ is the number of inbound links into n (i.e., $l_{in}(n) = \mathbf{card}(\{l \mid l = \{n_i, n_j\} \wedge n_i, n_j \in V \wedge n = n_j \wedge i \neq j\})$) and $l_{out}(n)$ is the number of outbound links from the node n (i.e., $l_{out}(n) = \mathbf{card}(\{l \mid l = \{n_i, n_j\} \wedge n_i, n_j \in V \wedge n = n_i \wedge i \neq j\})$). The in-degree is a measure of the "popularity" of node n in the graph G^T, whereas the out-degree is node n's "usage" of other types in the graph G^T [19].

We can further refine the notions of in-degree and out-degree in the context of the analysis of component-based applications. Each component in a given system may comprise several classes and interfaces. The most frequent techniques used to construct these composites are *aggregation*, an approach based on inheritance and interface composition, respectively, and *containment*, a delegation-based approach to compose the often orthogonal behavior.[1] These techniques give rise to a refinement of the measures in-degree and out-degree in which we also distinguish between *intra-* and *inter-*component links. A given link to or from a node n may or may not cross the boundary of the containing component, depending on some organizational, structural, and/or functional features. For example, if an outbound link from node n ends in a node n_j that occurs within the boundary of the component in question, then we call this link an *internal* outbound link and denote by $l^i_{out}(n)$ it's corresponding *internal out-degree*. On the other hand, if an outbound link ends in a node $n_{j'}$ that lies outside of the component's boundary, then we call this link an *external* outbound link and denote by $l^e_{out}(n)$ it's corresponding *external out-degree*. Hence, the out-degree of node n is $l_{out}(n) = l^i_{out}(i) + l^e_{out}(n)$.

The refinement of in-degree is defined similarly. That is, we denote by $l^i_{in}(n)$ the *internal in-degree* and by $l^e_{in}(n)$ the *external in-degree* of a type node n. The total in-degree of a node n is $l_{in}(n) = l^i_{in}(i) + l^e_{in}(n)$.

Finally, for any given node n in a type dependency graph G^T, we can measure a number of additional, yet very meaningful, attributes related to its size, such as

- the total number of methods m^n defined by n;
- the number of defined *public* methods p^n;
- the number of branch instructions b^n; and
- the digital measure of inheritance i^n indicating whether node n inherits from another node n_k (apart from the language default).

2.3 Layering

The measures *in-degree* and *out-degree* provide a powerful, size-oriented tool to discover, monitor, and analyze the architectural composition of a software system. In particular, we are able to observe the forming of application-specific boundaries or *layers*.

---

[1] The notions aggregation and containment have been popularized by the COM/ActiveX component model [21].

These layers are constituted by types, whose in-degree and out-degree share similar characteristics. Every software system (i.e., the whole application and its individual components) exhibits the layer-building behavior. For the purpose of this study, we classify each type to belong to one of four distinct layers. These layers are:

- **Foundation:** The types in the Foundation Layer F only provide their services to other types occurring *within* a given component (or system). The types in the Foundation Layer do not depend on any types except those defined in external libraries and the runtime environment. For every type $n \in F$ it holds that $l_{in}^i(n) > 0$, $l_{in}^e(n) \geq 0$, $l_{out}^i(n) = 0$, and $l_{out}^e(n) \geq 0$.
- **Central:** The types in the Central Layer C both provide services to and require services from other types occurring within a given component (or system). For every type $n \in C$, we have $l_{in}^i(n) > 0$, $l_{in}^e(n) \geq 0$, $l_{out}^i(n) > 0$, and $l_{out}^e(n) \geq 0$.
- **Top:** The types in the Top Layer T do not provide any services to other types occurring within a given component (or system). However, types in the Top Layer depend on at least one other type occurring within a given component (or system). As a result, for every $n \in T$, we have $l_{in}^i(n) = 0$, $l_{in}^e(n) \geq 0$, $l_{out}^i(n) > 0$, and $l_{out}^e(n) \geq 0$.
- **Free:** The types in the Free Layer U neither provide any services to types occurring within a given component (or system) nor require any services from the other three layers. For every type $n \in U$ it holds that $l_{in}^i(n) = 0$, $l_{in}^e(n) \geq 0$, $l_{out}^i(n) = 0$, and $l_{out}^e(n) \geq 0$. Types of the Free Layer denote either dormant software artifacts that do not contribute to the overall behavior of a component (or system) or their usage cannot be detected statically.

The reader should note that all types can be assigned to exactly one of the four layers given above, hence if V is the set of all types of a given component, then it holds that $V = T \cup C \cup F \cup U$. It also holds that $l_{in}^e(n) \geq 0$ and $l_{out}^e(n) \geq 0$ for types in any of the four layers. Hence, we can optimize our analysis and do not need to consider external inbound links and external outbound links when assigning types to layers.

Once a software system has been represented as a dependency graph G^T, we can apply appropriate graph theoretical techniques to discover, monitor, analyze, and predict how this given system will evolve in the future. By constructing a dependency graph G^T for each new version of a given software system and comparing the new graph with the one built for previous versions, we can refine the analysis process and obtain early indicators for potential risks.

3 Methodology

Both the version-specific type dependency graphs and the deduced structural layer-based decomposition of live systems provide us with suitable means not only to unveil the inherent nature of component-based software systems, but also to predict reliably their anticipated growth patterns with respect to size and complexity.

To demonstrate our approach in greater detail, we have selected five representative open-source projects and present our findings in the remainder of this work. For all systems, we have catalogued their corresponding reoccurring size and growth patterns.

Table 1. Components under analysis

Name	Releases	Initial Size N_1	Current Size N_k	Description
Acegi	17	135	368	Role-based security framework
Active MQ	26	205	2295	Message queue framework
Hibernate	44	120	1053	Object-relational mapping framework
Spring	39	386	1527	Light-weight container
Xalan	13	207	919	XML parsing/transformation library

Based on these patterns, we can create simple *predictive models* being able to capture relevant aspects associated with the nature of how a given component-based software system evolves.

3.1 Input Data Set Selection

Our primary focus in this work is on open-source Java-based systems. In order to identify suitable systems for our empirical study, we define a number of selection criteria that are expected to yield the best results with respect to assessing the complexity, size, and evolution history of a given system. Our selection criteria are as follows:

1. The system is a single *component* or *application framework*, that is, it cannot be used as a stand-alone application and, as a consequence, has to be analyzed as a part of a bigger, composite system.
2. At least *10 builds* of the system are available. Only complete releases are considered builds. Branches and releases not derived from the main system tree are ignored.
3. The system has been in active development and use for at least *24 months* to increase the likelihood of the existence of a significant development history.
4. The system should comprise of at least *200 types* (i.e., classes and interfaces) at some point in its lifetime and should consist of no less than 100 types when being analyzed. This ensures the anaysis of components of a realistic complexity.
5. Availability of change logs that indicate defect fixes, addition of new features, and highlight structural changes. This data aids us in understanding and attributing changes.

Using these selection criteria, we have identified five systems (cf. Table 1), which provide a best match for our study with respect to time and resource constraints. The reader should note that we have initially been able to identify over 100 systems that met our selection criteria [26].

In addition, we use a *Release Sequence Number* (RSN) [4] as the pseudo-time measure for all systems under investigation. RSNs are universally applicable and independent of any release numbering scheme and/or schedule. A RSN is a sequential number allocated based on release dates, where the first version is 1 and then each subsequent version increases by one.

3.2 Extracting Metrics

In order to perform the required data mining, we developed a *metrics extraction* tool [26], especially designed to analyze Java programs and to extract growth-related data to capture the degree of change of a system with respect to its size and complexity. This tool takes as input the core JAR files for each version of the system being investigated and generates the desired metric data.

Our extraction tool uses ASM, a Java Bytecode manipulation framework,[2] to collect static dependency information from the classes contained within the core JARs. For each type, the set of dependencies are extracted and recorded. However, the following types are ignored, as they do not add any specific value to the analysis process [26]:

1. All primitive Java types like `int`,
2. The class `java.lang.String`,
3. The root class `java.lang.Object`, and
4. `self`-references (i.e., all occurrences of `this`).

The reader should note that all systems that we have analyzed require also some additional Java-based third party libraries. However, these third party libraries as well as all Java standard libraries do not impact the size and complexity of the analyzed software system. For this reason, our metric extraction tool ignores dependencies associated with types originating from those libraries, an approach that does not compromise the overall quality and precision of the collected data in our study.

4   Observations and Analysis

In the previous sections, we have outlined the selection criteria required to identify five suitable Java-based systems for analysis and briefly discussed the measures in which we are particularly interested in. In this section, we illustrate how the notion of *power-scaling relationship* [16] in software dependency graphs can be used as a means to discover and analyze recurring structural and evolutionary patterns in the component-based systems.

4.1   Power-Scaling Relationship

In our previous work on detecting structural changes in object-oriented software systems [26], we developed a *growth estimation model* for calculating the total number of type links L in a software dependency graph G^T given the total number of type nodes N. This model is based on a *power-scaling relationship* [16] that can be established between L and N. More specifically, if N denotes the total number of types (as defined in Section 2) and L the total number of dependencies between types (i.e., associations, inheritance, and interface refinements) [26], then it holds that

$$L = N^{\beta}, \quad \text{where } \beta \approx 1.4 \tag{1}$$

The reader should note, however, that β is *not* a constant! It changes marginally between successive versions and usually stabilizes around the value 1.4 as a software system matures [26].

---

[2] ASM is available at *http://asm.objectweb.org*

As we will outline in the following, power-scaling relationships are central to our study as they are commonly found in software dependency graphs, most notably between the total number of types and methods, both public and private. Therefore, such relationships will allow us to create estimation models for the corresponding dependencies over a number of versions of a given software component.

4.2   Relationship Between Types and Methods

As the first item in our study, we analyze the relationship between the number of types in a component with (i) the total number of methods (denoted by M) and (ii) the total number of *public* methods (denoted by P). The number of methods in a software component[3] can be considered as a measure that denotes the *volume of functionality* of this component. The public methods of a component, on the other hand, can be seen to be the potential *external interface* of that component, although in practice only a small part of this interface may be used by external parties. However, analyzing the use of the external interface of a component is beyond the scope of this study.

Analyzing the five selected systems, our data reveals that the total number of methods M and the number of public methods P grow predictably along with the number of types N. More significantly, there is a power-scaling relationship between the total number of types and the total number of (public) methods. We observe that

$$M = N^{\beta^M}, \quad \text{where } \beta^M \approx 1.35 \tag{2}$$

$$P = N^{\beta^P}, \quad \text{where } \beta^P \approx 1.30 \tag{3}$$

The reader should note that a linear model (i.e., $M = \alpha N$) for the relationship between types and (public) methods cannot be used, as it is not sensitive enough to pick up slight slopes in data and, therefore, would be unsuitable to recognize medium-sized architectural changes from one version of a system to another.

Our data also indicates that as the size of a component increases, the rate at which the public methods are added starts to decrease. Additionally, we notice that public methods are added at a faster rate early in the development life-cycle. Once a component becomes more mature and has stabilized, our data shows that it will resist an increase in its public interface. A similar observation can also be made for non-public methods.

Based on these two observations, we can estimate the total number of public methods that a given system will have in the current version given the corresponding information from the previous version. If N_v and β_v^P denote the total number of types and the scaling factor for version v of a given component, respectively, then it holds that the estimated scaling factor for version $v+1$, denoted by $^*\beta_{v+1}^P$, is

$$^*\beta_{v+1}^P = \beta_v^P + \gamma^P \cdot \mathbf{sng}(N_v - N_{v+1}) \quad \text{where } \gamma^P \approx 0.001 \tag{4}$$

with **sng** being the *signum* function.[4] γ^P in the formula above encodes the observation that β^P tends to slowly decrease as the size of a component increases. Furthermore, the

---

[3] We use the term *component* as a synonym for both a whole software system and individual, self-contained software artifacts.

[4] The signum function returns $+1, -1$ or 0 if it is applied to a positive number, negative number, or zero, respectively.

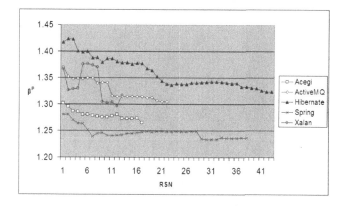

Fig. 1. Evolution of scaling factor β^P

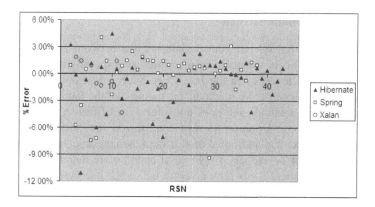

Fig. 2. Estimation error for public methods P

more mature a component becomes, the rate at which β^P changes decreases. The distribution of the scaling factor β^P for all five components under investigation is illustrated in Figure 1. A similar relationship can be defined for methods M with a scaling factor β^M, and the estimation model holds with $\gamma \approx 0.002$. The reader may note that γ is a constant in our model, but further analysis may result in a revised model where γ is a function.

We have derived this model based on our analysis of Acegi and ActiveMQ and then applied it to the other three components to verify our growth estimation model. Our data shows that this model is able to estimate the total number of public methods in a component with no more than 3% error rate in 75% of the time (cf. Figure 2). If the error rate is beyond a given, project-dependent threshold, then this is an indication that substantial changes have been made between two versions, a situation that deserves special documentation and analysis, in particular with respect to an emerging risk.

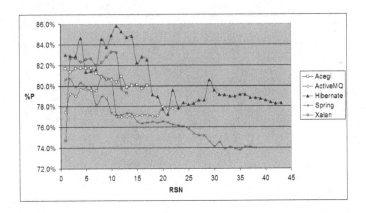

Fig. 3. Percentage of public methods %P

4.3   Percentage of Public Methods

Accross all five analyzed systems, our data shows that between 74% and 86% of all methods are public. This is unusually large and deserves special attention. We suspect that there is a natural tendency in the Java Open Source development community to create a larger number of public methods, indicating that the language makes it very easy to define public methods and does not offer a set of features that would allow the developers to choose a greater level of control over the "visibility" of the code that they write. We feel that additional modifiers in the language, in combination with appropriate training of developers, might yield better, more maintainable, outcomes. Ideally, a component should only have a very small public interface that is available to outside developers.

Our data also reveals that, with few exceptions, the proportion of public methods in a given component tends to fluctuate in the 5% range. Hence, if in the initial version 75% of the methods are public, then our data indicates that we are likely to see a range of in-between 70% and 80% over the duration of the project. However, the tendency for this measure is to decrease rather than to increase. So, over time the percentage of public methods will tend to go down from 80% to 75% rather than the other way.

Similar to the growth estimation model illustrated in Section 4.2, we are able to define a model to estimate the number of public methods in the next version of a component or systems, denoted by $^*P$, as

$$^*P_{v+1} = N_{v+1}^{^*\beta_{v+1}^P} \tag{5}$$

This model allows us to estimate the total number of public methods in a system (i) within 2% accuracy 70% of the time and (ii) within 5% accuracy 90% of the time. When the estimated value is not within a small margin of error compared to the "real" value, it provides a good indicator for the development team to reflect on what changes were made to the component/framework in order to provide additional documentation. The threshold should be determined by the development team based on observations from

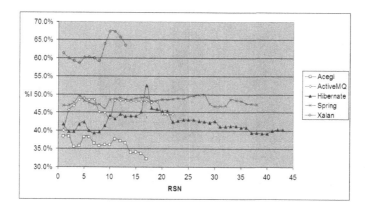

Fig. 4. Percentage of derived types

their product data over the recent past. Further, our data shows that as time progresses, the estimation accuracy increases because less changes are made and, as a consequence, the error threshold should be reduced accordingly. Figure 3 illustrates the evolution of the percentages of public methods for all analyzed systems.

4.4   Growth Proportion in Inheritance

Our study also reveals a rather intriguing property, namely that the proportion of types that extend (i.e., are derived from) another type is strongly bounded and does not change significantly. We found that, in general, between 35% and 50% of the types are derived from another type. On average, there is a 45% chance that a type is derived from another type. The exception is Xalan, which has a much higher number of derived types (cf. Figure 4). Further analysis showed that Xalan, being an XML parser, exhibits a strong relationship to the underlying hierarchical structure of XML documents. This seems to be an architectural choice made by the development team.

Our data also demonstrates that the variation in the proportion of types that are derived from another type, although system dependent, is very low. Generally, the observed variation is around 5%. There is no strong tendency over time for the components/frameworks to either have more or less types that (i) are derived or (ii) derive another type. This might indicate that there is a certain cultural bias and developer habit at work and the overall size/maturity does not have a direct impact on the rate of change. This, however, is something that needs further investigation. In the five systems that we have analyzed, the probability of significant change in the number of types deriving from another type (i.e., more than 2%) between two subsequent versions is very low (on average, less than 0.15%). This is further illustrated in Figure 4.

4.5   Type Distribution in Layers

In all five systems, we consistently find that the Central Layer (c.f. Section 2.3) contains the majority of the types. On average, the Central Layer C contains about 80% of the

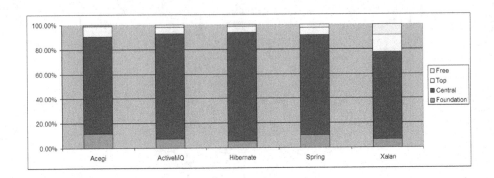

Fig. 5. Type distribution in layers

types in the component, the Top Layer T and the Foundation Layer F contain 9% each, and the Free Layer U contains the remaining 2% of the types. Figure 5 illustrates the type distribution of the *last* available release for each analyzed system.

Although the precise values change from component to component, it is interesting to note that the Foundation Layer has a small number of types (i.e., around 9%). This indicates that developers naturally tend to keep the number of the types in the layer that has the highest *ripple impact* low.

The natural interface exposed by the components is most likely located in the Top Layer since it contains types that are not directly used internally. Our study shows that compared with the Central Layer, the Top Layer is also fairly small, indicating that component designers tend to keep the interface of a component as small as possible. Although the Top Layer contains the set of types that external users of this component are most likely to access, it does not restrict types in other layers to be used. It would be ideal, if languages like Java provide better language abstractions that allow developers to explicitly tag the external interface to a component, allowing for further analysis.

To further illustrate the distribution of types between layers, consider Table 2, where the layer distribution for the first 18 versions of Hibernate is recorded. Besides the version number/name, Table 2 lists the number of classes for a given RSN, the number of types (classes or interfaces) that are derived from another type (denoted by I), and the percentage of classes in the Foundation, Central, Top, and Free layers (denoted by $\%F$, $\%C$, $\%T$, and $\%U$, respectively). Table 2 also lists the total number of methods as well as the number of public methods (denoted by M and P, respectively).

We would like to highlight that between RSN 3 and 4, an unusual amount of change can be observed in type distribution across layers. An inspection of the available change logs reveals that a major refactoring of the core code was performed. The reader may note that this change could also be detected purely by observing the growth in size (i.e., N and P). However, between RSN 14 and 15, another change in the distribution of types between layers occurs. This change cannot be detected by observing size measures. N, P, and I all remain unchanged.

Further, as documented in the change logs and discussion groups, we would like to note that the team changed the underlying structure between version 1.2.2 and 2.0. This change can be observed in the distribution of types between layers (cf. Figure 6).

Table 2. History of Hibernate

RSN	Version	N	I	$\%F$	$\%C$	$\%T$	$\%U$	M	P	β^M	β^P
1	0.9.1	120	50	0.075	0.850	0.075	0.000	1065	873	1.456	1.415
2	0.9.2	126	50	0.087	0.841	0.071	0.000	1175	963	1.462	1.421
3	0.9.3	126	50	0.079	0.849	0.071	0.000	1174	962	1.461	1.420
4	0.9.5	144	60	0.049	0.833	0.104	0.014	1246	1044	1.434	1.399
5	0.9.6	163	69	0.049	0.834	0.104	0.012	1523	1229	1.439	1.397
6	0.9.9	185	74	0.065	0.827	0.092	0.016	1829	1473	1.439	1.397
7	0.9.10	201	79	0.060	0.821	0.104	0.015	1923	1553	1.426	1.386
8	0.9.14	222	88	0.068	0.815	0.104	0.014	2136	1789	1.419	1.386
9	1.0.0	242	100	0.062	0.822	0.103	0.012	2312	1920	1.411	1.377
10	1.1.0.b7	270	119	0.059	0.826	0.104	0.011	2762	2329	1.415	1.385
11	1.1.0	296	128	0.071	0.821	0.098	0.010	3102	2647	1.413	1.385
12	1.1.6	342	152	0.070	0.816	0.102	0.012	3690	3131	1.408	1.379
13	1.2.0	367	161	0.084	0.798	0.104	0.014	4047	3337	1.406	1.374
14	1.2.1	377	166	0.082	0.801	0.103	0.013	4198	3469	1.406	1.374
15	1.2.2	377	166	0.069	0.878	0.040	0.013	4260	3439	1.409	1.373
16	2.0b1	390	176	0.074	0.885	0.028	0.013	4489	3630	1.410	1.374
17	2.0.0	364	191	0.038	0.926	0.033	0.003	4083	3280	1.410	1.373
18	2.1.0	446	206	0.040	0.910	0.047	0.002	5301	4154	1.406	1.366

However, this level of change cannot be detected by purely looking at size growth – the number of classes N only increases by 13 (cf. Table 2). It is interesting to note that both, β^M and β^P, do not change significantly between version 1.2.2 and 2.0, either, yet another indication that a range of measures is needed to truly understand evolution of software.

4.6   Proportional Growth in Layers

Another result of our study is that components undergo phases of changes and that the proportion of types in the various layers slightly changes over time. When a component is not very mature (i.e., early in its development life span), the distribution of types in the various layers changes much more frequently than in a component that has reached a certain level of maturity. Hibernate, for example, underwent three distinct phases so far. Early in its life span, the proportion of types in various layers has changed much more than in later releases of Hibernate, as is illustrated in Figure 6.

But why is it interesting to study the evolution in the layers themselves? In software development, there are two distinct development strategies, namely *top-down* and *bottom-up*. In the top-down approach, we develop the interface of a component and then slowly add the functionality to support this interface. Hence, as per our layer definition, the Top Layer components are defined first, followed by the Central Layer and finally the Foundation Layer components are added. In the bottom-up development approach, however, this sequence is reversed and the Foundation Layer is developed first. In practice, one would expect a mixture of both approaches to be used by software developers, with the tendency to favor one approach over the other, when we take a distinct time interval.

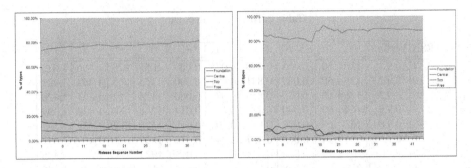

Fig. 6. Type evolution of the Spring framework (left) and Hibernate (right)

In order to identify a bottom-up development approach, we should be able to observe the proportion of the number of classes in the Foundation Layer decreasing over time, while the Central Layer and the Top Layer increase. This would indicate that the Foundation layer types have matured and the developers are working on the code in other layers. However, only the Spring framework shows more of a bottom-up approach rather than the top-down approach (cf. Figure 6). We hypothesize that this upwards trend in the Central Layer will stabilize as the product matures. It does not seem to be practical, however, to have a system where more than 95% of the types are in the Central Layer. On the contrary, our study shows that there is a natural tendency to host around 80% of the types in the Central Layer.

Developers working on the Hibernate project exhibit a tendency to add types equally in all layers. This seems to be the case for all analyzed systems and we cannot identify any periods where either a top-down or the bottom-up approach is clearly visible. Our data reveals that evolution of components tends to happen in vertical slices, where the types are distributed over all layers. A larger sample size may provide further information and other trends, however this is beyond the scope of our current anaylsis.

5   Related Work

Modern software systems are built from of a large number of interacting and mutual-dependent parts. One way to study these systems is to use *complex systems theory* [14], which suggests that in order to understand a complex system, one should use a *top-down* approach in which the system properties are inferred from its observable behavior rather than focusing on the individual parts in the beginning. This position is also taken by Newmann [17], who argues that complex systems exhibit a certain set of *emergent* properties, which become only visible at the system level and may not have been intentionally created by the system designers. Understanding and cataloguing emergent properties can provide us with valuable insights and a new prospective to grasp the complexity and evolutionary growth patterns of modern, complex component-based software systems.

Much of the seminal work in the field of software evolution has been done over a number of years by Lehman et al. [11]. Their work suggests that at the system level, the evolutionary behavior of a software system is systemic and not completely under the control of the individual developers. Turski [25] made a similar observation. Based on his analysis of the nature of software evolution, he presented an *inverse-square* model [25] that suggests that the growth of a software system is inversely proportional to its complexity, and as complexity increases, the rate of growth is constrained. However, while analyzing the Linux operating system, Godfrey et al. [9, 8] discovered that some systems have a *hyper-linear* growth curve. As a consequence, the models proposed by Turski and Lehman et al. do not always hold. Godfrey et al. concluded that the architecture of a system determines the evolutionary growth potential and a modular architecture allows for a system to grow faster than otherwise possible.

Mockus et al. [15] studied the evolution of Mozilla and the Apache web server, both open source software systems. They, like Godfrey et al., argue that the design structure of the software system has a direct impact on the development speed. A highly modular, component-based architecture allows for fast evolution, whereas a highly interdependent architecture generally requires a longer period of time between released versions.

In our previous work on software evolution [26], we presented a growth estimation model built on top of an observed *power-scaling relationship* between the total number of nodes and the total number of links in a software dependency graph G^T. We also showed that when the estimation model fails to predict the growth within a 7% error margin, then this error is induced by significant architectural shifts in the analyzed version of the software system. However, these architectural shifts may also signify a potential risk that needs to be addressed in a proactive manner. This proactive risk management is at the heart of our growth estimation model as it provides a powerful feedback mechanism for both to improve the development process and to offer guidance to a more controllable evolution practice of software systems. Furthermore, the results of our work also lend renewed support to Turski's hypothesis [24] that, as system complexity increases, the rate of growth of the software systems tends to decrease.

6 Conclusions and Future Work

Developers constructing components in a software system can mitigate risks by better understanding typical patterns of software evolution. Using an emperical investigation of popular software components with a substantial development history, we presented recurring structural and evolutionary patterns in this work. Supported by quantitative analysis and the patterns identified, we have highlighted atypical evolution of components and discussed the reasons that caused such changes. In this context, we have observed that for certain types of changes, more than one measure may be needed to highlight deviations from normal growth patterns. However, we have not yet been able to identify which measure can detect what kind of atypical change; this is a topic for future investigations.

Although our analysis shows that software grows over time, the structure and scope of growth is in general not erratic. We have observed that the percentage of derived types in a given component does not change significantly over time. Also, the naturally exposed interface of a component does not change as much as commonly perceived.

Our investigation into the nature of software evolution lead us to construct type dependency graphs and classify the types within a component into four orthogonal layers. We noticed that, in general, the distribution of the proportion of types in these layers is relatively stable. Where substantial changes in the proportional distribution were observed, they could always be attributed to significant architectural changes. As a side-effect of the layering, we were also able to detect the high-level construction methodology (e.g, top-down, bottom-up) that was most likely used to build a given component.

The growth estimation models presented in this work rely on information of the previous version of a component and offer low error rates. It is likely that we can improve the accuracy of our estimations by using information of more than one previous version. This, however, is still the topic of ongoing work.

References

1. Appel, W.A.: Modern Compiler Implementation in Java, 2nd edn. Cambridge University Press, Cambridge (2002)
2. Bergel, A., Ducasse, S., Nierstrasz, O., Wuyts, R.: Classboxes: Controlling Visibility of Class Extensions. Journal of Computer Languages, Systems & Structures 31(3–4), 107–126 (2005)
3. Clifton, C., Leavens, G.T., Chambers, C., Millstein, T.: MultiJava: Modular Open Classes and Symmetric Multiple Dispatch for Java. In: Proceedings OOPSLA 2000, ACM SIGPLAN Notices, vol. 35, pp. 130–146 (October 2000)
4. Cox, D.R., Lewis, P.A.W.: The Statistical Analysis of Series of Events. In: Monographs on Applied Probability and Statistics, Chapman and Hall, Sydney, Australia (1966)
5. Dami, L.: Software Composition: Towards an Integration of Functional and Object-Oriented Approaches. PhD thesis, Centre Universitaire d'Informatique, University of Geneva, CH (1994)
6. Fenton, N.E., Pfleeger, S.L.: Software Metrics: A Rigorous & Practical Approach, 2nd edn. Thomson Publishing (1996)
7. Gamma, E., Helm, R., Johnson, R., Vlissides, J.: Design Patterns. Addison-Wesley, Reading (1995)
8. Godfrey, M., Tu, Q.: Growth, Evolution, and Structural Change in Open Source Software. In: IWPSE 2001. Proceedings of the 4th International Workshop on Principles of Software Evolution, Vienna, Austria, pp. 103–106. ACM Press, Vienna (2001)
9. Godfrey, M.W., Tu, Q.: Evolution in Open Source Software: A Case Study. In: ICSM 2000. Proceedings of the 16th International Conference on Software Maintenance, San Jose, California, IEEE Computer Society Press, Los Alamitos (2000)
10. Kemerer, C.F.: Empirical Research on Software Complexity and Software Maintenance. Annals of Software Engineering 1(1), 1–22 (1995)
11. Lehman, M.M., Perry, D.E., Ramil, J.C.F., Turski, W.M., Wernik, P.: Metrics and Laws of Software Evolution – The Nineties View. In: Metrics 1997. Proceedings of the Fourth International Symposium on Software Metrics, Albuquerque, New Mexico, pp. 20–32 (November 1997)
12. Lehman, M.M.: Programs, Life Cycles, and Laws of Software Evolution. Proceedings of the IEEE 68(9), 1060–1076 (1980)
13. Lumpe, M., Schneider, J.-G.: On the Integration of Classboxes into C#. In: Löwe, W., Südholt, M. (eds.) SC 2006. LNCS, vol. 4089, pp. 307–322. Springer, Heidelberg (2006)
14. Mitchell, M., Newmann, M.: Complex Systems Theory and Evolution. In: Pagel, M. (ed.) Encyclopedia of Evolution, Oxford University Press, Oxford (2002)

15. Mockus, A., Fielding, R., Herbsleb, J.: A Case Study of Open Source Software Development: The Apache Server. In: Proceedings ICSE 2000, Limerick, Ireland, pp. 263–272 (June 2000)
16. Myers, C.R.: Software systems as complex networks: Structure, function, and evolvability of software collaboration graphs. Physical Review E 68(4), 46–116 (2003)
17. Newmann, M.E.J.: The Structure and Function of Complex Networks. SIAM Review 45(2), 167–256 (2003)
18. Nierstrasz, O., Gibbs, S., Tsichritzis, D.: Component-Oriented Software Development. Communications of the ACM 35(9), 160–165 (1992)
19. Potanin, A., Noble, J., Frean, M., Biddle, R.: Scale-free Geometry in OO Programs. Communications of the ACM 48(5), 99–103 (2005)
20. Pressman, R.S.: Software Engineering: A Practitioner's Approach, 6th edn. McGraw-Hill, New York (2005)
21. Rogerson, D.: Inside COM: Microsoft's Component Object Model. Microsoft Press (1997)
22. Sametinger, J.: Software Engineering with Reusable Components. Springer, Heidelberg (1997)
23. Szyperski, C.: Component Software: Beyond Object-Oriented Programming, 2nd edn. Addison-Wesley / ACM Press (2002)
24. Turski, W.M.: Reference Model for Smooth Growth of Software Systems. IEEE Transactions on Software Engineering 22(8), 599–600 (1996)
25. Turski, W.M.: The Reference Model for Smooth Growth of Software Systems Revisited. IEEE Transactions on Software Engineering 28(8), 814–815 (2002)
26. Vasa, R., Schneider, J.-G., Woodward, C., Cain, A.: Detecting Structural Changes in Object-Oriented Software Systems. In: Verner, J., Travassos, G.H. (eds.) ISESE 2005. Proceedings of 4th International Symposium on Empirical Software Engineering, Noosa Heads, Australia, pp. 463–470. IEEE Computer Society Press, Los Alamitos (2005)

An Approach for Structural Pattern Composition

Imed Hammouda and Kai Koskimies

Institute of Software Systems
Tampere University of Technology
P.O.BOX 553, FI-33101 Tampere, Finland
`firstname.lastname@tut.fi`

Abstract. Pattern composition has been recognized as a key element for the adoption of pattern languages and systems. This paper discusses the challenges of structural pattern composition and proposes an approach for role-based pattern composition, with two alternative composition mechanisms. To demonstrate the applicability of the proposed composition model, we have extended an existing pattern-driven architecting environment with an implementation of the approach.

1 Introduction

Different kinds of patterns (like analysis patterns [1], design patterns [2], architectural patterns [3], etc) have become a central part of contemporary software engineering. Patterns are typically organized into pattern languages or systems, which provide a framework for building solutions composed of elementary patterns. Indeed, pattern composition has been considered as a key requirement for the automation of software industry [4]. Even though tool support for patterns has been improved considerably in recent IDE's and CASE tools (e.g. [5,6]), support for pattern composition is still relatively modest.

Requirements on the pattern composition mechanisms depend on the way the patterns themselves are specified and applied in practice. For instance, depending on the used pattern specification technique, composition can be *structural* where pattern structures are glued together or *behavioral* where objects play several roles in different patterns [7]. Furthermore, pattern specification and usage influence very much the kind of composition constraints needed [8] (e.g. whether composition is mandatory, optional or forbidden) and the way these constraints should be formulated.

In this work, we study the challenges and pragmatics of structural pattern composition assuming a role-based specification of patterns. We mainly discuss how composition manifests itself in the generative usage of patterns, where patterns are instantiated to create the design of a software system. In this context, there is still a number of influential decisions to be made concerning the definition of the composition operator and the implementation of tool support for the composition. In particular, we will discuss the following issues:

M. Lumpe and W. Vanderperren (Eds.): SC 2007, LNCS 4829, pp. 252–265, 2007.
© Springer-Verlag Berlin Heidelberg 2007

- *Role specification.* In role-based specification of patterns, roles have different kinds of properties (e.g. constraints, relationships). An important question is how the individual properties of two composed roles are reflected in the resulting unified role.
- *Role binding.* In role-based specification of patterns, roles have multiplicities specifying the number of instances of the roles (number of elements playing the roles). Accordingly, we may have situations of *role scattering*: multiple objects playing the same role and *role tangling*: the same element playing different roles. This leads to new kinds of composition constraints such as the number of allowed composition instances between two roles and the kind of elements that may be involved in composition.
- *Role dependencies.* Roles may depend or relate to other roles. Composition constraints should follow the implications of such dependencies. In addition, we may want certain composition constraints to be validated only if certain conditions are met. This suggests a need of a dependency model of composition constraints.
- *Kind of composition.* Pattern composition can be carried out at different levels. In particular, two patterns can either be merged into a new pattern (combinative composition), or the participating patterns may remain separate, with additional information indicating the overlapping parts (conservative composition). The need for a certain kind of composition may depend, for example, on whether the pattern (system) is being applied for generative purposes [9] (conservative is preferred) or in a reverse engineering mode [10] (combinative is more suitable).
- *Effect on constraints.* The constraints imposed on the composed pattern can be either the conjunction or disjunction of the constraints on the participating patterns. That is, the participating patterns can either widen or limit each other's constraints.

In this paper, we discuss the various options and propose rules for the pattern composition. In order to demonstrate the concrete usage of the concepts, we have implemented pattern composition support for a pattern-driven development environment known as INARI [11]. The tool assumes a role-based specification of patterns and provides a task-based pattern instantiation mechanism.

The remaining of the paper is organized as follows. Section 2 presents a role-based specification of patterns. Section 3 discusses in detail role-based pattern composition and introduces an example composition algorithm. Concrete tool support for the proposed pattern composition approach is presented in Section 4. In Section 5, we compare our work to other related approaches. Finally, Section 6 concludes the paper.

2 Role-Based Specification of Patterns

To be able to discuss pattern composition independently of any particular pattern kind (e.g. design patterns [2], architectural patterns [3], etc), we use the

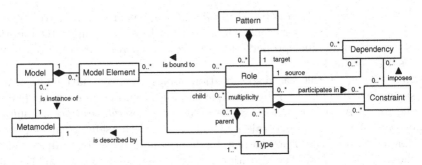

Fig. 1. Conceptual model for generic patterns

concept of a generic pattern as depicted in Figure 1. A generic pattern (or simply a pattern) is an arrangement of software elements for solving a problem. A pattern is defined in terms of element roles rather than concrete elements; a pattern is instantiated in a particular context by creating instances for each role and by binding the role instances to concrete elements.

A role has a type, which determines the kind of software elements that can be bound to the instances of that role; the set of all the role types is called the domain of the pattern. An example domain could be UML; that is, the roles are played by UML model elements.

Each role may have a set of constraints. Constraints are structural conditions that must be satisfied by the concrete element bound to an instance of a role. Constraints may refer to the elements playing other roles, implying dependencies between the roles. For example, in a pattern that covers UML class diagrams, a constraint of an association role may require that the association bound to an instance of this role must appear between the classes playing certain class roles, thus implying a dependency from the association role to the two class roles. Another example constraint is the containment relationship between roles (e.g. operation roles are contained within class roles). In this case, a dependency exists from an operation role to its parent class role.

A multiplicity (i.e. cardinality) is defined for each role. The multiplicity of a role gives the lower and upper limits for the number of the instances of the role in the pattern. In this work, we assume that the multiplicity is given using the symbols '1' for exactly one, '?' for zero or one, '*' for zero or more, and '+' for one or more. For example, if an operation role has multiplicity '?', the operation is optional in the pattern, because the lower limit is zero.

The upper part of Figure 2 shows a *role diagram* of a simple pattern consisting of three class roles (*Client*, *Facade* and *Service*). The purpose of the pattern is to ensure that system services are accessed through a facade component. Role *Service* has a child attribute role *description* and a child operation role *getDescription*. Similarly, role *Facade* has a child operation role *getServiceDesc*. The multiplicity of role *Service* is + (marked after the role name), stating that the facade may encapsulate one or more services. There is a dependency from role *getServiceDesc* on role *getDescription*: there should be a *getServiceDesc* instance for each *getDescription* instance.

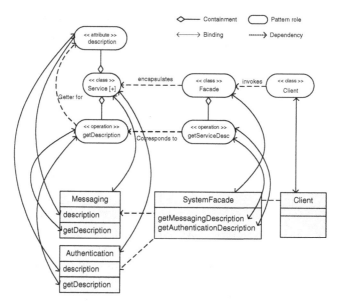

Fig. 2. Services pattern instance

The bottom part of Figure 2 gives an example binding of the *Services* pattern. The concrete element *SystemFacade* plays the role of *Facade*, this is marked by the double-arrowed line between *Facade* and *SystemFacade*. In addition, there are two elements that play the role *Service*, this is allowed by the multiplicity value of *Service* ('+'). Accordingly, there are two instances of roles *description* and *getDescription*. Because of the dependency between *getServiceDesc* and *get-Description*, there are two instances of *getServiceDesc*.

3   Role-Based Pattern Composition

The composition of two patterns results in a new pattern. The composition operator we define is a binary operator that takes two arbitrary patterns and returns a possibly larger one. Given two arbitrary patterns *patternX* and *patternY*, if *roleX* and *roleY* are roles in *patternX* and *patternY* respectively, we say that *roleX* and *roleY* overlap if their instances are bound to the same concrete elements. It is important to note that *roleX* and *roleY* can overlap only if (i) they are of the same role type and (ii) the parent roles of *roleX* and *roleY* (the roles where *roleX* and *roleY* are contained), if any, are overlapping too.

Considering an overlapping relationship between roleX and roleY, our role-based composition can be expressed as follows:
patternZ = Compose(patternX, patternY, {(roleX, roleY)}).
patternZ is said to be the composite pattern of *patternX* and *patternY*. The composition formula specifies the two patterns to be composed followed by a set of tuples defining the overlapping roles.

Table 1. Role multiplicity in pattern composition

roleX	roleY	Allowed number of role instances
*	*	*
*	?	?
*	1	1
*	+	+
1	?	1
1	1	1
1	+	1
+	?	1
+	+	+
?	?	?

In our work, we assume a restrictive pattern composition in the sense that the rules of *roleX* should restrict the binding of instances of *roleY* and vice versa. In contrast, an augmentive composition approach would relax the rules on both sides, requiring that either the rules on *roleX* or the rules on *roleY* apply for the bindings of both *roleX* and *roleY*. Given the above definition, the consequences of the composition operator are as follows.

- Interpreting role multiplicities as sets of numbers, the overlapping relationship between *roleX* and *roleY* implies that the number of elements that can be bound to instances of both roles is given by the intersection of the multiplicities of *roleX* and *roleY*. For example, if the multiplicity of roleX is '+' and the multiplicity of roleY is '1', then exactly one element could play *roleX* and *roleY* in the composite pattern *patternZ*. The different cases are shown in Table 1.
- If *roleX* and *roleY* are two overlapping roles, then binding an element to instances of *roleX* and *roleY* should follow all the dependencies of *roleX* and *roleY*. Thus if *roleX* has n dependencies and *roleY* has m dependencies, then the bound element should follow at most n+m dependencies and at least max(n, m) dependencies. This is because some of the dependencies (dependencies having the same target role) of *roleX* and *roleY* can be the same.
- Similarly, the bound element to instances of *roleX* and *roleY* should satisfy the constraints of both *roleX* and *roleY*. Thus if *roleX* has n constraints and *roleY* has m constraints, then the bound element should satisfy at most n+m constraints and at least max(n, m) constraints. The constraints having the same type and value are treated to be the same.

Patterns *patternX* and *patternY* are said to be disjoint if they have no overlapping roles. Patterns *patternX* and *patternY* are said to be fully composed if there is a one-to-one overlapping relationship between all roles of *patternX* and *patternY*.

In order to illustrate pattern composition in terms of role diagrams, let us consider a second simple pattern called *WatchDogs*. The purpose of the pattern,

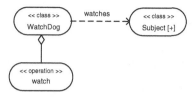

Fig. 3. WatchDogs pattern

in our example case, is to verify the availability of system services. Figure 3 depicts a role diagram of the pattern: A *WatchDog* class role has an operation role *watch* for watching an instance of role *Subject*. The pattern allows an instance of *WatchDog* for every instance of Subject. The motivation for the composition here is that we want system services (playing role *Service* in the *Services* pattern discussed earlier) to be watched for availability. In other words, system services will play role *Subject* in the *WatchDogs* pattern.

Supposing that the composite pattern is named *WatchedServices*, the composition formula can be given as follows:

WatchedServices = Compose(*Services, WatchDogs, {(Service, Subject)}*).

As we discussed earlier, composition in role-based specification of patterns can be combinative or conservative. This is discussed in more detail in the next two subsections.

3.1   Combinative Composition

Combinative composition means that the two composed patterns are statically merged into a single pattern forming a new role structure. Each pair of overlapping roles merges into a unified role in the new role structure. Assuming the composition of *patternX* (consisting of n roles) and *patternY* (consisting of m roles) and that there are k pairs of overlapping roles, the number of roles in the composite role structure is n+m-k.

Figure 4 shows an example of a combinative composition of patterns *Services* and *WatchDogs*. Roles *Subject* and *Service* are merged into a unified role named *WatchedService*. The properties of the unified role are restricted to those of Subject and Service in their respective role structures. Instantiating the composite pattern is trivial, it is carried out in the same way as discussed in Figure 2.

3.2   Conservative Composition

Conservative composition means that the two composed patterns keep their own identities during composition; no new role strcuture is formed because of the composition. This is illustrated in Figure 5 using the example of *Services* and *WatchDogs*: An overlapping relationship is made between *Subject* and *Service* without merging them. The composition is made by binding instances of *Subject* to the same elements that are bound to instances of *Service*. As a result, there are as many instances of *Subject* as there are for *Service*.

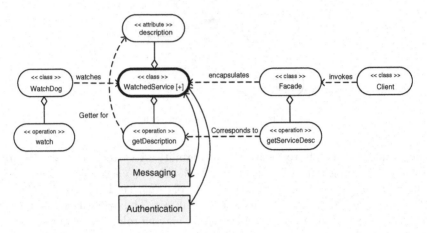

Fig. 4. Combinative composition of Services and WatchDogs patterns

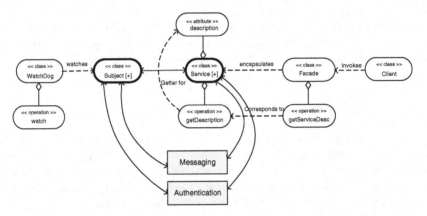

Fig. 5. Conservative composition of Services and WatchDogs patterns

Compared to combinative composition, instantiating the composite structure shown in Figure 5 is tricky. The reason is that because the multiplicity of the two overlapping roles is '+', we have to maintain the right correspondence between individual bindings of *Subject* and *Service*. If not maintained, there is the risk that an instance of role *WatchDog* is watching a wrong instance of Subject, or that two different instances of *WatchDog* are watching the same instance of *Subject*. We need an algorithm for conservative composition that eliminates these two problems.

In our approach, conservative composition is implemented using the following algorithm. The algorithm assumes a stepwise instantiation process. Furthermore, at any time, a role instance of a composed role is either in state 'doable' (an instance can be bound to a concrete element) or state 'not doable' (an instance cannot be bound to a concrete element).

```
Compose(roleX, roleY)
  While more instances of the pair (roleX, roleY) are allowed, do
    1. Select roleX to instantiate
    2. Create a 'not doable' role instance of roleX
    3. Create a 'not doable' role instance of roleY
    4. Associate 'not doable' role instances of roleX and roleY
    5. Change the state of 'not doable' role instances to 'doable'
  end while
```

Figure 6 shows a graphical illustration of an example execution of the the algorithm. The algorithm creates an instance of *roleX* named *X1* (Figure 6 A, algorithm step 1 and 2). The role instance cannot be bound to a concrete element since the corresponding instance of *roleY* has not been created yet. The state of node *X1* is set to 'not doable'. This is marked by the label on top of the node.

The algorithm then creates a 'not doable' node *Y1* (Figure 6 B, algorithm step 3). Because a 'not doable' node of *roleX* exists, both states of *X1* and *Y1* change to 'doable' and the association between *X1* and *Y1* is made (Figure 6 C, algorithm steps 4 and 5). The association is marked by a dashed line linking the two nodes. It is now possible to bind the 'doable' instances of *roleX* and *roleY* to the same concrete element. In a similar fashion, a second 'not doable' instance of *roleX* named *X2* is created (Figure 6 C, algorithm steps 1 and 2) and a second 'not doable' instance of *roleY* named *Y2* is added (Figure 6 D, algorithm step 3). The structure grows as more instances are allowed.

It can be shown that the algorithm eliminates the risk of wrong correspondences between instances of *roleX* and *roleY*. In other words, there is no risk that both *X1* and *X2* be associated with *Y1* for example. Also, there is no risk that *X1* is associated with *Y2* or *X2* is associated with *Y1*. A proof of the algorithm correctness is presented in [12].

3.3   Composition Constraints

Composition constraints have been defined as binary relationships between roles [8] stating whether an overlapping relationship between two roles is a 'must be' (the roles must be played by the same elements), 'must not be' (the roles must not be played by the same elements), or 'may be' (the roles may be played by the same elements). In fact, the properties of the composition operator discussed earlier represent other kinds of composition constraints as well, for example how the multiplicity is calculated when two roles overlap. These constraints highly depend on the interpretation of the composition, for example whether it is restrictive or augmentive. In addition, we may suggest other kinds of constraints including:

– Number of allowed composition instances: We may want to further restrict the number instances of two overlapping roles. Considering the example of *Service* and *WatchDog*, we may want for performance reasons to restrict the number of instances *WatchedService*: we do not want to have a *WatchDog* for every system service.

Fig. 6. Example illustration of the algorithm

- Kinds of elements bound: We may want to restrict the kind of elements to be bound to instances of the two overlapping roles. For example, for performance or security reasons only certain kinds of services are allowed to be watched
- Conditional composition constraints: a 'may be' composition constraint in a certain situation may change to a 'must be' constraint in another situation. For instance, if our example system should be of high availability, then the composition of *Subject* and *Service* becomes a 'must be'. However, we may want the same constraint to become 'must not be' if performance is prioritized: the use of *WatchDog* degrades the performance of the system.

4 Tool Support for Pattern Composition - INARI

In order to implement our proposed approach to pattern composition, we use a prototype tool environment known as INARI (Integrated Development Environment) [11]. The INARI tool has been developed as a pattern-driven stepwise modeling and architecting environment, it is currently integrated with Rational Software Architect [5]. An INARI pattern is a role-based structure that is applied by binding instances of its element roles to concrete model elements. Currently the tool supports UML, Java and XML elements.

We have extended the tool with pattern composition capabilities for both combinative and conservative compositions. For composition constraint evaluation, INARI uses two levels of constraints: constraints applied to the pattern model (checking constraints on role relationships, role bindings, etc) and constraints applied to the concrete elements bound to the patterns. Within the first

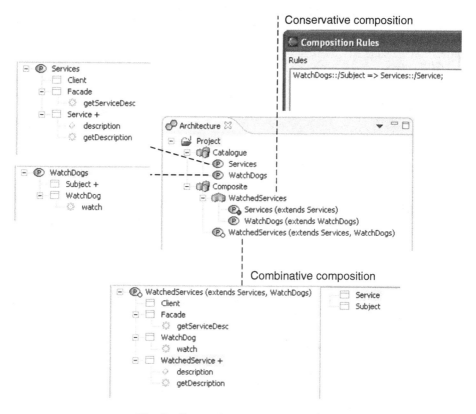

Fig. 7. Composing patterns in INARI

level, composition constraints are specified as OCL expressions [13] evaluated on an EMF-based representation [14] of the pattern model. This can, for example, be used to monitor for mandatory or forbidden compositions. Within the second level, INARI incorporates constraints that are evaluated on the concrete models to be able, for example, to verify the kind of concrete elements that are involved in a composition.

Figure 7 shows the specification of patterns *Services* and *WatchDogs* in the INARI environment (under node Catalogue in the Architecture view). For the combinative composition, a new pattern *WatchedServices*, under node Composite is formed. The detailed specification of the pattern shows that role *Watched-Service* merges the two roles *Service* and *Subject*.

As an example of conservative composition, Figure 7 shows a composite structure named *WatchedServices* under the node Composite. In this case, the two patterns *Services* and *WatchDogs* are not merged but rather connected with a composition rule. The composition rule states that the overlapping relationship is from *Subject* to *Service*. The reason is that INARI adopts a unidirectional composition relationship. This is exploited to enforce a partial order of applying patterns. Role *Subject* is said to be 'outgoing' and *Service* is said to be

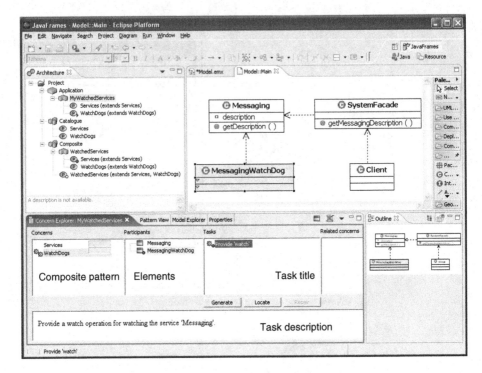

Fig. 8. Applying composite patterns in INARI

'incoming'. When the composition is applied, an instance of 'incoming' role gets bound before an instance of its 'outgoing' counterpart is bound to the same element.

Figure 8 depicts an example application of the *WatchedServices* composite pattern, the conservative composition is used. The pattern instance is named *MyWatchedServices* and is shown in the Architecture view of the tool (top left corner) under the node Application. INARI transforms a role-based specification of a pattern into a task list. This is done by generating a task for each unbound role instance that can be bound in the current situation, taking into account the dependencies and multiplicities of roles as well as the composition rules.

In Figure 8, the user has provided a *Messaging* service (by binding it to an instance of role *Service*). As a result, *Messaging* gets automatically bound to an instance of the *Subject* role of *WatchDog*. The bound elements of a pattern instance are shown in the lower part of the figure (Elements). The user has then provided a *WatchDog* for the service (*MessagingWatchDog*). The next task is to provide a *watch* method for the *WatchDog* component. This is shown in the task view in the bottom part of the figure. This task would not have appeared if the composition between *Subject* and *Service* was not made. Adaptive text is used in the task prompt (the use of term 'Messaging' in the task description).

The INARI environment maintains the identity of the constituent patterns as shown in the left bottom part of the figure. It is possible to show the effect of one pattern in the model by highlighting (coloring) the corresponding bound elements or by generating separate view of the bound elements.

5   Related Work

The pattern composition presented in [7] is an example of structural pattern composition. The authors base their composition approach on a class diagram representation of patterns. We, however, use role modeling to study the composition mechanism. The POD [15] tool implements a design environment for visual composition of design patterns, called constructional patterns. The advantage of the approach is that it maintains a view of the design as a composition of patterns and it provides traceability mechanism in both the top/down and bottom/up directions. Similarly, we propose a conservative composition approach that enable the constituent patterns to keep their identities. However, we do also present a combinative version of the composition that allow the formation of new patterns based on existing ones.

A formal approach to structural pattern composition has been introduced in [16]: the two composed patterns are statically merged into a single pattern, which is then added to the pattern system. The approach in [16] does not support conservative composition.

In [8], the author uses role diagrams to document object collaboration based patterns. The author further defines the notion of composite pattern to be a pattern described as a composition of other patterns and suggests a technique to cope with the complexity of the composition. Composition constraints on any two roles can be of one of three values: 'must be', 'must not be', or 'don't care'. Compared to [8], we propose new kinds of composition constraints such as the number of allowed composition instances and we discuss situations where composition between two roles is conditional. We also propose an algorithm for the composition and tool support.

Behavioral pattern composition techniques are generally based on assigning runtime objects to roles [17,18]. In our work, we apply role modeling to structural pattern composition. However, if we assume that the structural elements participating in a composition are eventually instantiated into objects at runtime, then we can consider that these objects play the roles that are played by their corresponding structural elements.

Tool support for pattern composition has been provided by various tools [5,6,15]. Compared to these, the INARI tool allows a task-based pattern composition approach where the composition is carried out under the control of the user. INARI also supports a larger set of composition constraints.

6   Conclusions

In this work, we have discussed a model for structural pattern composition by making explicit the kind of decisions one should consider when defining and implementing pattern composition. We have defined a composition operator for role-based patterns assuming a restrictive interpretation of composition. The proposed approach distinguishes between combinative composition where the constituent patterns are statically merged forming a new composite pattern and a conservative composition where the the identity of the composed patterns are kept.

Furthermore, we have proposed an algorithm for conservative composition. The algorithm has been implemented for INARI [11], a pattern-oriented development environment. The tool is capable to address both combinative and conservative pattern composition and to model different kinds of composition constraints. Our future work consists of applying the proposed composition approach to a large pattern catalogue and to provide support for behavioral composition using the same role-based mechanism.

References

1. Fowler, M.: Analysis Patterns: Reusable Object Models. Addison-Wesley, Reading (1997)
2. Gamma, E., Helm, R., Johnson, R., Vlissides, J.: Design Patterns: Elements of Reusable Object-Oriented Software. Addison-Wesley, Reading (1994)
3. Buschmann, F., Meunier, R., Rohnert, H., Sommerland, P., Stal, M.: Pattern-Oriented Software Architecture: A System of Patterns. Wiley, Chichester (1996)
4. Greenfield, J., Short, K., Cook, S., Kent, S.: Software Factories: Assembling Applications with Patterns, Models, Frameworks, and Tools. Wiley, Chichester (2004)
5. IBM Rational Software:Rational Software Architect (2007), At URL http://www-306.ibm.com/software/rational
6. IBM Rational Software: Rational XDE. (2007), At URL http://www.rational.com/products/xde/index.jsp
7. Sherif, M.Y., Hany, H.A.: Pattern-Oriented Analysis and Design: Composing Patterns to Design Software Systems. Addison-Wesley, Reading (2003)
8. Riehle, D.: Composite design patterns. In: Proc. OOPSLA 1997, pp. 218–228 (1997)
9. Cornils, A.: Patterns in Software Development. PhD thesis, University of Aarhus (2001)
10. Keller, R., Schauer, R., Robitaille, S., Page, P.: Pattern-based reverse engineering of design components. In: Proc. ICSE 1999, Los Angeles, USA, pp. 226–235 (1999)
11. Practise Research Group: Integrated Architecting Environment (INARI) (2007), At URL http://practise.cs.tut.fi/project.php?project=inari
12. Hammouda, I.: Towards tool-support for pattern composition. Technical report, Tampere University of Technology (2004), http://www.cs.tut.fi/~imed/reports/PatternComposition.pdf
13. OMG: UML 2.0 OCL Specification (2007), http://www.omg.org/docs/ptc/03-10-14.pdf
14. Eclipse: Eclipse Modeling Framework (EMF) (2007), http://www.eclipse.org/emf/
15. Sherif, M.Y., Hengyi, X., Hany, H.A.: POD: A composition environment for pattern-oriented design. In: Proc. TOOLS 34 2000, Santa Barbara, California, pp. 263–272 (2000)

16. Mikkonen, T.: Formalizing design patterns. In: Proc. ICSE 2000, pp. 115–124. IEEE Computer Society Press, Los Alamitos (1998)
17. Reenskaug, T.: Working with Objects: The OOram Software Engineering Method. Manning Publishing (1996)
18. Gottlob, G., Schrefl, M., Röck, B.: Extending object-oriented systems with roles. ACM Transactions on Information Systems 14(3), 268–296 (1996)

Composite Connectors for Composing Software Components

Kung-Kiu Lau, Ling Ling, Vladyslav Ukis and Perla Velasco Elizondo

School of Computer Science, The University of Manchester
Manchester M13 9PL, United Kingdom
{kung-kiu,lling,ukisv,pvelasco}@cs.man.ac.uk

Abstract. In a component-based system, connectors are used to compose components. Connectors should have a semantics that makes them simple to construct and use. At the same time, their semantics should be rich enough to endow them with desirable properties such as genericity, compositionality and reusability. For connector construction, compositionality would be particularly useful, since it would facilitate systematic construction. In this paper we describe a hierarchical approach to connector definition and construction that allows connectors to be defined and constructed from sub-connectors. These composite connectors are indeed generic, compositional and reusable. They behave like design patterns, and provide powerful composition connectors.

1 Introduction

A component-based system can be described as a software architecture [14] with components (boxes) and connectors (lines). Components represent parts of the system, while connectors represent interactions between components. Connectors are therefore composition operators for the components.

Clearly, in a component model, the ease of building systems and reasoning about the process depends directly on the varieties of connectors available and their semantics. A crucial question therefore is how to define and construct suitable connectors.

Connectors should have a semantics that makes them simple to construct and use. At the same time, their semantics should be rich enough to endow them with desirable properties such as genericity, compositionality and reusability. For connector construction, compositionality would be particularly useful, since it would allow connectors to be constructed a systematic manner.

In this paper we describe a hierarchical approach to connector definition and construction. Using a set of basic exogenous composition connectors, we can define and construct a composite connector as a composition of the basic connectors. The resulting composite connectors are indeed generic, compositional and reusable.

Because our basic connectors define control structures, our composite connectors represent composite control structures, or composite control flow patterns. As such, they behave like certain design patterns [6], and provide powerful composition operators that can be used to perform complicated compositions involving many components all in a single step.

M. Lumpe and W. Vanderperren (Eds.): SC 2007, LNCS 4829, pp. 266–280, 2007.
© Springer-Verlag Berlin Heidelberg 2007

The paper is organised as follows. In Section 2 we describe related work on the issue of composite connectors. In Section 3 we briefly describe the concept of exogenous composition connectors and present a basic set of these connectors. In Section 4 we explain composite connectors in detail and how they are implemented. In Section 5 we show how they can be used in practice. Finally, in Section 6 we discuss our approach for creating composite connectors.

2 Related Work

As far as we know, our approach to composite connectors is new and unique. There are two main related areas: *software architectures* [14] and *coordination languages* [13].

In *software architectures*, there is work on compositional approaches to connector construction, but it does not construct connectors from sub-connectors. Rather it tries to construct only a *single* connector. This construction consists in a composition of elements with the desired properties, yielding a new connector; or a composition of the necessary adaptations or transformations of an existing connector to achieve these properties. In [15], an ADL (Architecture Description Language [11]) connector can be adpated by composing a set of transformations. The transformations can modify the connector's properties, e.g. protocol, data policy. Typically they also change the code of the components involved since connector code is embedded in component code.

In [4,5] a connector is composed from a set of *connector elements*. The elements model certain non-functional properties of some basic connector types supported in middleware technologies. In [10], an existing connector's aspects, e.g. security, monitoring, etc., can be specified separately and then composed and integrated with the connector.

These approaches only deal with the construction of a single connector. Furthermore, in these approaches either connectors are not distinct from components, e.g. [15], or when they are, their implementations are customized solutions for a specific system [4,5]. Therefore in all these approaches, both components and connectors cannot be reused.

In *coordination languages*, composite connectors can be constructed. In these languages, connectors are used to coordinate component interactions. Compared to ADL connectors, these connectors can represent much more sophisticated coordination policies for sets of components. In the coordination language Reo [2,1] connectors are composed of channels. The channels are compositional, and therefore composite connectors can be defined.

However, Reo composite connectors are very different in nature from our composite connectors. In Reo, components only perform I/O operations, and connectors are data channels. Consequently, a composite connector in Reo is not a control structure, and so it differs form our composite connector. In particular, a Reo composite connector does not behave like any design pattern.

3 Exogenous Composition Connectors

Our approach is based on exogenous connectors. In this section we briefly explain what exogenous connectors are, and how they are used as composition operators for software components.

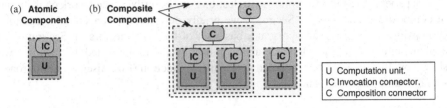

Fig. 1. Atomic and composite components

Exogenous connectors are defined within the context of our component model [8]. In our component model, there are two kinds of basic entities: (i) *exogenous connectors* [7] and (ii) *computation units*. Components are constructed from exogenous connectors and computation units. A computation unit performs only computation (by providing a set of methods) and does not invoke any computation outside itself. Exogenous connectors coordinate all the computation performed by components.

There are two kinds of components: *atomic* and *composite*. An atomic component (Fig.1 (a)), consists of a computation unit (U) and an exogenous connector for invoking the methods in the computation unit.

This connector is called an *invocation connector* (IC). A composite component is composed from (atomic or composite) components by using a *composition connector* (C in Fig. 1 (b), which shows two composite components). This is an exogenous connector that defines a piece of control that coordinates all the calls to the methods in the sub-components. In a system, the set of all the composition connectors encapsulate all the control in the system. For example, a *Sequencer* connector that composes two atomic components A_1 and A_2 can call a method m_1 in A_1, and a method m_2 in A_2, in that order. A *Pipe* connector composing A_1 and A_2 behaves similarly, but can also pass the result of m_1 to A_2 and use it in calling m_2. Components do not initiate any control, and just provide services when invoked by the connectors.

Every component thus has a top-level connector: this is either an invocation connector (for an atomic component) or a composition connector (for a composite component). This connector acts as an interface for the component, and is also used by other connectors for composition.

In [7], we have introduced these basic exogenous composition connectors which encapsulate different control structures that are necessary for building systems. The control encapsulated in these connectors corresponds to the three standard control structures: *sequencing*, *branching* and *looping*; therefore this set of connectors is Turing complete [12,3].

3.1   A Hierarchy of Composition Connectors

Exogenous composition connectors are defined in a hierarchical way (as can be seen in Fig. 1). For example, a *Sequencer* connector, or a *Pipe* connector, that composes two atomic components A_1 and A_2 is clearly defined in terms of the invocation connectors in A_1 and A_2.

In general, exogenous composition connectors form a hierarchy built on top of invocation connectors for atomic components. The lowest level (level 1) of composition connectors connect invocation connectors, and the second-level (level 2) composition connectors are of variable arities and types. In general, composition connectors at any level can be of variable arities; composition connectors at any level higher than 1 can be of variable arities and types; and we can define any number of levels of connectors. Connectors at level n for any $n > 1$ can be defined in terms of connectors at levels 1 to $(n - 1)$. In particular, the types of the former are defined in terms of the types of the latter. The connector type hierarchy can be defined in terms of dependent types and polymorphism as follows (omitting methods and their parameters):

$Basic\ types:$ Atomic Component, Result;
$Connector\ types:$

$$I \equiv \text{Atomic Component} \longrightarrow \text{Result};$$
$$L1 \equiv I \times \ldots \times I \longrightarrow \text{Result};$$
$$\text{For } 1 < i \le n, \quad Li \equiv L(j_1) \times \ldots \times L(j_m) \longrightarrow \text{Result, for some } m$$
$$\text{where } j_k \in \{1, \ldots, (i - 1)\} \text{ for } 1 \le k \le m,$$
$$\text{and } L(i) = \begin{cases} L1 \ , \ i = 1 \\ L2 \ , \ i = 2 \\ \vdots \\ Ln \ , \ i = n. \end{cases}$$

where I is the Invocation Connector type, and Li is the Level-i Composition Connector type, for $1 \le i \le n$.

Accordingly we have implemented composition connectors as a hierarchy of classes[1] which extend a common superclass called **Connector** (Fig. 2).

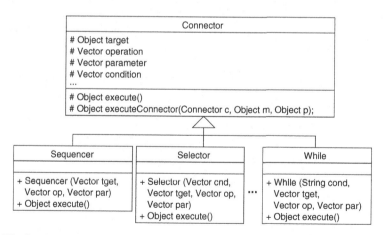

Fig. 2. Hierarchy of composition connector classes with the superclass Connector

At any level of the hierarchy, a connector can be defined in a generic manner as a class that extends and overrides selected methods of the superclass **Connector**. We have implemented a set of five basic composition connectors: *Sequencer* and *Pipe*, *Selector*,

---

[1] We have two implementations, one in Java and another in .NET C#.

and *While* and *Repeat*, which correspond to sequencing, branching and looping control respectively.

Each connector is made up of a *signature* and *code*. The signature, implemented by the connector's *constructor*, indicates how the connector can be used. The code implements the connector's functionality, and is defined as a method called **execute**.

As shown in Fig. 2, the constructors of all the connector receive a common set of parameters, i.e. tget, op and par. For a connector, tget specifies the set of connectors it is connected to; op is the set of operations to be executed via those connectors; and par is the set of parameters required to support the executions. The implementations of the constructors are all similar; the constructors only verify the type and number of the arguments they receive, and store them into the corresponding superclass fields, i.e. target, operation and parameter.

The execute method of a composition connector is inherited from the **Connector** superclass and overridden by the connector class. The execute methods of all the connectors are very similar and only differ in the specific code required for the control scheme they encapsulate, e.g. a *Selector* connector requires some code for evaluating its condition. All execute methods call the executeConnector method implemented in the **Connector** superclass. This method contains the code for executing any connector at any level of the hierarchy.

Fig. 3(a) shows an outline of the code for the executeConnector method. This illustrates the hierarchical execution of connectors. First, the subtype of the connector is identified via specific supporting functions arranged in an "if-then-else" control structure. Once the connector subtype is identified, it is stored in a variable of this subtype by casting it. For example, if the connected sub-connector is of type *Sequencer*, it needs to be cast to this type, which is a subtype of **Connector** as shown in Fig. 2. Finally, the connected connector is executed by calling its corresponding execute method. This process is repeated for all the connected connectors in a hierarchy until the invocation connectors are encountered.

(a)

```
class Connector {
    ...
    Object executeConnector(Object connToExecute,...){
        ...
        if (isInvocation(connToExecute)){
            Invocation ic = (Invocation) connToExecute;
            ...
            r = ic.execute(oper, params);
        else if (isSequencer(connToExecute)){
            Sequencer seq = (Sequencer) connToExecute;
            ...
            r = seq.execute();
        else if (...){
            ...
        } else if (isWhile(connToExecute)){
            While whi = (While) connToExecute;
            ...
            r = whi.execute();
        }
        return r;
    }
}
```

(b)

```
class Invocation extends Connector {
    private Object cu;

    public Object execute(
    Method operationToExecute, Object[] par){
        r = operationToExecute.invoke(cu, par);
        return r
    }
}
```

Fig. 3. Outline of the codes for (a) the executeConnector method in the Connector superclass and (b) the execute method in the Invocation connector class

Invocation connectors are not composition connectors, and so their `execute` methods are different. Fig. 3 (b) shows an outline of the code for the `execute` method of a invocation connector. This method requires two arguments: `operationToExecute` and `par`, which correspond to the name of the operation to invoke in the computation unit, and its parameters, respectively. We use the `invoke` method provided by the class Method in the java.lang.reflect package to dynamically execute the required operation in a computation unit (`cu`).

The hierarchical nature of composition connectors means that every system has one, and only one, top-level connector, which initiates control flow for the entire system calling the **execute** methods of connected connectors following a top-down approach. To illustrate this, consider the architecture with exogenous composition connectors in Fig. 4. The architecture corresponds to a Coffee Machine system. For simplicity and clarity, we have not explicitly distinguished between atomic and composite components in the architecture. The Coffee Machine consists of a hierarchical structure of composition connectors (*Sequencers SQ2* and *SQ1, Selector SEL* and *Pipe PIPE*) representing the system's control flow, sitting on top of independent components (Card Manager, Cash Manager, Coffee Maker, Cup Dispenser, Coffee Dispenser, Water Dispenser, Milk Dispenser and Sugar Dispenser) that provide the computation performed by the system. The execution of the system starts with the composition operator at the highest level, namely the *Sequencer SQ2*. The customers of the system can pay for a

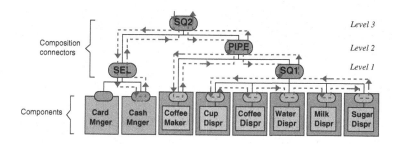

Fig. 4. An architecture with our basic composition operators

coffee either by cash or by card. Consider the use case of buying a coffee with cash. The control flow path for this is shown by the dotted line in Fig. 4. The first action is the execution of the level-3 connector *SQ2*, which firstly calls the level-1 *Selector SEL*. The latter chooses the component Cash Manager, and invokes the required method in it to process the transaction. Then, *SQ2* calls the level-2 *Pipe PIPE*, which invokes one of the operations in the component CoffeeMaker to get from a recipe the amount of each ingredient for the selected product. The amounts are passed through *PIPE* to *SQ1* which uses them as parameters for invoking methods in each one of the dispenser components. Finally the control flow goes back across the composition hierarchy until it reaches *SQ2*, whereupon the transaction is completed. If any data is generated by the dispenser, e.g. an error or success code, it is also transmitted back across the hierarchy with the control flow.

4   Composite Composition Connectors

The hierarchical nature of composition connectors means that the connectors them-selves can be composed into composite composition connectors. In this section, we explain composite connectors in detail.

4.1   Composite Connectors are Patterns

It should be clear from the previous section that a set of connectors that are inter-connected can be regarded as a single composite connector *CC*, which in turn can be used in hierarchical composition subsequently. It should also be clear that *CC* is a *pat-tern*, since it represents a composite control structure that composes a set of components.

For example, in the Coffee Machine example (Fig. 4), the level-2 *Pipe PIPE* and level-1 *Sequencer SQ1* can be composed into a composite composition connector, as shown in Fig. 5.

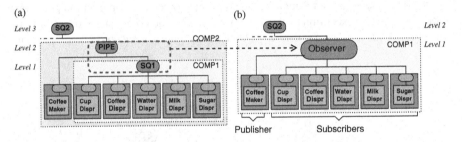

Fig. 5. Coffee Machine with (a) basic connectors and (b) composite connector Observer

This composite connector is equivalent to the object-oriented *Observer* design pat-tern [6]. This is because it defines the *publish-subscribe* dependency between the Cof-feeMaker component and the Dispenser components. In Fig. 5(a), when *PIPE* invokes the CoffeeMaker, it gets the recipe data and then pipes it to *SQ1*. *SQ1* then invokes all the Dispenser components so that they dispense different amounts of ingredients according to the piped-in recipe data.[2] Thus the Pipe-Sequencer hierarchy is an *Observer* com-posite connector (Fig. 5(b)). Of course here *Observer* is used to compose components rather than objects.

As in its object-oriented counterpart, there are two main roles for components com-posed by an *Observer* composite connector: Publisher and Subscriber. When the Pub-lisher is called, the Subscribers must be notified and must behave accordingly. Like its object-oriented counterpart, an *Observer* composite connector defines the one-to-many dependencies between the Publisher and Subscribers.

In general, a composite composition connector *CC* can be composed from a set of (basic or composite) composition connectors $C_1, \ldots, C_n$. *CC* can be used to perform a

---

[2] In the Observer pattern, the order in which the subscribers are notified is not specified. Here we have chosen a sequential order.

composite composition involving all the components that are composed by $C_1, \ldots, C_n$, but all in a single step. Therefore, composite connectors are patterns, and as such, are much more powerful than their sub-connectors.

Using such connectors can make composition more efficient by reducing the number of (levels of) composition. For example comparing Fig. 5(a), with only basic connectors, and Fig. 5(b), with the Observer composite connector, the level of composition is reduced by 1 in the latter.

Finally, composing connectors into composite ones is clearly one form of connector reuse.

4.2   Constructing Composite Connectors

To construct a composite connector CC from a set of inter-connected sub-connectors $C_1, \ldots, C_n$ requires the generation of the correct signature for CC as a single connector. CC connects different and more connectors (components) than its sub-connectors. In particular its signature is not the same as those of its top-level sub-connector.

For example in Fig. 5, the top-level sub-connector of *Observer* is PIPE (Fig. 5(a)). PIPE actually connects two components: CoffeeMaker and Comp1. Comp1 is a composite component constructed by the lower level connector SQ1. By contrast, the *Observer* in Fig. 5(b) connects CoffeeMaker and all the Dispenser components.

Therefore, to construct a composite connector correctly, we have to take care of its signature, by considering the signatures of its sub-connectors, and their composition structure.

To express the composition structure of a composite constructor, we use the notation $C_1[C_2, C_3]$ recursively to denote a composite connector whose top-level connector C_1 is connected to C_2 and C_3 at the next level down, and so on. Fig. 6 shows a general composite connector (denoted by the shaded box).

This connector can be written as $C1[C2, C3[C4, C5, C6]]$.

Once the composition structure of a composite composition connector has been determined, we can implement the connector by using the implementation of its sub-connectors. For simplicity, we shall assume that all the sub-connectors in a composite composition connector are the basic connectors that we described in Section 3.1. As before, each connector is made up of a signature and code. We represent this as *Connector(Sig, Code)*. In general, the signature of a composite connector is generated from the signatures of all the connectors involved in the composition. Specifically, the signature of a composite connector is the union of the signatures of those connectors,

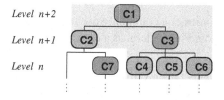

Fig. 6. A general composite connector

including the top-level one, that connect to at least one connector (component) outside of the boundary of the composition. For example, for the composite connector in Fig. 6, its signature is generated from the union of the signatures *Sig1*, *Sig2*, *Sig4*, *Sig5* and *Sig6* of the connectors $C1$, $C2$, $C4$, $C5$, and $C6$. Dependencies between these signatures should be analysed and taken care of while constructing the signature of the composite. In particular, any redundancies resulting from these dependencies should be identified and removed.

The code of the composite connector is implemented by calling its sub-connectors' implementation codes. For instance in Fig. 6, the codes *Code1 . . . Code6* of the sub-connectors $C1 . . . C6$ already exist, and are used to generate the code for the composite connector, by implementing their dependencies (as specified in the composite connector) as method calls from higher level sub-connectors to the lower level ones. In $C1$'s code *Code1*, $C2$ and $C3$ are specified in the sub-connector list. When $C1$'s execute method is called, it invokes every connector in the sub-connector list, i.e. the execute methods of $C2$ and $C3$. Since $C3$ is composed from $C4$, $C5$ and $C6$, it further invokes *Code4*, *Code5* and *Code6* to implement the functionalities.

In this way, we construct a composite connector from its sub-connectors. We get a new signature as well as new code for the new connector. The new signature prescribes the usage of the new connector, and typically contains more parameters than the signatures of the sub-connectors. The new connector's code is a collaboration of the sub-connectors' codes performed according to the composition structure of the new connector.

Clearly the composition structure of a composite connector of course determines the nature of the connector. The same set of sub-connectors will result in different composite connectors when composed differently. This is particularly alarming when you consider that composite connectors are patterns. For example, given a connector C, whereas the composite *Pipe[C,Sequencer]* is the Observer pattern, as we have seen, by reversing the order of the sub-connectors we get a totally different pattern: *Pipe[Sequencer, C]* is the AND-join Pipe pattern (which we will describe below).

Another point worth noting is that in theory, it is possible to build arbitrary composite connectors of unlimited complexity. In practice, some of these connectors may be useless or too hard to use. So there must be some intent when building any composite connector. In other words, useful composite connectors must reflect commonly occurring or recurring control flow patterns, such as the set of workflow control-flow patterns identified in [16].

4.3   Example

Now we show how to construct a commonly occurring workflow control-flow pattern [16], namely the AND-Join Pipe pattern, as a composite connector.

AND-Join Pipe. The intent of the *AND-Join Pipe* composite connector is to allow more than one predecessors in a binary piping composition scheme. It is an "AND" relationship between these predecessors, i.e. only after all the predecessors have been called that the results are gathered and delivered to the successor. This pattern of control can be achieved by composing the *Pipe* and the *Sequencer* together. This composite connector is equivalent to the *Generalised AND-Join* workflow control-flow pattern [16].

Fig. 7 (a) shows the composition structure of the *AND-Join Pipe* connector. The *Pipe* connects to the *Sequencer* at the predecessor position. The *Sequencer* connects to multiple predecessor connectors (components), i.e. *pred1*, ..., *predN*; and the successor connector (component), i.e. *succ*, is connected to the *Pipe* directly. The dotted line denotes the control-flow path of this connector. It first invokes the *Sequencer* and then, and then the *Sequencer* invokes all the connecting predecessor connectors (components) and returns all the resulting data (denoted with circled D). Finally, the *Pipe* delivers all the results to the successor connector (component) which it takes for its execution.

Fig. 7 (b) shows the signatures of the basic connectors *Pipe* and *Sequencer* and the values they could take for the composition depicted in Fig. 7 (a). As shown in the figure, the signatures require the parameters `tget`, `op` and `par` which correspond to the connectors (components) they connect, the operations to execute through these connectors (on this components), and the required parameters for these executions.

Fig. 7 (c) shows the signature generated for the *AND-Join Pipe*. As can be seen, it differs from those of its sub-connectors, since it connects different and more connectors (components) than its sub-connectors. Note how its signature is not the same as that of its top-level sub-connector (*Pipe*). As we have explained, the signature of the *AND-Join Pipe* is the union of the signatures of all sub-connectors that connect to at least one

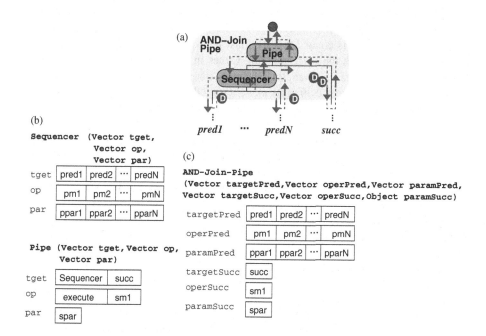

Fig. 7. (a) Composition structure of AND-Join Pipe connector, (b) Signatures of its subconnectors and (c) Signature of AND-Join Pipe connector.

```
class AND-Join-Pipe extends Connector {
  Sequencer seq;
  AND-Join-Pipe(Vector targetPred, ...){
    ...
    seq = new Sequencer(targetPred, ...);
    ...
  }
  Object execute (){
    ...
    result = seq.execute();
    ...
    result = executeConnector(targetSucc.elementAt(0), ...);
    ...
    return result;
  }
}
```

Fig. 8. Outline of the code for the AND-Join-Pipe composite connector's class

connector (component) outside of the boundary of the composition. Thus, as shown in Fig. 7 (c), the signature of a *AND-Join Pipe* includes those for *Sequencer* and *Pipe*.

In the signature of the AND-Join Pipe, we have removed redundancies arising from the signatures of *Sequencer* and *Pipe*. Notice how the signature elements corresponding to the *Pipe* connector (targetSucc, operSucc and paramSucc) do not include an entry for referring to the *Sequencer* connector. The connection to *Sequencer* is defined in the composition structure of the composite connector and so has been coded in.

The connectors' code of the *AND-Join Pipe* connector is a collaboration of the sub-connectors' codes and, as in basic connectors, it is encapsulated in its execute method. Fig. 8 shows an outline of it.

When the connector is created, via its constructor, an instance of a *Sequencer* connector is generated with the corresponding values in the signature, i.e. targetPred, operPred and paramPred. Then, this instance (seq) is used in the execute method to execute the *Sequencer* by calling its execute method. Later, and given that the type of the successor connector is unknown at this point, the execution of the successor connector is carried out by calling the executeConnector method.

The process of creating composite connectors can be partially automated by using a graphical tool. We have implemented such a tool. The tool provides a visual way to drag connectors into a composition environment, connect them and generate the skeleton for the resulting connector's class. The skeleton has to be filled in; this is done manually at present. Then the completed connector can be deposited in the tool's repository.

Fig. 9 shows an example of using this tool. On the left hand side, we can see a *Pipe* and a *Sequencer*. These connectors are connected together using a line. The line indicates to the tool that these connectors should be composed to make a composite connector. The tool then generates a skeleton for the composite connector, and the user fills in the skeleton. On the right hand side of Fig. 9, we can see the constructed connector, *AND-Join Pipe* in the connector repository.

Analogously, a *Pipe* is composed with the *Selector* on the left hand side of Fig. 9. The composition result is an *Exclusive OR-Split Pipe* connector. This composite connector models the piping control that allows multiple successors but chooses only one depending on the output value of the predecessor. This connector is constructed from composing a *Selector* to the successor position of a *Pipe*. It behaves like the Exclusive

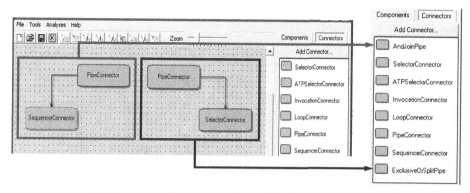

Fig. 9. Building composite connectors by using a graphical tool

OR-Split workflow control-flow pattern [16]. In Fig. 9, the *Exclusive OR-Split Pipe* has also been constructed and put in the connector repository.

An example using these two composite connectors will be shown in next section.

5   Using Composite Connectors in Practice

Having explained how composite connectors are constructed, in this section, we show to use composite connectors to build a complete system. We will use the example of an Automatic Train Protection (ATP) system.

To construct a system from our components and composition connectors, we use an assembler-container tool [9] that we have built. The assembler-container hosts components and connectors and manages their assembly. It takes three main inputs: (a) a set of components; (b) a set of composition connectors; and (c) an XML description of the connector hierarchy of the system. The three inputs are independent from each other. The output of the assembler-container is a run-time system constructed in accordance with the XML description, with the top level connector as an interface to the system.

The assembler-container does not distinguish between basic and composite composition connectors. So we can use our composite connectors to build systems in the assembler-container. As an illustration we will show how the ATP system can be built both with and without composite composition connectors.

The ATP system is located on board a train to ensure safety. The system consists of the following components: Sensor 1, 2 and 3, SensorAggregator, ATPController, Brakes, Alarm, Speedometer and CautionStateProcessor. The sensors are attached to the side of the train and detect information on the track-side signals. Each sensor generates a signal in the range {DANGER, CAUTION, PROCEED}. The overall resulting signal is then sent to the other components. The components must respond to the signal accordingly, e.g. Alarm and Brakes must be enabled when the signal is DANGER.

Using only basic connectors, the ATP system can be built with the architecture shown in Fig. 10.

This architecture consists of 9 components and 13 composition connectors on 6 levels.

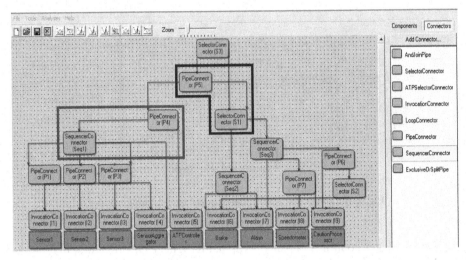

Fig. 10. Automated Train Protection System without composite connectors

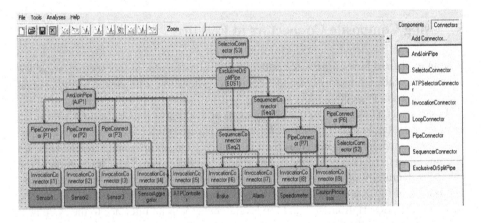

Fig. 11. Automated Train Protection System with composite connectors

Looking at the connector hierarchy in Fig. 10, it is clear that we can compose some basic connectors into composite connectors. The latter are indicated in the figure by two groups of basic connectors encircled by a bold line. These two composite connectors are in fact an *AND-Join Pipe* and an *Exclusive OR-Split Pipe* (Section 4.3).

The graphical tool for building composite connectors (Section 4.3) is integrated with the assembler-container, so we can build the *AND-Join Pipe* and *Exclusive OR-Split Pipe* connectors in the assembler-container, and then use them to build the ATP system.

Using these composite connectors, we can reduce the complexity of the ATP system, and change its architecture to that in Fig. 11.

From the system architecture in Fig. 11 we can see that a composite connector is used in the same manner as the basic ones in hierarchical composition. Also, comparing

Fig. 10 and Fig. 11, we see that using composite connectors reduces the complexity of ATP system by 2 connectors and 1 hierarchy level.

6   Discussion

As pointed out in [15], software systems are getting increasingly complex, and so building them will require more powerful connectors than basic ones such as RPC (remote procedure call). We believe our approach to composite connectors can be used to build suitable connectors. By building composite connectors hierarchically from subconnectors, we can build composites of arbitrary complexity and functionality.

Our connectors are generic, compositional and reusable. Their genericity and compositionality are demonstrated by the fact that they are control flow patterns. They behave like object-oriented design patterns [6] that coordinate communications between objects, e.g. the Observer pattern, as we saw in Section 4.1. Furthermore, because they coordinate components that do not initiate communication with other components, they correspond even more closely to workflow control-flow patterns [16].

However, in contrast to object-oriented design patterns and workflow control-flow patterns, our composite connectors are reusable as real pieces of implementation. Object-oriented design patterns are generic solutions. The idea behind such a pattern can be used for many applications, but the pattern itself has no generic implementation and has to be coded into every application. A workflow control-flow pattern also does not have any generic implementation. This is because it represents a process, and it is only defined when the workflow (with the activities involved) has been fixed.

Clearly there are object-oriented design patterns that cannot be represented by our composite connectors, namely (i) patterns that do not coordinate communications, (ii) patterns that are specific only to objects, e.g. creational patterns. Conversely, there are object-oriented design patterns that can be represented as a basic connector in our model. For example, the Mediator pattern can be implemented as a *Sequencer* that has been enhanced with an iterator.

Equally, there are many workflow control-flow patterns that cannot be represented by our composite connectors. In particular, those that involve concurrency. We have no concurrency in our model as yet.

7   Conclusion

In this paper we have presented a set of composite composition connectors for component composition, which are ready-to-use for building systems out of reusable components encapsulating computation only. These operators are defined within the context of our component model, and are based on the idea of exogenous connectors.

We have demonstrated that the hierarchical nature of our exogenous composition connectors makes it not only possible, but also easy to generate composite composition connectors. We have demonstrated the use of our connectors for constructing systems by means of an example. Additionally, these composite composition connectors can also be seen as patterns that can be used to perform complicated compositions involving many components all in a single step.

To further enhance its usefulness and efficiency, we plan to extend our set of basic operators to concurrency, so that we get composites able to deal with multi-threading issues, etc.

References

1. Arbab, F.: Reo: A channel-based coordination model for component composition. Mathematical Structures in Computer Science 14(3), 329–366 (2004)
2. Arbab, F.: Abstract behavior types: a foundation model for components and their composition. Sci. Comput. Program. 55(1-3), 3–52 (2005)
3. Böhm, C., Jacopini, G.: Flow diagrams, turing machines and languages with only two formation rules. Communications of the ACM 9(5), 366–371 (1966)
4. Bures, T., Plasil, F.: Composing connectors of elements. Technical Report 2003/3, Dep. of SW Engineering, Charles University, Prague (2003)
5. Bures, T., Plasil, F.: Scalable-element based connectors. In: Ramamoorthy, C.V., Lee, R., Lee, K.W. (eds.) SERA 2003. LNCS, vol. 3026, pp. 198–204. Springer, Heidelberg (2004)
6. Gamma, E., Helm, R., Johnson, R., Vlissides, J.: Design Patterns: Elements of Reusable Object-Oriented Software. Professional Computing Series. Addison-Wesley, Reading (1995)
7. Lau, K.-K., Elizondo, P.V., Wang, Z.: Exogenous connectors for software components. In: Heineman, G.T., Crnkovic, I., Schmidt, H., Stafford, J., Szyperski, C., Wallnau, K. (eds.) Proceedings of 8th Int. SIGSOFT Symposium on Component-based Software Engineering, pp. 90–106. Springer, Heidelberg (2005)
8. Lau, K.-K., Ornaghi, M., Wang, Z.: A software component model and its preliminary formalisation. In: de Boer, F.S., Bonsangue, M.M., Graf, S., de Roever, W.-P. (eds.) FMCO 2005. LNCS, vol. 4111, pp. 1–21. Springer, Heidelberg (2006)
9. Lau, K.-K., Ukis, V.: Automatic control flow generation from software architectures. In: Löwe, W., Südholt, M. (eds.) SC 2006. LNCS, vol. 4089, pp. 323–338. Springer, Heidelberg (2006)
10. Lopes, A., Wermelinger, M., Fiadeiro, J.L.: A compositional approach to connector construction. In: Cerioli, M., Reggio, G. (eds.) WADT 2001. LNCS, vol. 2267, pp. 201–220. Springer, Heidelberg (2002)
11. Medvidovic, N., Taylor, R.N.: A classification and comparison framework for software architecture description languages. Software Engineering 26(1), 70–93 (2000)
12. Le Metayer, D., Nicolas, V.-A., Ridoux, O.: Programs, Properties, and Data: Exploring the Software Development Trilogy. IEEE Software 15(6), 75–81 (1998)
13. Papadopoulos, G.A., Arbab, F.: The Engineering of Large Systems. Advances in Computers 46, 329–400 (1998)
14. Shaw, M., Garlan, D.: Software Architecture: Perspectives on an Emerging Discipline. Prentice-Hall, Englewood Cliffs (1996)
15. Spitznagel, B., Garlan, D.: A compositional approach for constructing connectors. In: WICSA 2001. In: Proceedings of the Working IEEE/IFIP Conference on Software Architecture (August 2001)
16. van der Aalst, W.M.P., ter Hofstede, A.H.M., Kiepuszewski, B., Barros, A.P.: Workflow patterns. In: Distributed and Parallel Databases, pp. 5–51 (2003)

Author Index

Lecture Notes in Computer Science

Sublibrary 2: Programming and Software Engineering

For information about Vols. 1– 4214
please contact your bookseller or Springer

Vol. 4551: J.A. Jacko (Ed.), Human-Computer Interaction, Part II. XXIII, 1253 pages. 2007.

Vol. 4550: J.A. Jacko (Ed.), Human-Computer Interaction, Part I. XXIII, 1240 pages. 2007.

Vol. 4542: P. Sawyer, B. Paech, P. Heymans (Eds.), Requirements Engineering: Foundation for Software Quality. IX, 384 pages. 2007.

Vol. 4536: G. Concas, E. Damiani, M. Scotto, G. Succi (Eds.), Agile Processes in Software Engineering and Extreme Programming. XV, 276 pages. 2007.

Vol. 4530: D.H. Akehurst, R. Vogel, R.F. Paige (Eds.), Model Driven Architecture - Foundations and Applications. X, 219 pages. 2007.

Vol. 4523: Y.-H. Lee, H.-N. Kim, J. Kim, Y.W. Park, L.T. Yang, S.W. Kim (Eds.), Embedded Software and Systems. XIX, 829 pages. 2007.

Vol. 4498: N. Abdennahder, F. Kordon (Eds.), Reliable Software Technologies - Ada-Europe 2007. XII, 247 pages. 2007.

Vol. 4486: M. Bernardo, J. Hillston (Eds.), Formal Methods for Performance Evaluation. VII, 469 pages. 2007.

Vol. 4470: Q. Wang, D. Pfahl, D.M. Raffo (Eds.), Software Process Dynamics and Agility. XI, 346 pages. 2007.

Vol. 4468: M.M. Bonsangue, E.B. Johnsen (Eds.), Formal Methods for Open Object-Based Distributed Systems. X, 317 pages. 2007.

Vol. 4467: A.L. Murphy, J. Vitek (Eds.), Coordination Models and Languages. X, 325 pages. 2007.

Vol. 4454: Y. Gurevich, B. Meyer (Eds.), Tests and Proofs. IX, 217 pages. 2007.

Vol. 4444: T. Reps, M. Sagiv, J. Bauer (Eds.), Program Analysis and Compilation, Theory and Practice. X, 361 pages. 2007.

Vol. 4440: B. Liblit, Cooperative Bug Isolation. XV, 101 pages. 2007.

Vol. 4408: R. Choren, A. Garcia, H. Giese, H.-f. Leung, C. Lucena, A. Romanovsky (Eds.), Software Engineering for Multi-Agent Systems V. XII, 233 pages. 2007.

Vol. 4406: W. De Meuter (Ed.), Advances in Smalltalk. VII, 157 pages. 2007.

Vol. 4405: L. Padgham, F. Zambonelli (Eds.), Agent-Oriented Software Engineering VII. XII, 225 pages. 2007.

Vol. 4401: N. Guelfi, D. Buchs (Eds.), Rapid Integration of Software Engineering Techniques. IX, 177 pages. 2007.

Vol. 4385: K. Coninx, K. Luyten, K.A. Schneider (Eds.), Task Models and Diagrams for Users Interface Design. XI, 355 pages. 2007.

Vol. 4383: E. Bin, A. Ziv, S. Ur (Eds.), Hardware and Software, Verification and Testing. XII, 235 pages. 2007.

Vol. 4379: M. Südholt, C. Consel (Eds.), Object-Oriented Technology. VIII, 157 pages. 2007.

Vol. 4364: T. Kühne (Ed.), Models in Software Engineering. XI, 332 pages. 2007.

Vol. 4355: J. Julliand, O. Kouchnarenko (Eds.), B 2007: Formal Specification and Development in B. XIII, 293 pages. 2006.

Vol. 4354: M. Hanus (Ed.), Practical Aspects of Declarative Languages. X, 335 pages. 2006.

Vol. 4350: M. Clavel, F. Durán, S. Eker, P. Lincoln, N. Martí-Oliet, J. Meseguer, C. Talcott, All About Maude - A High-Performance Logical Framework. XXII, 797 pages. 2007.

Vol. 4348: S. Tucker Taft, R.A. Duff, R.L. Brukardt, E. Plödereder, P. Leroy, Ada 2005 Reference Manual. XXII, 765 pages. 2006.

Vol. 4346: L. Brim, B.R. Haverkort, M. Leucker, J. van de Pol (Eds.), Formal Methods: Applications and Technology. X, 363 pages. 2007.

Vol. 4344: V. Gruhn, F. Oquendo (Eds.), Software Architecture. X, 245 pages. 2006.

Vol. 4340: R. Prodan, T. Fahringer, Grid Computing. XXIII, 317 pages. 2007.

Vol. 4336: V.R. Basili, H.D. Rombach, K. Schneider, B. Kitchenham, D. Pfahl, R.W. Selby (Eds.), Empirical Software Engineering Issues. XVII, 193 pages. 2007.

Vol. 4326: S. Göbel, R. Malkewitz, I. Iurgel (Eds.), Technologies for Interactive Digital Storytelling and Entertainment. X, 384 pages. 2006.

Vol. 4323: G. Doherty, A. Blandford (Eds.), Interactive Systems. XI, 269 pages. 2007.

Vol. 4322: F. Kordon, J. Sztipanovits (Eds.), Reliable Systems on Unreliable Networked Platforms. XIV, 317 pages. 2007.

Vol. 4309: P. Inverardi, M. Jazayeri (Eds.), Software Engineering Education in the Modern Age. VIII, 207 pages. 2006.

Vol. 4294: A. Dan, W. Lamersdorf (Eds.), Service-Oriented Computing – ICSOC 2006. XIX, 653 pages. 2006.

Vol. 4290: M. van Steen, M. Henning (Eds.), Middleware 2006. XIII, 425 pages. 2006.

Vol. 4279: N. Kobayashi (Ed.), Programming Languages and Systems. XI, 423 pages. 2006.

Vol. 4262: K. Havelund, M. Núñez, G. Roşu, B. Wolff (Eds.), Formal Approaches to Software Testing and Runtime Verification. VIII, 255 pages. 2006.

Vol. 4260: Z. Liu, J. He (Eds.), Formal Methods and Software Engineering. XII, 778 pages. 2006.

Vol. 4257: I. Richardson, P. Runeson, R. Messnarz (Eds.), Software Process Improvement. XI, 219 pages. 2006.

Vol. 4242: A. Rashid, M. Aksit (Eds.), Transactions on Aspect-Oriented Software Development II. IX, 289 pages. 2006.

Vol. 4229: E. Najm, J.-F. Pradat-Peyre, V.V. Donzeau-Gouge (Eds.), Formal Techniques for Networked and Distributed Systems - FORTE 2006. X, 486 pages. 2006.

Vol. 4227: W. Nejdl, K. Tochtermann (Eds.), Innovative Approaches for Learning and Knowledge Sharing. XVII, 721 pages. 2006.

Vol. 4218: S. Graf, W. Zhang (Eds.), Automated Technology for Verification and Analysis. XIV, 540 pages. 2006.